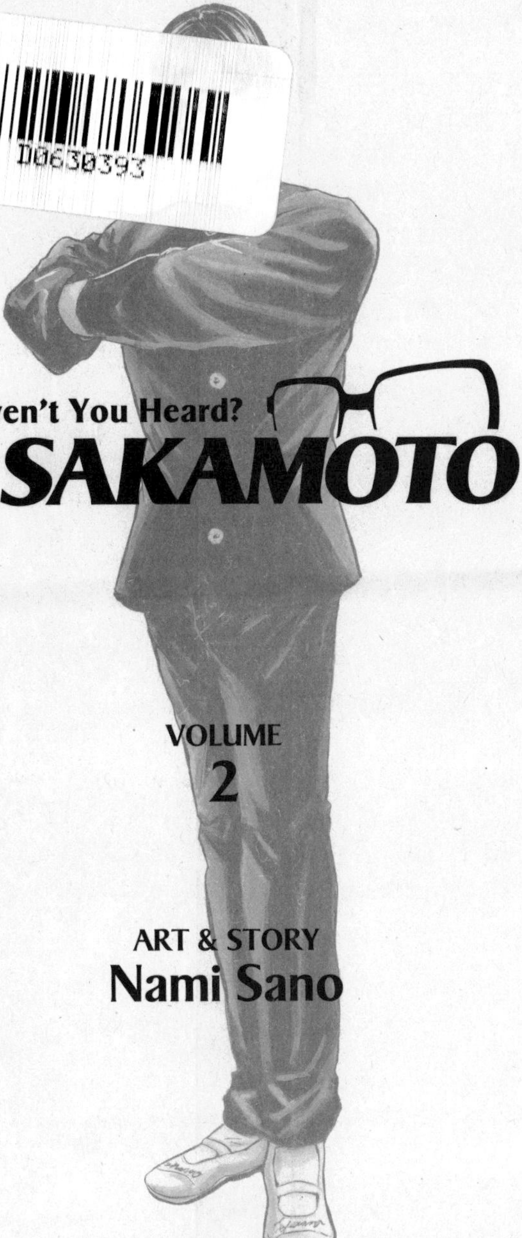

Haven't You Heard? I'M SAKAMOTO

VOLUME
2

ART & STORY
Nami Sano

SEVEN SEAS ENTERTAINMENT PRESENTS

Haven't You Heard?
I'M SAKAMOTO

story and art by NAMI SANO   VOLUME 2

TRANSLATION
Adrienne Beck

ADAPTATION
Janet Gilbert
Karis Page

LETTERING AND LAYOUT
Lys Blakeslee

COVER DESIGN
Nicky Lim

PROOFREADER
Shanti Whitesides

ASSISTANT EDITOR
Lissa Pattillo

MANAGING EDITOR
Adam Arnold

PUBLISHER
Jason DeAngelis

Sakamoto Desuga? Vol.2
©2013 Nami Sano
All Rights reserved.
First published in Japan in 2013 by KADOKAWA CORPORATION ENTERBRAIN.
English translation rights arranged with KADOKAWA CORPORATION
ENTERBRAIN through TOHAN CORPORATION., Tokyo.

Seven Seas books may be purchased in bulk for educational, business, or
promotional use. For information on bulk purchases, please contact Macmillan
Corporate & Premium Sales Department at 1-800-221-7945 (ext 5442)
or write specialmarkets@macmillan.com.

Seven Seas and the Seven Seas logo are trademarks of
Seven Seas Entertainment, LLC.

ISBN: 978-1-626922-20-4

Printed in Canada

First Printing: November 2015

10 9 8 7 6 5 4 3 2 1

FOLLOW US ONLINE: *www.gomanga.com*

READING DIRECTIONS

The manga prelude and epilogue sections that
bookend this light novel read from right to left,
Japanese style. If this is your first time reading
manga, you start reading from the top right panel on
each page and take it from there. If you get lost, just
follow the numbered diagram here. Enjoy!!

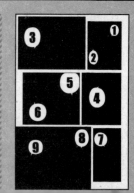

CHAPTER 6: PLAYING HARD TO GET

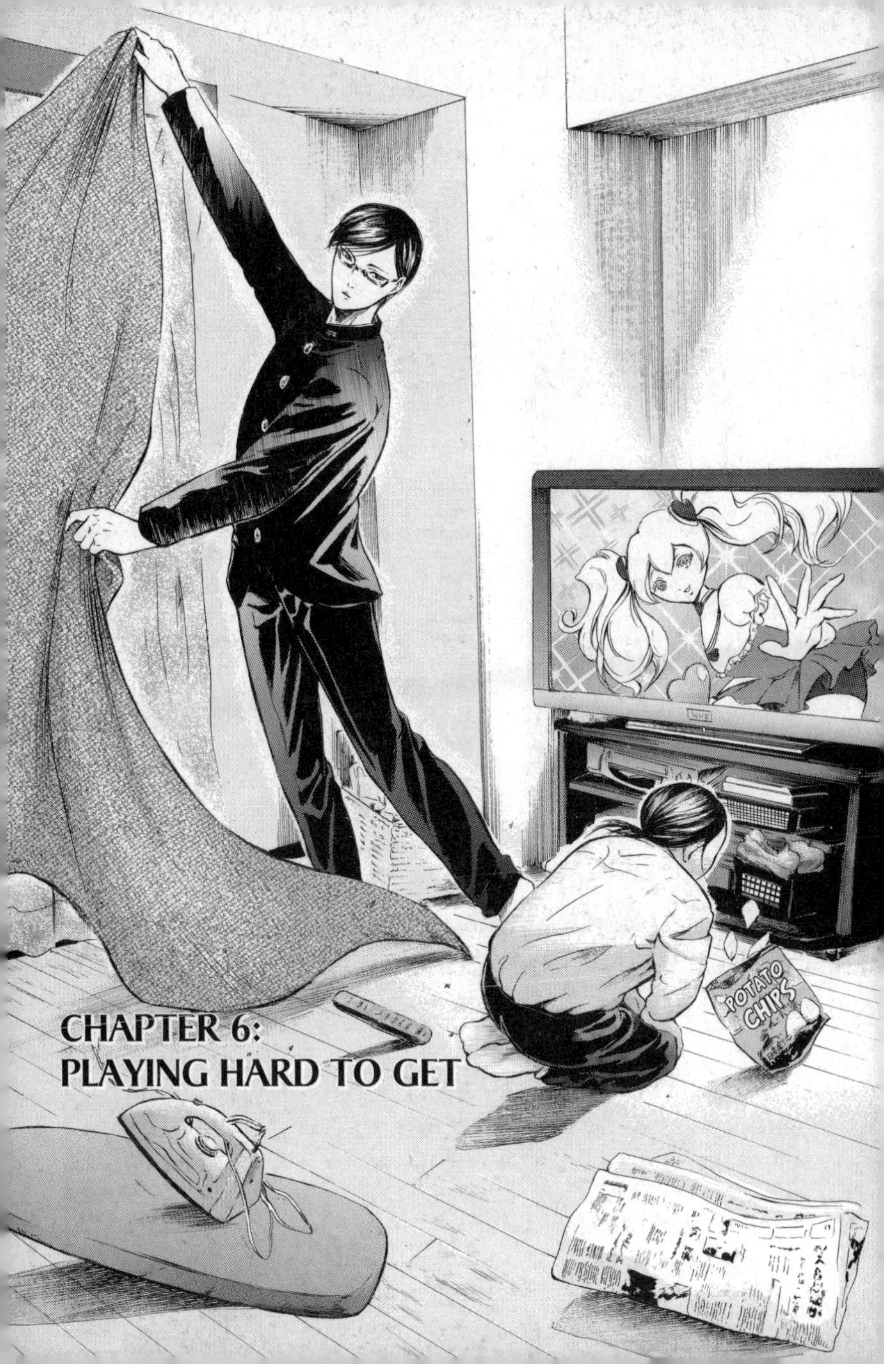
POTATO CHIPS

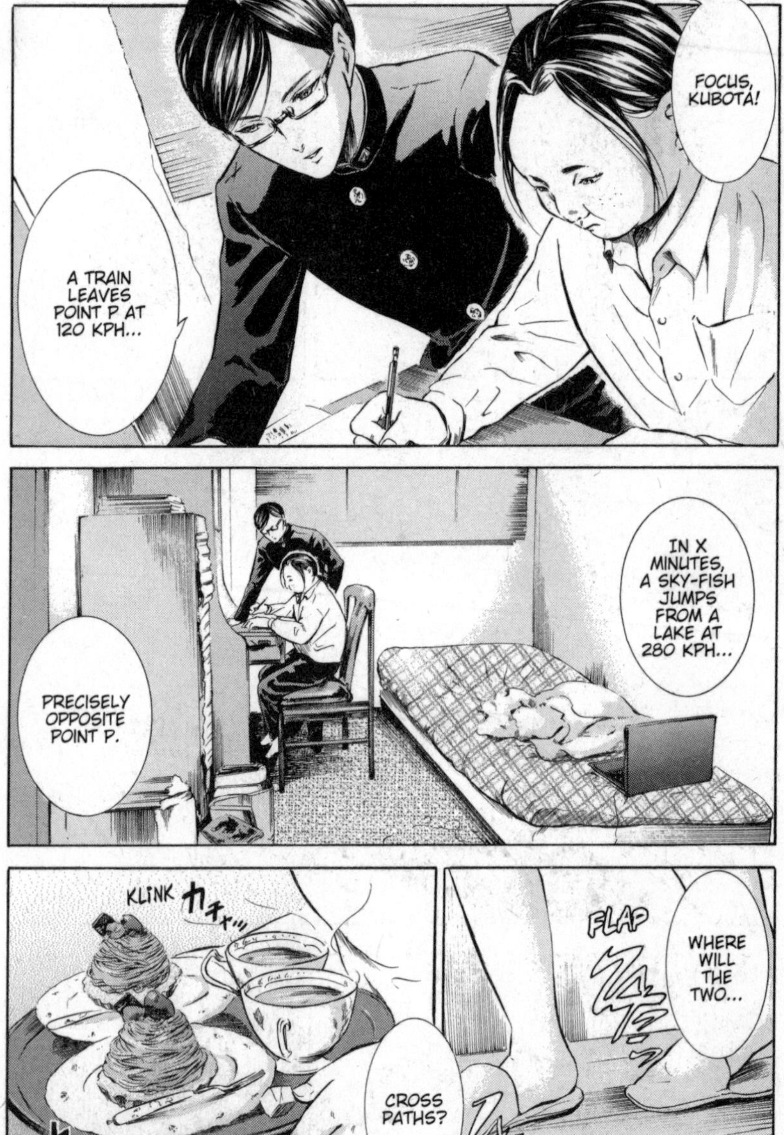
FOCUS, KUBOTA!
A TRAIN LEAVES POINT P AT 120 KPH...
IN X MINUTES, A SKY-FISH JUMPS FROM A LAKE AT 280 KPH...
PRECISELY OPPOSITE POINT P.
FLAP
WHERE WILL THE TWO...
FLAP
KLINK
カチャッ
CROSS PATHS?
カチャ
TINK

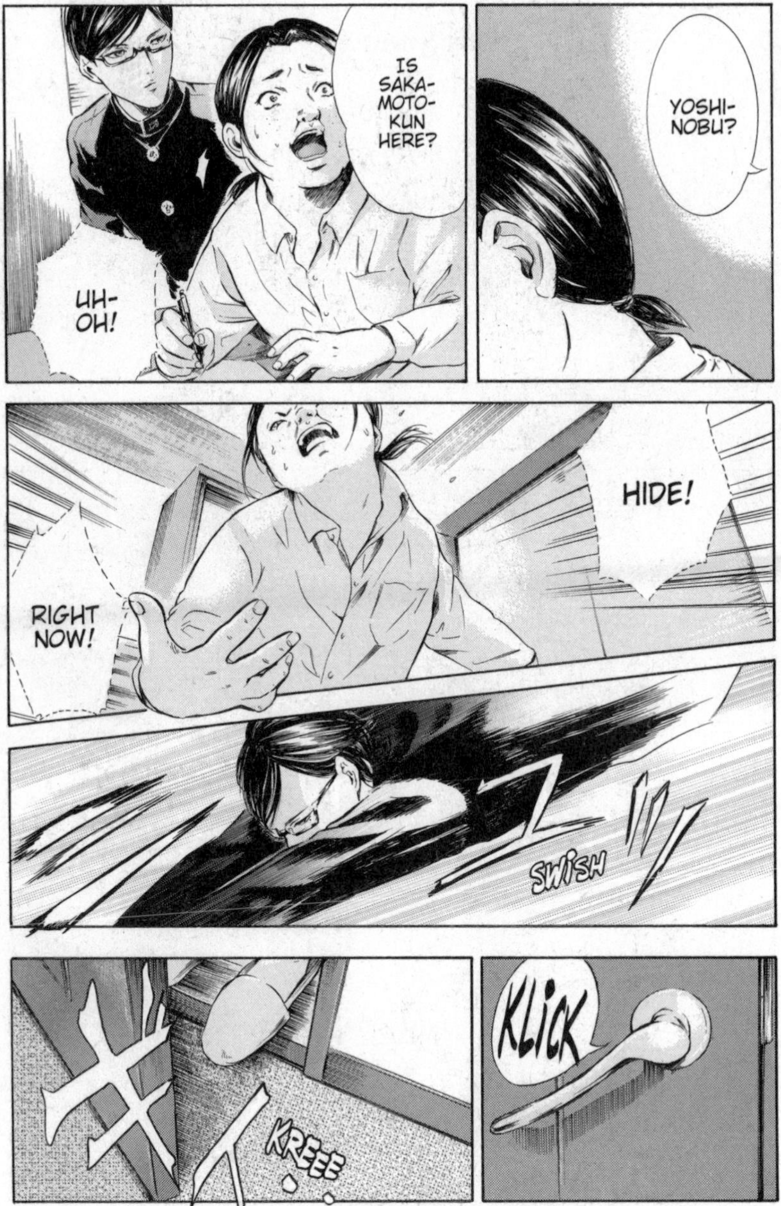
YOSHI-NOBU?
IS SAKA-MOTO-KUN HERE?
UH-OH!
HIDE!
RIGHT NOW!
SWISH
KLICK
KREEE

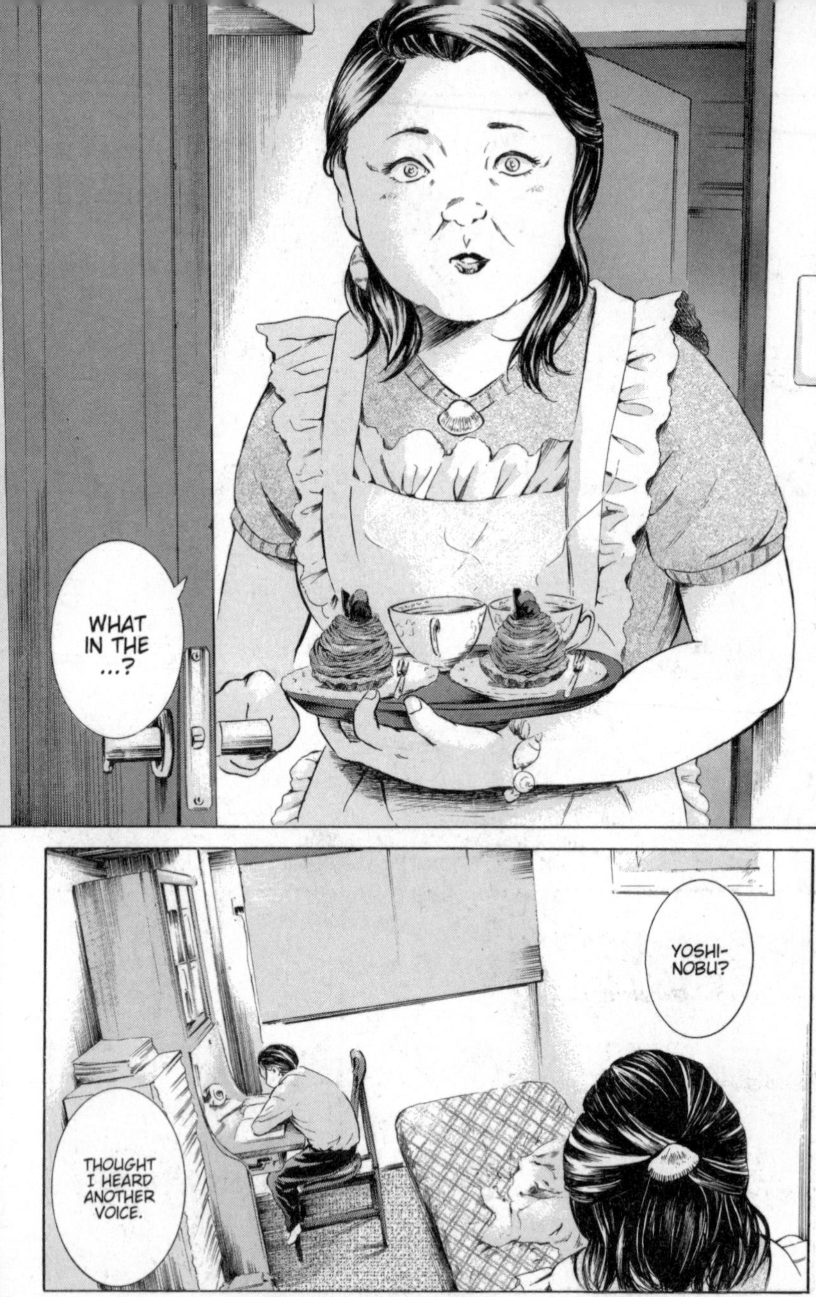
WHAT IN THE ...?
YOSHI-NOBU?
THOUGHT I HEARD ANOTHER VOICE.

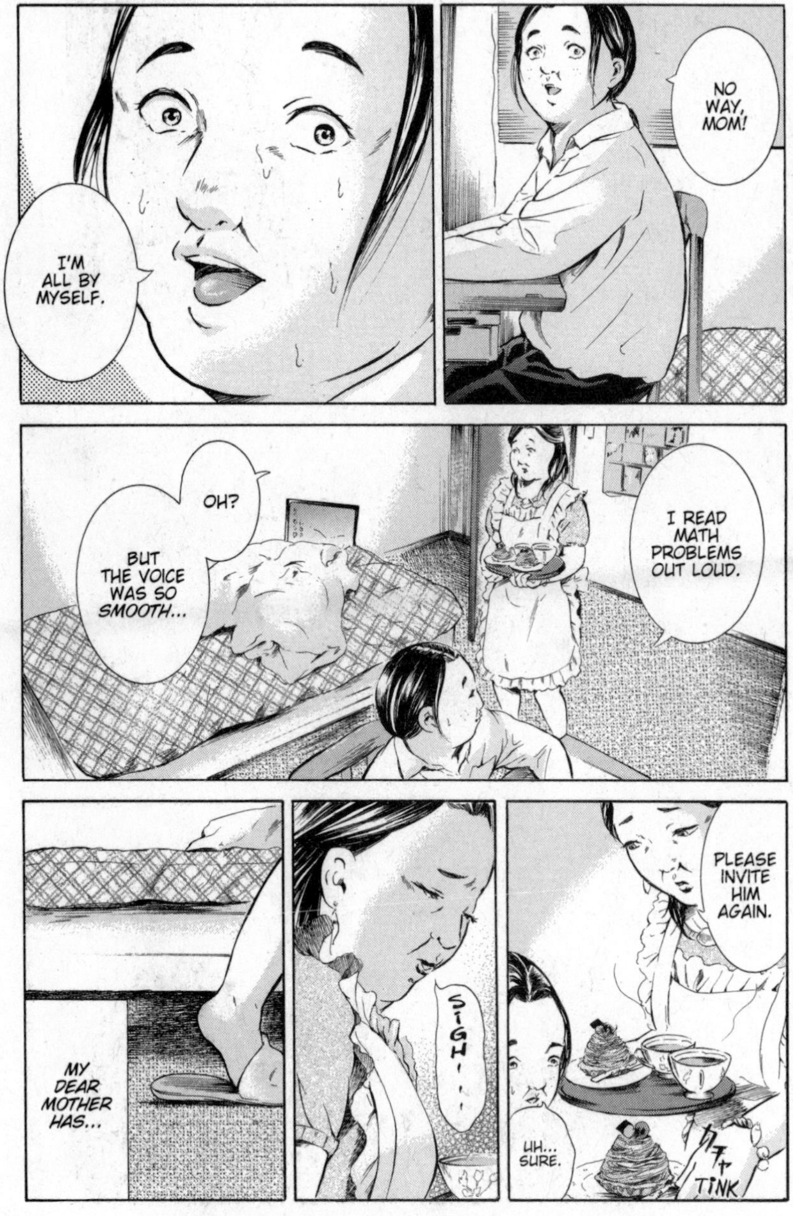
NO WAY, MOM!
I'M ALL BY MYSELF.
I READ MATH PROBLEMS OUT LOUD.
OH?
BUT THE VOICE WAS SO SMOOTH...
PLEASE INVITE HIM AGAIN.
UH... SURE.
カチャ
TINK
SIGH...
MY DEAR MOTHER HAS...

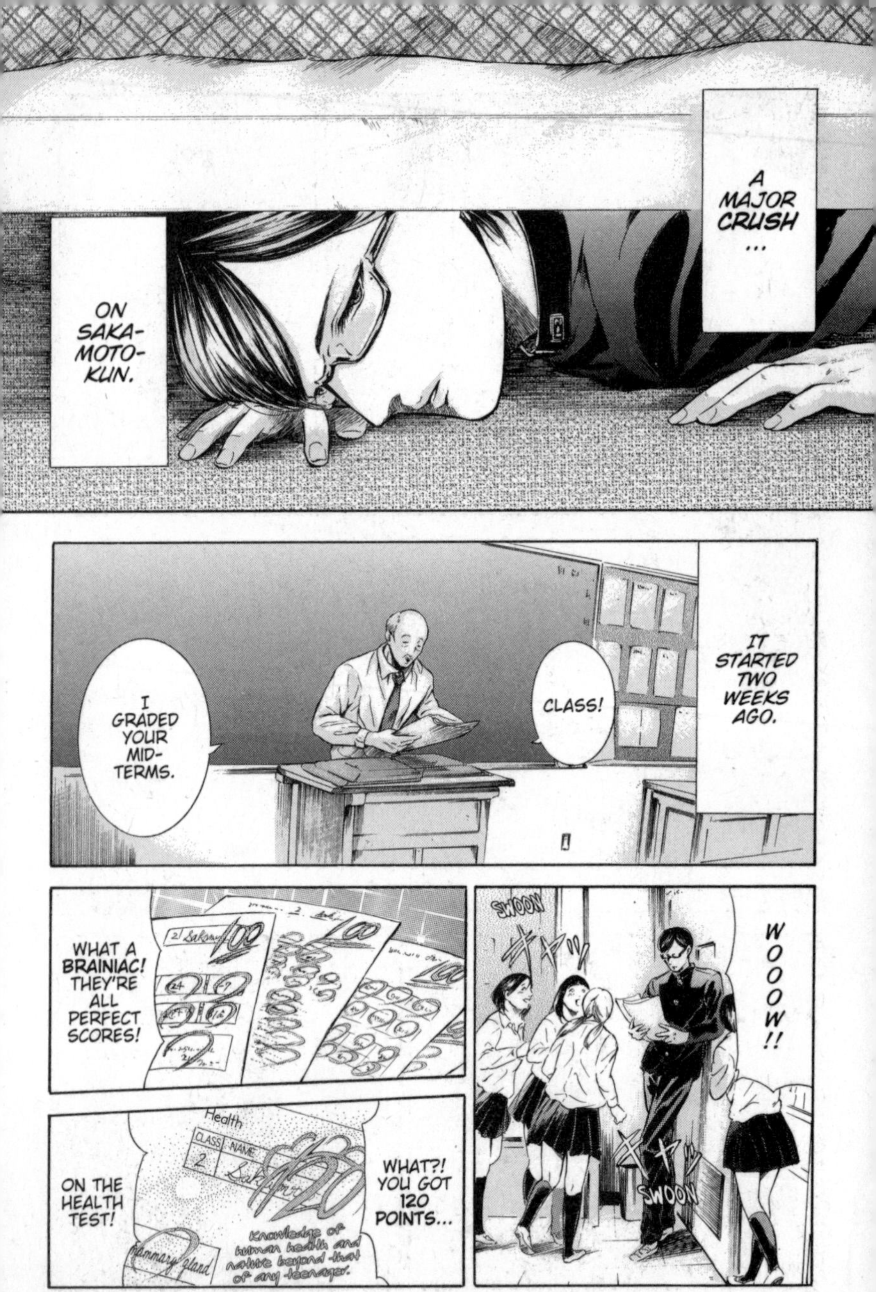
A MAJOR CRUSH ...
ON SAKAMOTO-KUN.
IT STARTED TWO WEEKS AGO.
CLASS!
I GRADED YOUR MID-TERMS.
WOOOOW!!
SWOON
SWOON
WHAT A BRAINIAC! THEY'RE ALL PERFECT SCORES!
WHAT?! YOU GOT 120 POINTS...
ON THE HEALTH TEST!
Health
CLASS
NAME
2
Knowledge of human health and nature beyond that of any teenager.
mammary gland

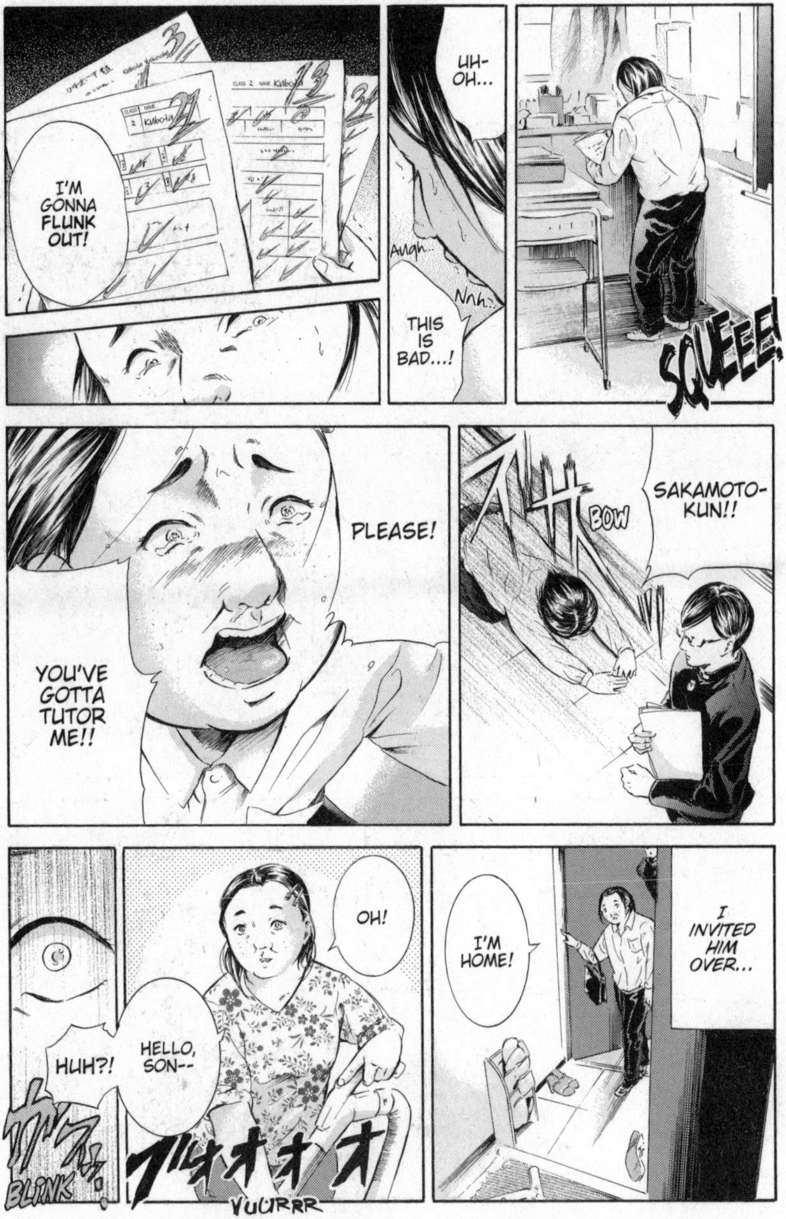
SQUEEE!
UH-OH...
Augh...
Nnh...
THIS IS BAD...!
I'M GONNA FLUNK OUT!
SAKAMOTO-KUN!!
BOW
PLEASE!
YOU'VE GOTTA TUTOR ME!!
I INVITED HIM OVER...
I'M HOME!
OH!
HELLO, SON--
VUURRR
HUH?!
BLINK

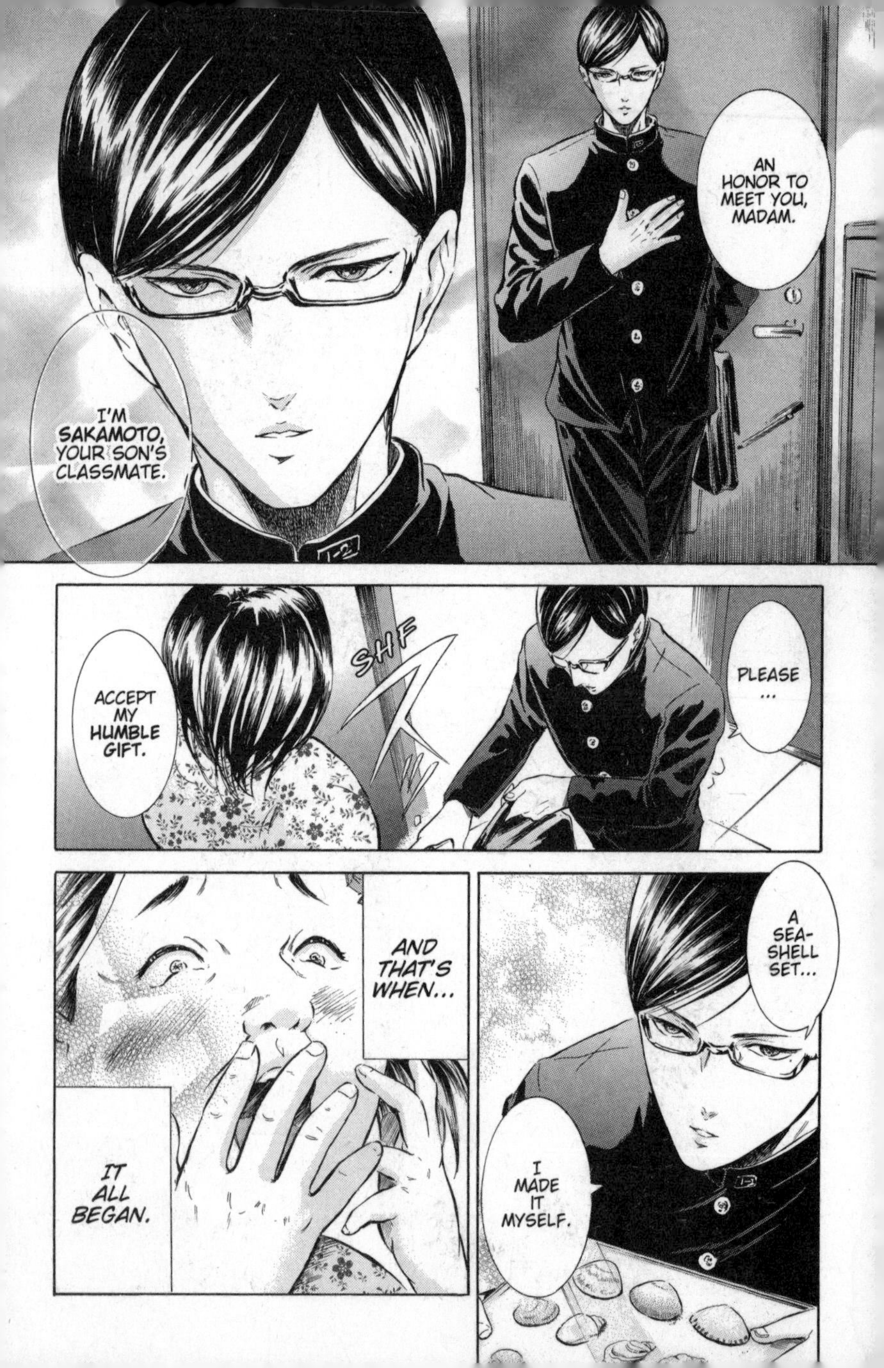
AN HONOR TO MEET YOU, MADAM.
I'M SAKAMOTO, YOUR SON'S CLASSMATE.
PLEASE...
SHF
ACCEPT MY HUMBLE GIFT.
A SEA-SHELL SET...
I MADE IT MYSELF.
AND THAT'S WHEN...
IT ALL BEGAN.

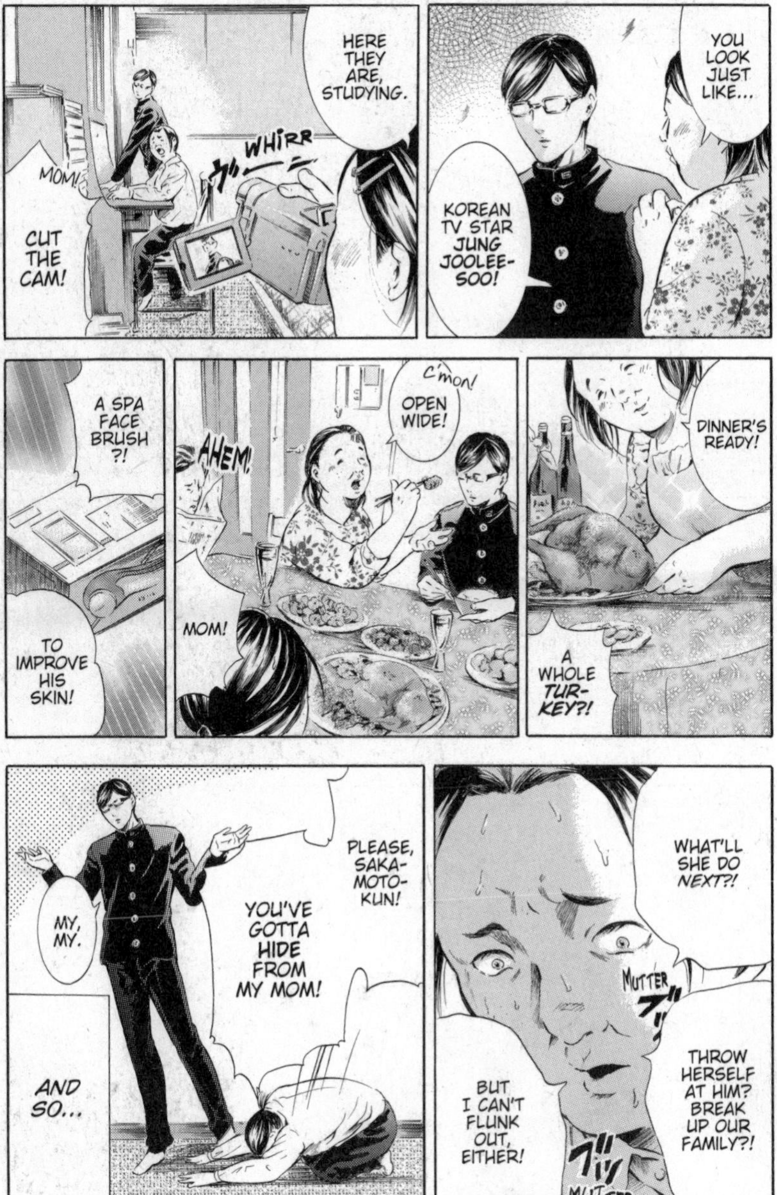
YOU LOOK JUST LIKE...
KOREAN TV STAR JUNG JOOLEE-SOO!
HERE THEY ARE, STUDYING.
WHIRR
MOM!
CUT THE CAM!
DINNER'S READY!
A WHOLE TURKEY?!
C'MON!
OPEN WIDE!
AHEM!
MOM!
A SPA FACE BRUSH?!
TO IMPROVE HIS SKIN!
WHAT'LL SHE DO NEXT?!
THROW HERSELF AT HIM? BREAK UP OUR FAMILY?!
MUTTER
BUT I CAN'T FLUNK OUT, EITHER!
MUT-TER
PLEASE, SAKAMOTO-KUN!
YOU'VE GOTTA HIDE FROM MY MOM!
MY, MY.
AND SO...

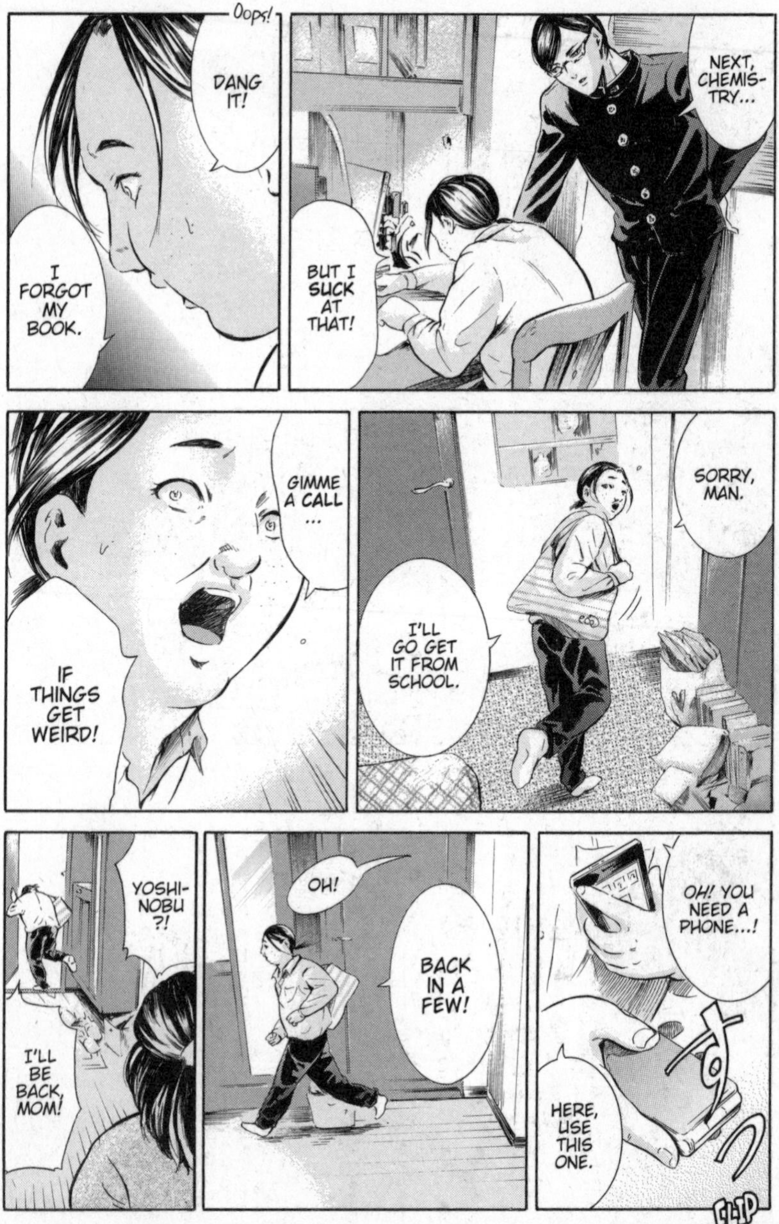
NEXT, CHEMISTRY...
BUT I SUCK AT THAT!
Oops!
DANG IT!
I FORGOT MY BOOK.
SORRY, MAN.
I'LL GO GET IT FROM SCHOOL.
GIMME A CALL ...
IF THINGS GET WEIRD!
OH! YOU NEED A PHONE...!
HERE, USE THIS ONE.
FLIP
OH!
BACK IN A FEW!
YOSHI-NOBU?!
I'LL BE BACK, MOM!

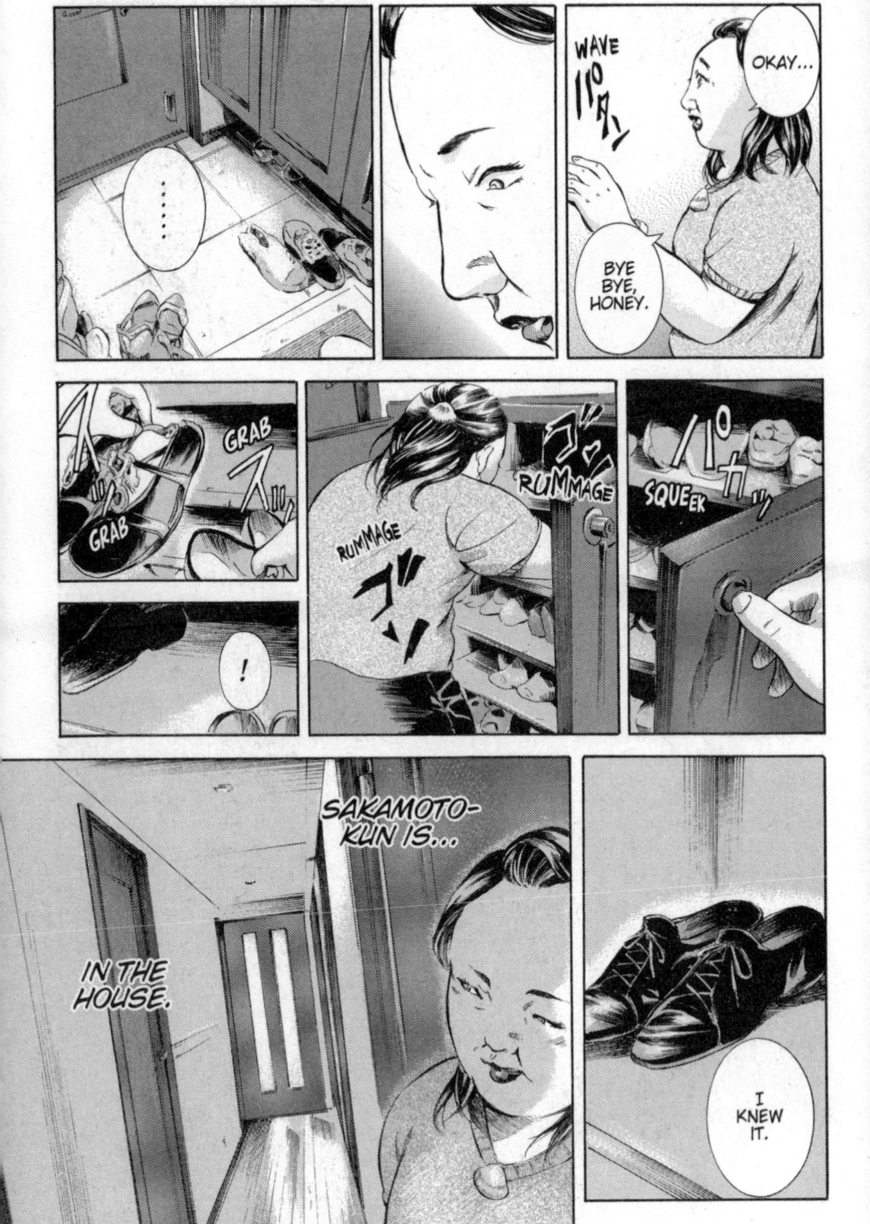
OKAY...
WAVE
BYE BYE, HONEY.
......
SQUEEK
RUMMAGE
RUMMAGE
GRAB
GRAB
!
I KNEW IT.
SAKAMOTO-KUN IS...
IN THE HOUSE.

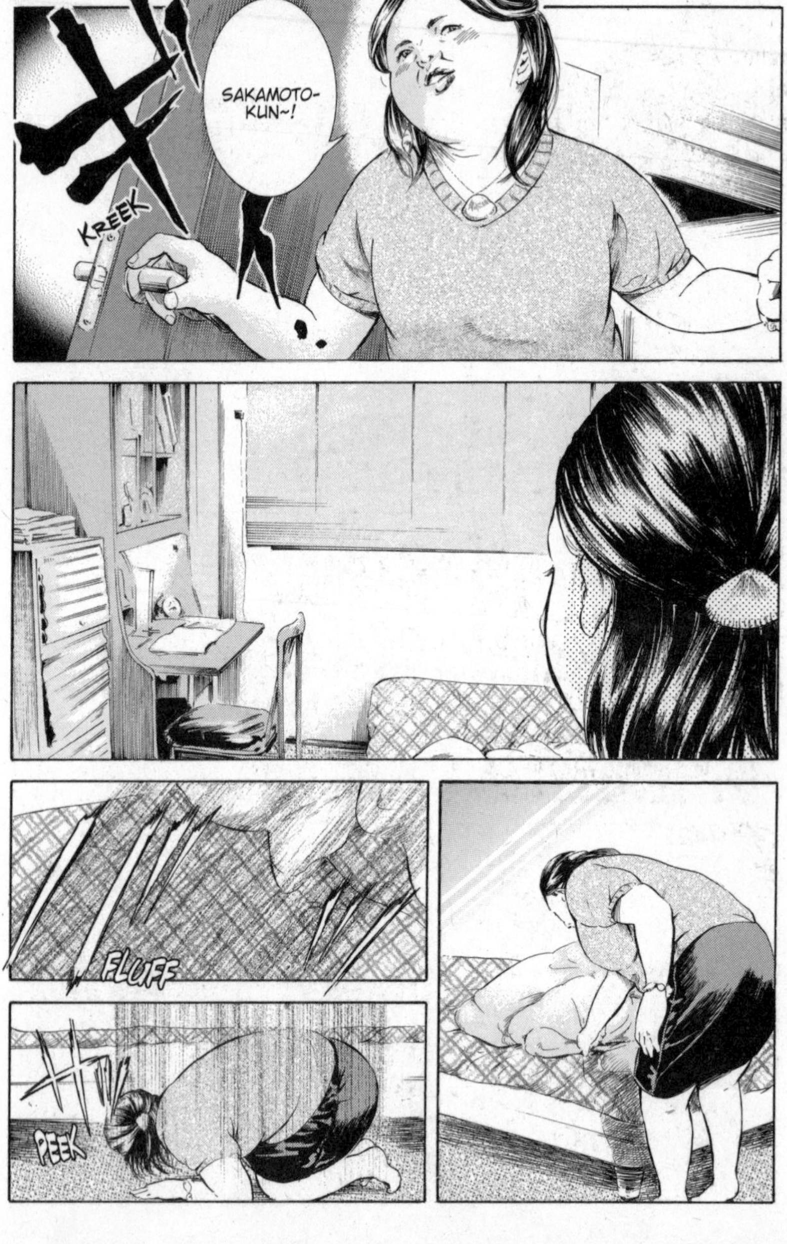
SAKAMOTO-KUN~!
KREEK
FLUFF
PEEK

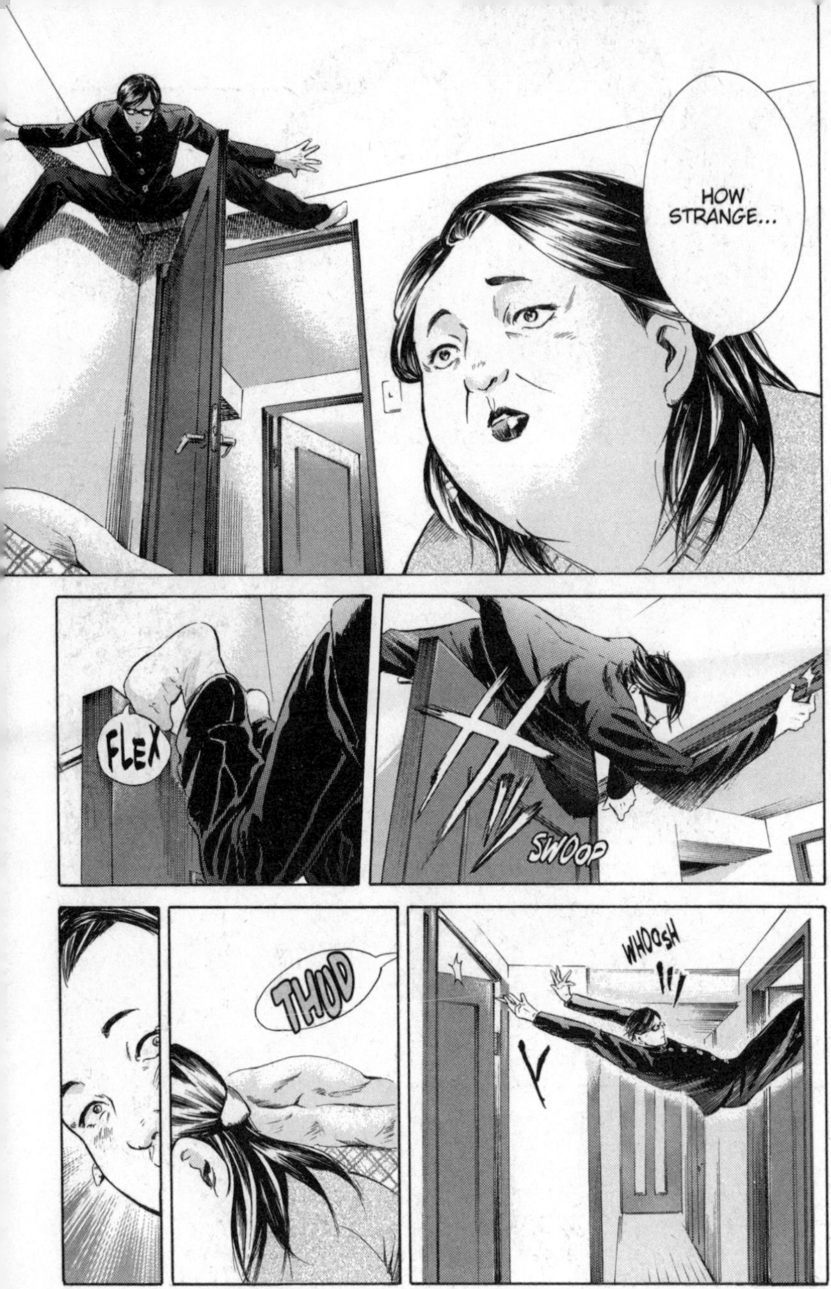
HOW STRANGE...
SWOOP
FLEX
WHOOSH
THUD

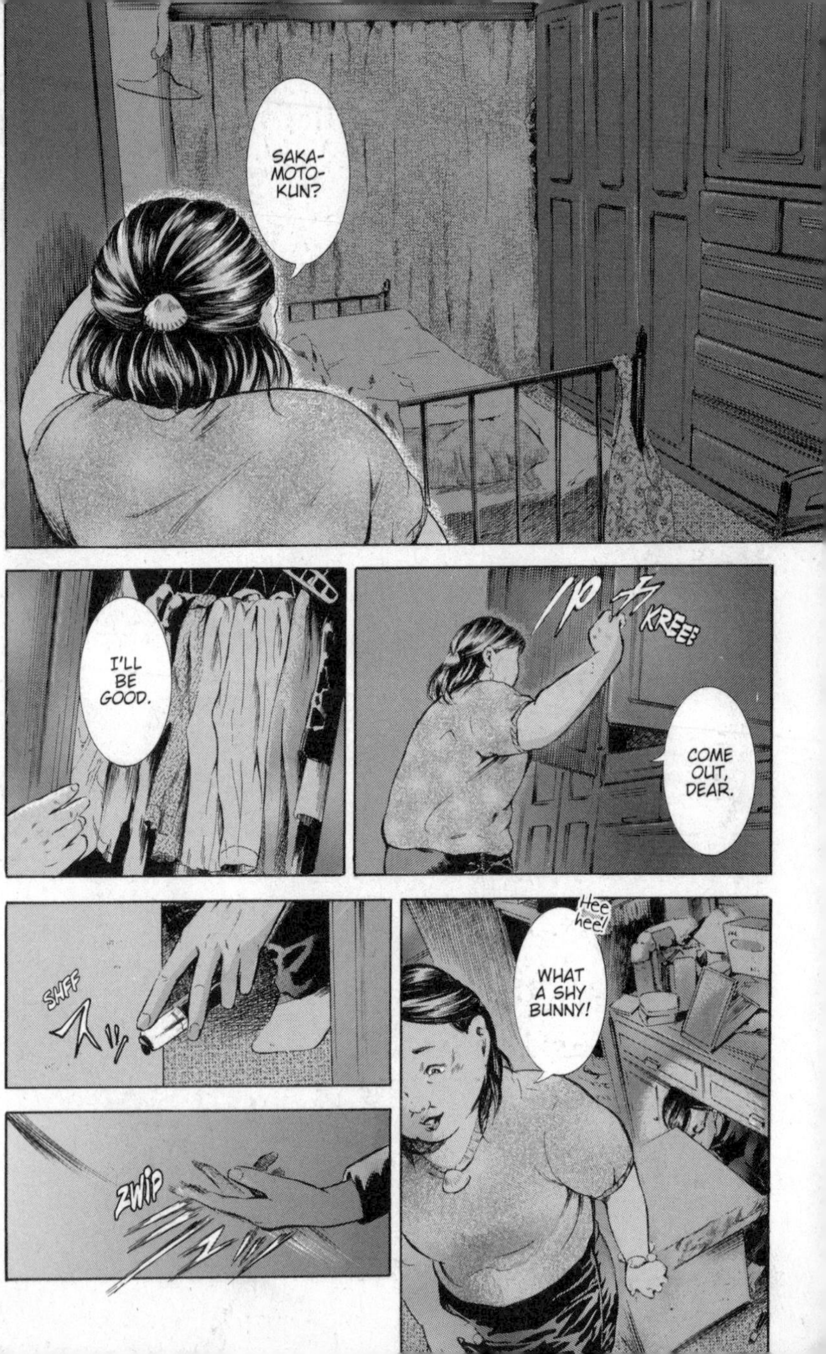
SAKA-MOTO-KUN?
KREE!
COME OUT, DEAR.
I'LL BE GOOD.
Hee hee!
WHAT A SHY BUNNY!
SHFF
ZWIP

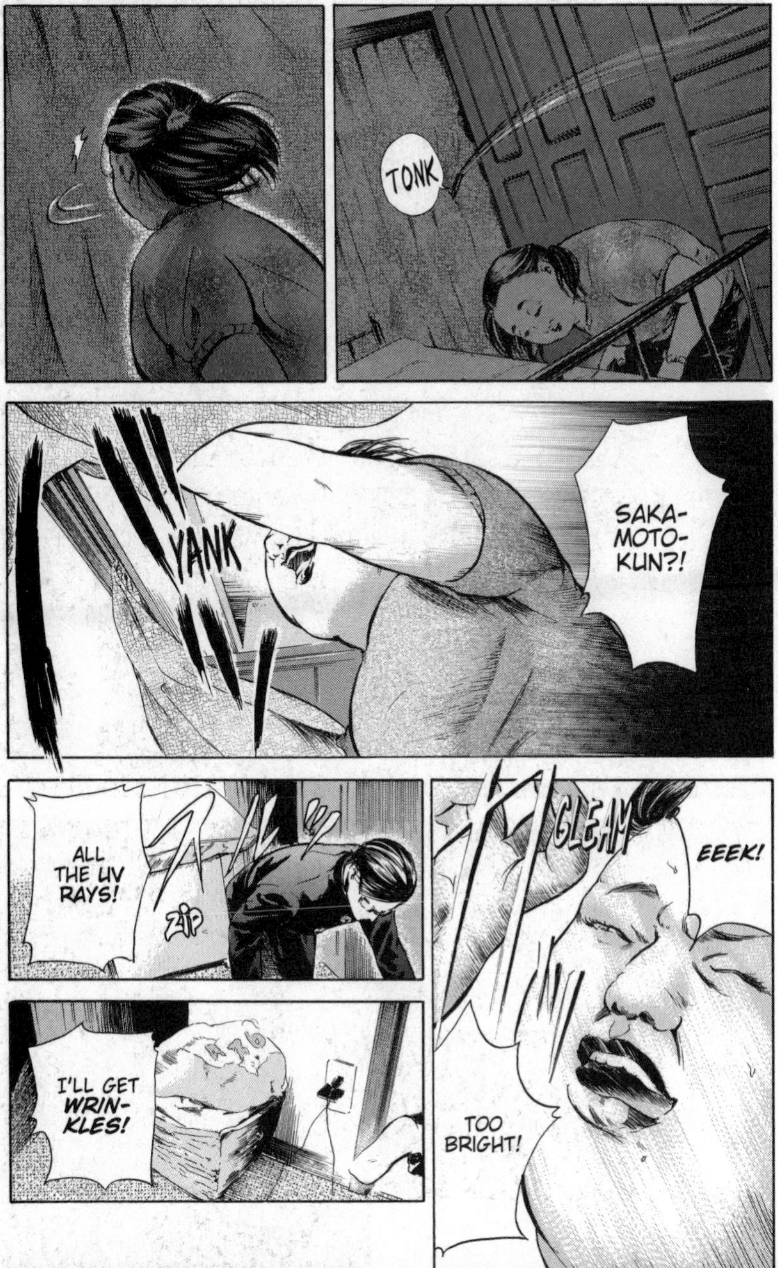
TONK
SAKA-MOTO-KUN?!
YANK
EEEK!
GLEAM
TOO BRIGHT!
ALL THE UV RAYS!
ZIP
I'LL GET WRIN-KLES!

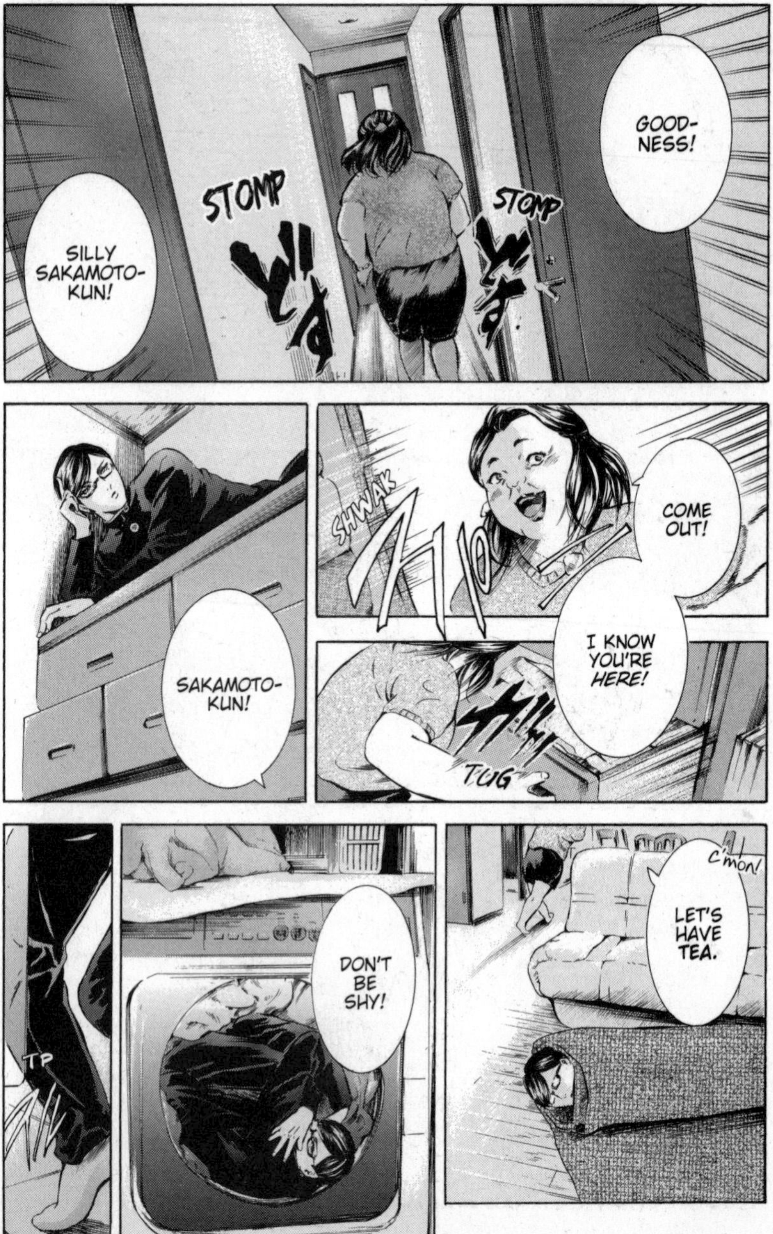
GOOD-NESS!
STOMP
STOMP
SILLY SAKAMOTO-KUN!
COME OUT!
SHWAK
I KNOW YOU'RE HERE!
TUG
SAKAMOTO-KUN!
C'mon!
LET'S HAVE TEA.
DON'T BE SHY!
TP

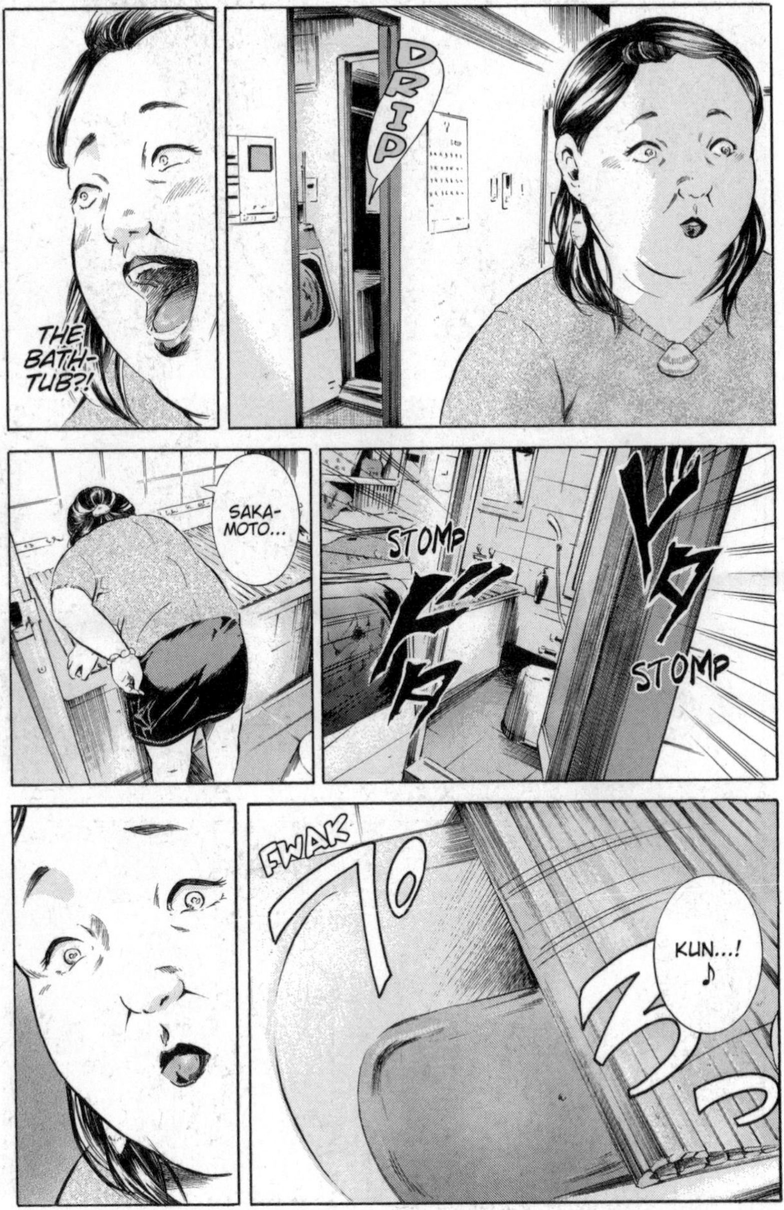
DRIP
THE BATH-TUB?!
STOMP
STOMP
SAKA-MOTO...
FWAK
KUN...! ♪

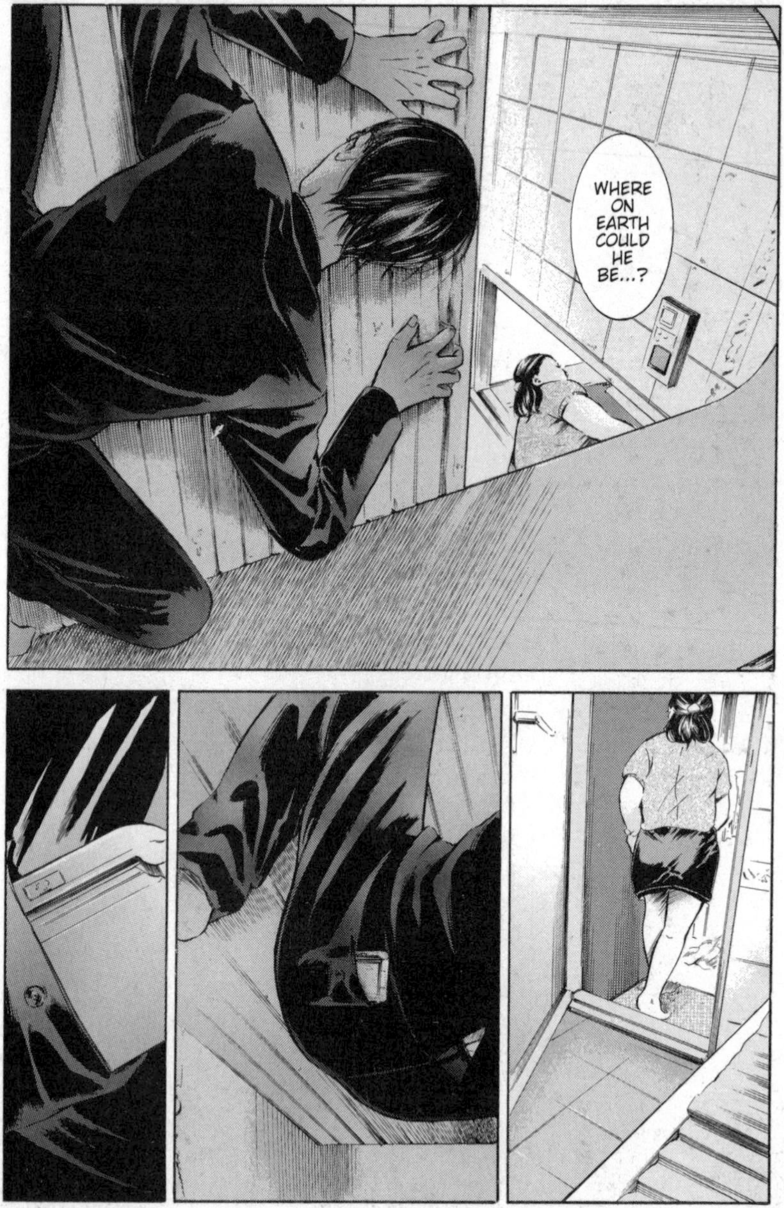
WHERE ON EARTH COULD HE BE...?

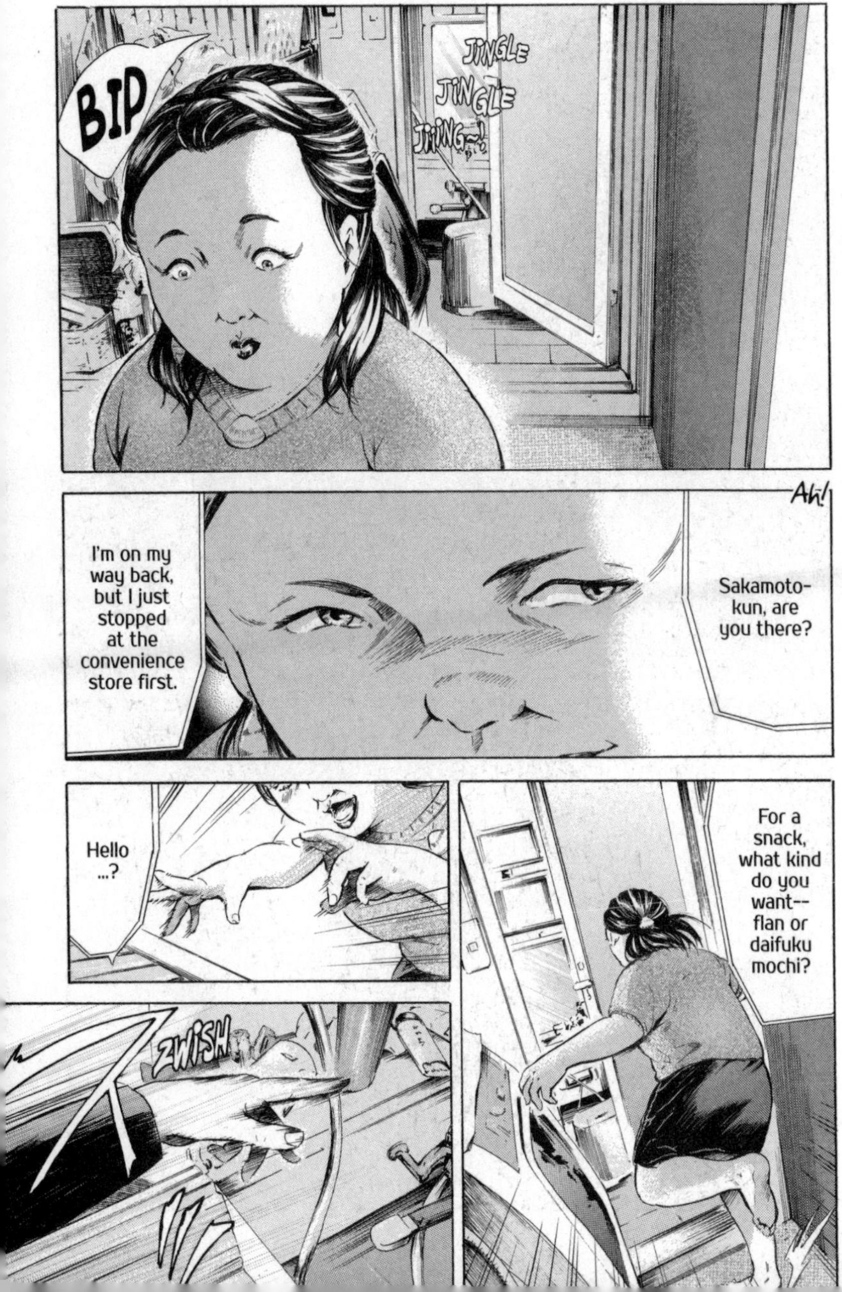
JINGLE
JINGLE
JIIING~!
BIP
Ah!
Sakamoto-kun, are you there?
I'm on my way back, but I just stopped at the convenience store first.
For a snack, what kind do you want-- flan or daifuku mochi?
Hello ...?
ZWISH

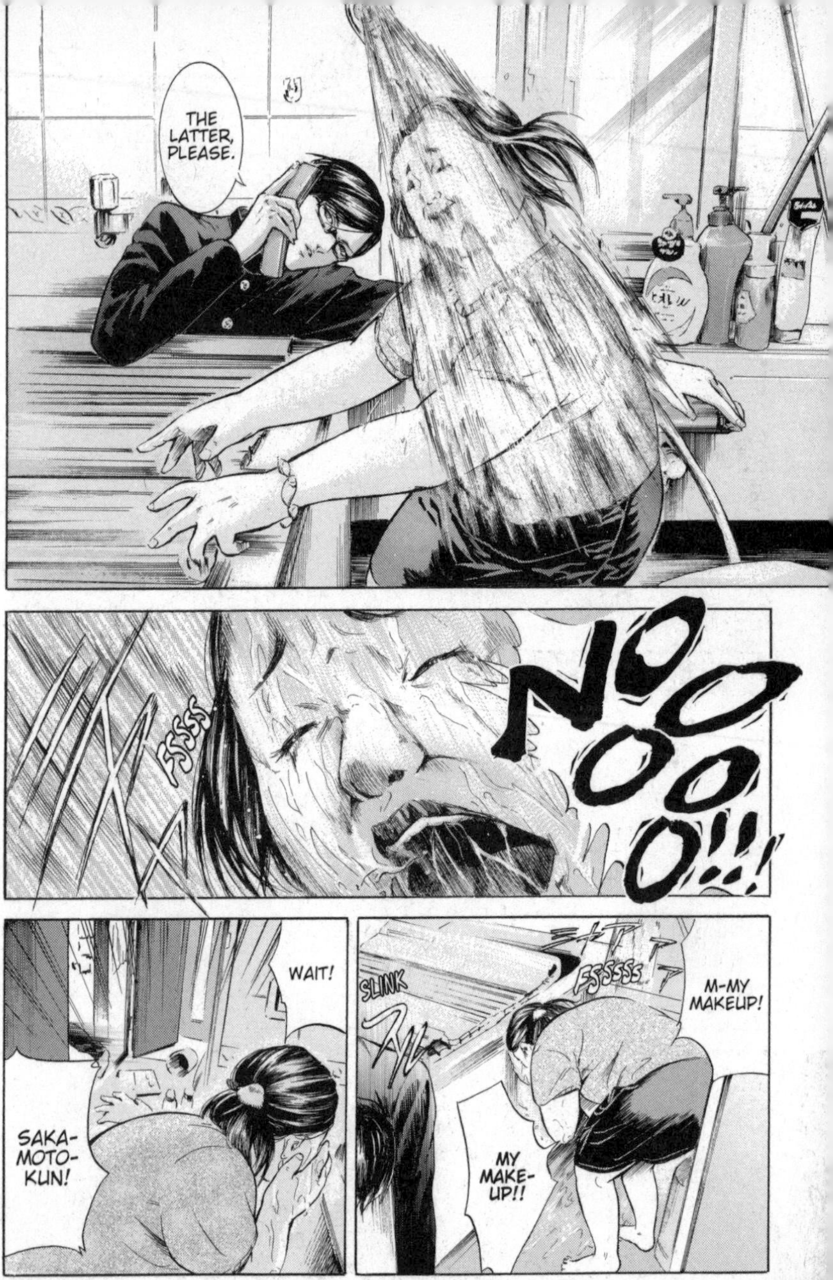
THE LATTER, PLEASE.
FSSSS
NOOOOOO!!!
M-MY MAKEUP!
FSSSSS
SLINK
MY MAKE-UP!!
WAIT!
SAKA-MOTO-KUN!

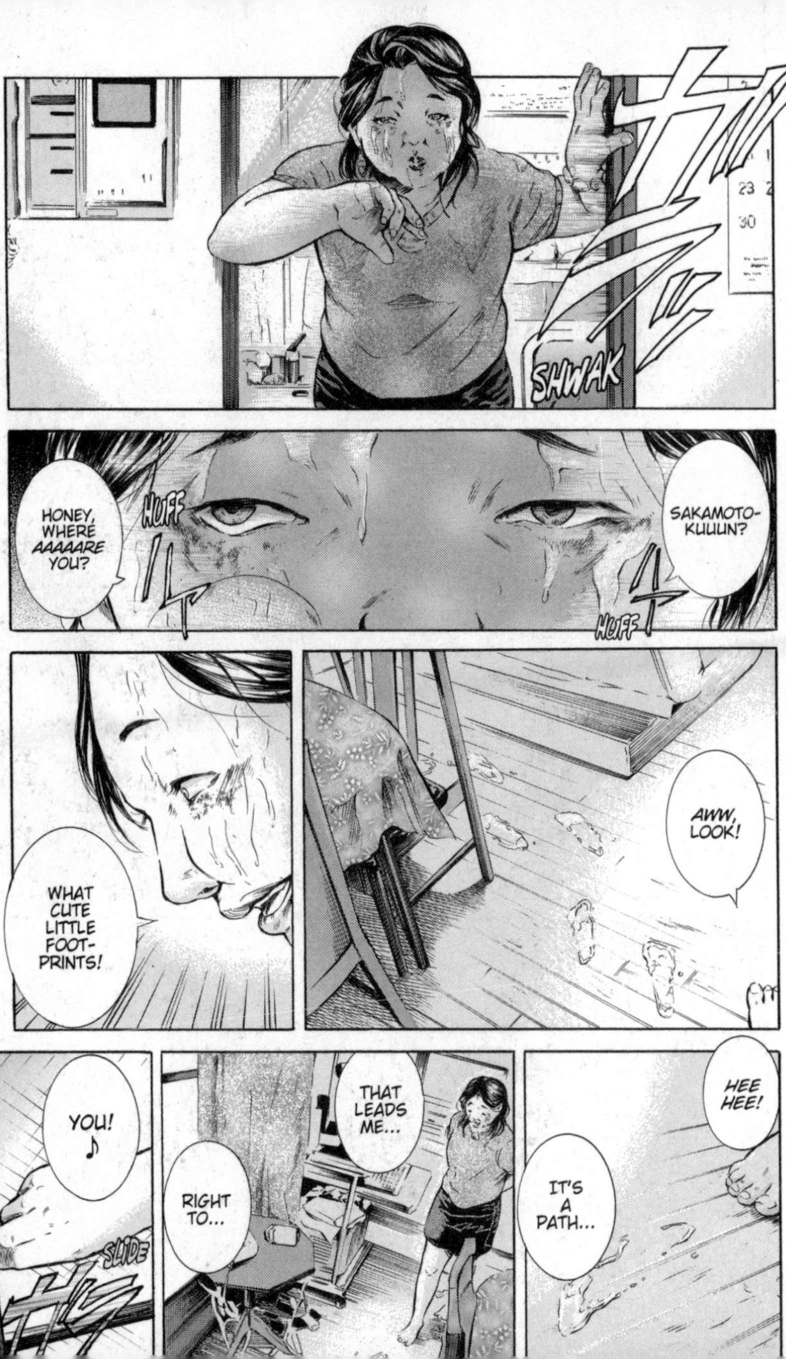
SHWAK
SAKAMOTO-KUUUN?
HUFF
HUFF
HONEY, WHERE *AAAAARE* YOU?
AWW, LOOK!
WHAT CUTE LITTLE FOOT-PRINTS!
HEE HEE!
IT'S A PATH...
THAT LEADS ME...
RIGHT TO...
YOU! ♪
SLIDE

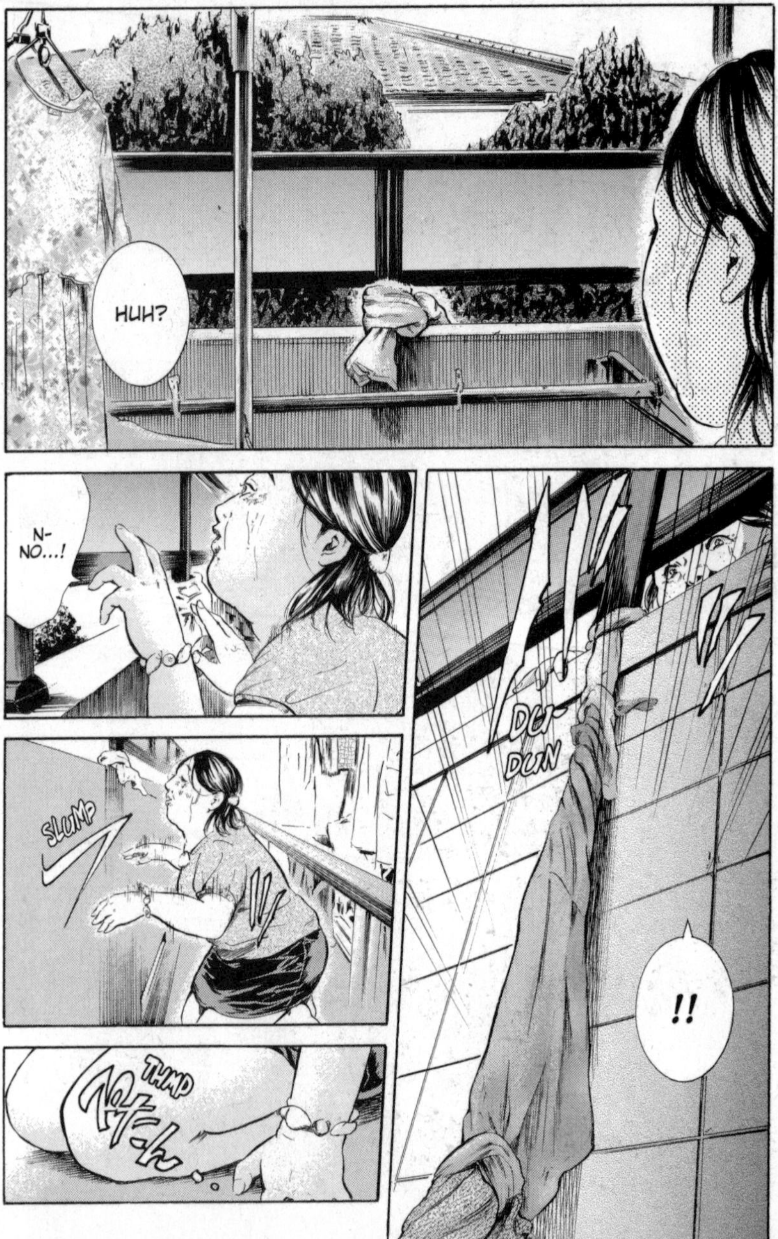
HUH?
DU-
DUN
!!
N-
NO...!
SLUMP
THMP

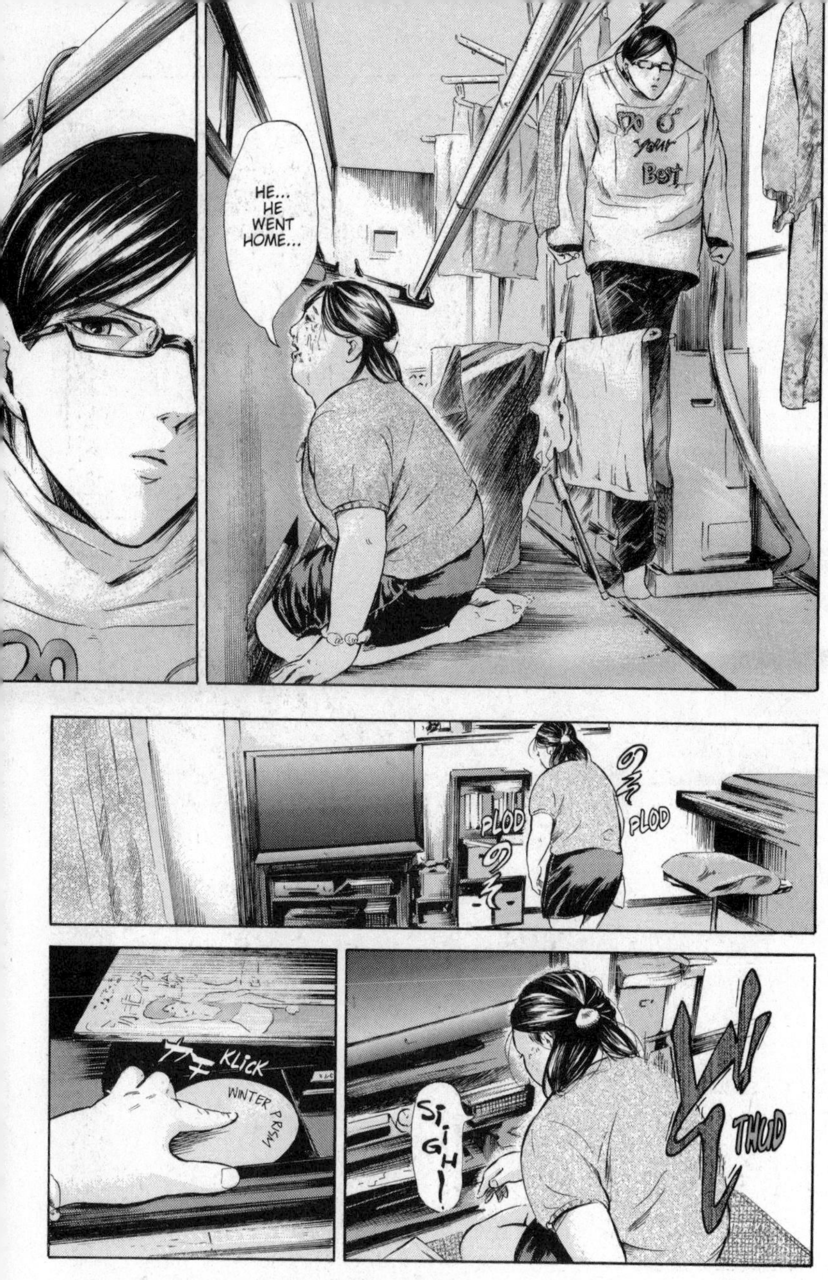
HE... HE WENT HOME...
PLOD
PLOD
THUD
SIGH!
KLICK
WINTER PRISM

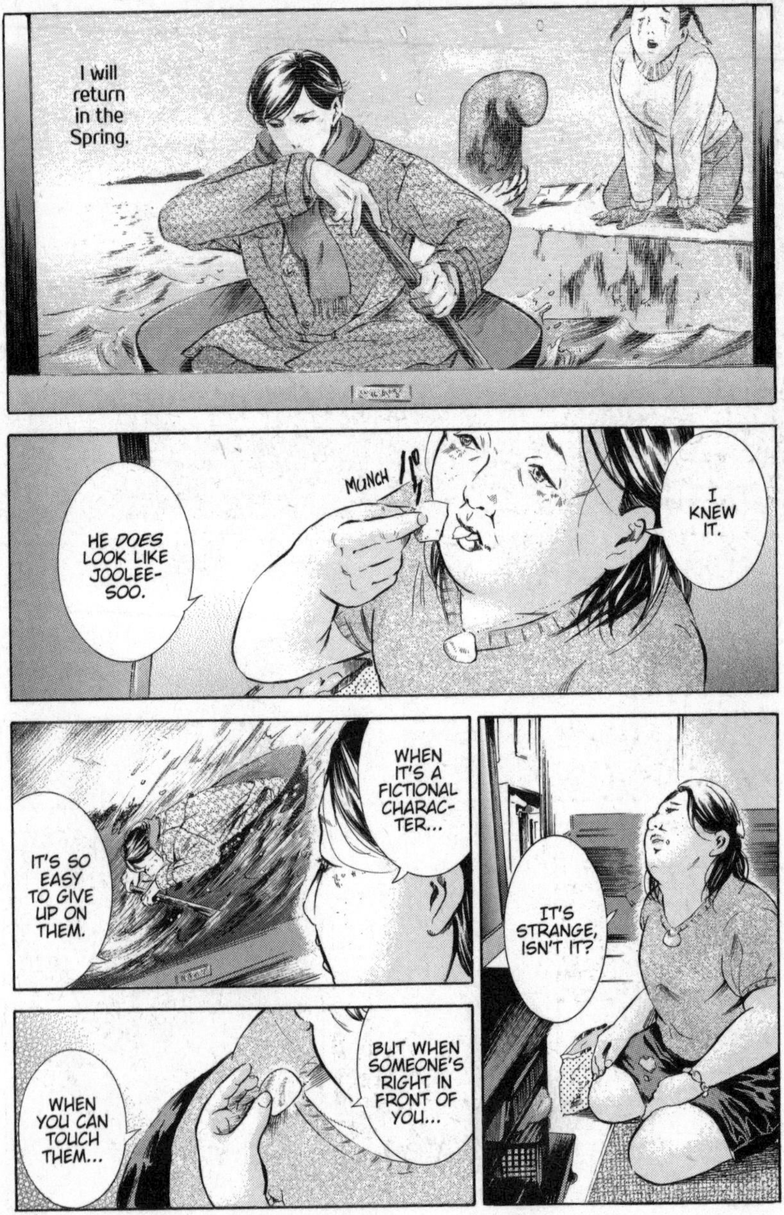
I will return in the Spring.
I KNEW IT.
MUNCH
HE *DOES* LOOK LIKE JOOLEE-SOO.
IT'S STRANGE, ISN'T IT?
WHEN IT'S A FICTIONAL CHARACTER...
IT'S SO EASY TO GIVE UP ON THEM.
BUT WHEN SOMEONE'S RIGHT IN FRONT OF YOU...
WHEN YOU CAN TOUCH THEM...

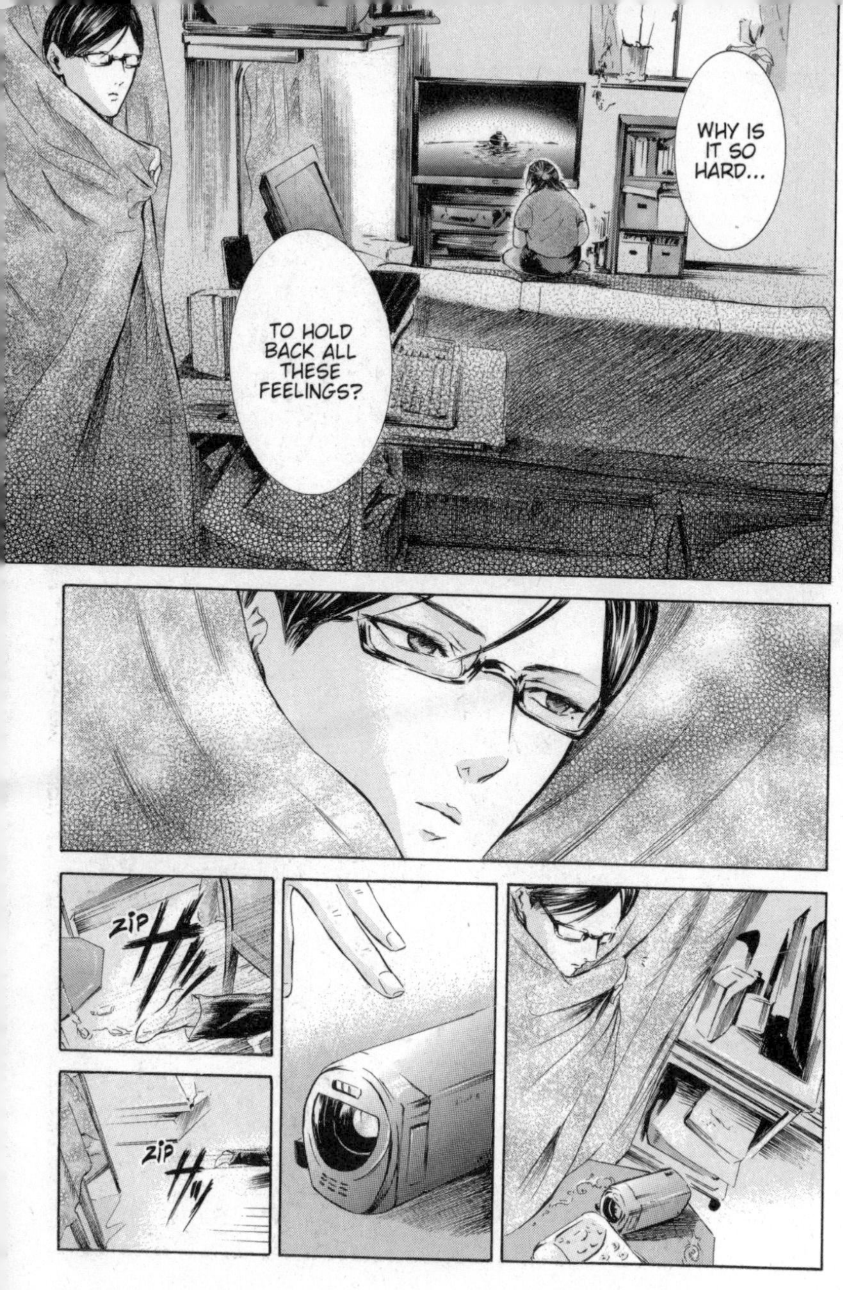
WHY IS IT SO HARD...
TO HOLD BACK ALL THESE FEELINGS?
zip
zip

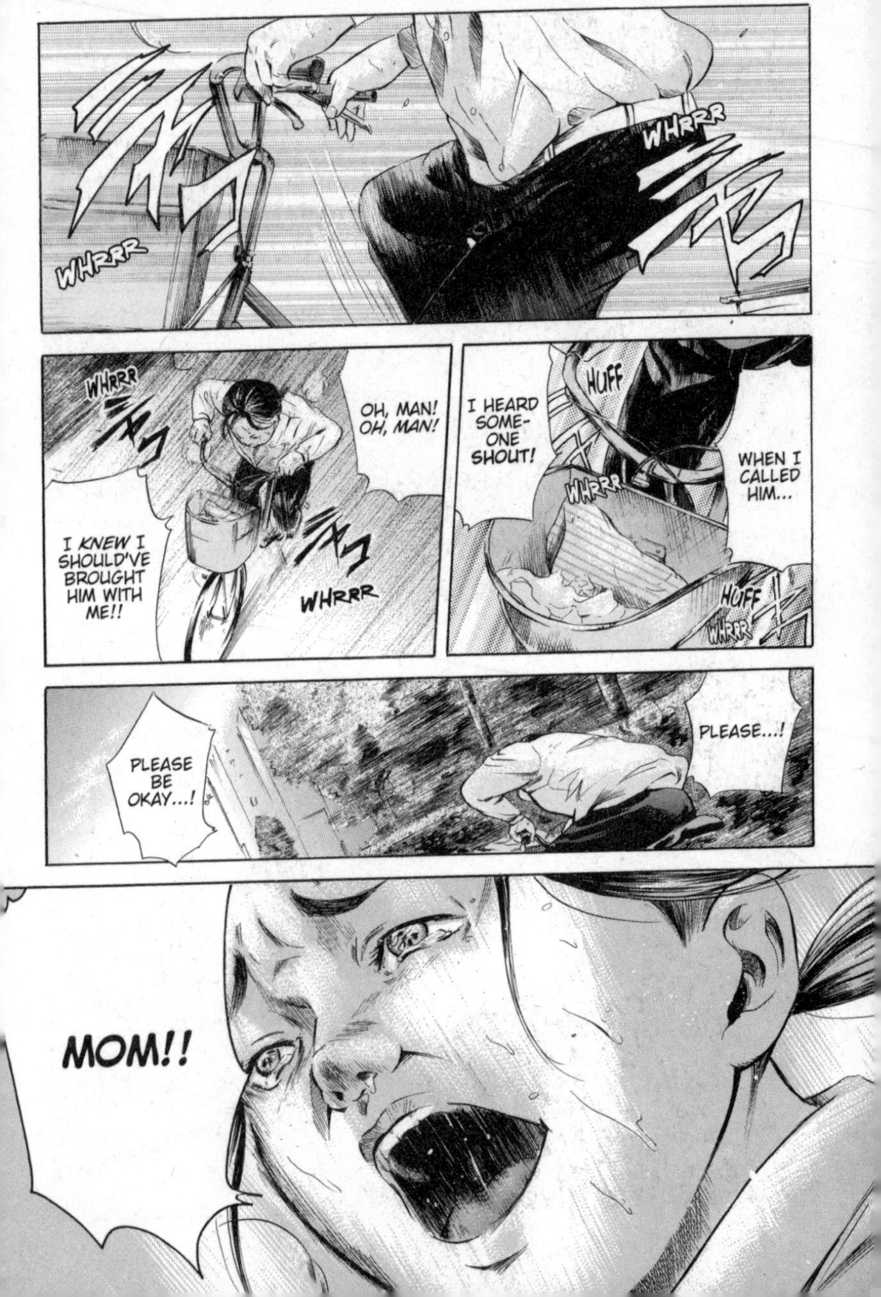
WHRRR
WHRRR
HUFF
WHEN I CALLED HIM...
I HEARD SOME-ONE SHOUT!
WHRRR
HUFF
WHRRR
WHRRR
OH, MAN! OH, MAN!
I KNEW I SHOULD'VE BROUGHT HIM WITH ME!!
WHRRR
PLEASE...!
PLEASE BE OKAY...!
MOM!!

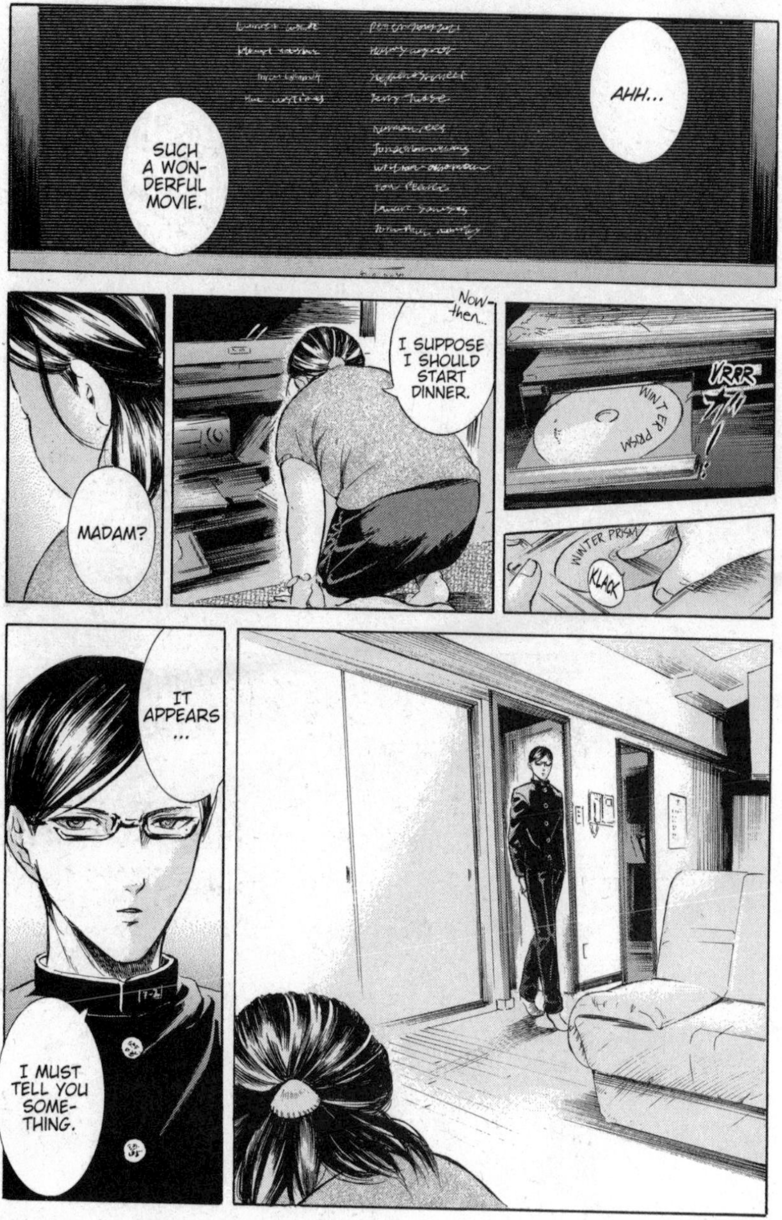
AHH...
SUCH A WON-DERFUL MOVIE.
VRRR
WINTER PRISM
WINTER PRISM
KLACK
Now—then...
I SUPPOSE I SHOULD START DINNER.
MADAM?
IT APPEARS ...
I MUST TELL YOU SOME-THING.

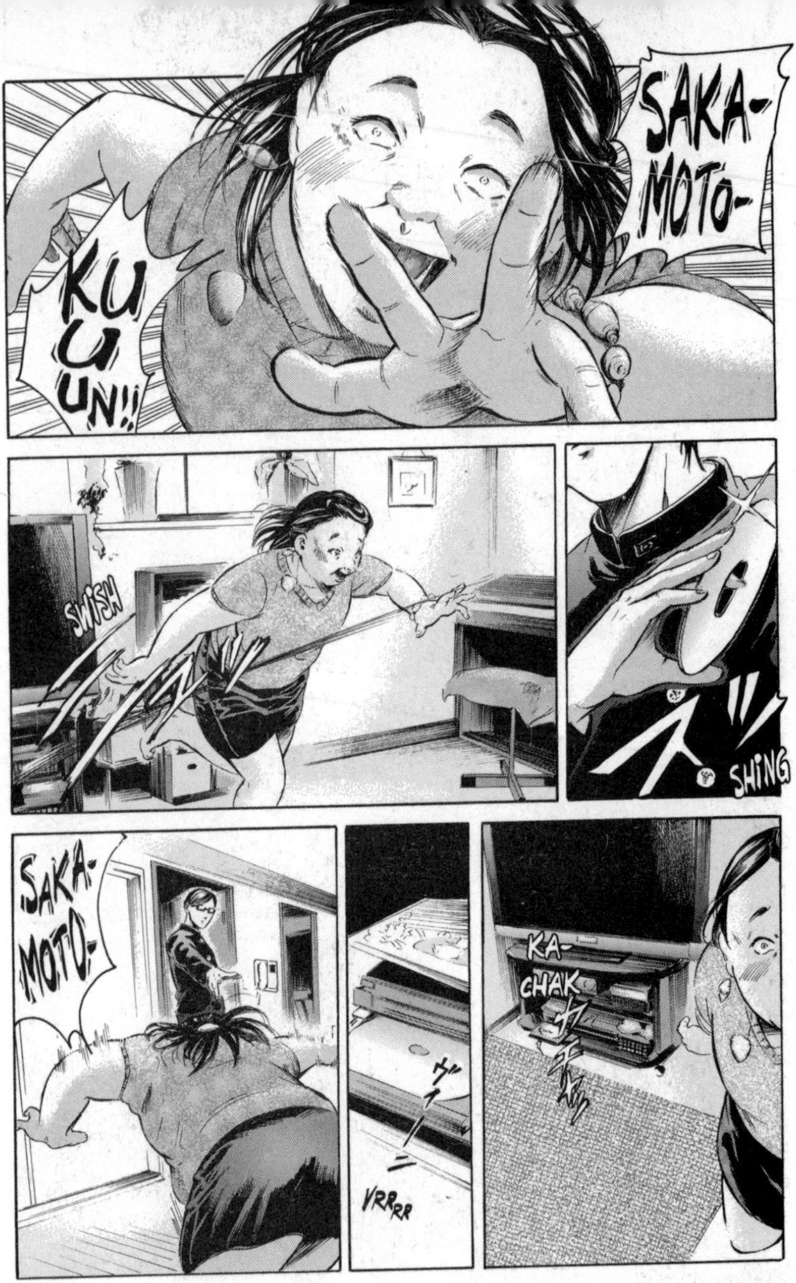
SAKA-MOTO-
KU U U UN!!
SHING
SWISH
KA-CHAK
VRRRR
SAKA-MOTO-

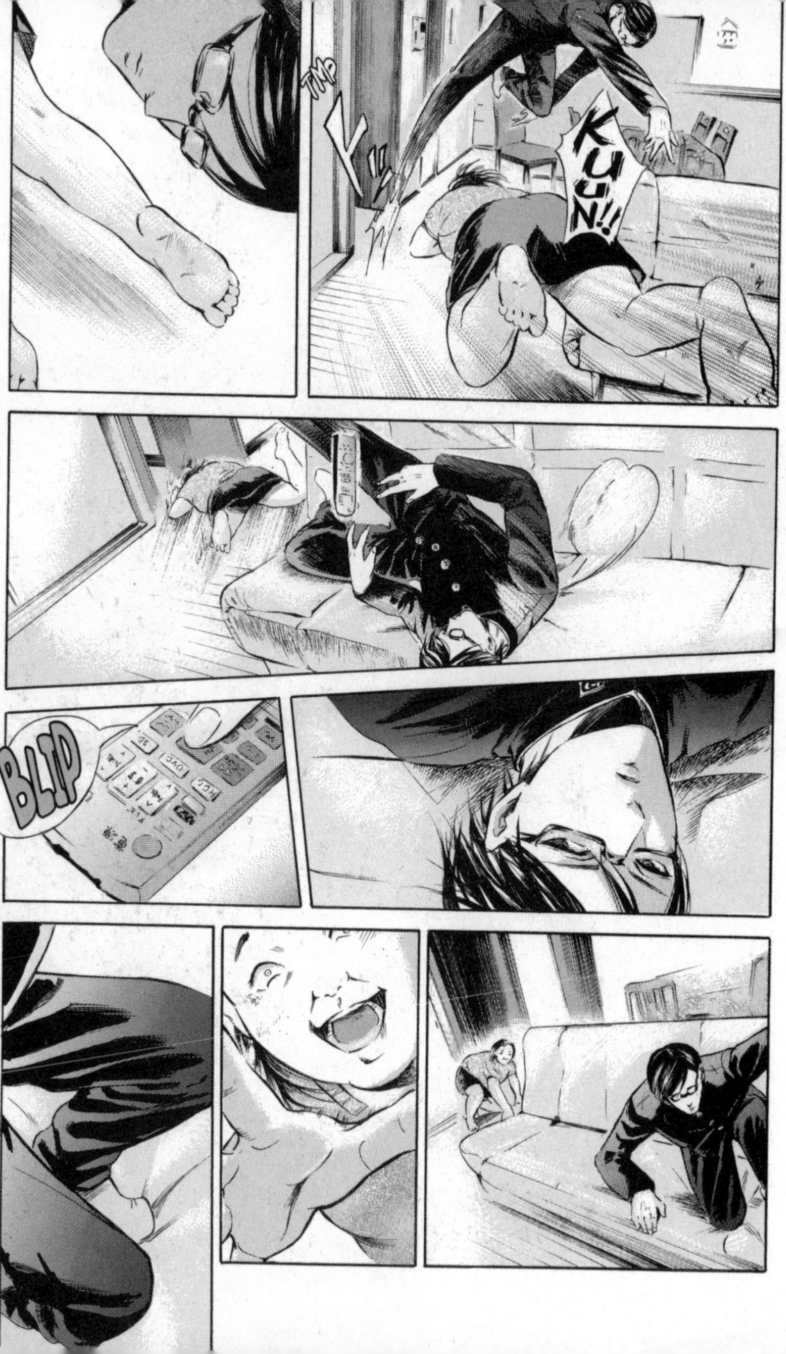
KUUN!!
TMP
BLIP

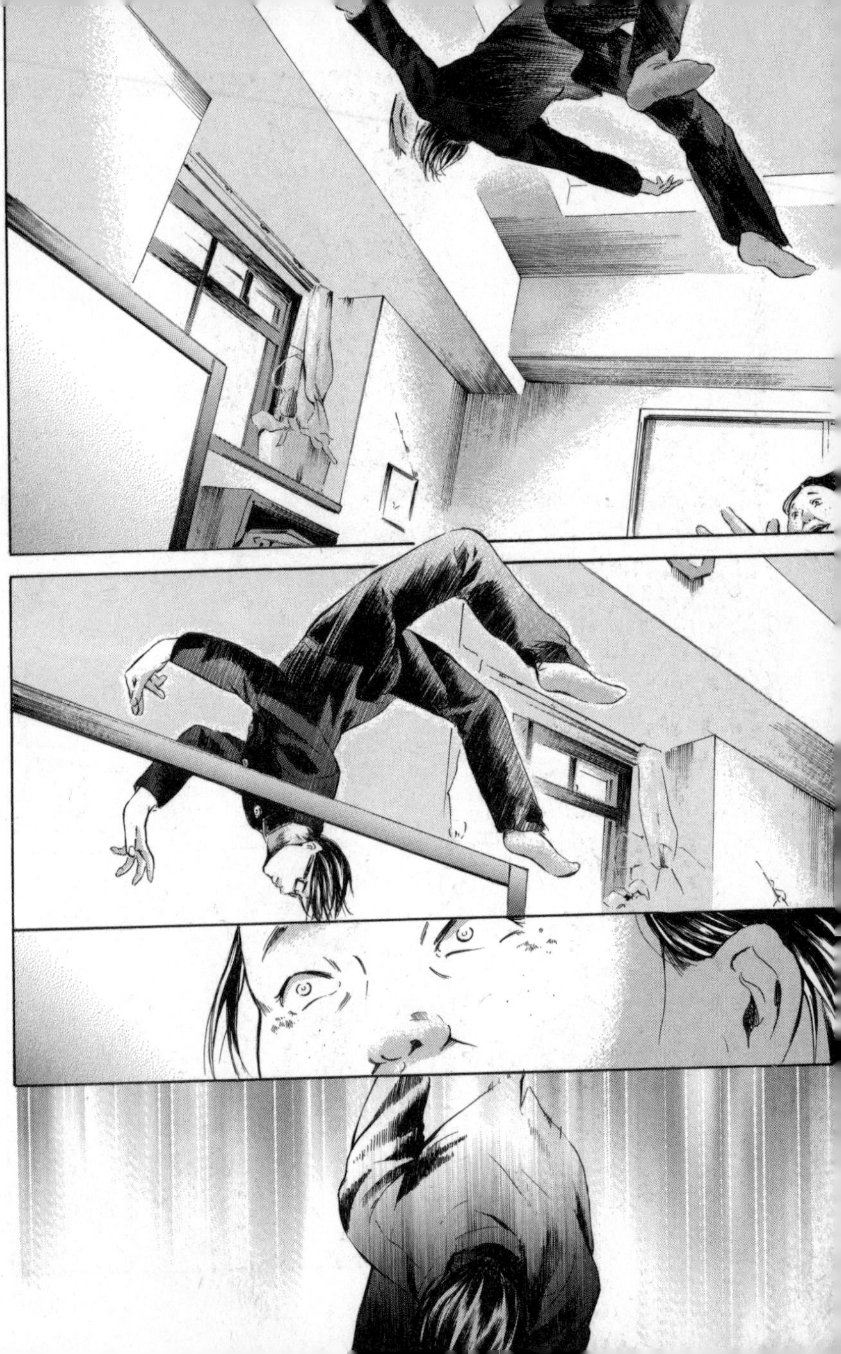

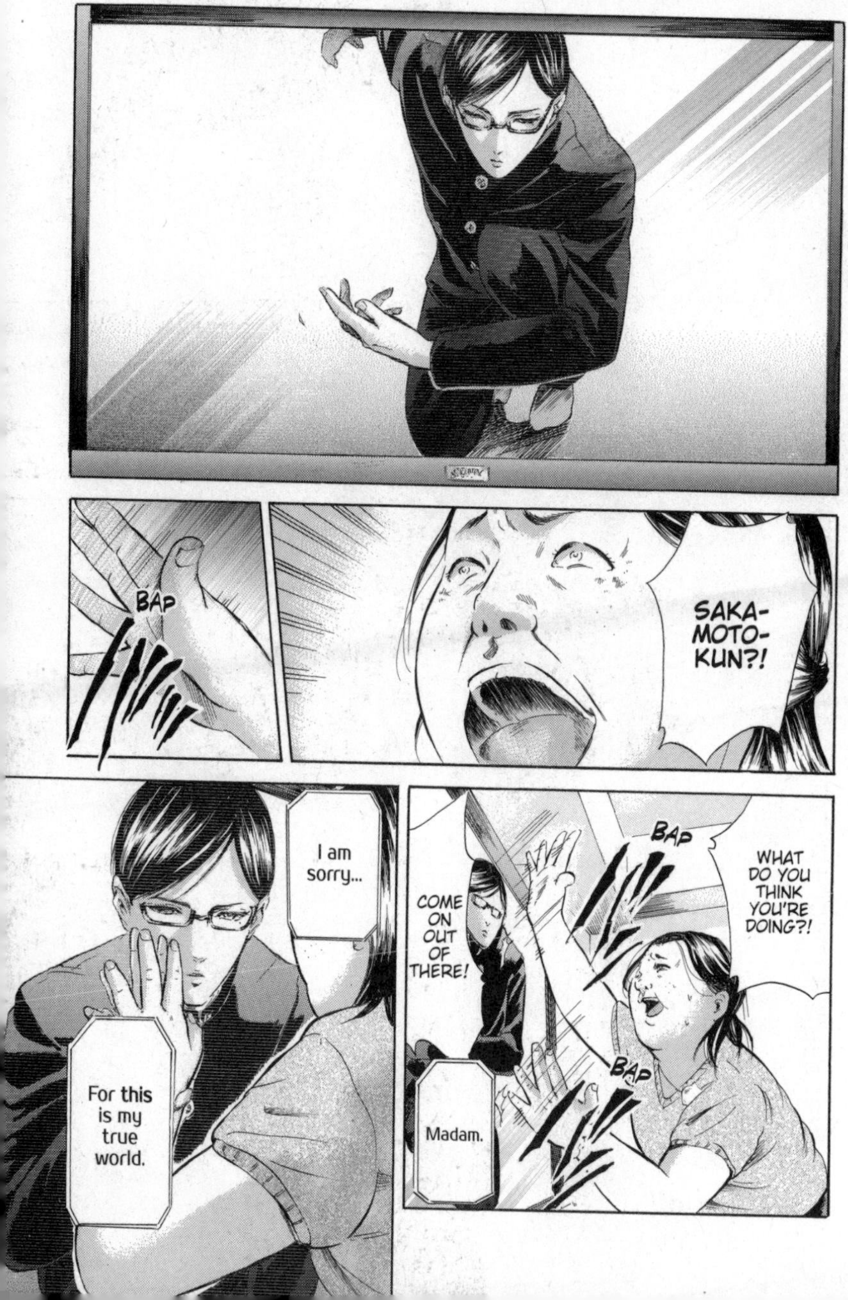
SAKA-MOTO-KUN?!
BAP
BAP
WHAT DO YOU THINK YOU'RE DOING?!
COME ON OUT OF THERE!
BAP
Madam.
I am sorry...
For this is my true world.

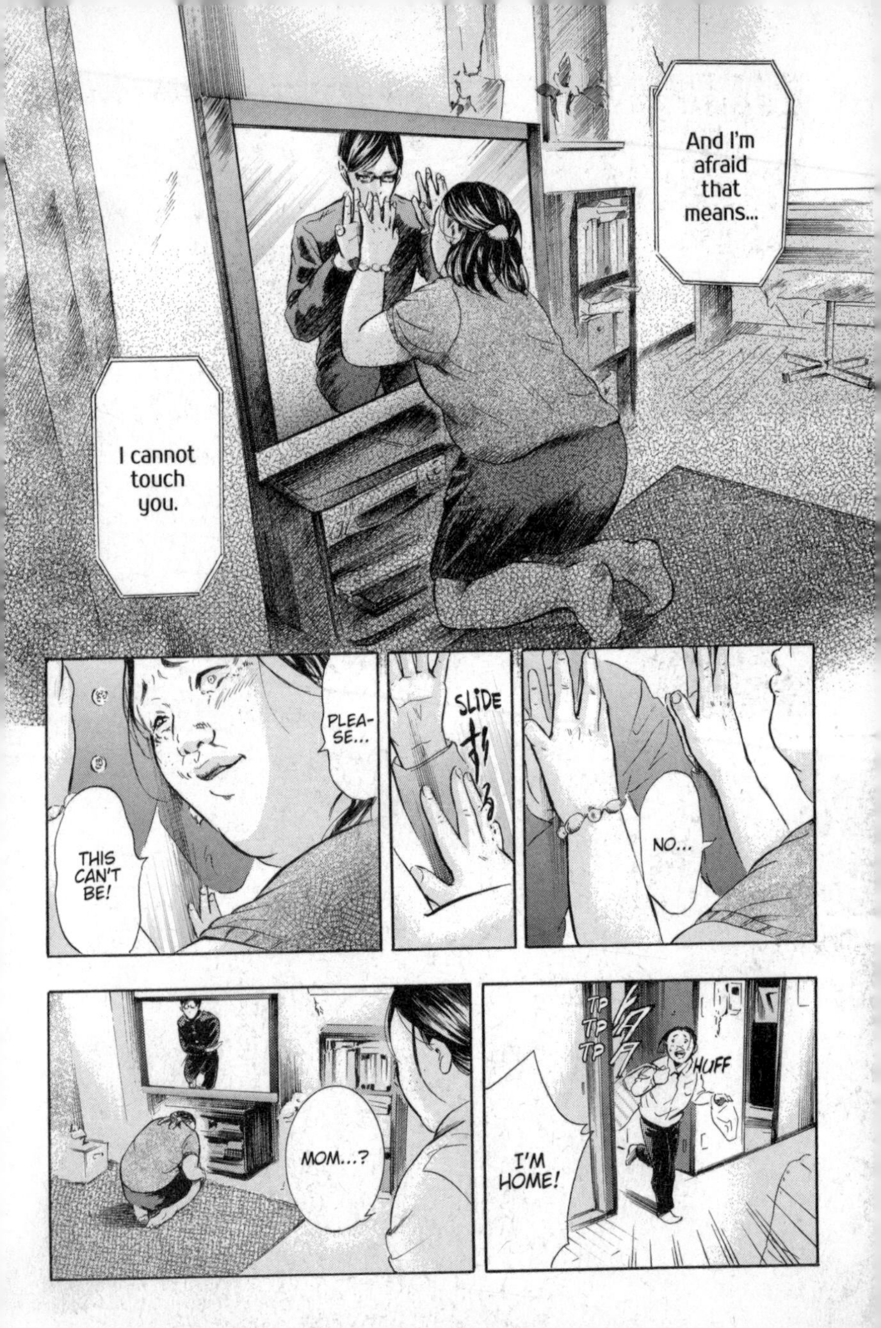
And I'm afraid that means...
I cannot touch you.
NO...
SLIDE
PLEASE-SE...
THIS CAN'T BE!
TP TP TP
HUFF
I'M HOME!
MOM...?

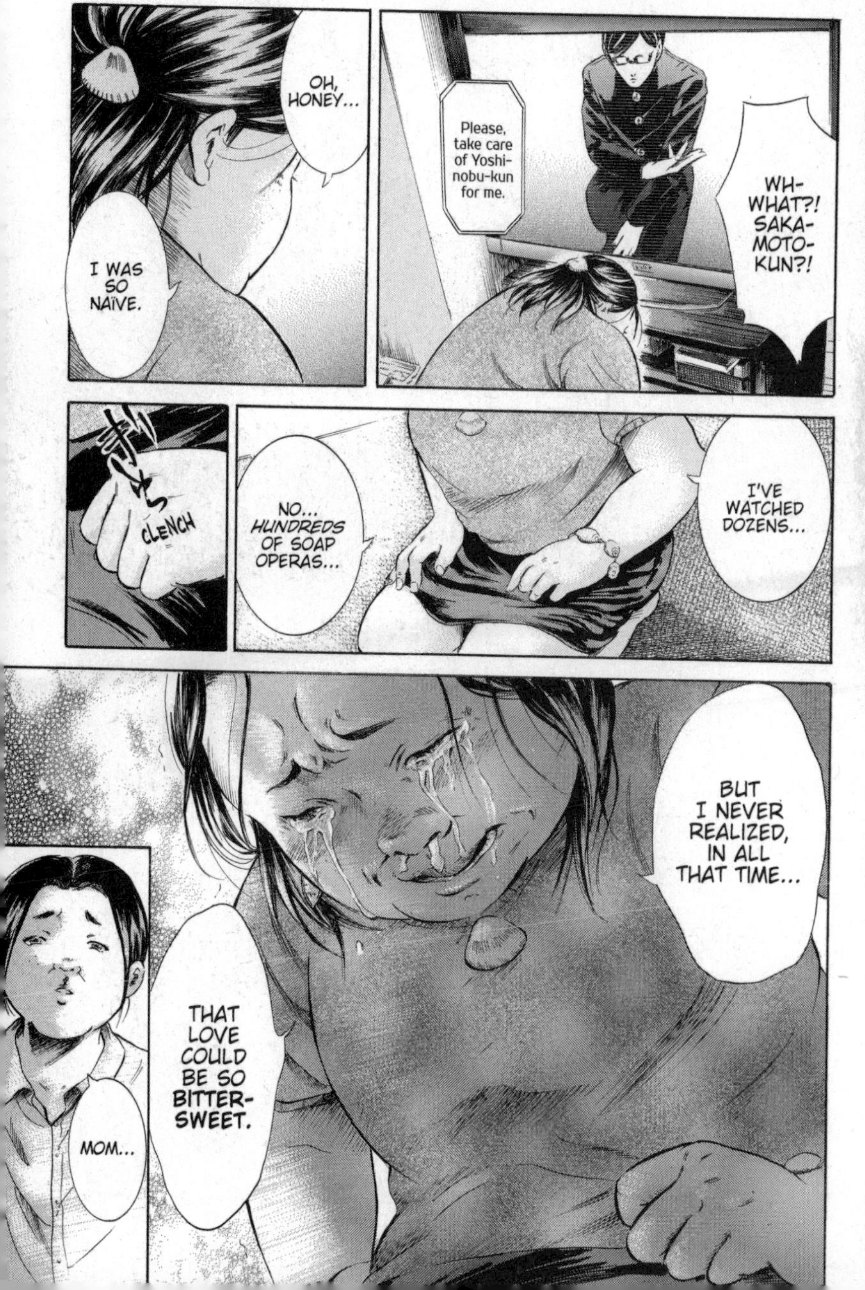
Please, take care of Yoshinobu-kun for me.
WH-WHAT?! SAKAMOTO-KUN?!
OH, HONEY...
I WAS SO NAÏVE.
I'VE WATCHED DOZENS...
NO... *HUNDREDS* OF SOAP OPERAS...
CLENCH
BUT I NEVER REALIZED, IN ALL THAT TIME...
THAT LOVE COULD BE SO BITTERSWEET.
MOM...

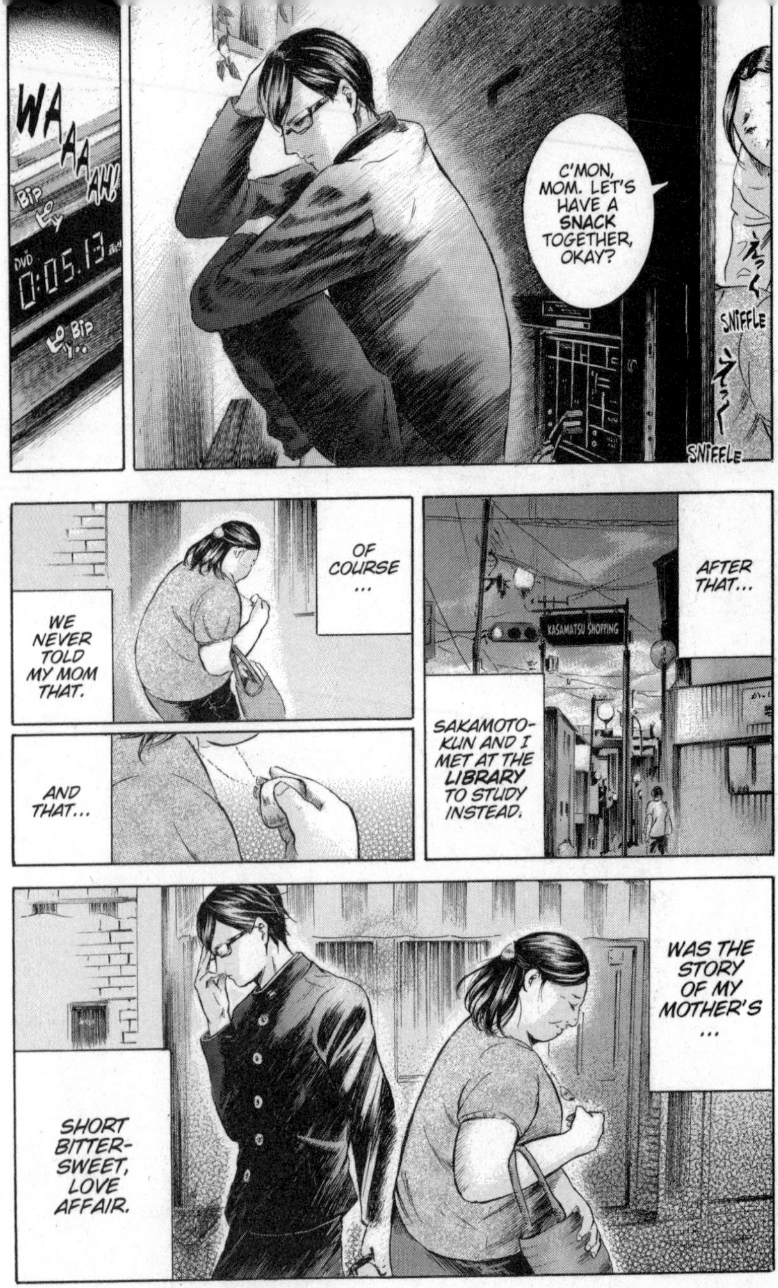
えっく
SNIFFLE
えっく
SNIFFLE
C'MON, MOM. LET'S HAVE A SNACK TOGETHER, OKAY?
WAAAAAH!
BIP
ピッ
DVD 0:05.13
ピッ
BIP
AFTER THAT...
KASAMATSU SHOPPING
SAKAMOTO-KUN AND I MET AT THE LIBRARY TO STUDY INSTEAD.
OF COURSE...
WE NEVER TOLD MY MOM THAT.
AND THAT...
WAS THE STORY OF MY MOTHER'S...
SHORT BITTER-SWEET, LOVE AFFAIR.

End of Chapter 6

SLIDE
スー
!

Physical Exam #1:
Standing
Height

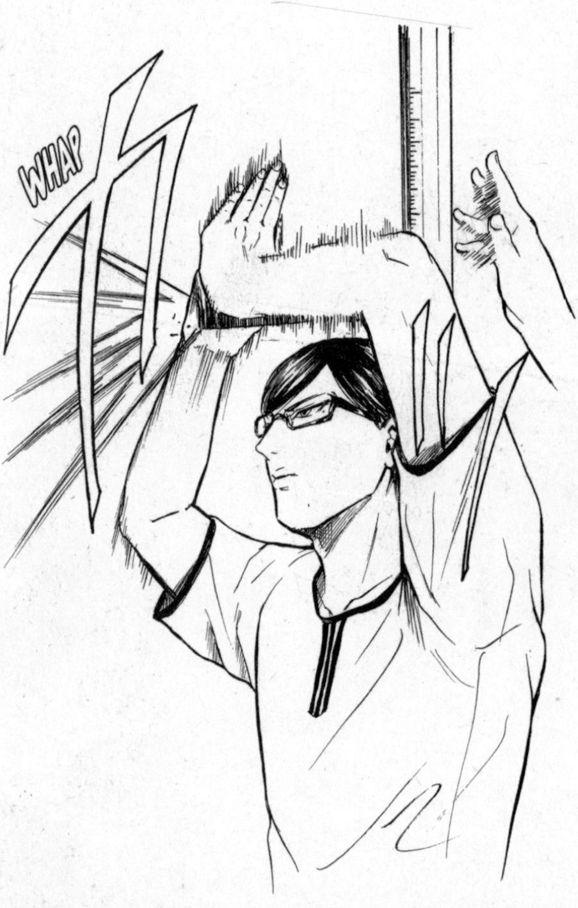
WHAP

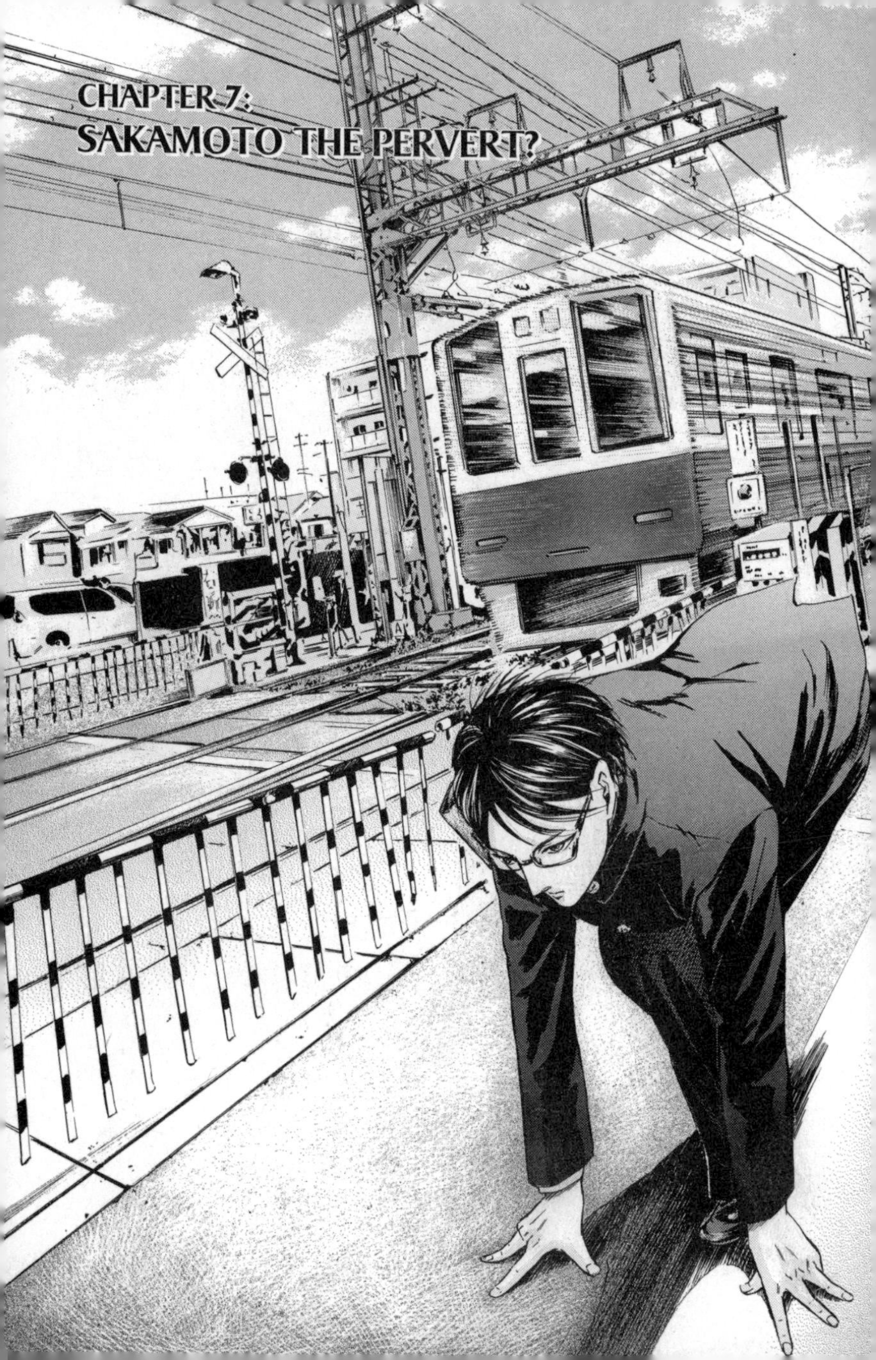
CHAPTER 7:
SAKAMOTO THE PERVERT?

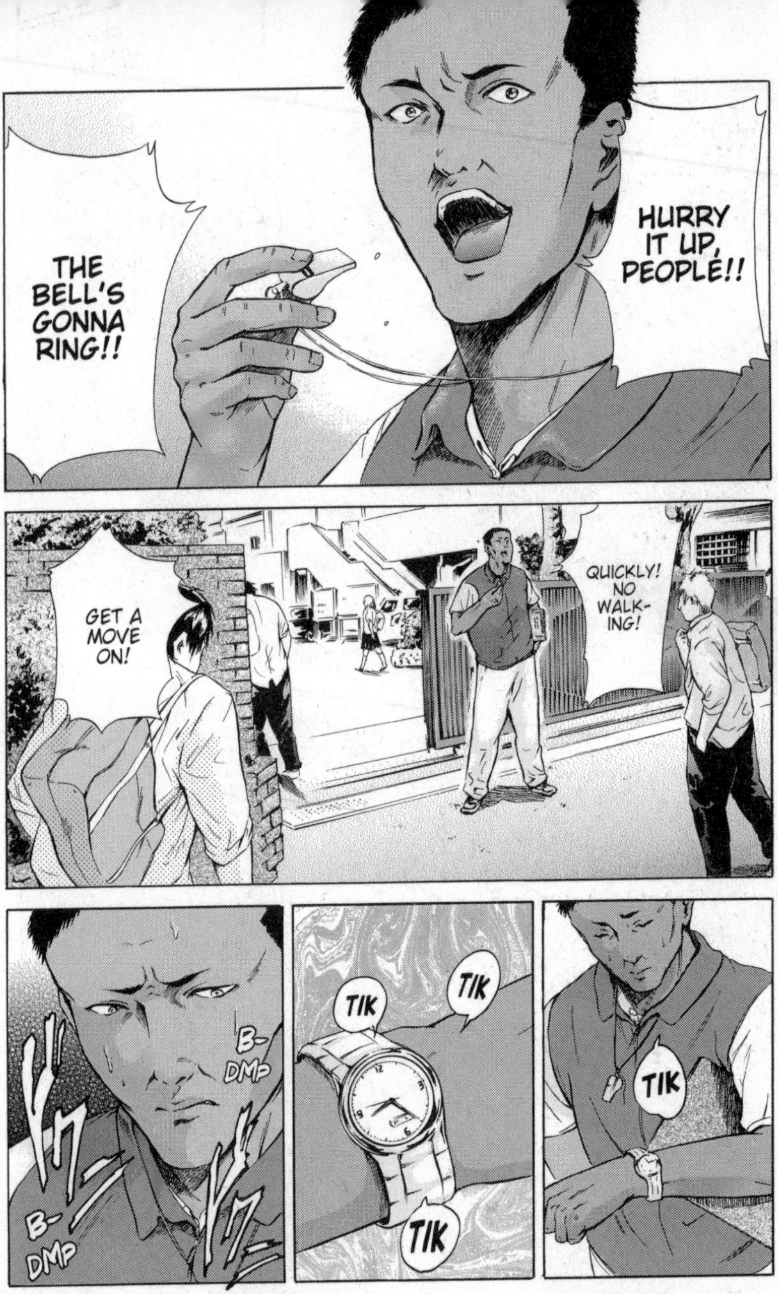
HURRY IT UP, PEOPLE!!
THE BELL'S GONNA RING!!
QUICKLY! NO WALKING!
GET A MOVE ON!
TIK
TIK
TIK
TIK
B-DMP
B-DMP

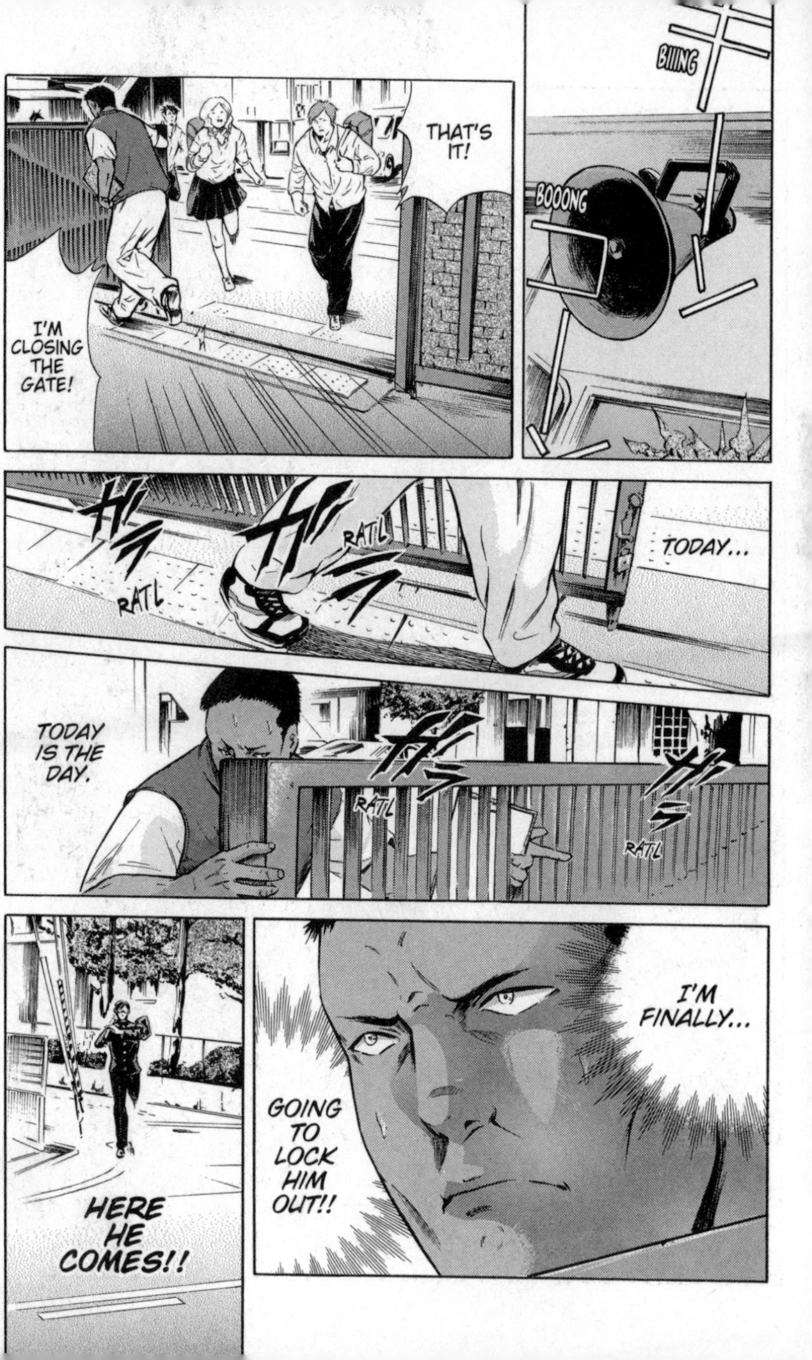
BIING
BOOONG
THAT'S IT!
I'M CLOSING THE GATE!
TODAY...
RATL
RATL
RATL
RATL
TODAY IS THE DAY.
I'M FINALLY...
GOING TO LOCK HIM OUT!!
HERE HE COMES!!

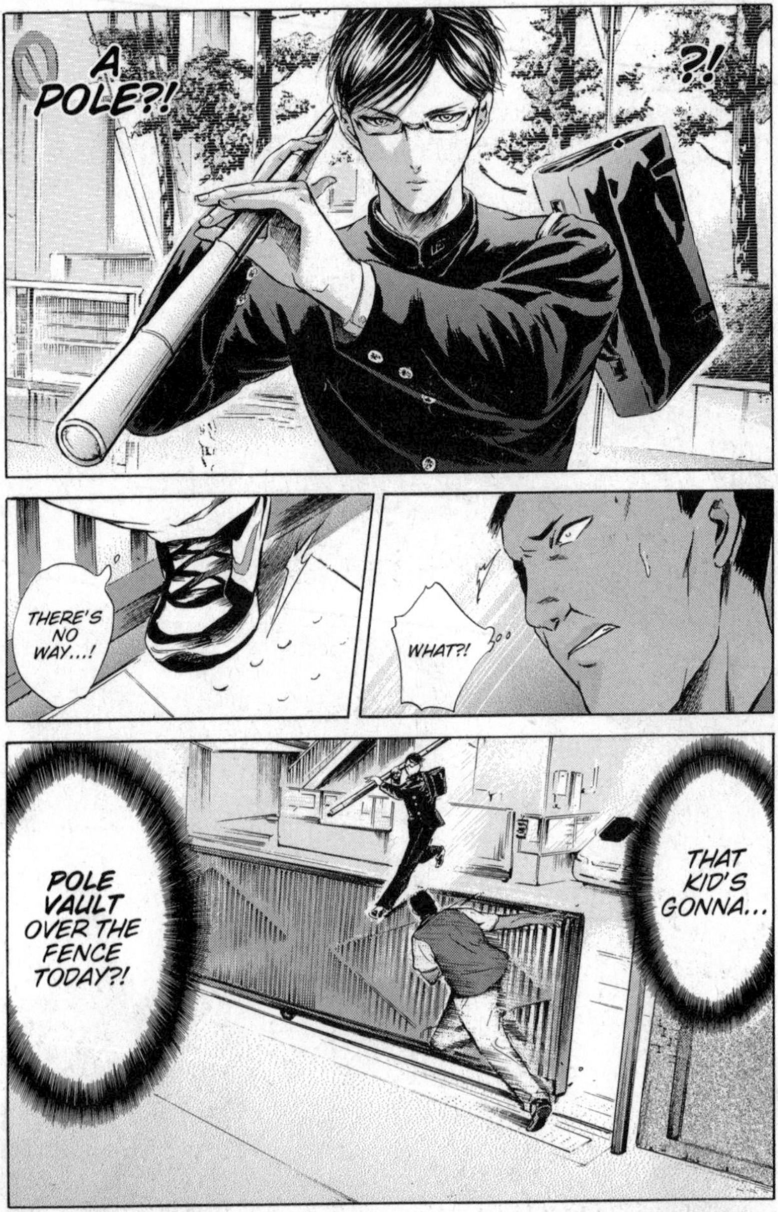
?!
A POLE?!
WHAT?!
THERE'S NO WAY...!
THAT KID'S GONNA...
POLE VAULT OVER THE FENCE TODAY?!

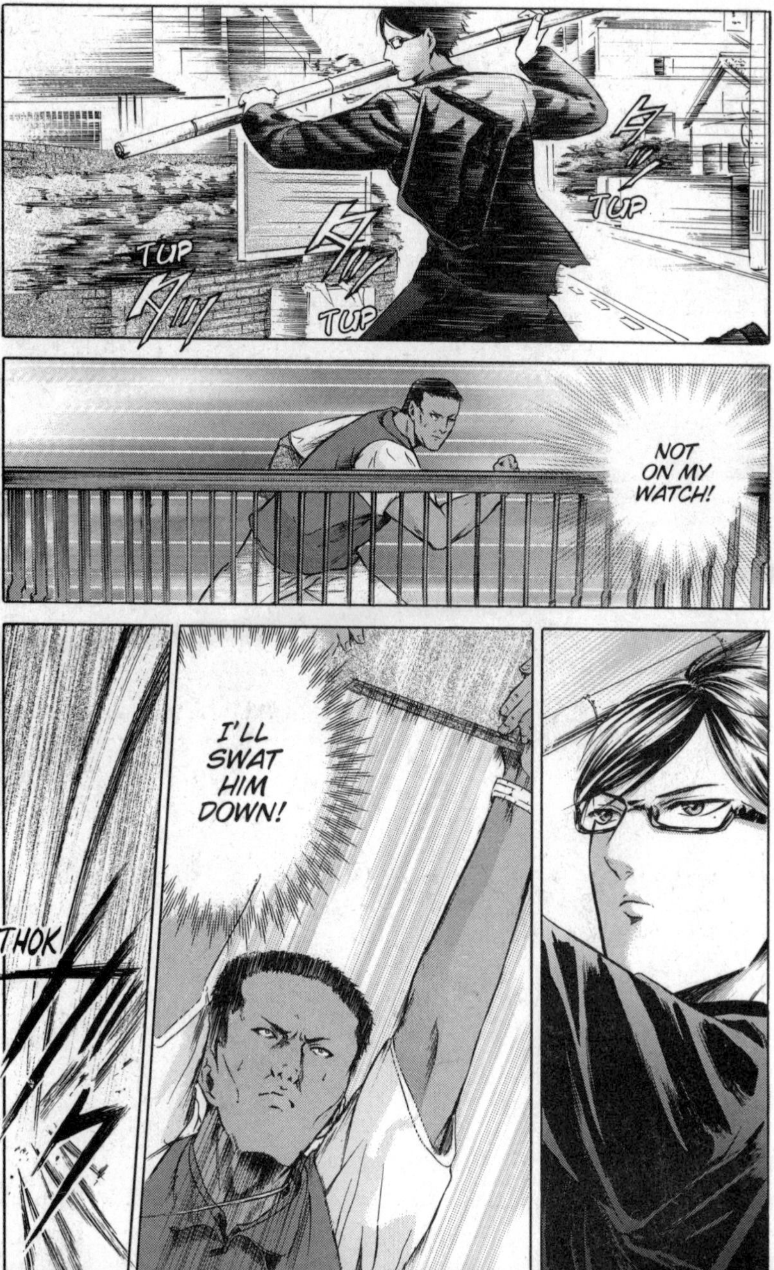
TUP
TUP
TUP
NOT ON MY WATCH!
I'LL SWAT HIM DOWN!
THOK

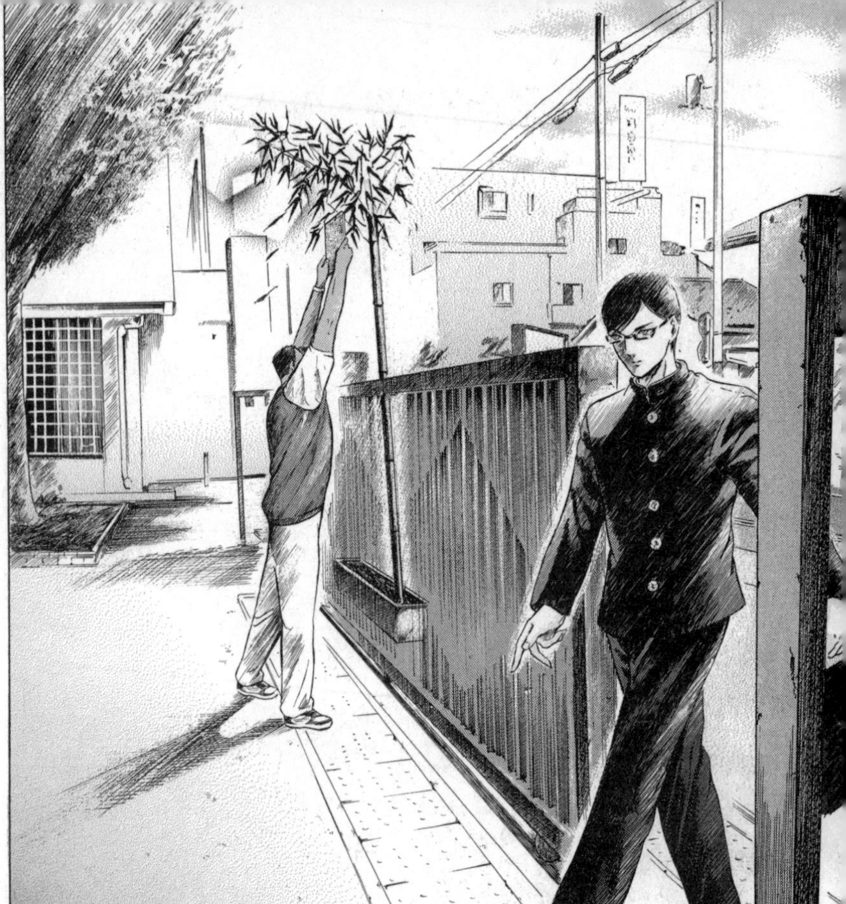

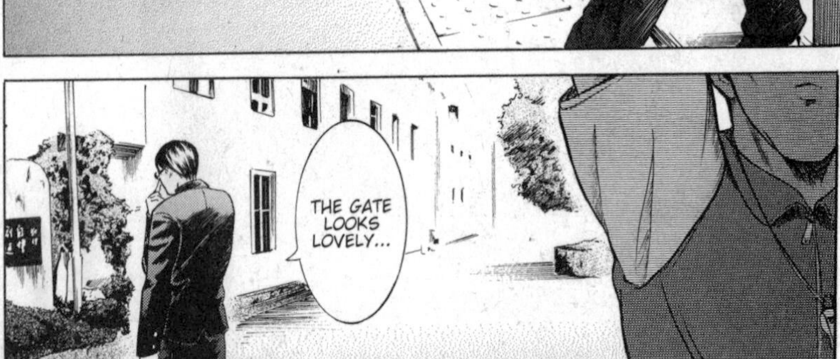
THE GATE LOOKS LOVELY...

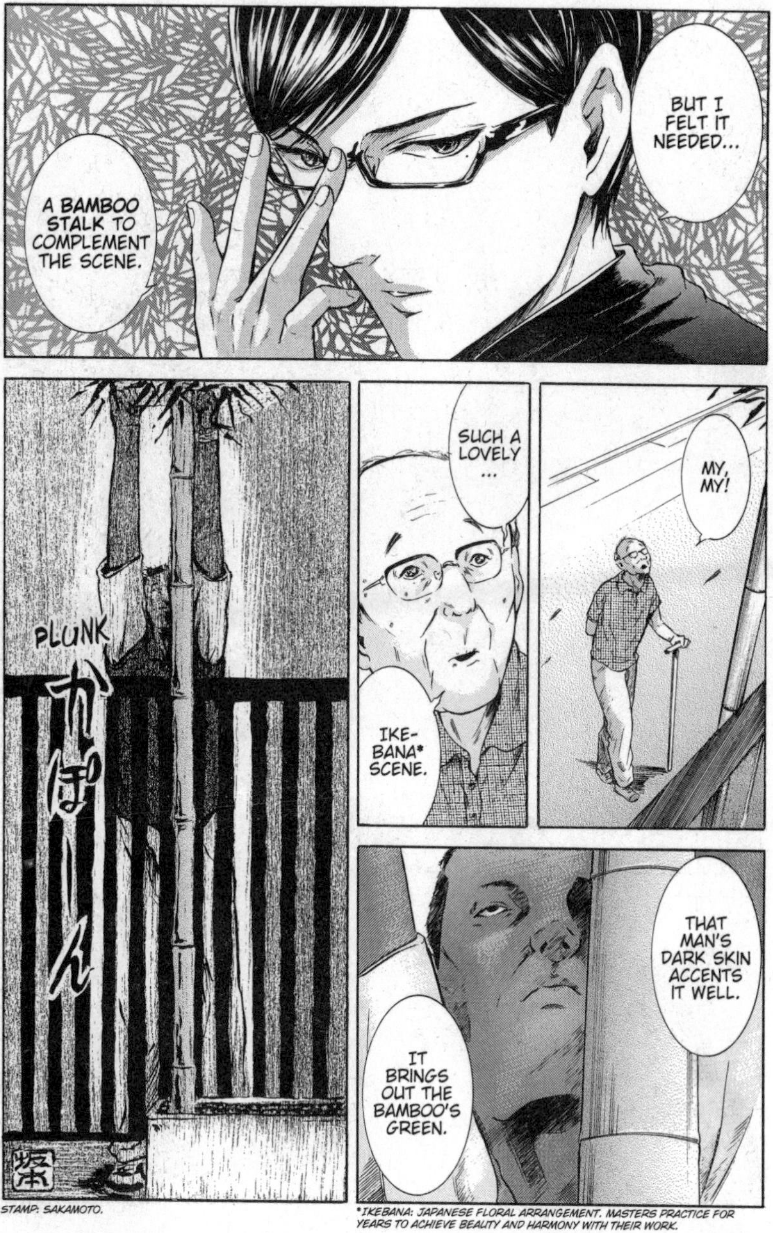
BUT I FELT IT NEEDED...
A BAMBOO STALK TO COMPLEMENT THE SCENE.
MY, MY!
SUCH A LOVELY ...
IKEBANA* SCENE.
THAT MAN'S DARK SKIN ACCENTS IT WELL.
IT BRINGS OUT THE BAMBOO'S GREEN.
PLUNK
かぽーん

STAMP: SAKAMOTO.

*IKEBANA: JAPANESE FLORAL ARRANGEMENT. MASTERS PRACTICE FOR YEARS TO ACHIEVE BEAUTY AND HARMONY WITH THEIR WORK.

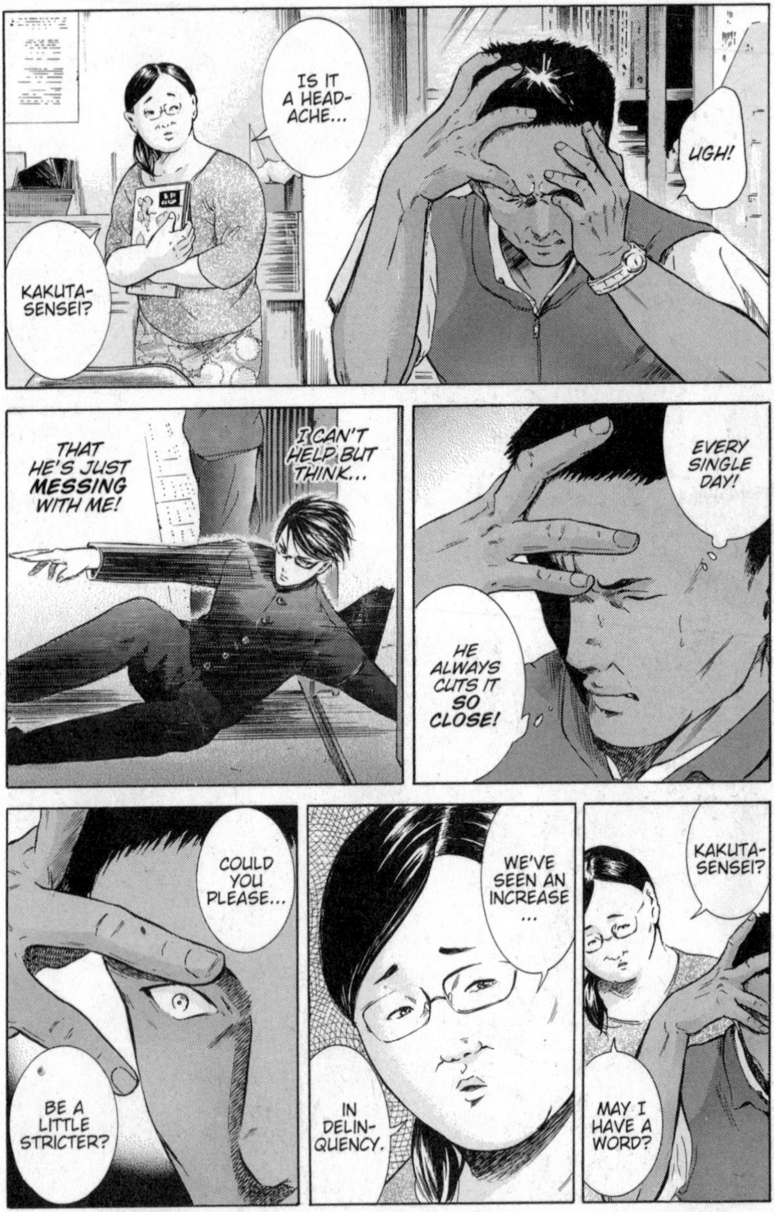
UGH!
IS IT A HEAD-ACHE...
KAKUTA-SENSEI?
EVERY SINGLE DAY!
HE ALWAYS CUTS IT SO CLOSE!
I CAN'T HELP BUT THINK...
THAT HE'S JUST MESSING WITH ME!
KAKUTA-SENSEI?
MAY I HAVE A WORD?
WE'VE SEEN AN INCREASE ...
IN DELIN-QUENCY.
COULD YOU PLEASE...
BE A LITTLE STRICTER?

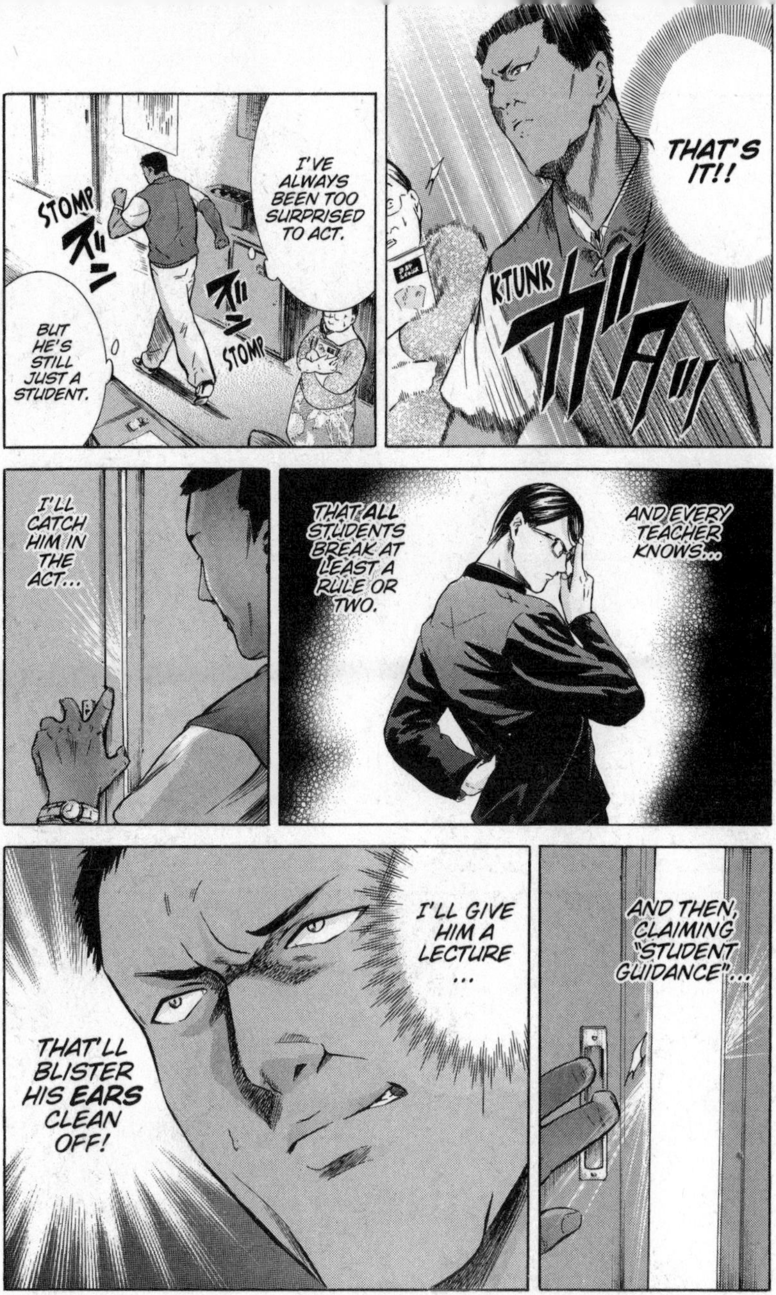
THAT'S IT!!
KTUNK
ガタッ
I'VE ALWAYS BEEN TOO SURPRISED TO ACT.
STOMP
ズン
ズン
STOMP
BUT HE'S STILL JUST A STUDENT.
AND EVERY TEACHER KNOWS...
THAT ALL STUDENTS BREAK AT LEAST A RULE OR TWO.
I'LL CATCH HIM IN THE ACT...
AND THEN, CLAIMING "STUDENT GUIDANCE"...
I'LL GIVE HIM A LECTURE ...
THAT'LL BLISTER HIS EARS CLEAN OFF!

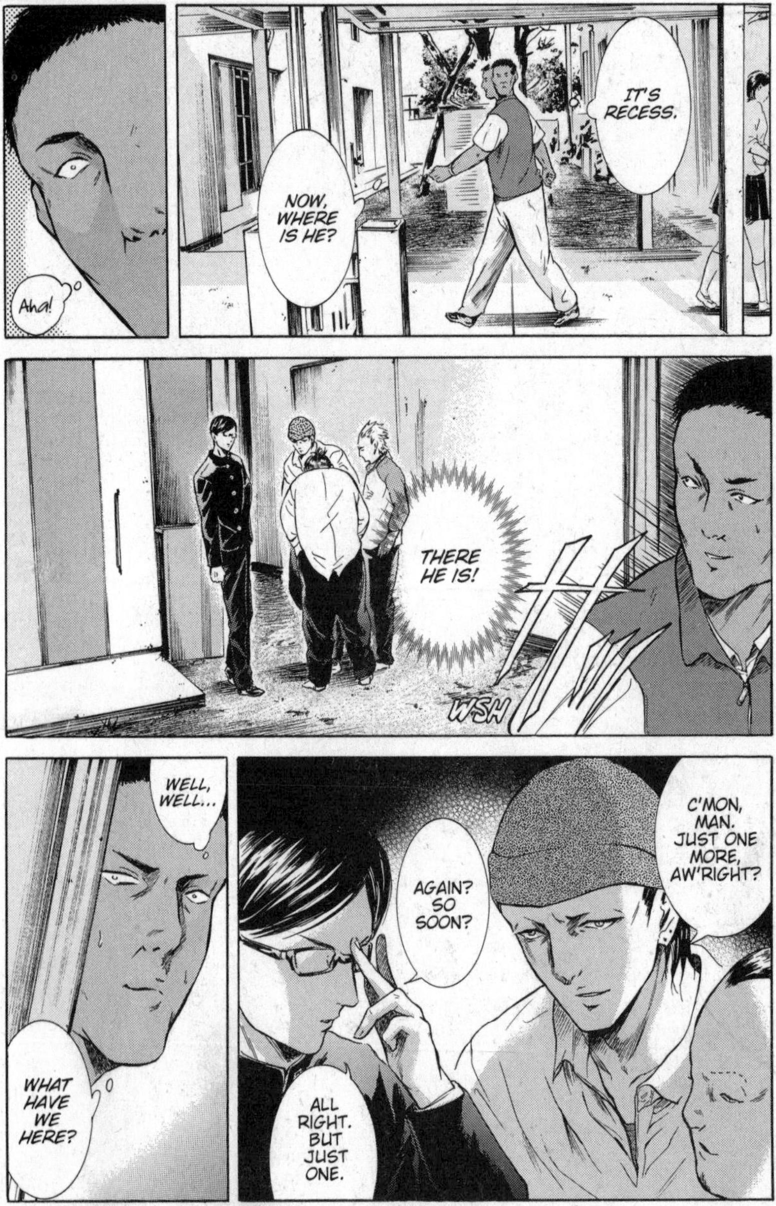
IT'S RECESS.
NOW, WHERE IS HE?
Aha!
THERE HE IS!
WSH
C'MON, MAN. JUST ONE MORE, AW'RIGHT?
AGAIN? SO SOON?
ALL RIGHT. BUT JUST ONE.
WELL, WELL...
WHAT HAVE WE HERE?

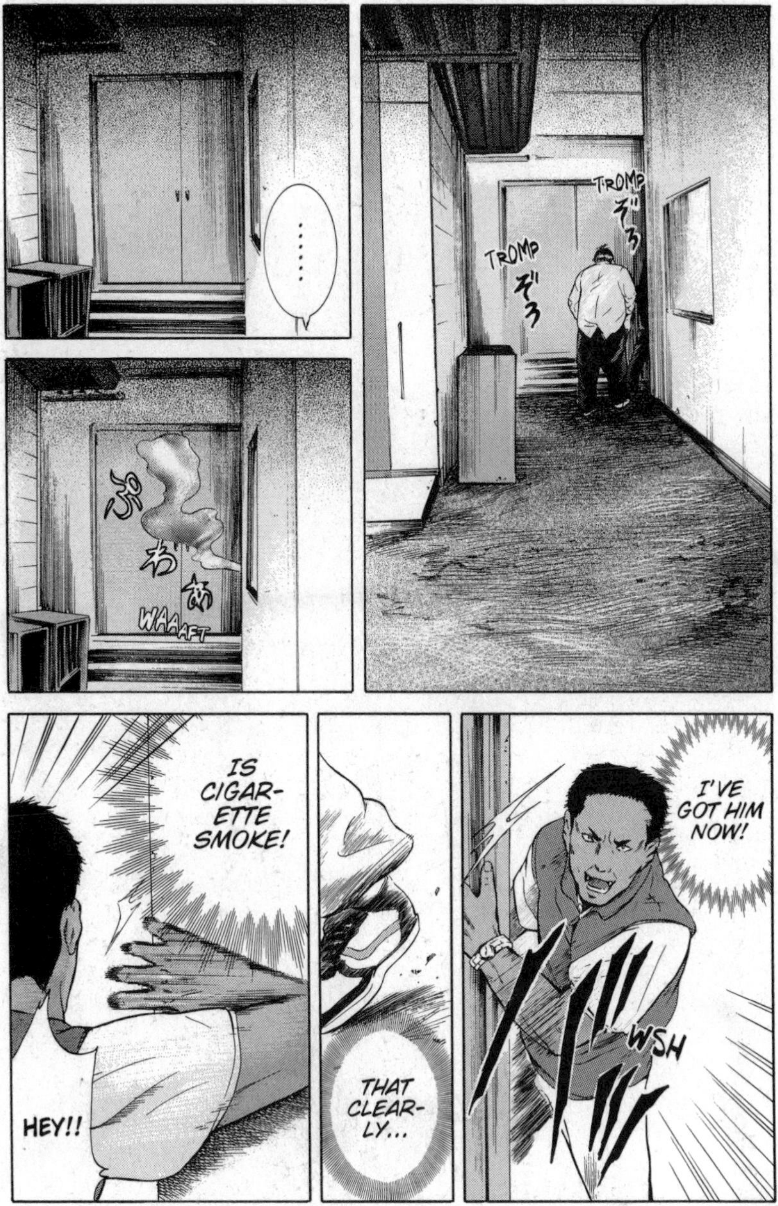
TROMP
ぞろ
TROMP
ぞろ
......
ぷわあ
WAAAFT
I'VE GOT HIM NOW!
WSH
THAT CLEAR-LY...
IS CIGAR-ETTE SMOKE!
HEY!!

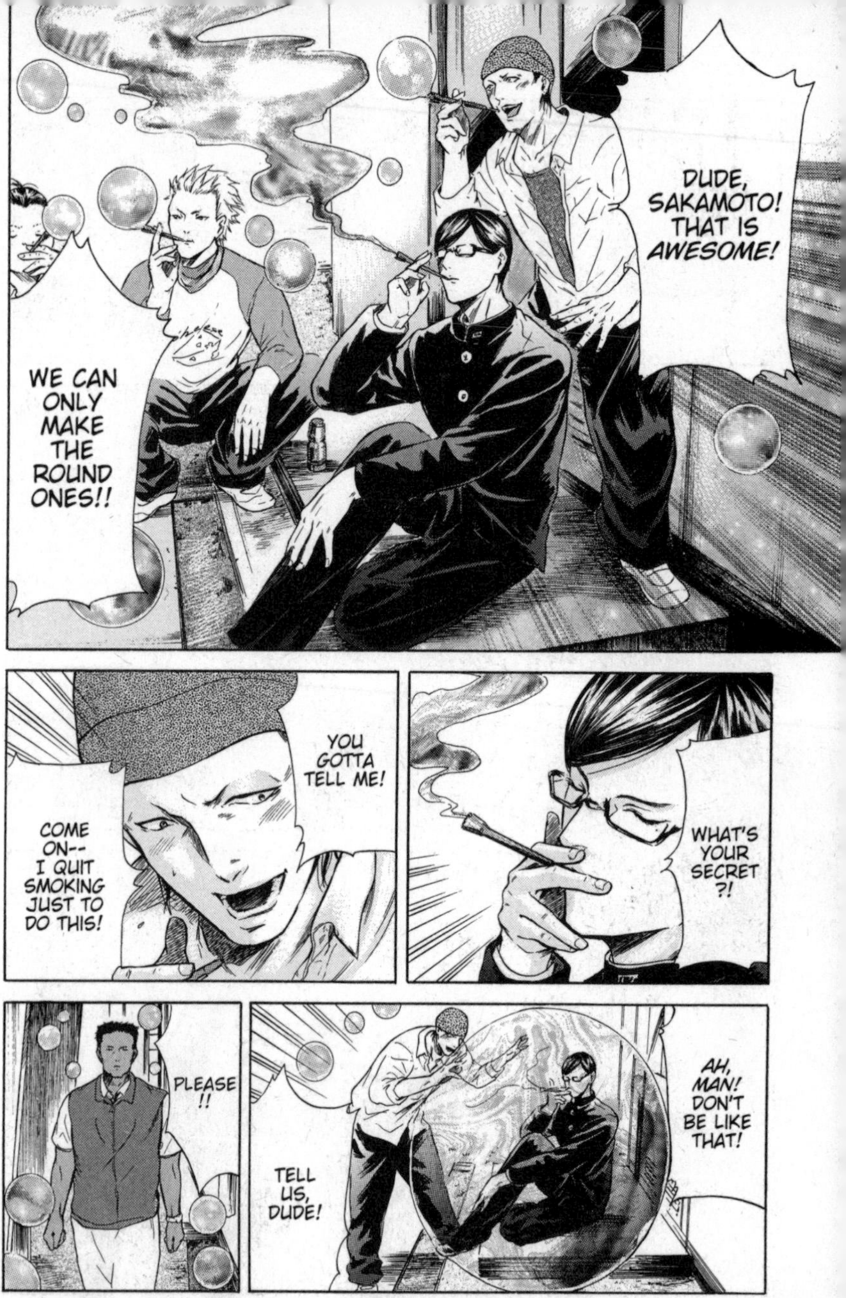
DUDE, SAKAMOTO! THAT IS AWESOME!
WE CAN ONLY MAKE THE ROUND ONES!!
WHAT'S YOUR SECRET ?!
YOU GOTTA TELL ME!
COME ON-- I QUIT SMOKING JUST TO DO THIS!
AH, MAN! DON'T BE LIKE THAT!
TELL US, DUDE!
PLEASE !!

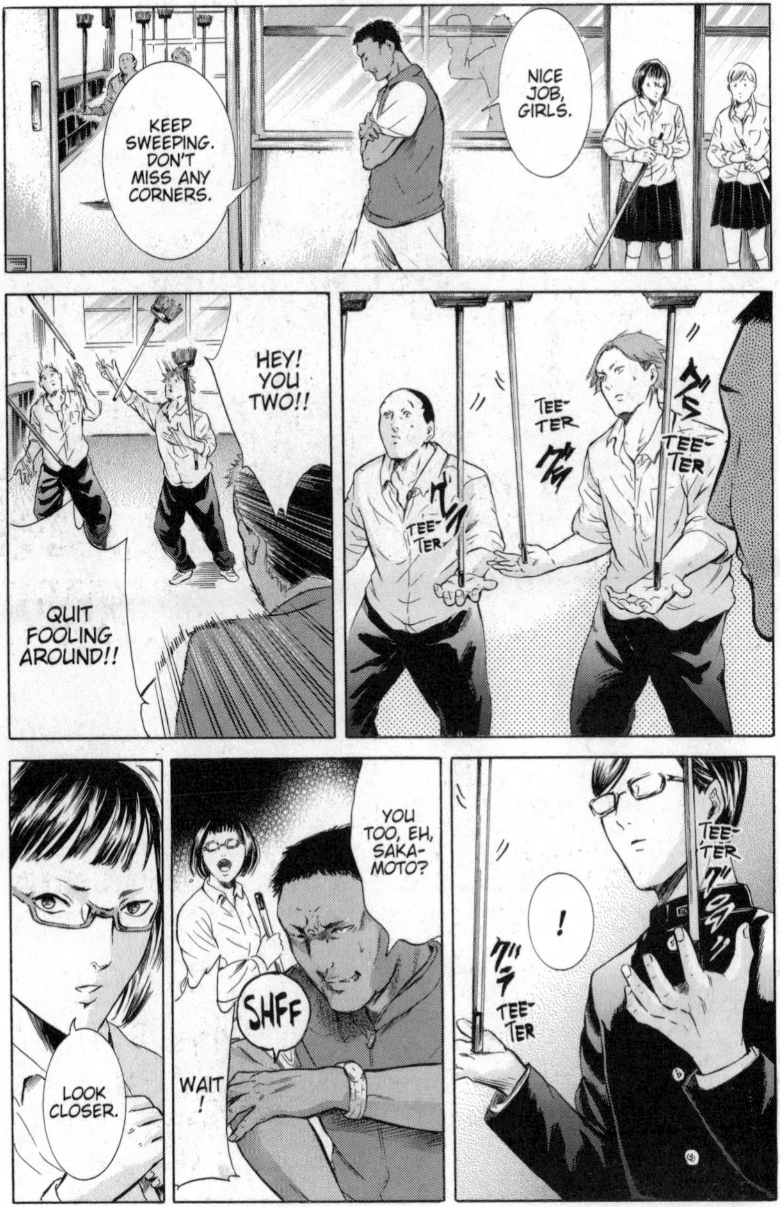
NICE JOB, GIRLS.
KEEP SWEEPING. DON'T MISS ANY CORNERS.
TEE-TER
TEE-TER
TEE-TER
HEY! YOU TWO!!
QUIT FOOLING AROUND!!
TEE-TER
!
TEE-TER
YOU TOO, EH, SAKAMOTO?
SHFF
WAIT!
LOOK CLOSER.

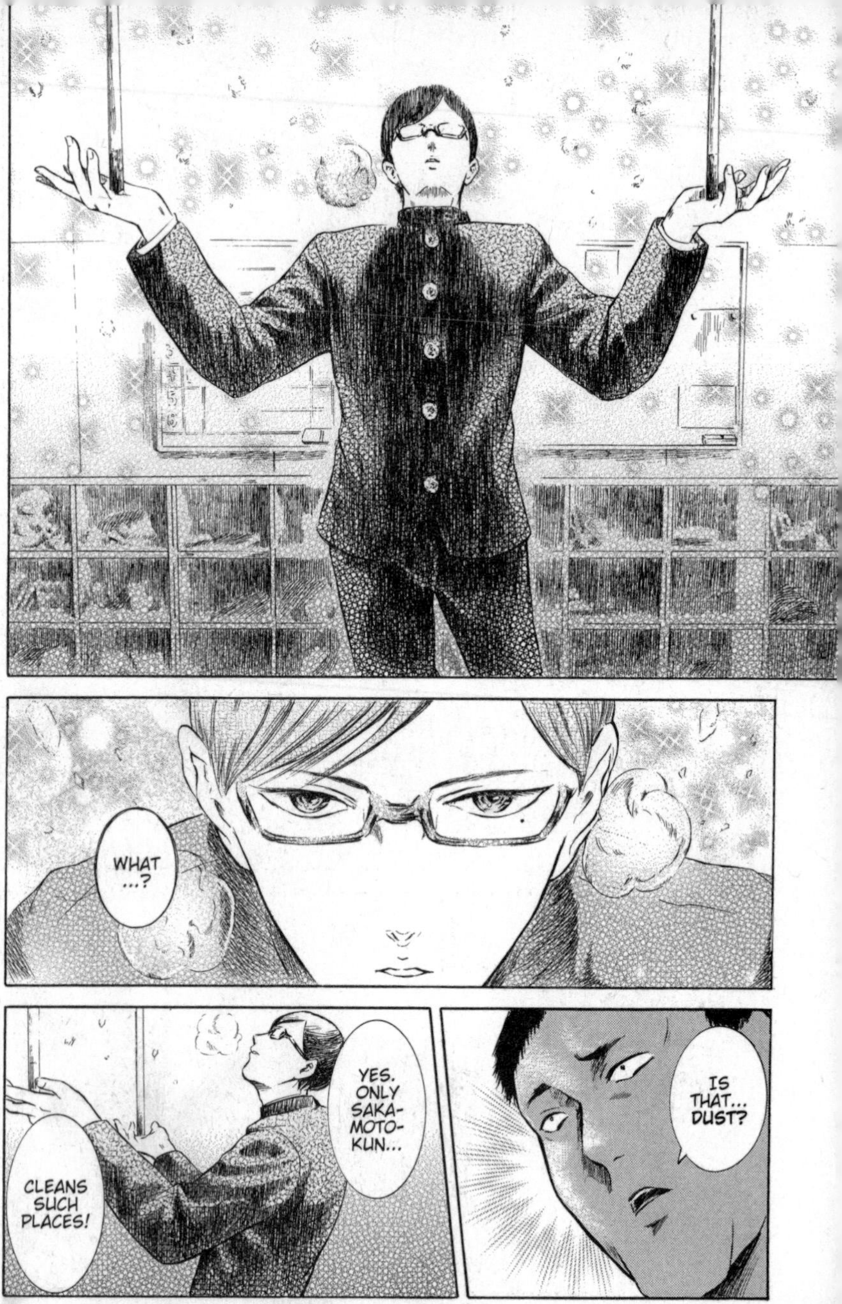
WHAT ...?
IS THAT... DUST?
YES. ONLY SAKA-MOTO-KUN...
CLEANS SUCH PLACES!

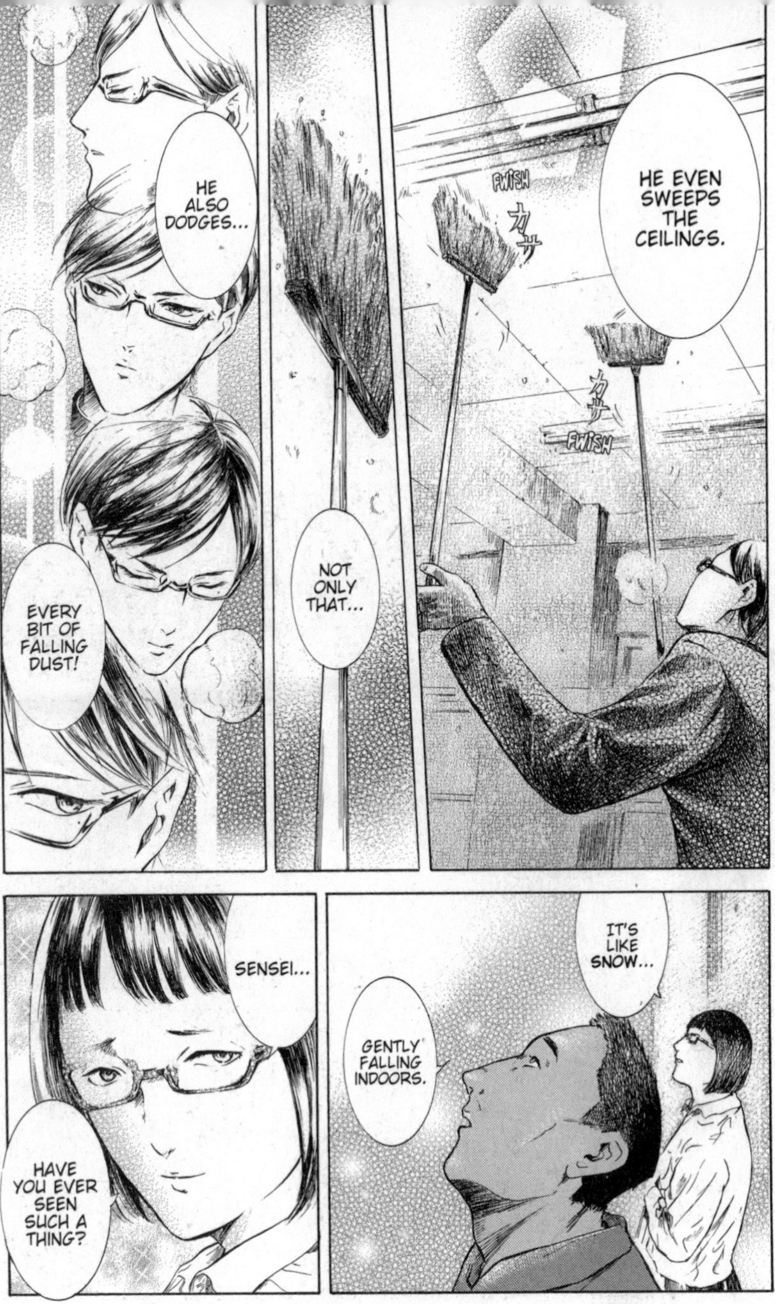
HE EVEN SWEEPS THE CEILINGS.
FWISH
カサ
カサ
FWISH
NOT ONLY THAT...
HE ALSO DODGES...
EVERY BIT OF FALLING DUST!
IT'S LIKE SNOW...
GENTLY FALLING INDOORS.
SENSEI...
HAVE YOU EVER SEEN SUCH A THING?

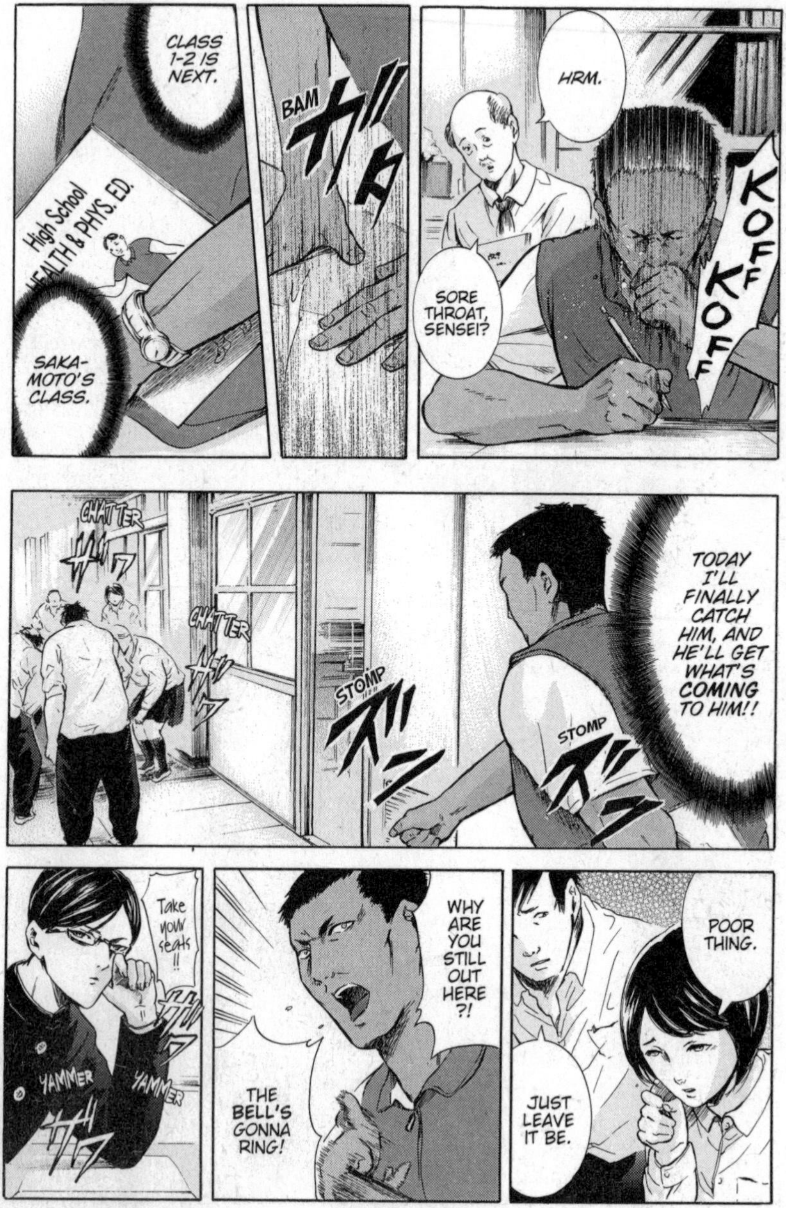
HRM.
KOFF KOFF KOFF
SORE THROAT, SENSEI?
BAM
CLASS 1-2 IS NEXT.
High School HEALTH & PHYS. ED.
SAKAMOTO'S CLASS.
TODAY I'LL FINALLY CATCH HIM, AND HE'LL GET WHAT'S COMING TO HIM!!
STOMP
STOMP
CHATTER
CHATTER
POOR THING.
JUST LEAVE IT BE.
WHY ARE YOU STILL OUT HERE?!
THE BELL'S GONNA RING!
Take your seats!!
YAMMER
YAMMER

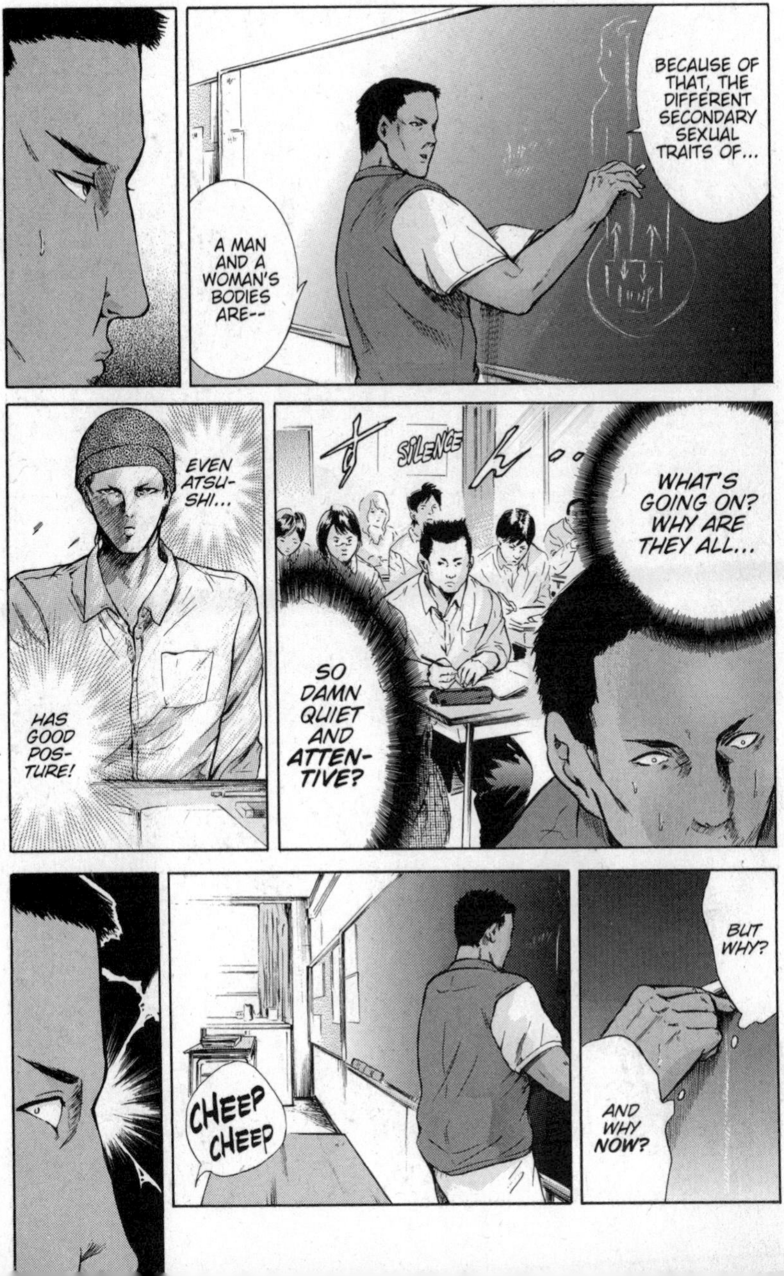
BECAUSE OF THAT, THE DIFFERENT SECONDARY SEXUAL TRAITS OF...
A MAN AND A WOMAN'S BODIES ARE--
SILENCE
WHAT'S GOING ON? WHY ARE THEY ALL...
SO DAMN QUIET AND ATTEN-TIVE?
EVEN ATSU-SHI...
HAS GOOD POS-TURE!
BUT WHY?
AND WHY NOW?
CHEEP CHEEP

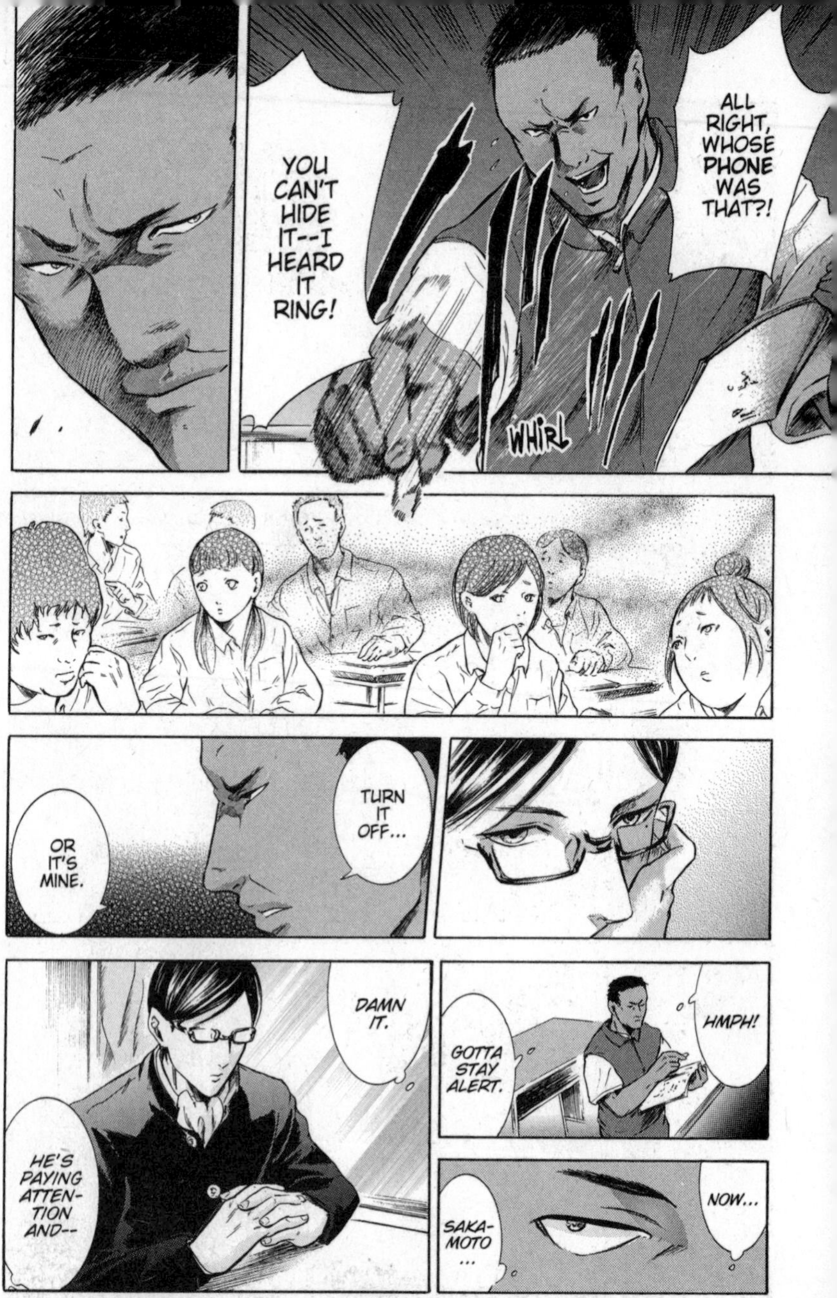
ALL RIGHT, WHOSE PHONE WAS THAT?!
YOU CAN'T HIDE IT--I HEARD IT RING!
WHIRL
TURN IT OFF...
OR IT'S MINE.
HMPH!
GOTTA STAY ALERT.
NOW...
SAKAMOTO...
DAMN IT.
HE'S PAYING ATTENTION AND--

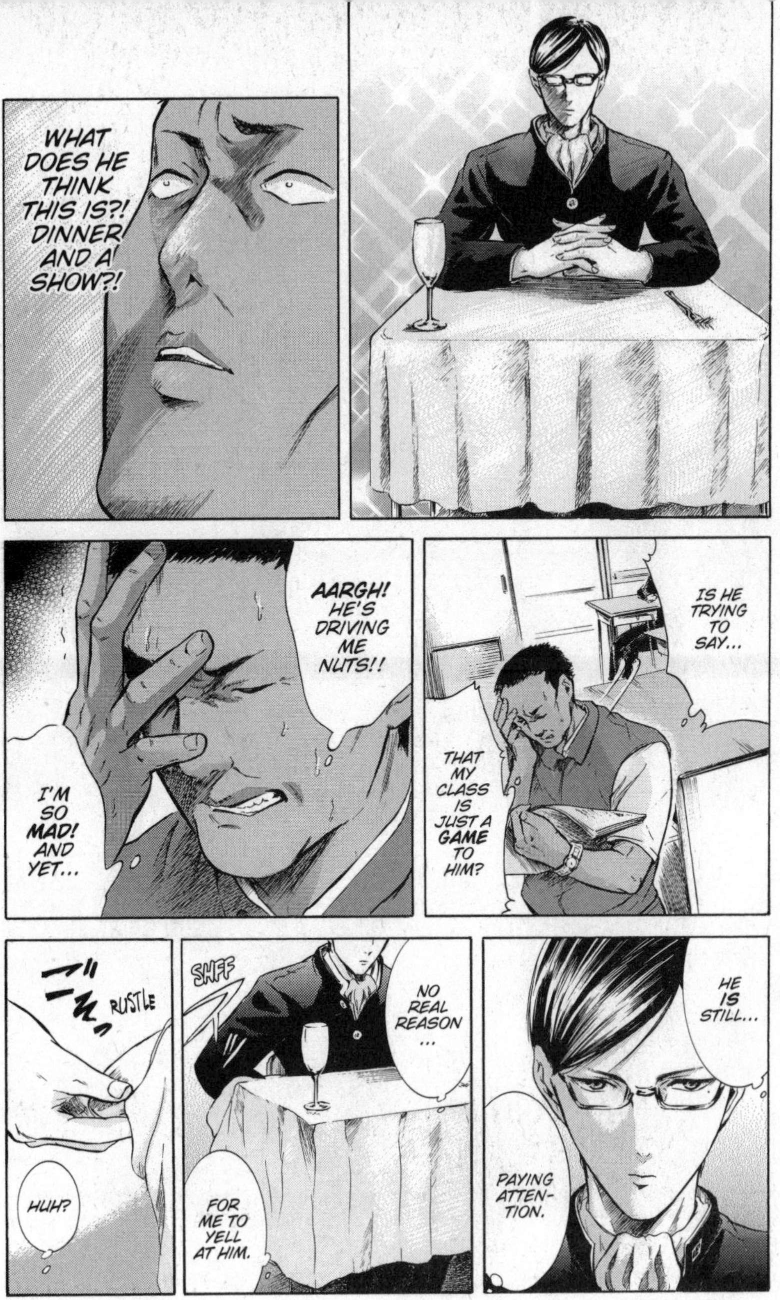
WHAT DOES HE THINK THIS IS?! DINNER AND A SHOW?!
IS HE TRYING TO SAY...
THAT MY CLASS IS JUST A GAME TO HIM?
AARGH! HE'S DRIVING ME NUTS!!
I'M SO MAD! AND YET...
HE IS STILL...
PAYING ATTEN-TION.
SHFF
NO REAL REASON...
FOR ME TO YELL AT HIM.
RUSTLE
HUH?

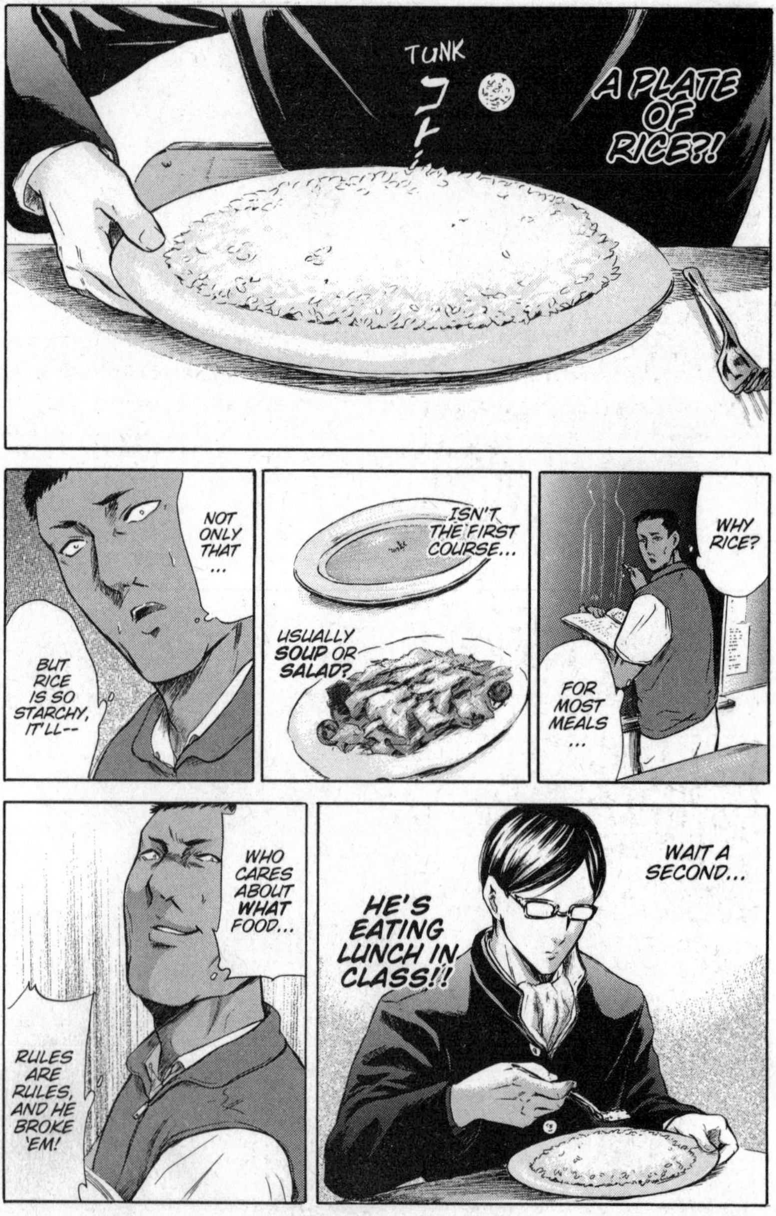
A PLATE OF RICE?!
TUNK
コト
WHY RICE?
FOR MOST MEALS...
ISN'T THE FIRST COURSE...
USUALLY SOUP OR SALAD?
NOT ONLY THAT...
BUT RICE IS SO STARCHY, IT'LL--
WAIT A SECOND...
HE'S EATING LUNCH IN CLASS!!
WHO CARES ABOUT WHAT FOOD...
RULES ARE RULES, AND HE BROKE 'EM!

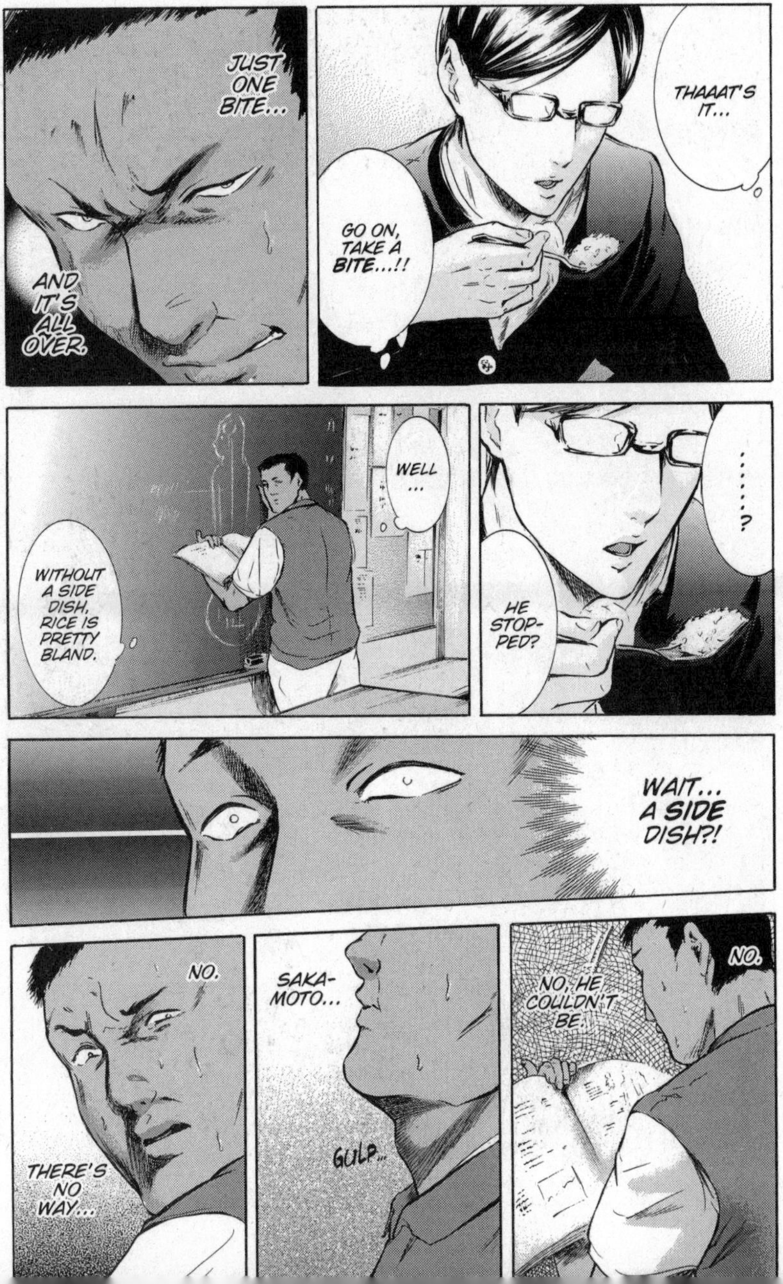
THAAAT'S IT...
GO ON, TAKE A BITE...!!
JUST ONE BITE...
AND IT'S ALL OVER.
......?
HE STOP-PED?
WELL...
WITHOUT A SIDE DISH, RICE IS PRETTY BLAND.
WAIT... A SIDE DISH?!
NO.
NO, HE COULDN'T BE.
SAKA-MOTO...
GULP...
NO.
THERE'S NO WAY...

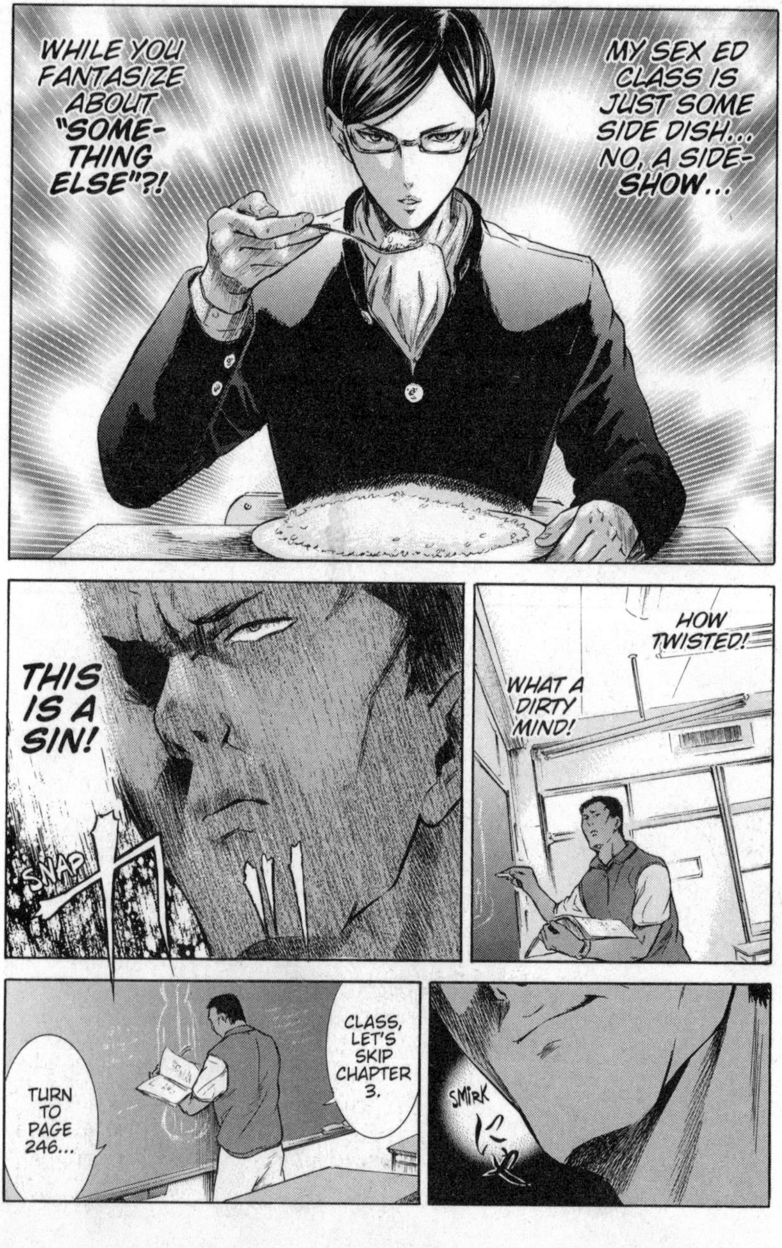
MY SEX ED CLASS IS JUST SOME SIDE DISH... NO, A SIDE-SHOW...
WHILE YOU FANTASIZE ABOUT "SOME-THING ELSE"?!
HOW TWISTED!
WHAT A DIRTY MIND!
THIS IS A SIN!
SNAP
SMIRK
CLASS, LET'S SKIP CHAPTER 3.
TURN TO PAGE 246...

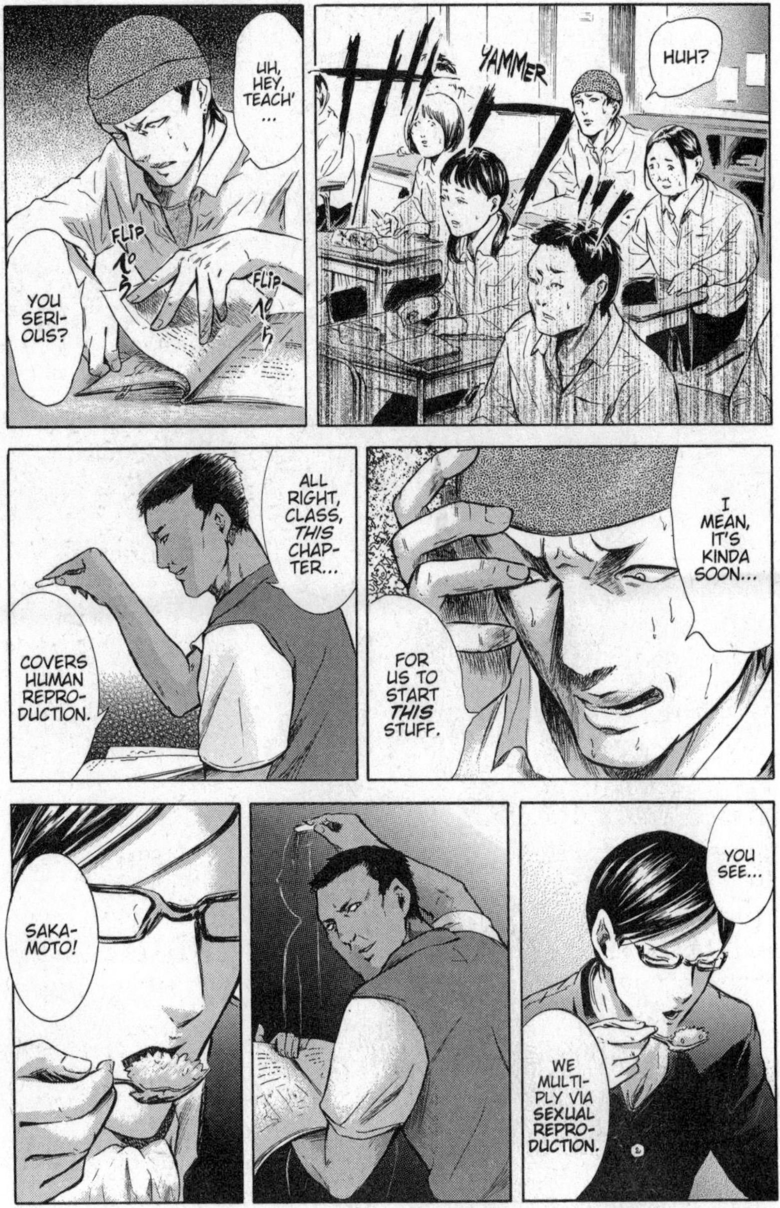
HUH?
YAMMER
UH, HEY, TEACH' ...
FLIP
FLIP
YOU SERI-OUS?
I MEAN, IT'S KINDA SOON...
FOR US TO START *THIS* STUFF.
ALL RIGHT, CLASS, *THIS* CHAPTER...
COVERS HUMAN REPRO-DUCTION.
YOU SEE...
WE MULTI-PLY VIA SEXUAL REPRO-DUCTION.
SAKA-MOTO!

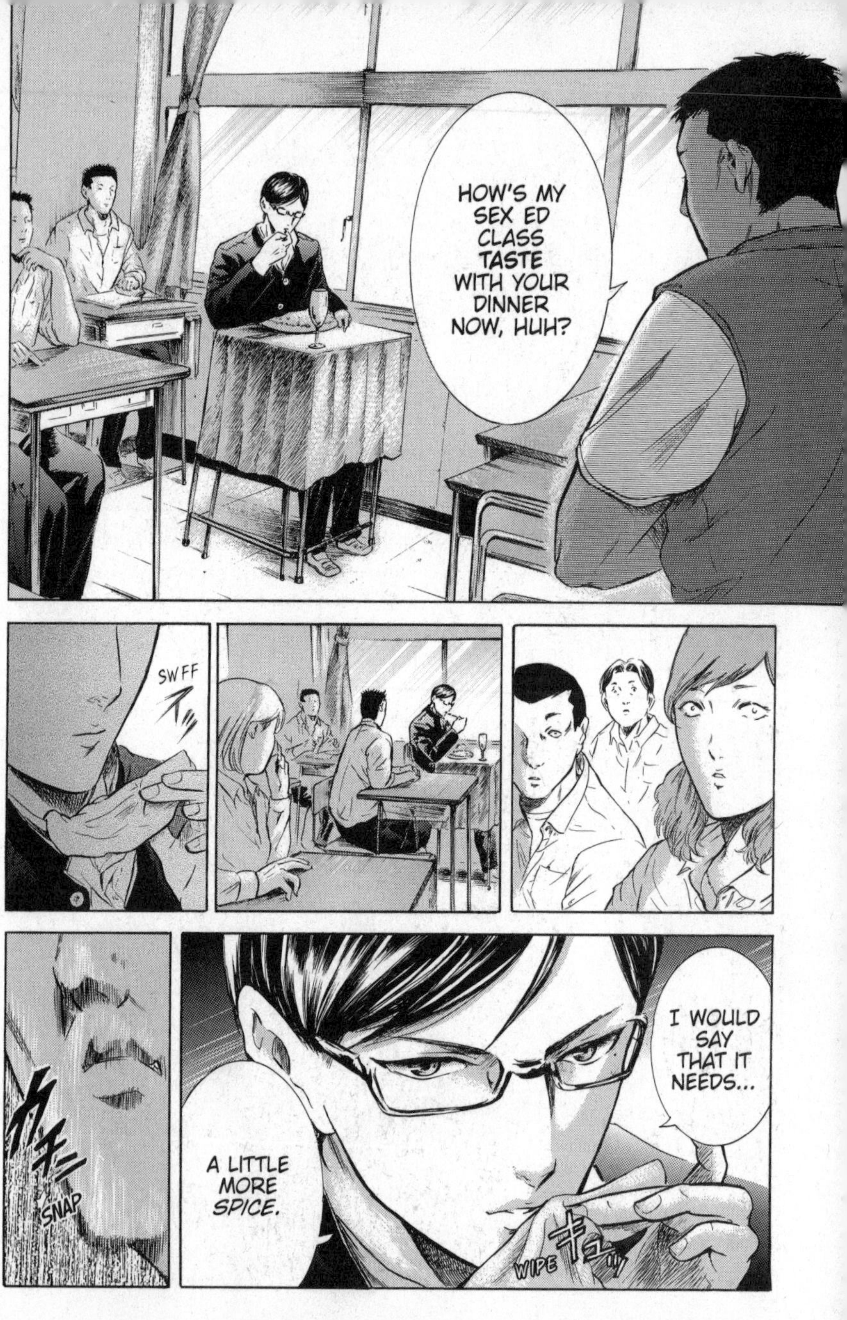
HOW'S MY SEX ED CLASS TASTE WITH YOUR DINNER NOW, HUH?
SWFF
I WOULD SAY THAT IT NEEDS...
A LITTLE MORE SPICE.
WIPE
SNAP

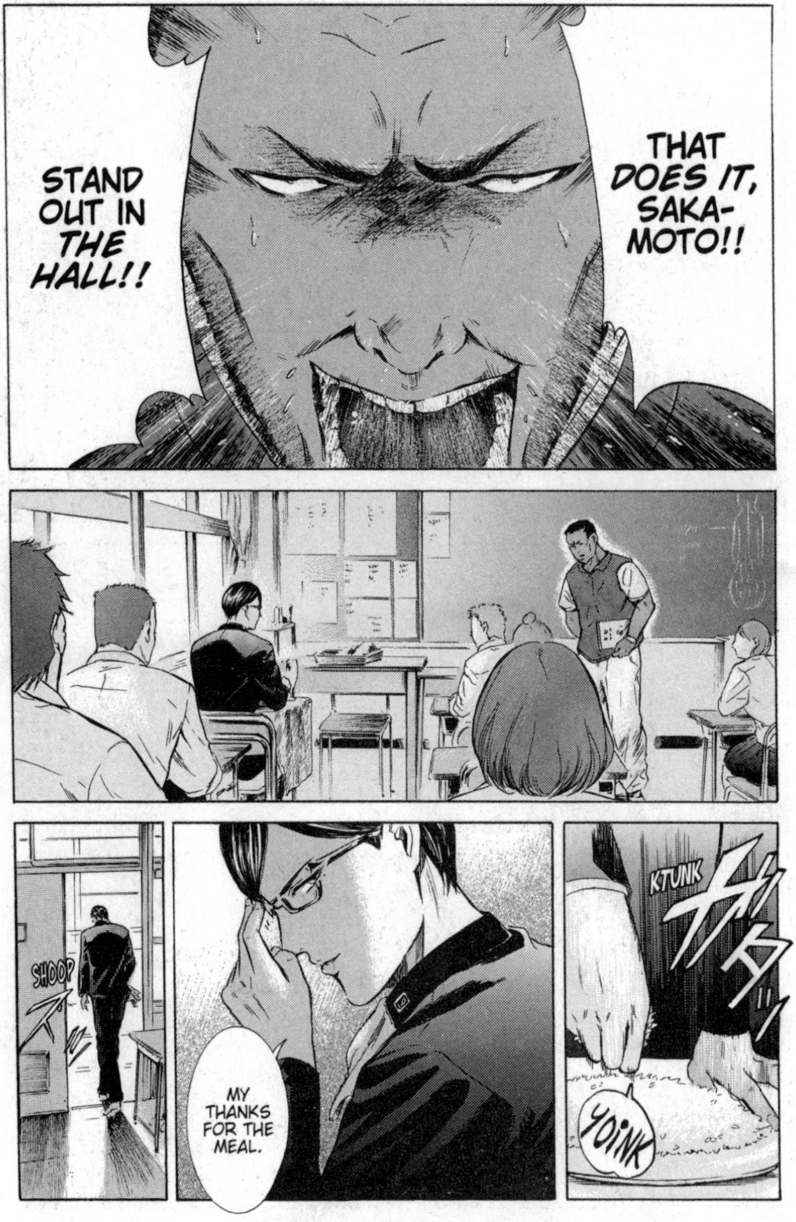
THAT DOES IT, SAKA-MOTO!!
STAND OUT IN THE HALL!!
KTUNK
YOINK
MY THANKS FOR THE MEAL.
SHOOP

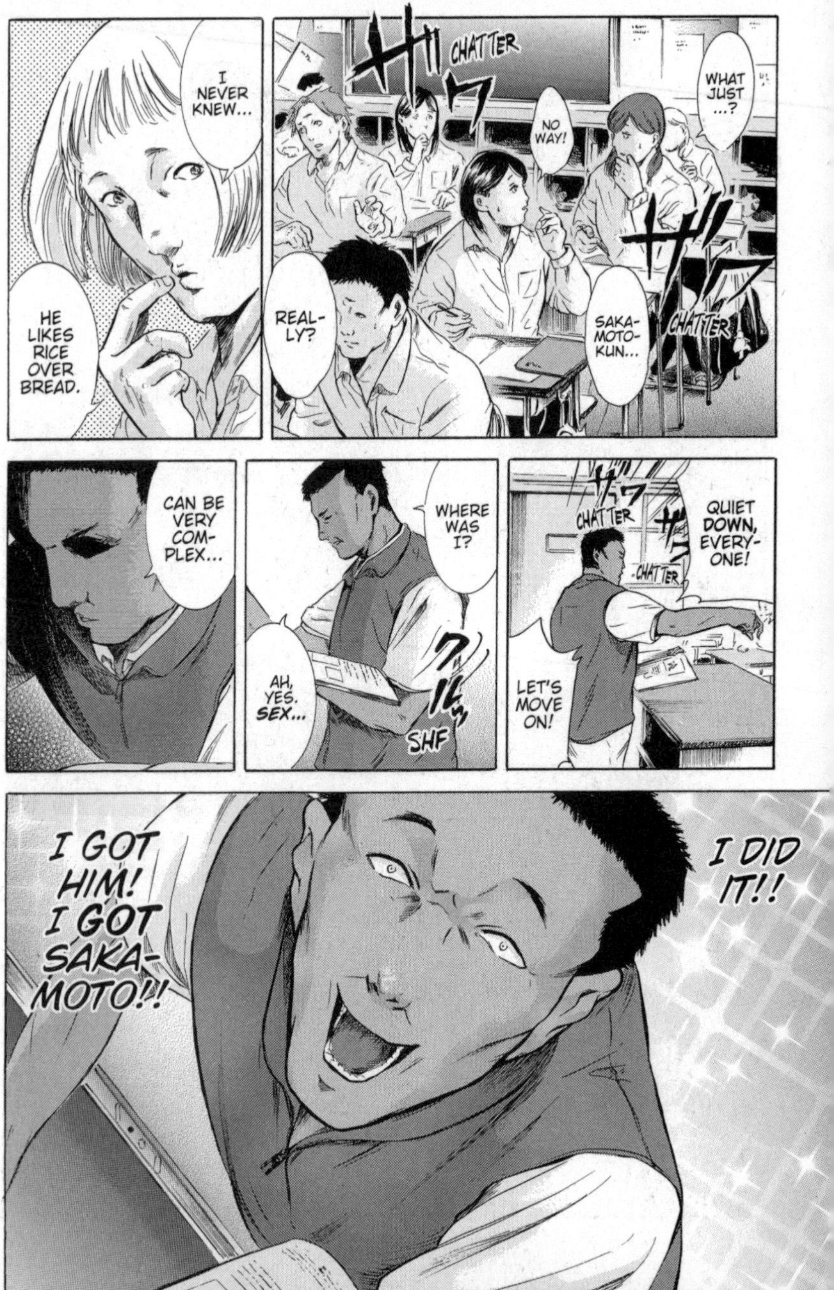
CHATTER
WHAT JUST ...?
NO WAY!
SAKA-MOTO-KUN...
CHATTER
REAL-LY?
I NEVER KNEW...
HE LIKES RICE OVER BREAD.
QUIET DOWN, EVERY-ONE!
CHATTER
CHATTER
LET'S MOVE ON!
WHERE WAS I?
SHF
AH, YES. SEX...
CAN BE VERY COM-PLEX...
I DID IT!!
I GOT HIM! I GOT SAKA-MOTO!!

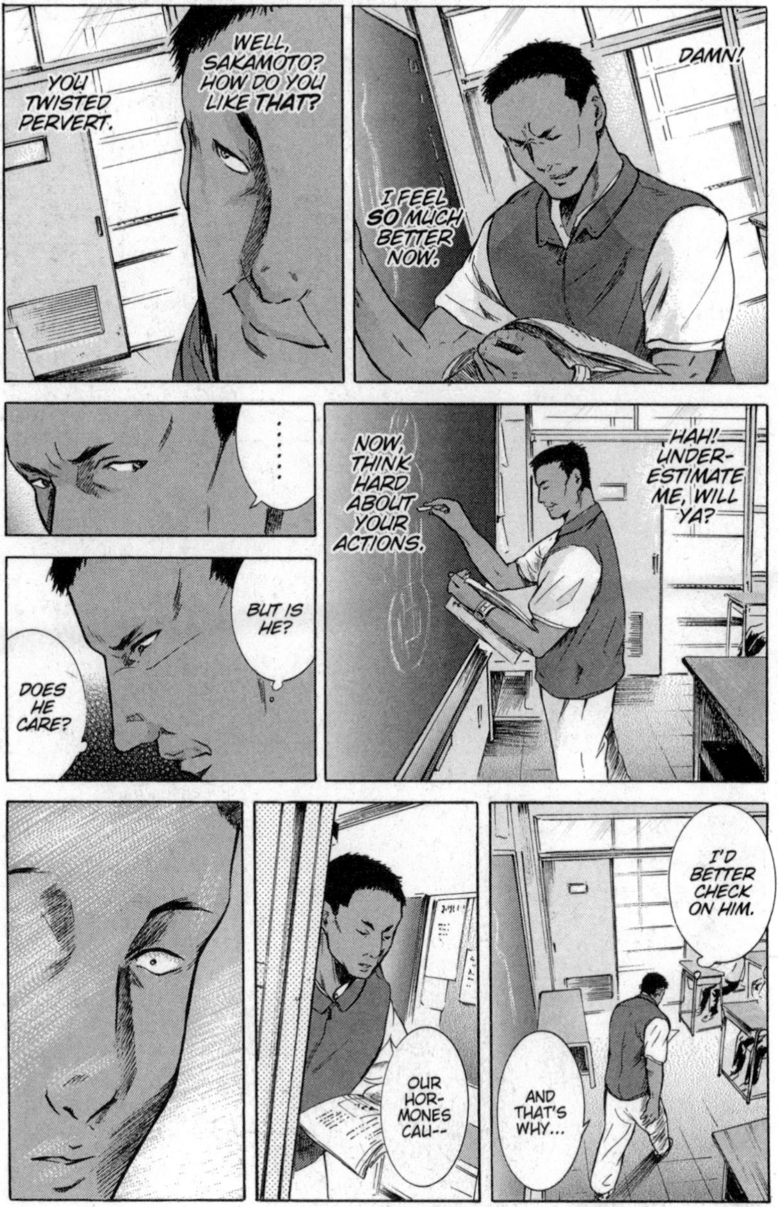
DAMN!
I FEEL SO MUCH BETTER NOW.
WELL, SAKAMOTO? HOW DO YOU LIKE THAT?
YOU TWISTED PERVERT.
HAH! UNDER-ESTIMATE ME, WILL YA?
NOW, THINK HARD ABOUT YOUR ACTIONS.
......
BUT IS HE?
DOES HE CARE?
I'D BETTER CHECK ON HIM.
AND THAT'S WHY...
OUR HOR-MONES CAU--

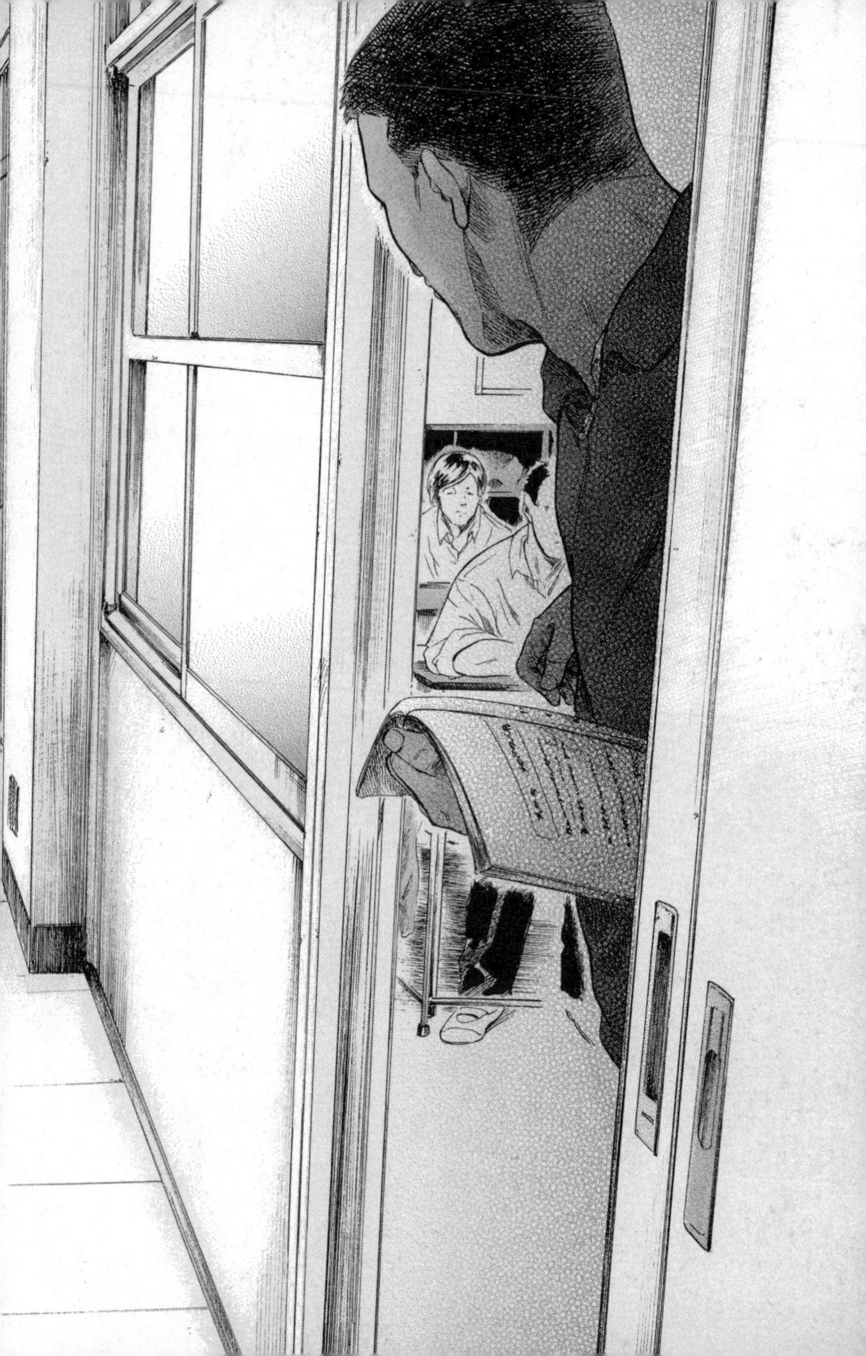

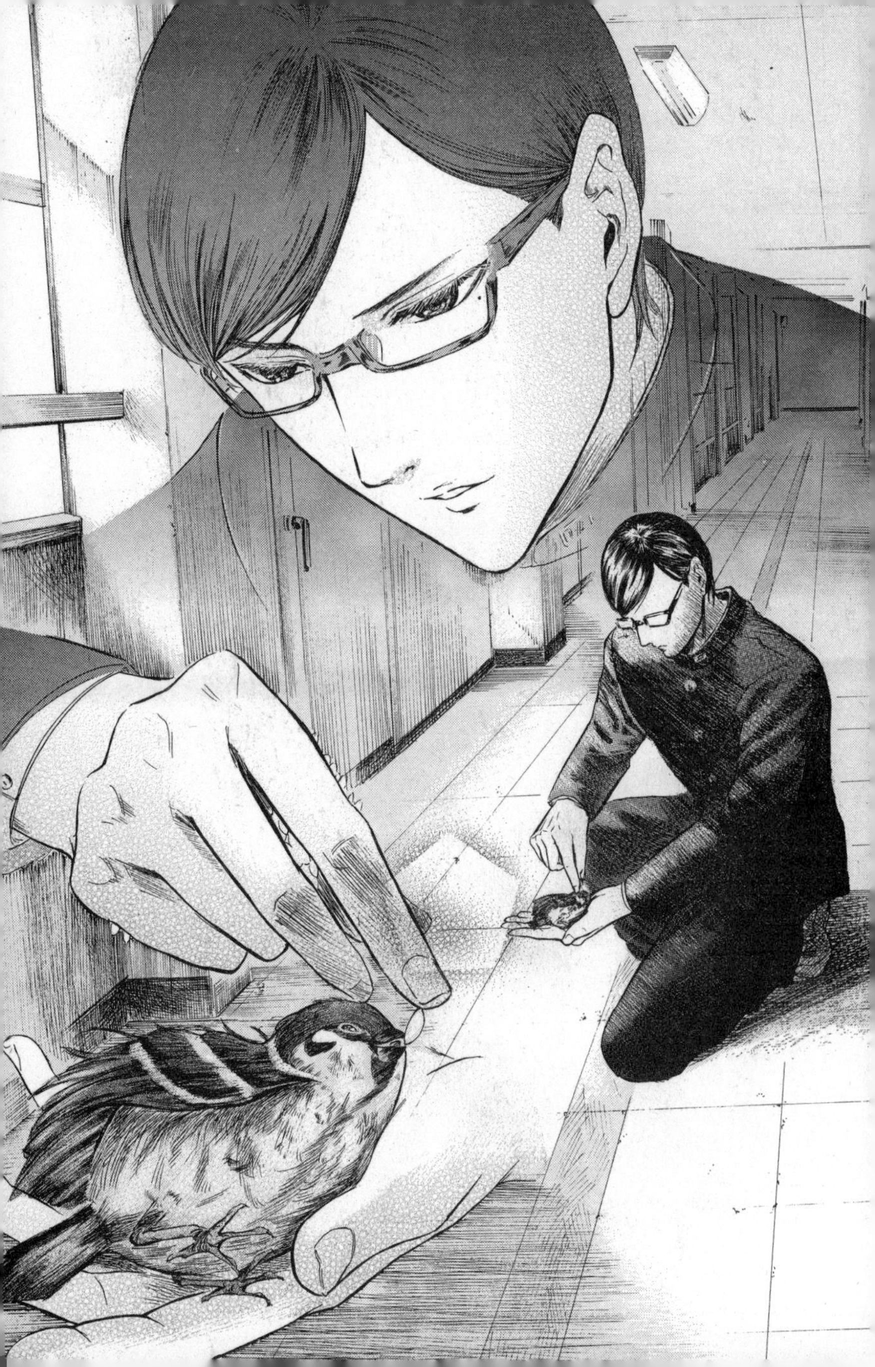

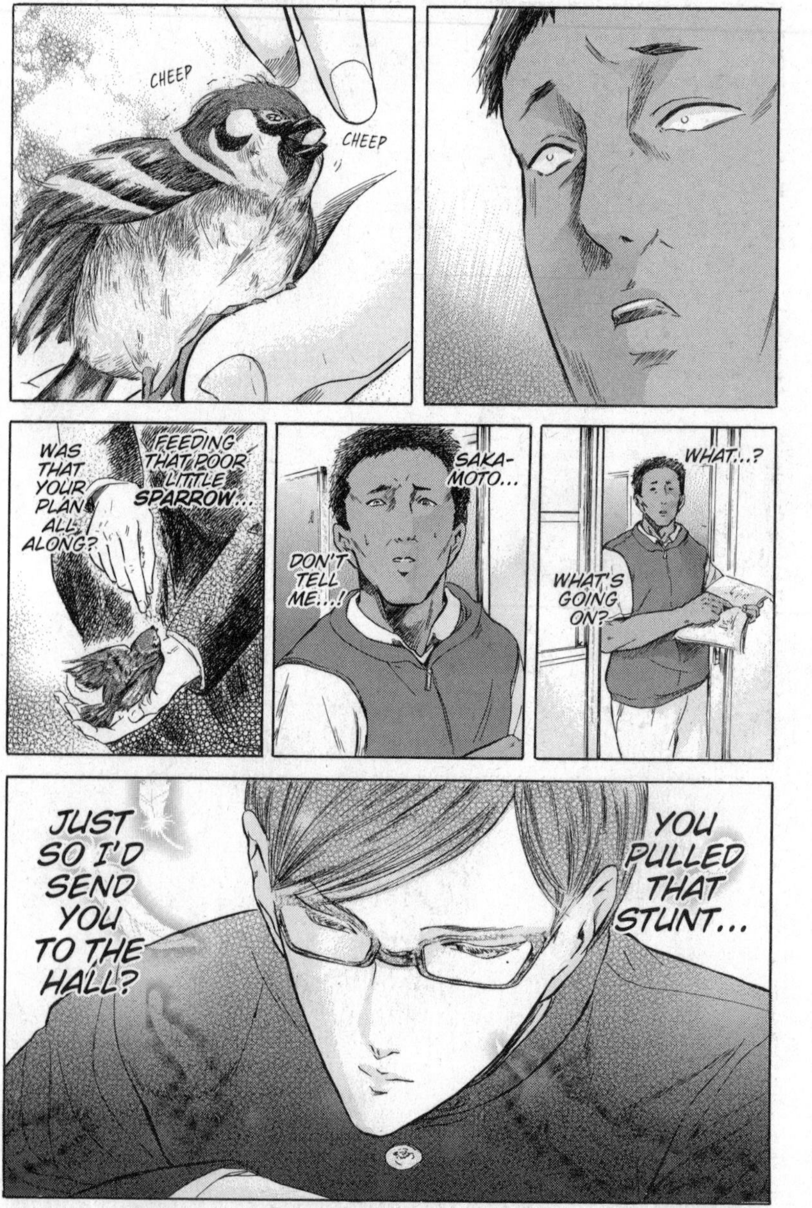
CHEEP
CHEEP
WHAT...?
WHAT'S GOING ON?
SAKA-MOTO...
DON'T TELL ME...!
FEEDING THAT POOR LITTLE SPARROW...
WAS THAT YOUR PLAN ALL ALONG?
YOU PULLED THAT STUNT...
JUST SO I'D SEND YOU TO THE HALL?

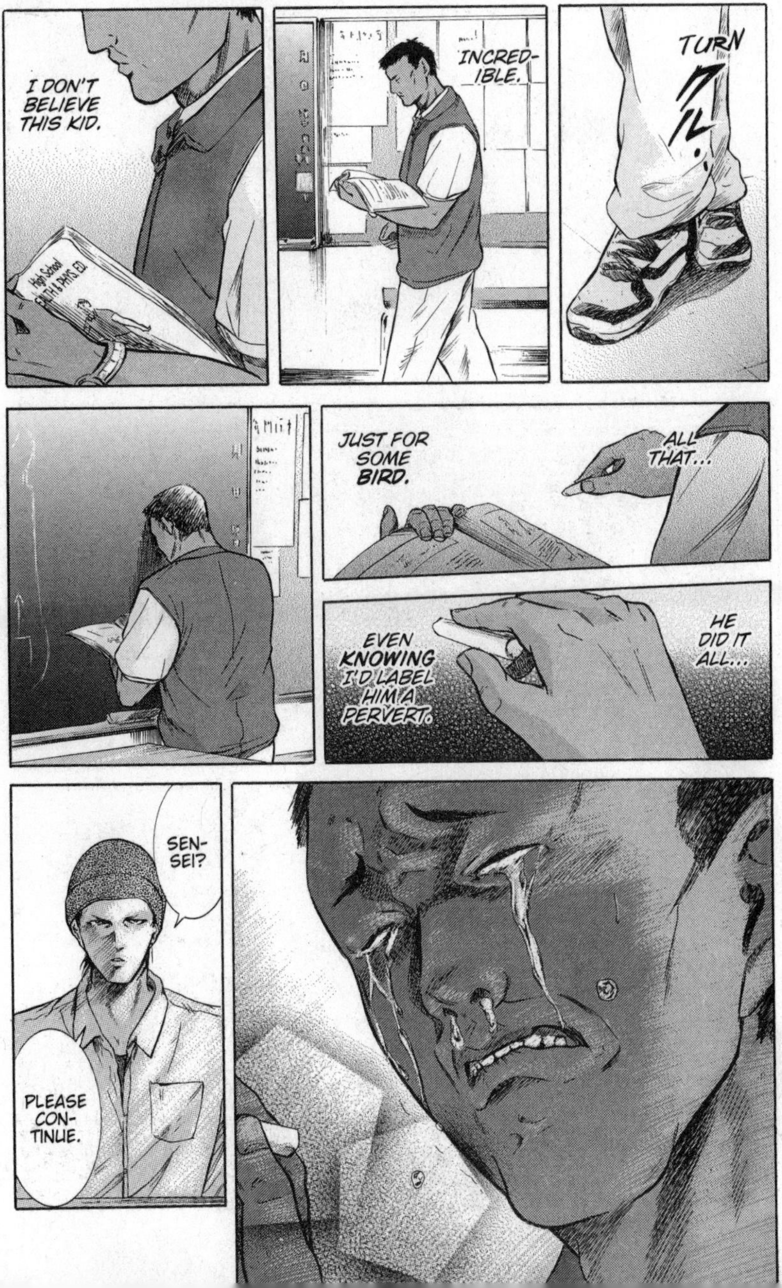
TURN
クル
INCRED-IBLE.
I DON'T BELIEVE THIS KID.
High School
ALL THAT...
JUST FOR SOME BIRD.
HE DID IT ALL...
EVEN KNOWING I'D LABEL HIM A PERVERT.
SEN-SEI?
PLEASE CON-TINUE.

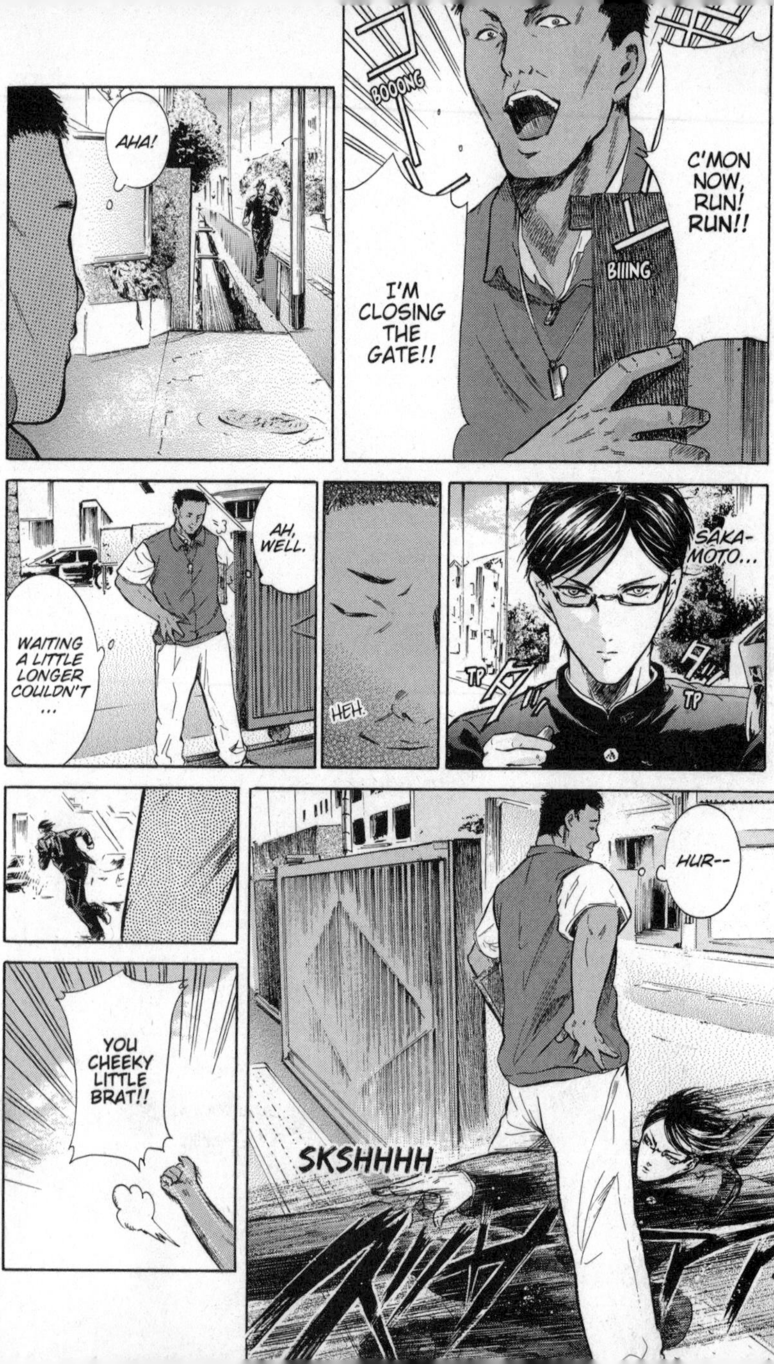
BOOONG
C'MON NOW, RUN! RUN!!
BIIING
I'M CLOSING THE GATE!!
AHA!
SAKA-MOTO...
TP
TP
HEH.
AH, WELL.
WAITING A LITTLE LONGER COULDN'T ...
HUR--
SKSHHHH
YOU CHEEKY LITTLE BRAT!!

End of Chapter 7

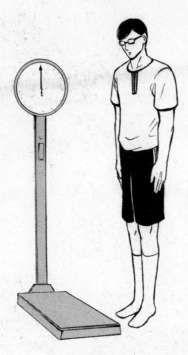

Physical Exam #2:
    Weight

CHAPTER 8: SCENES FROM CLASS LIFE

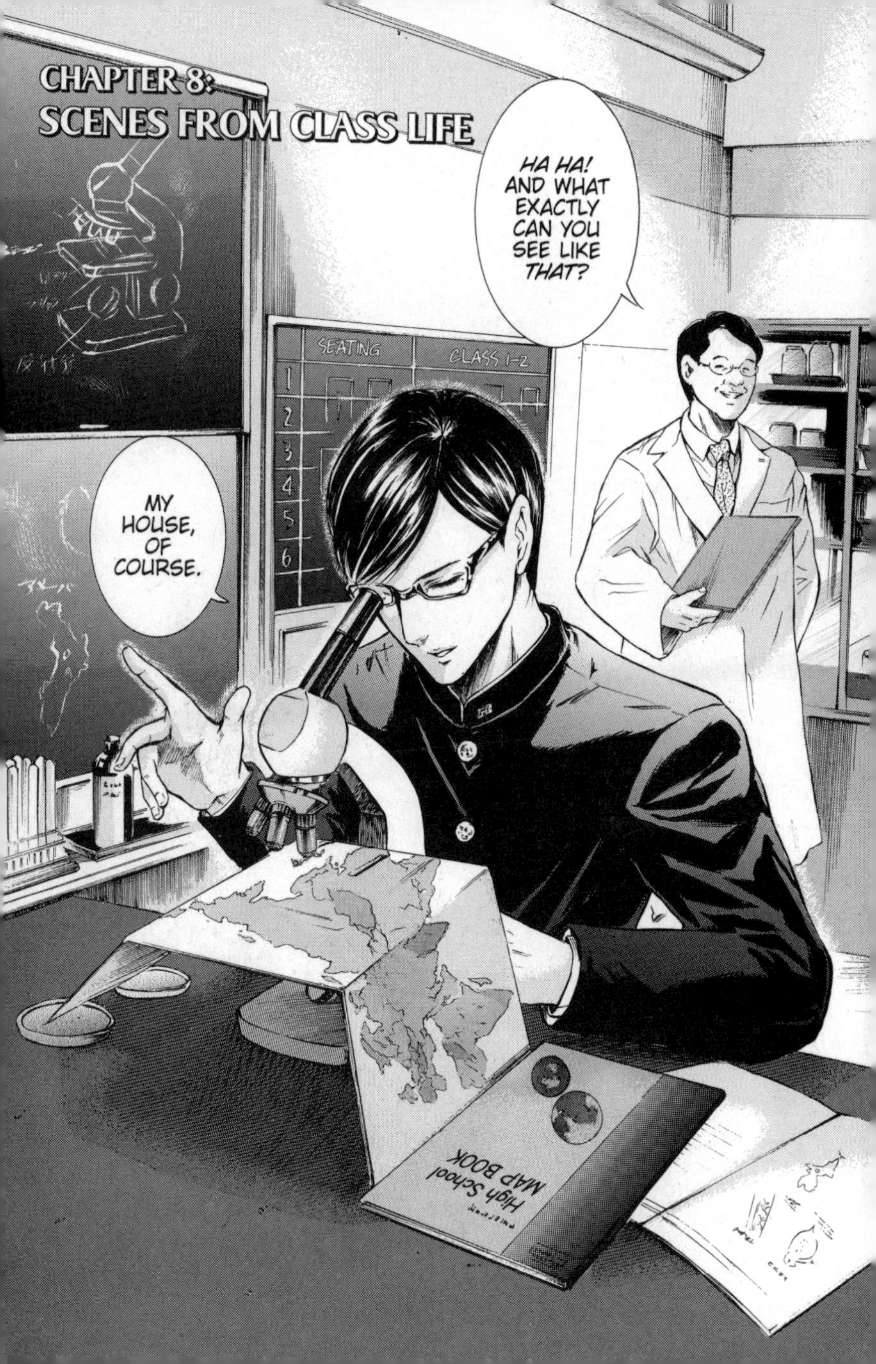
HA HA! AND WHAT EXACTLY CAN YOU SEE LIKE THAT?
SEATING
CLASS 1-2
MY HOUSE, OF COURSE.
High School MAP BOOK

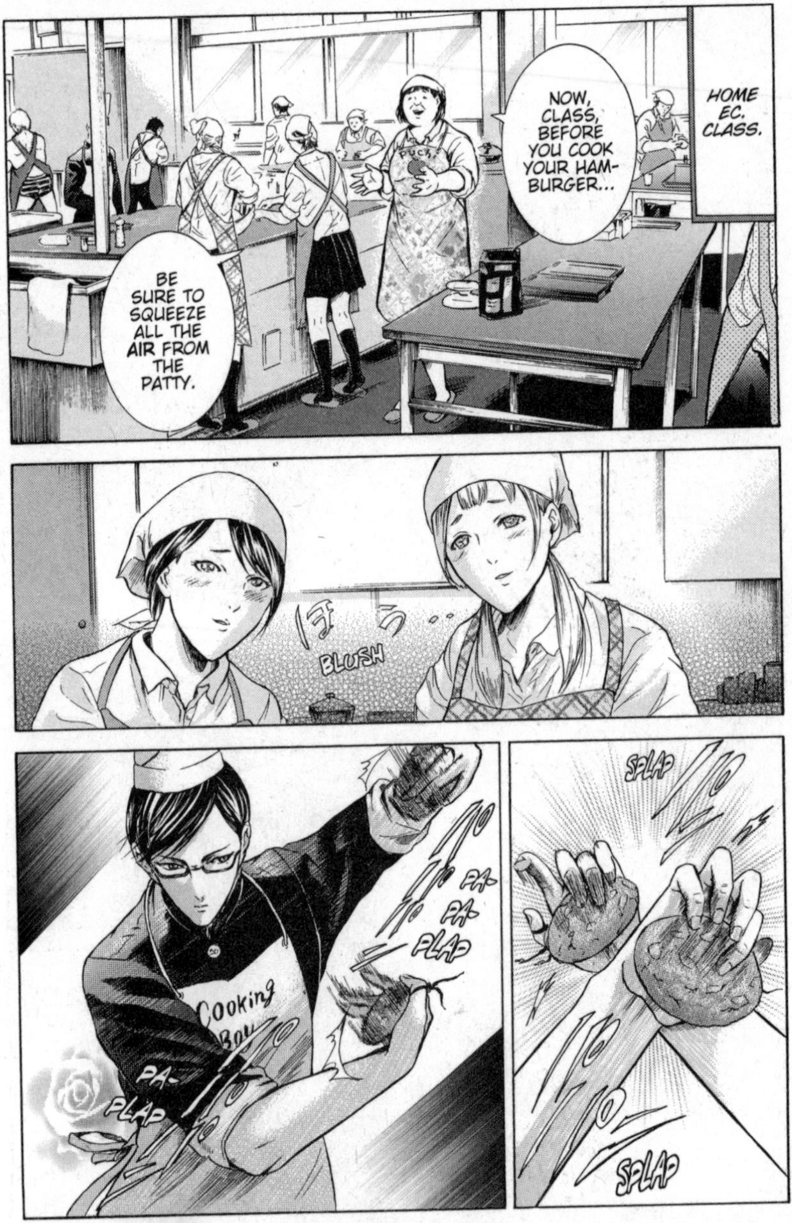
HOME EC. CLASS.
NOW, CLASS, BEFORE YOU COOK YOUR HAM-BURGER...
BE SURE TO SQUEEZE ALL THE AIR FROM THE PATTY.
ほう..
BLUSH
SPLAP
SPLAP
PA-PA-PLAP
Cooking Boy
PA-PLAP

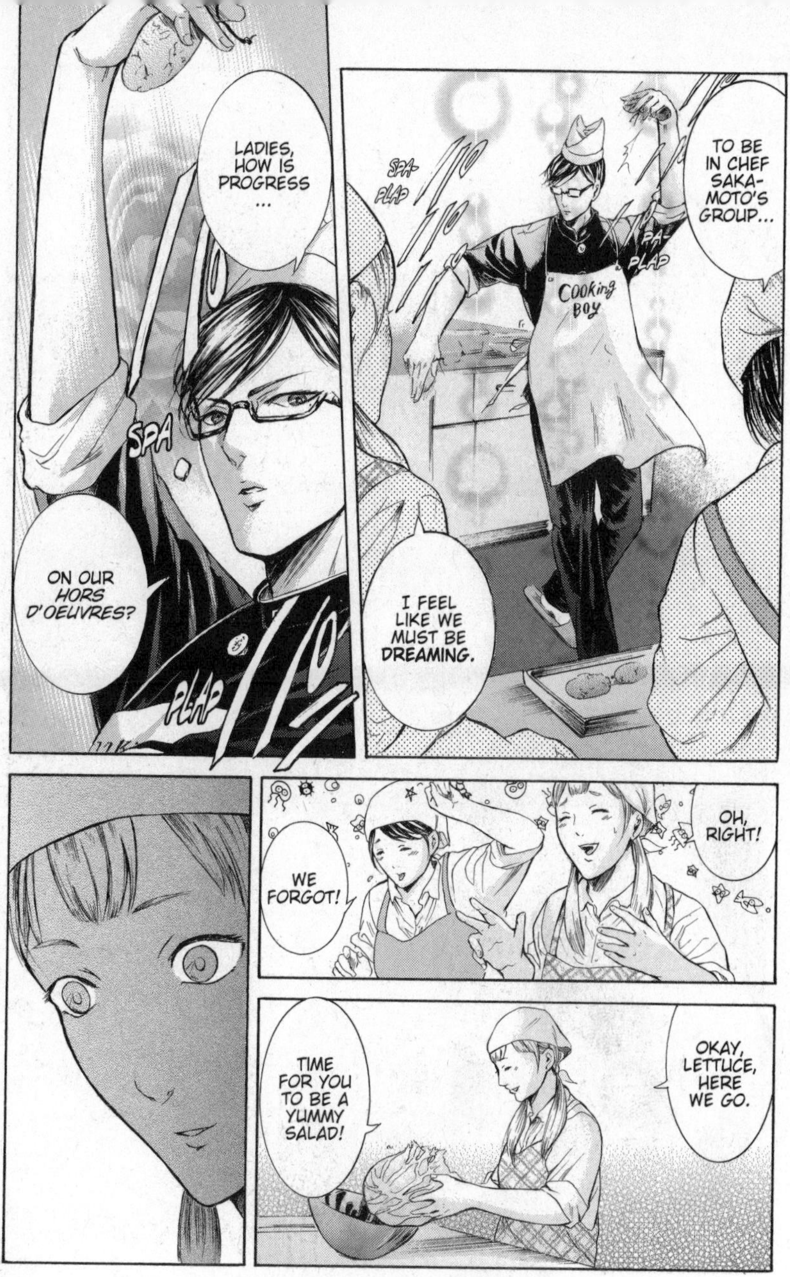
TO BE IN CHEF SAKA-MOTO'S GROUP...
SPA-PLAP
PA-PLAP
COOKing BOY
I FEEL LIKE WE MUST BE DREAMING.
LADIES, HOW IS PROGRESS ...
SPA
ON OUR HORS D'OEUVRES?
PLAP
OH, RIGHT!
WE FORGOT!
OKAY, LETTUCE, HERE WE GO.
TIME FOR YOU TO BE A YUMMY SALAD!

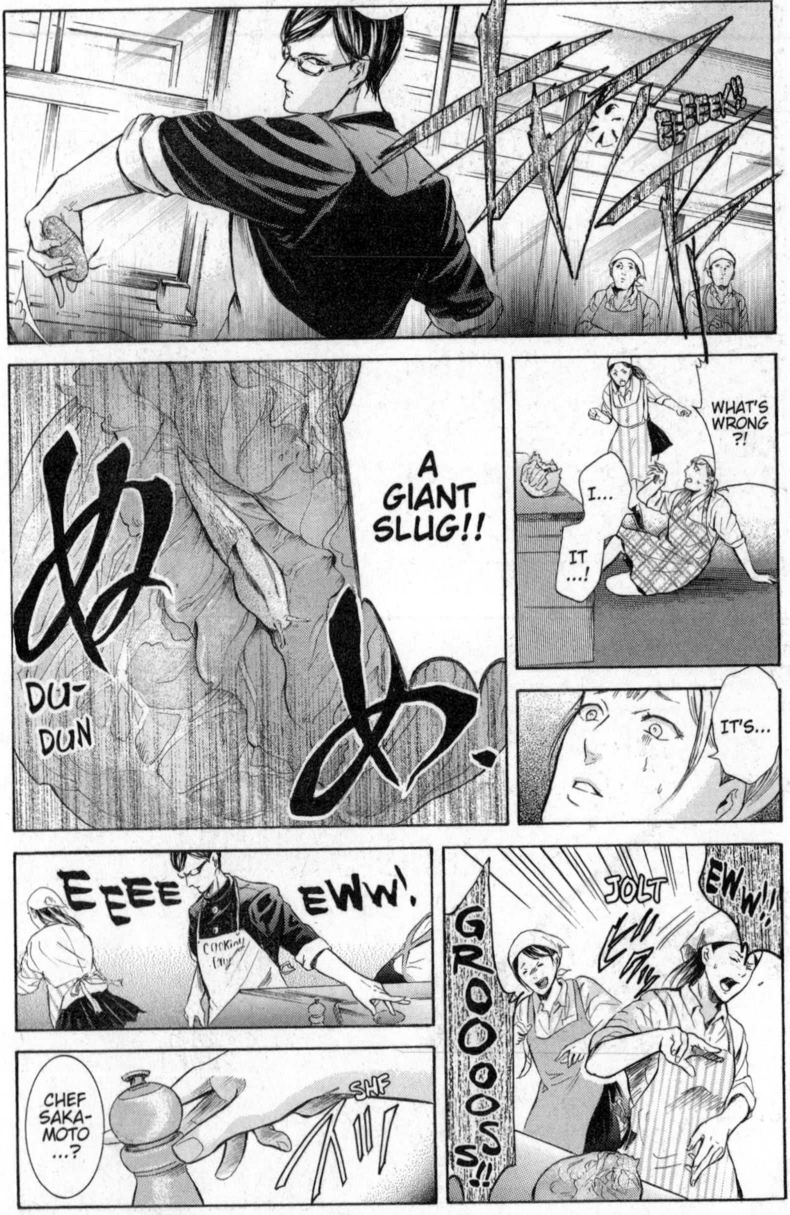
EEEEEK!!
WHAT'S WRONG ?!
I...
IT ...!
IT'S...
A GIANT SLUG!!
DU-DUN
JOLT
EWW!!
GROOOOOS S!!
EEEEEWW!
CHEF SAKAMOTO ...?
SHF

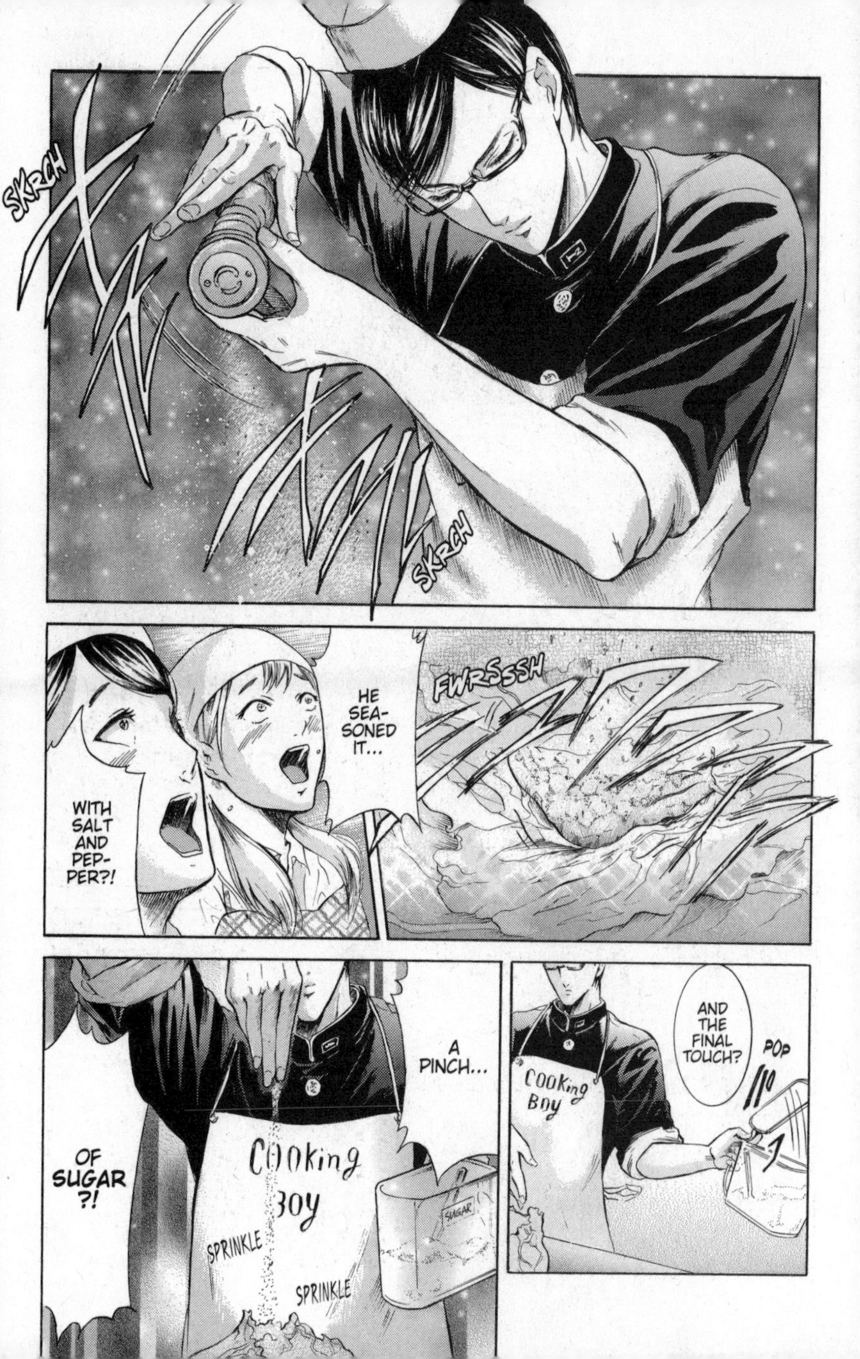
SKRCH
SKRCH
FWRSSSH
HE SEASONED IT...
WITH SALT AND PEPPER?!
AND THE FINAL TOUCH?
POP
COOKing Boy
A PINCH...
OF SUGAR?!
COOKing BOY
SUGAR
SPRINKLE
SPRINKLE

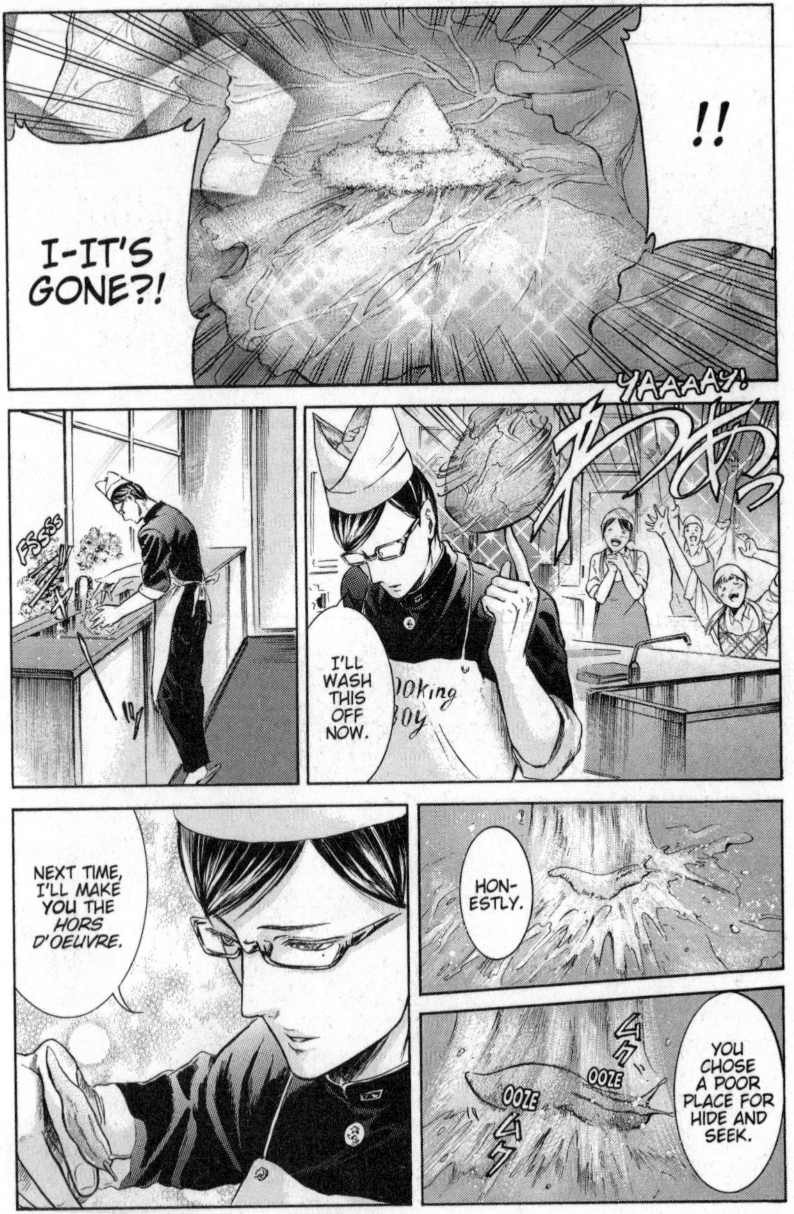
!!
I-IT'S GONE?!
YAAAAY!
I'LL WASH THIS OFF NOW.
FSSSS
HON-ESTLY.
YOU CHOSE A POOR PLACE FOR HIDE AND SEEK.
OOZE
OOZE
NEXT TIME, I'LL MAKE YOU THE *HORS D'OEUVRE*.

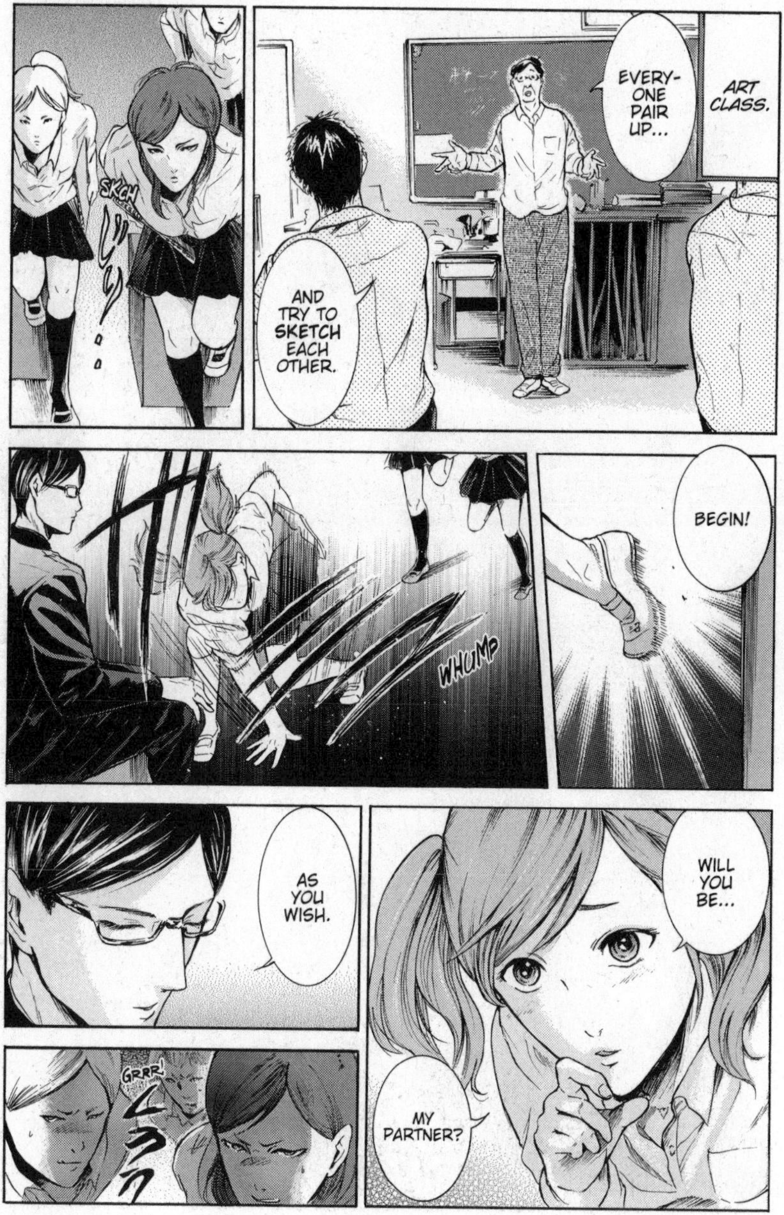
ART CLASS.
EVERY-ONE PAIR UP...
AND TRY TO SKETCH EACH OTHER.
SKCH
BEGIN!
WHUMP
WILL YOU BE...
MY PARTNER?
AS YOU WISH.
GRRR!

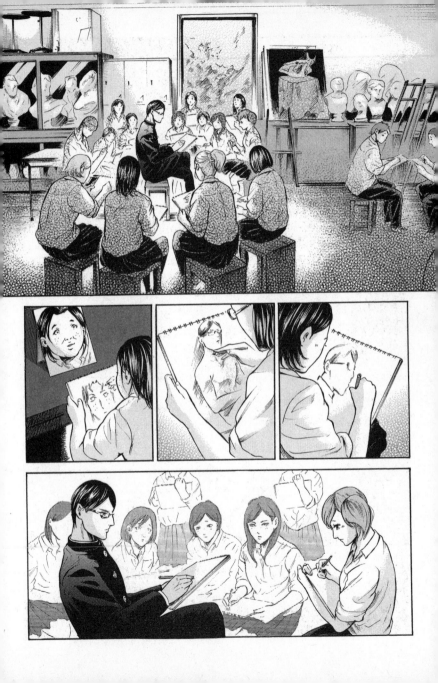

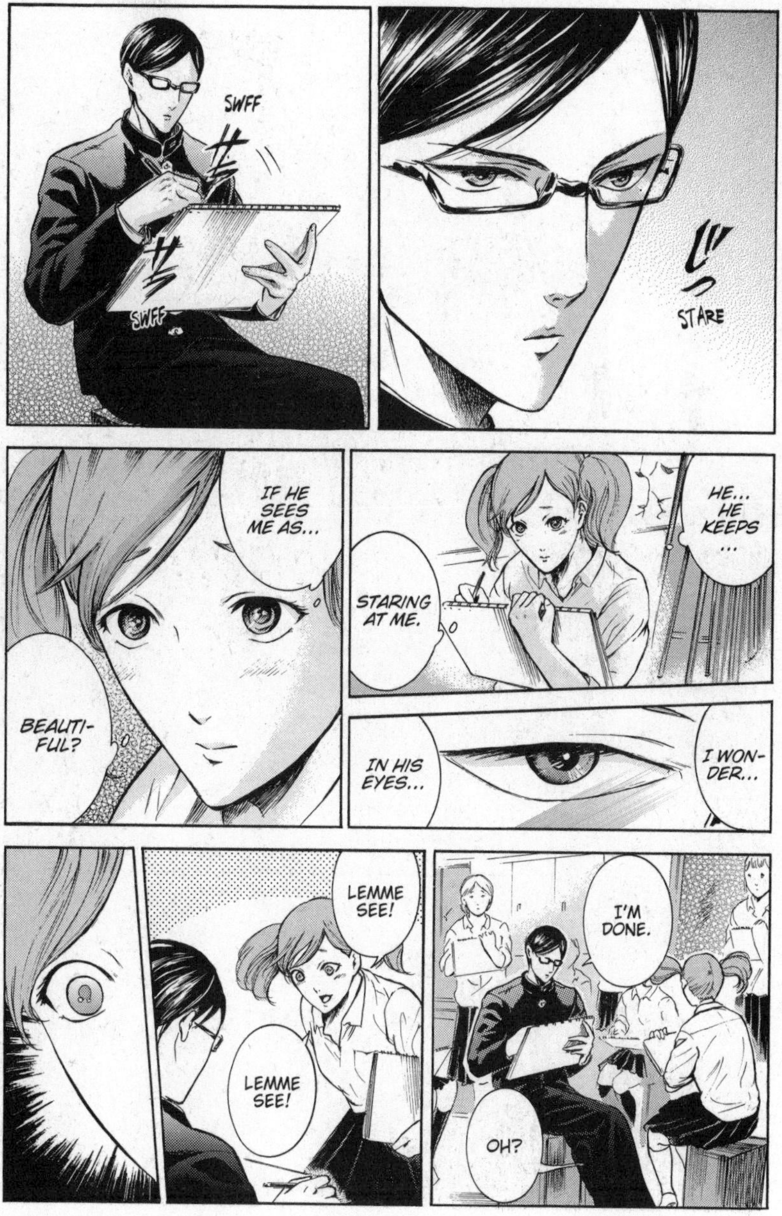
STARE
SWFF
SWFF
HE... HE KEEPS ...
STARING AT ME.
I WONDER...
IN HIS EYES...
IF HE SEES ME AS...
BEAUTIFUL?
I'M DONE.
OH?
LEMME SEE!
LEMME SEE!

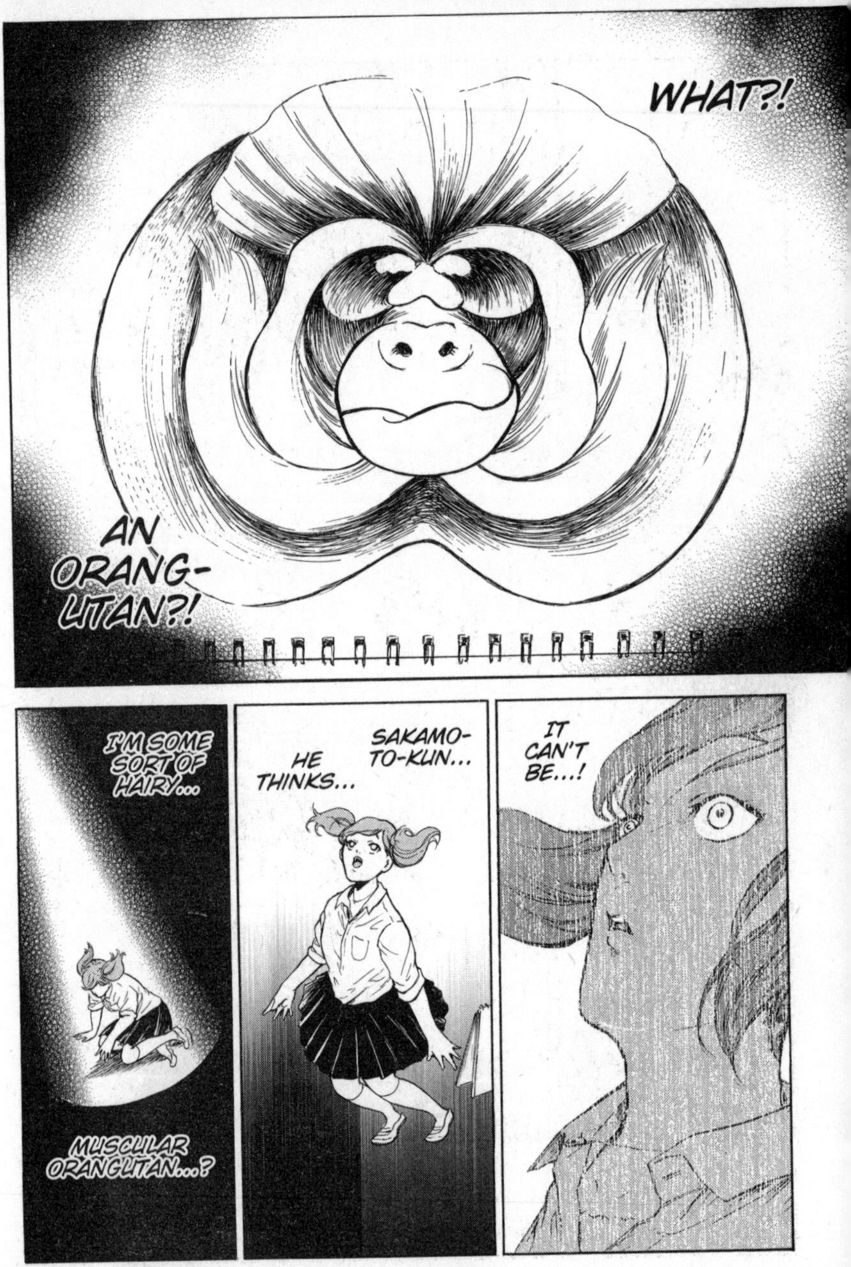
WHAT?!
AN ORANG-UTAN?!
IT CAN'T BE...!
SAKAMO-TO-KUN...
HE THINKS...
I'M SOME SORT OF HAIRY...
MUSCULAR ORANGUTAN...?

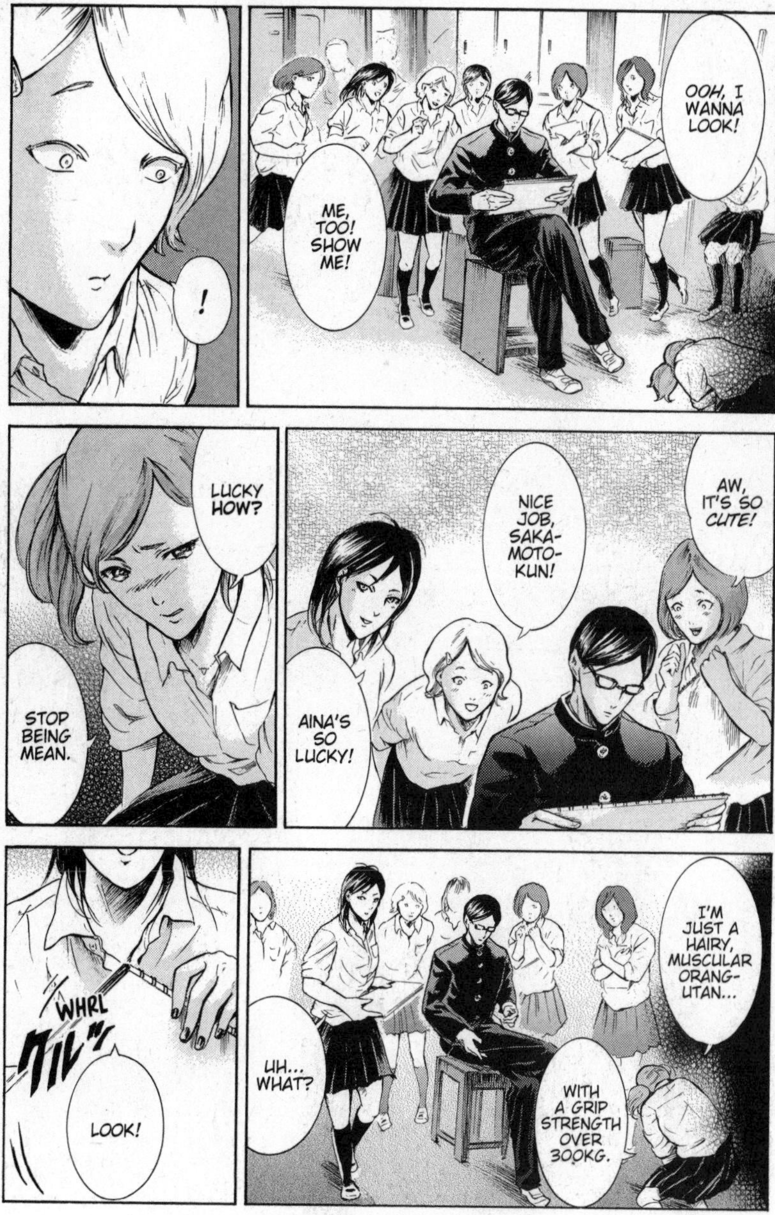
OOH, I WANNA LOOK!
ME, TOO! SHOW ME!
!
AW, IT'S SO CUTE!
NICE JOB, SAKAMOTO-KUN!
AINA'S SO LUCKY!
LUCKY HOW?
STOP BEING MEAN.
I'M JUST A HAIRY, MUSCULAR ORANGUTAN...
WITH A GRIP STRENGTH OVER 300KG.
UH... WHAT?
WHRL
クルッ
LOOK!

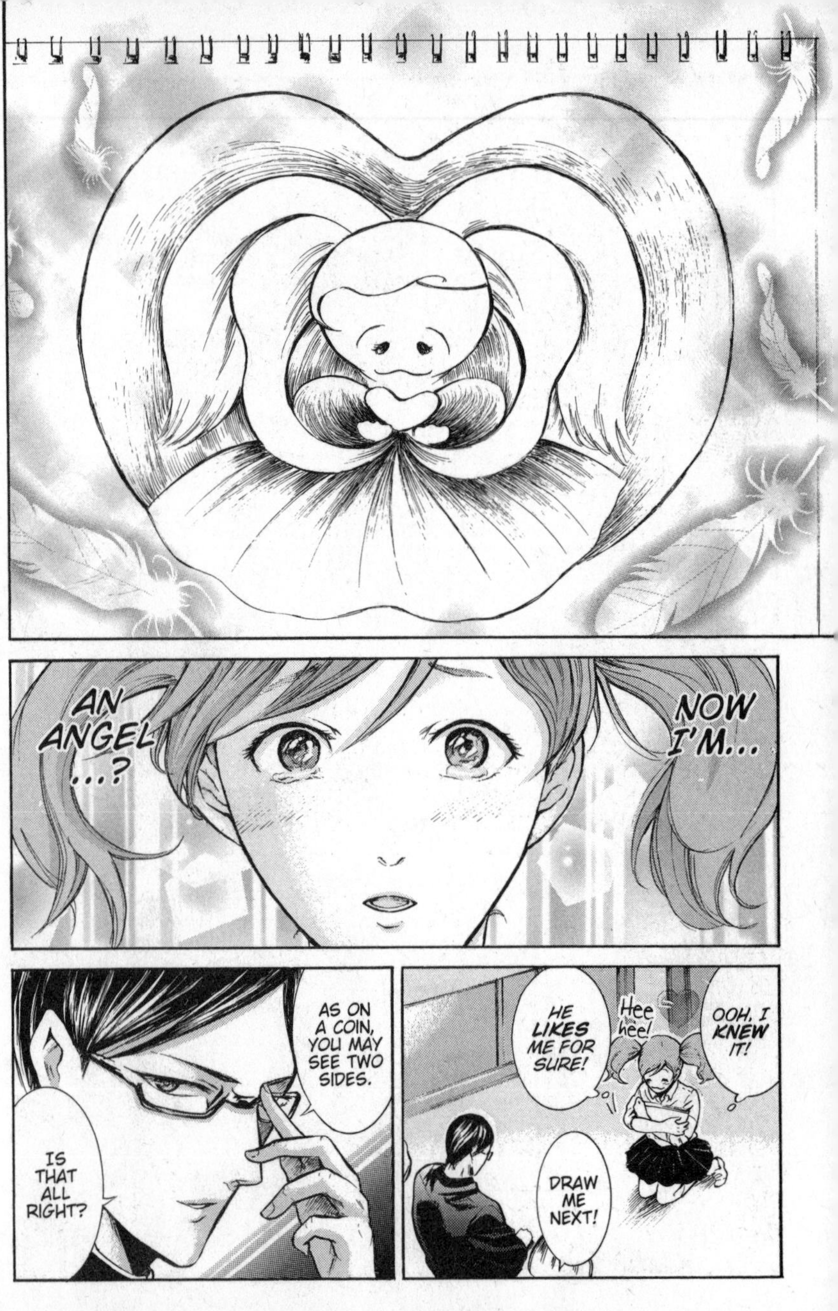
NOW I'M...
AN ANGEL ...?
OOH, I KNEW IT!
Hee hee!
HE LIKES ME FOR SURE!
DRAW ME NEXT!
AS ON A COIN, YOU MAY SEE TWO SIDES.
IS THAT ALL RIGHT?

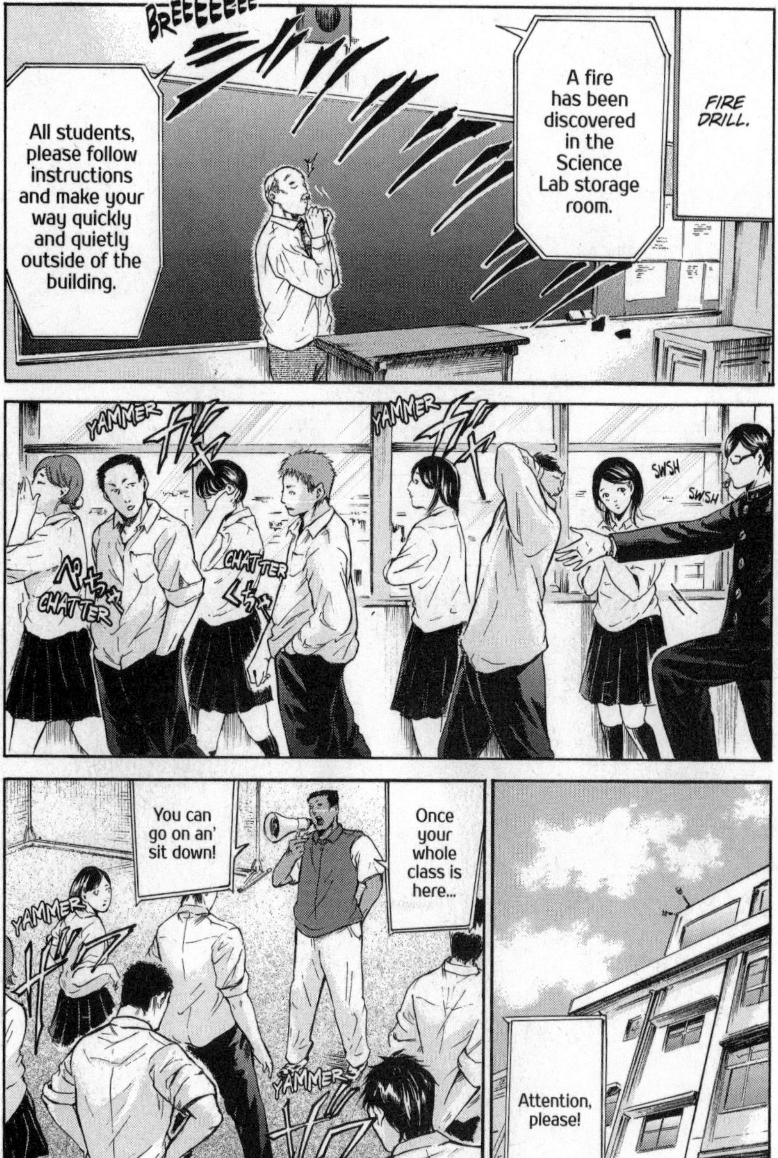
FIRE DRILL.
A fire has been discovered in the Science Lab storage room.
BREEEEEEEE
All students, please follow instructions and make your way quickly and quietly outside of the building.
SWSH
SWSH
YAMMER
CHATTER
YAMMER
CHATTER
Attention, please!
Once your whole class is here...
You can go on an' sit down!
YAMMER
YAMMER

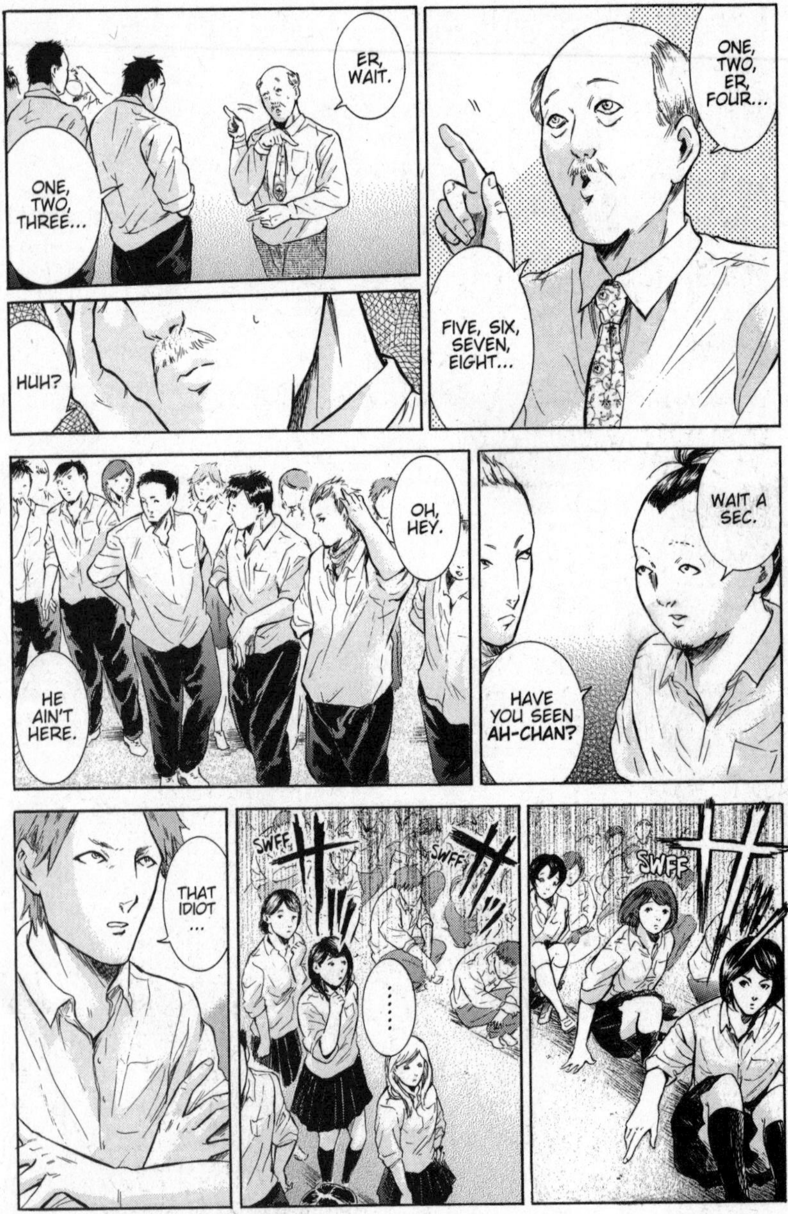
ONE, TWO, ER, FOUR...
FIVE, SIX, SEVEN, EIGHT...
ER, WAIT.
ONE, TWO, THREE...
HUH?
WAIT A SEC.
HAVE YOU SEEN AH-CHAN?
OH, HEY.
HE AIN'T HERE.
SWFF
SWFF
SWFF
......
THAT IDIOT ...

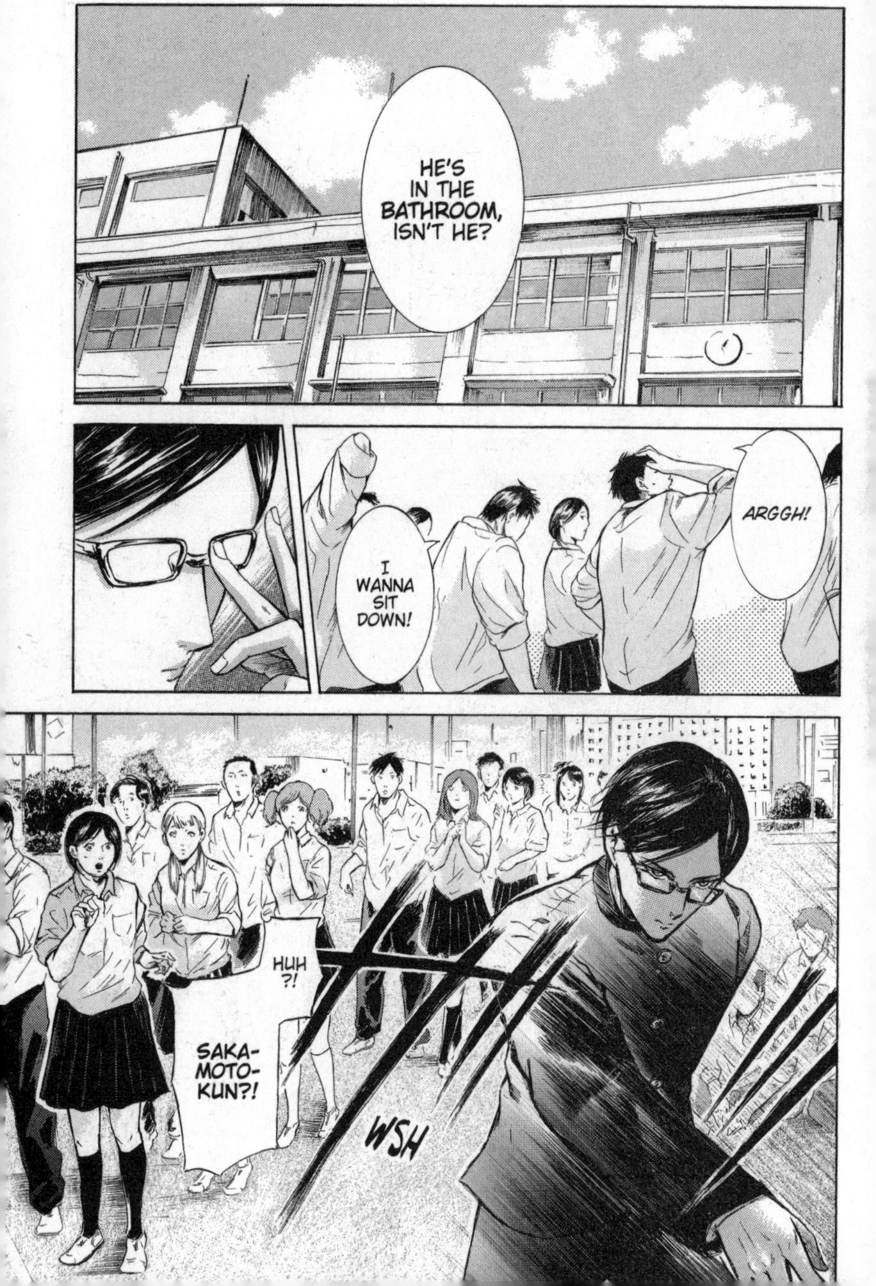
HE'S IN THE BATHROOM, ISN'T HE?
ARGGH!
I WANNA SIT DOWN!
WSH
HUH?!
SAKA-MOTO-KUN?!

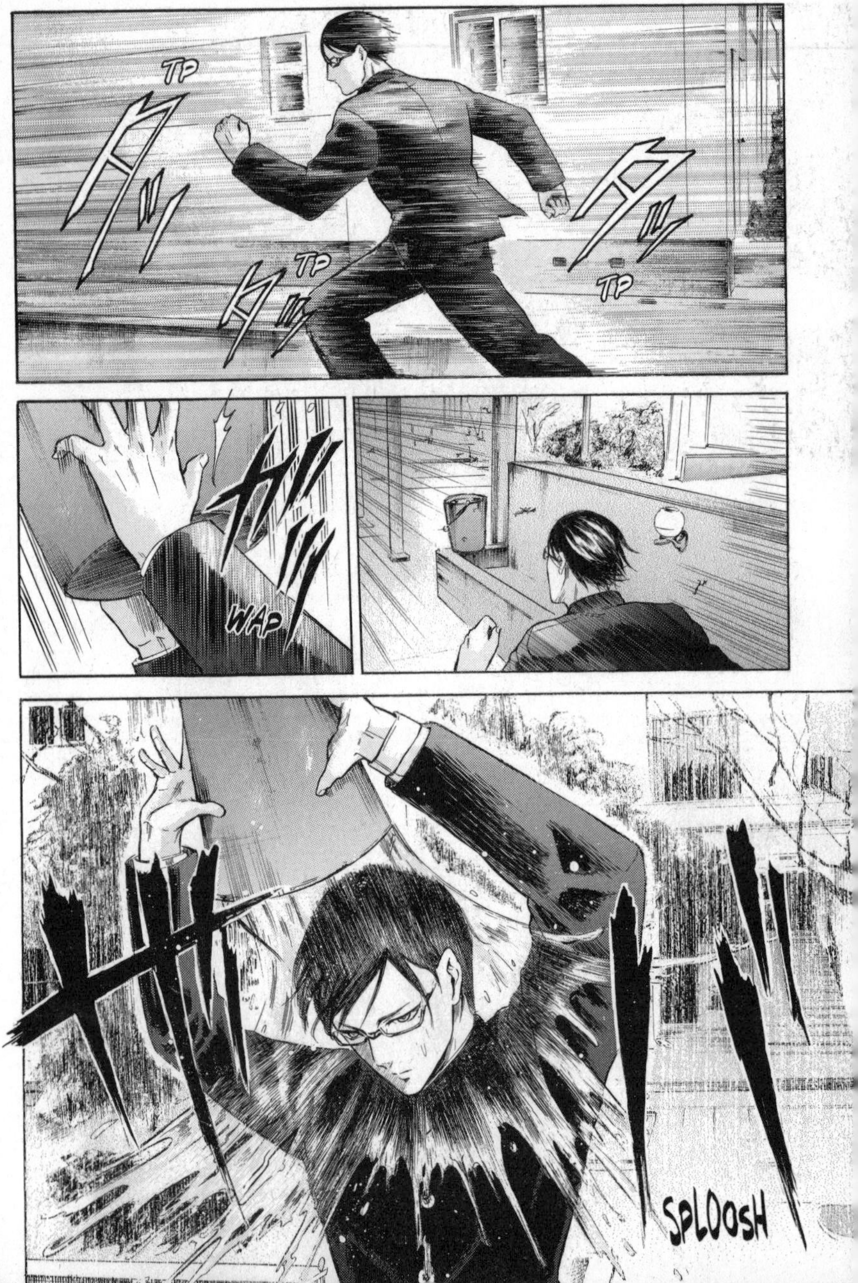
TP
TP
TP
WAP
SPLOOSH

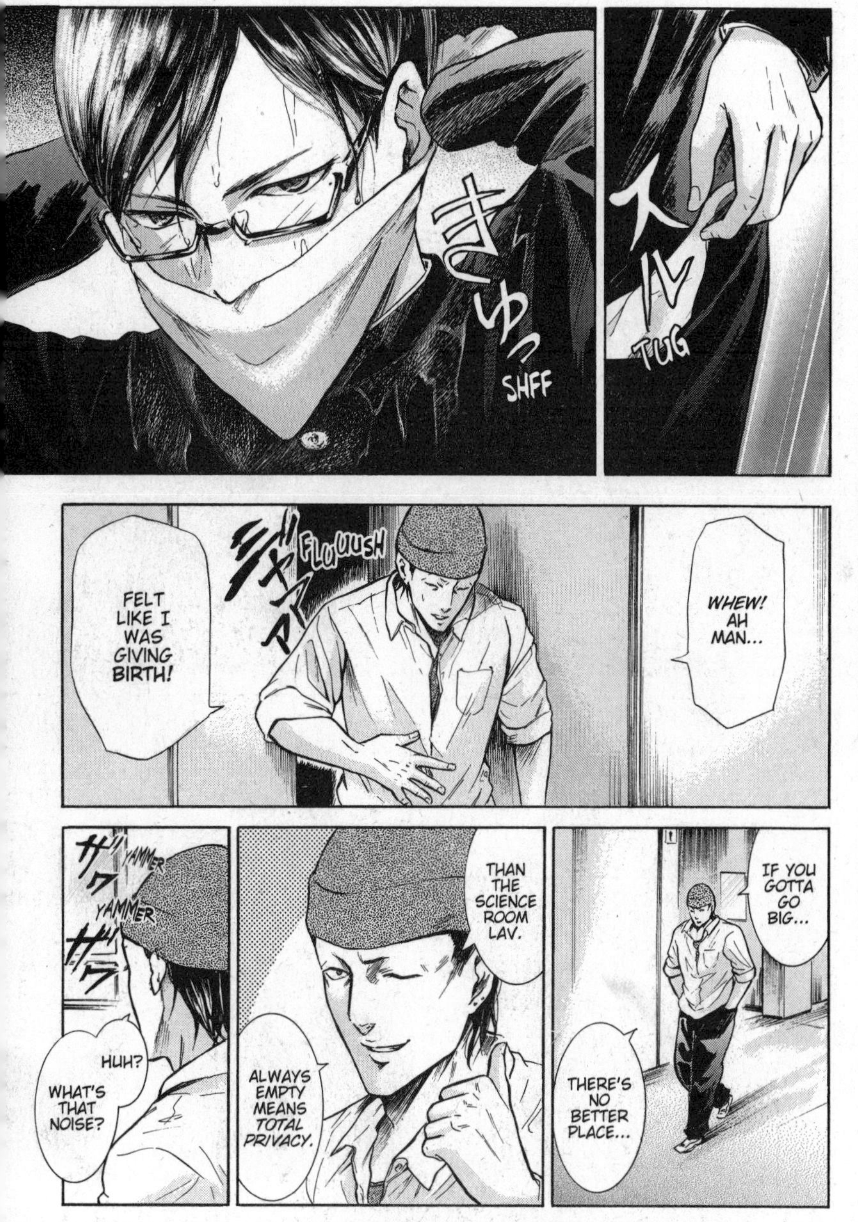
スル
TUG
きゅっ
SHFF
WHEW! AH MAN...
FELT LIKE I WAS GIVING BIRTH!
ジャアア
FLUUUSH
IF YOU GOTTA GO BIG...
THERE'S NO BETTER PLACE...
THAN THE SCIENCE ROOM LAV.
ALWAYS EMPTY MEANS *TOTAL* PRIVACY.
ザワ
YAMMER
ザワ
YAMMER
HUH?
WHAT'S THAT NOISE?

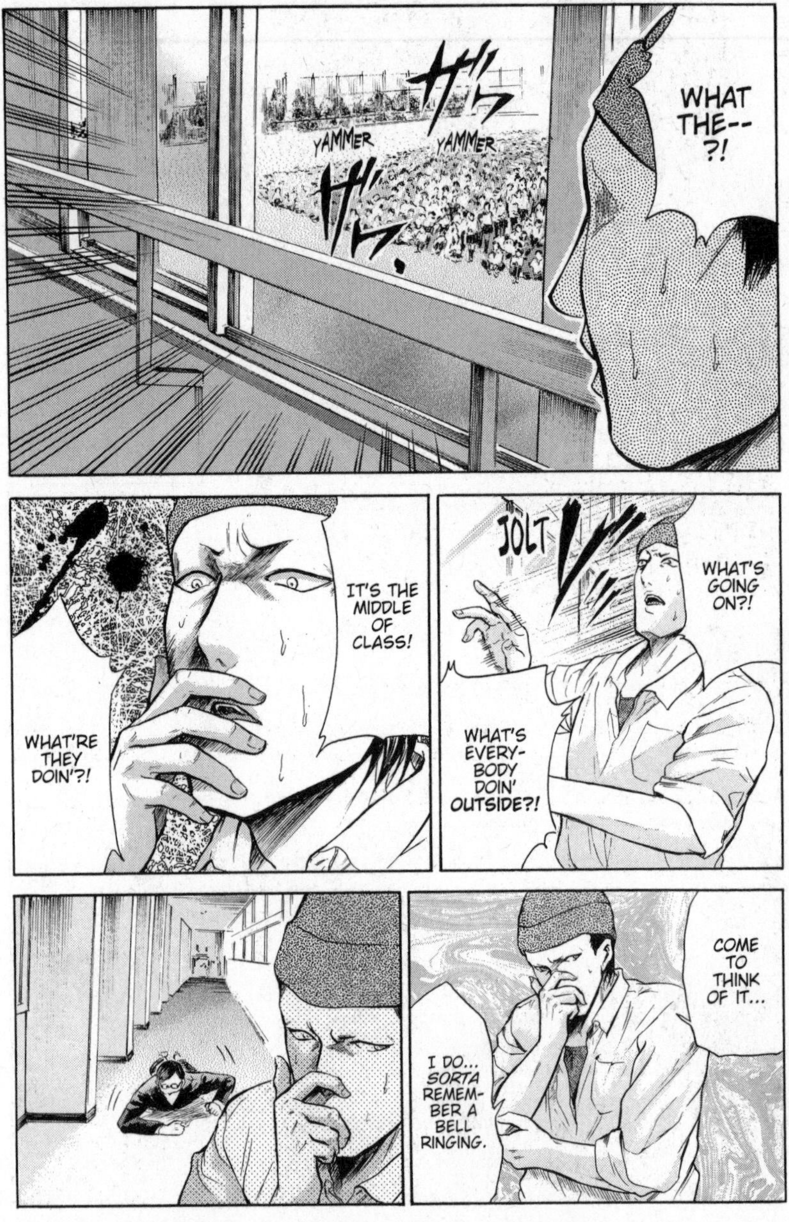
WHAT THE--?!
ザワ
YAMMER
YAMMER
ザワ
JOLT
WHAT'S GOING ON?!
WHAT'S EVERY-BODY DOIN' OUTSIDE?!
IT'S THE MIDDLE OF CLASS!
WHAT'RE THEY DOIN'?!
COME TO THINK OF IT...
I DO... *SORTA* REMEMBER A BELL RINGING.

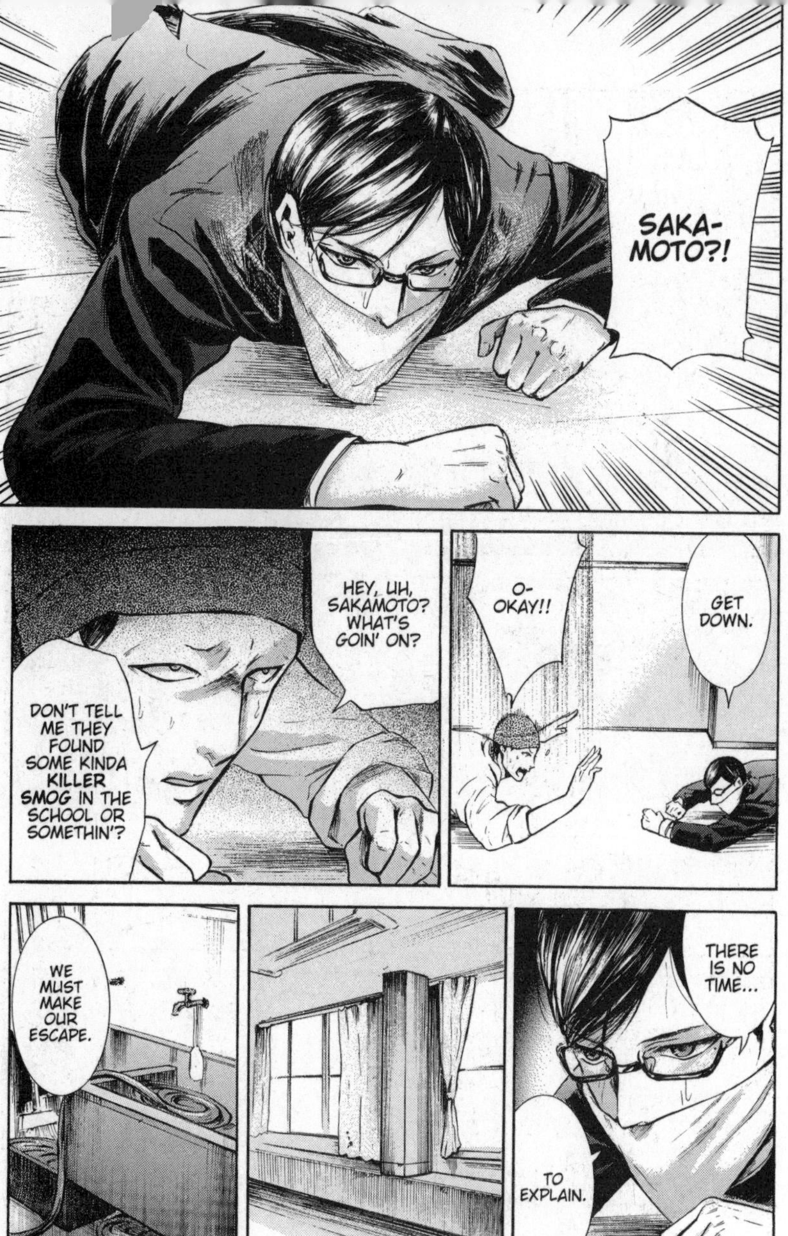
SAKA-MOTO?!
GET DOWN.
O-OKAY!!
HEY, UH, SAKAMOTO? WHAT'S GOIN' ON?
DON'T TELL ME THEY FOUND SOME KINDA KILLER SMOG IN THE SCHOOL OR SOMETHIN'?
THERE IS NO TIME...
TO EXPLAIN.
WE MUST MAKE OUR ESCAPE.

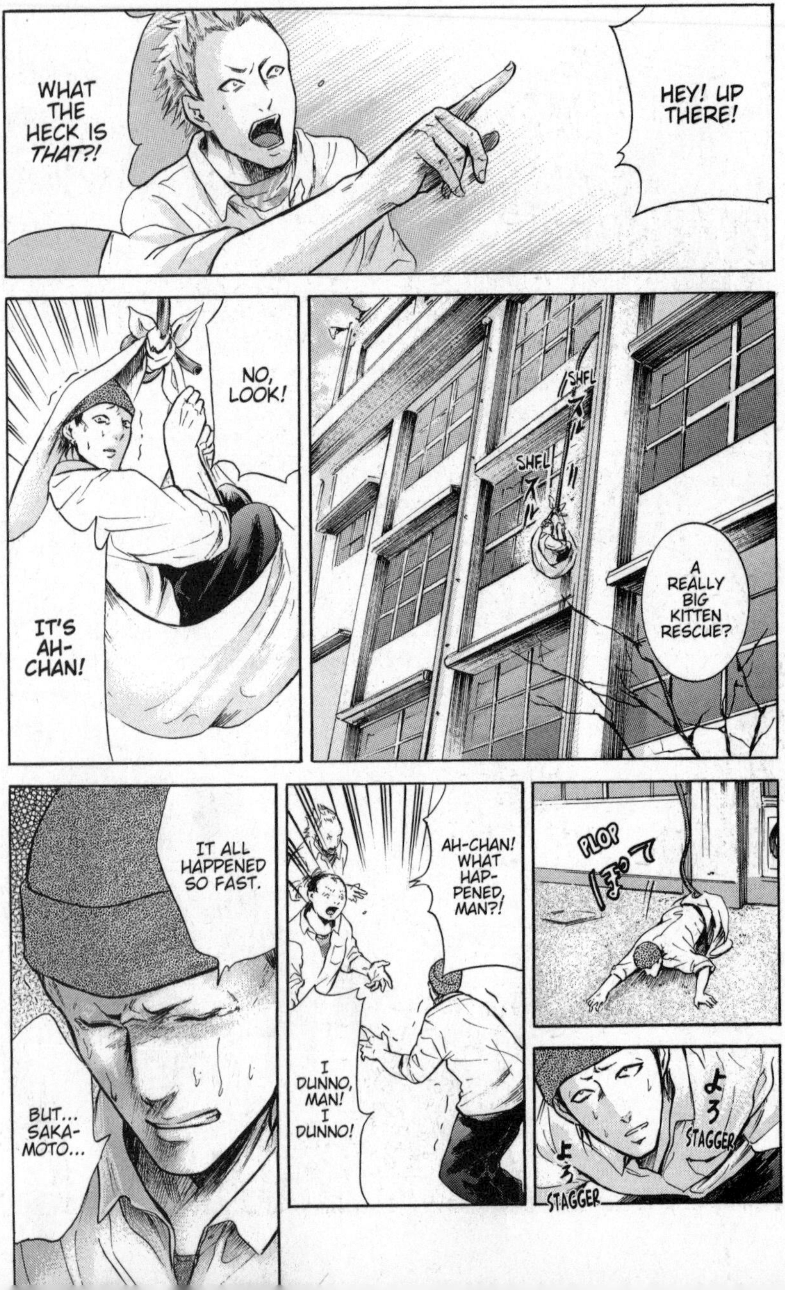

HEY! UP THERE!
WHAT THE HECK IS THAT?!
SHFL
SHFL
A REALLY BIG KITTEN RESCUE?
NO, LOOK!
IT'S AH-CHAN!
PLOP
よろ
STAGGER
よろ
STAGGER
AH-CHAN! WHAT HAP-PENED, MAN?!
I DUNNO, MAN! I DUNNO!
IT ALL HAPPENED SO FAST.
BUT... SAKA-MOTO...

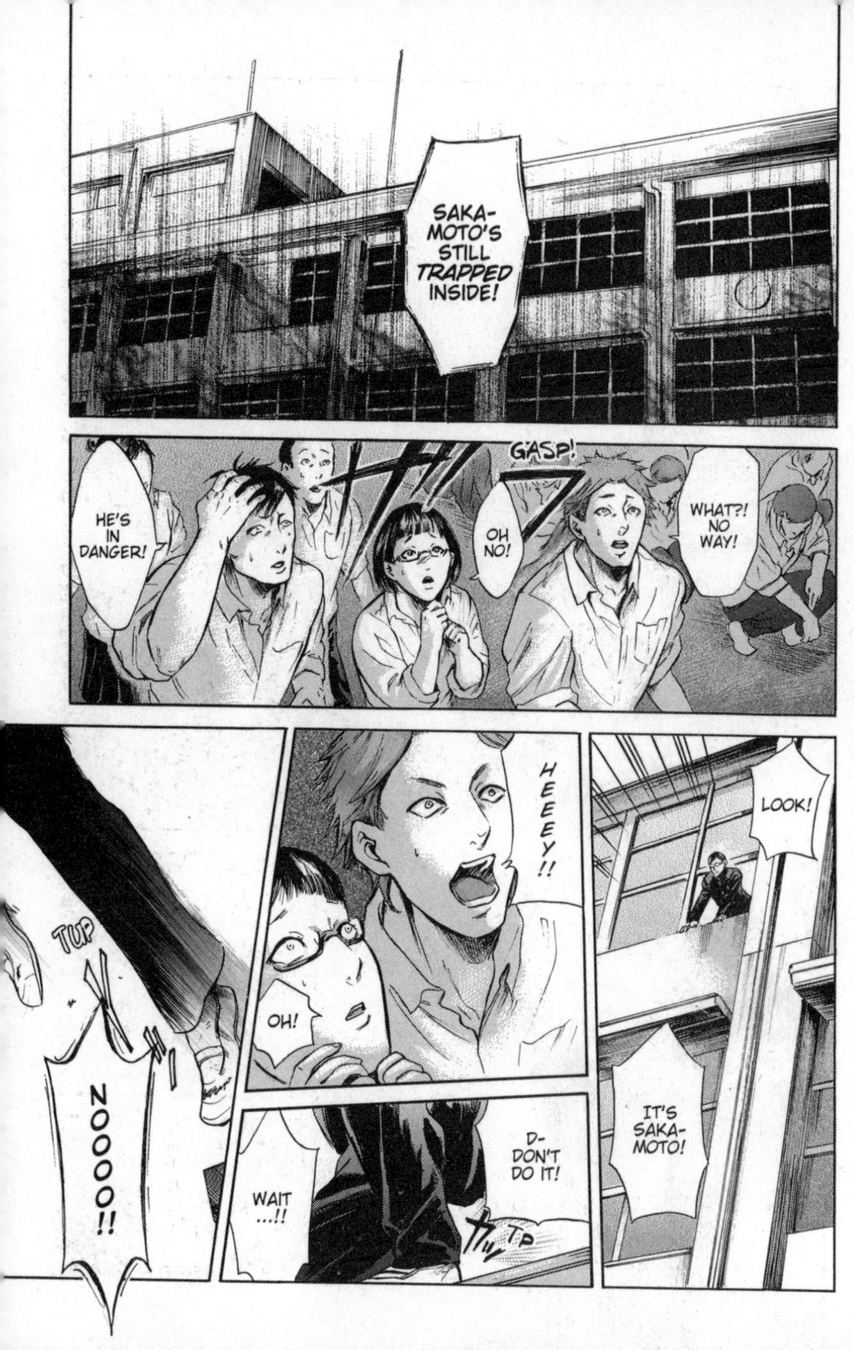
SAKA-MOTO'S STILL *TRAPPED* INSIDE!
WHAT?! NO WAY!
GASP!
OH NO!
HE'S IN DANGER!
LOOK!
IT'S SAKA-MOTO!
HEEEY!!
OH!
D-DON'T DO IT!
WAIT ...!!
TP
TUP
NOOOOO!!

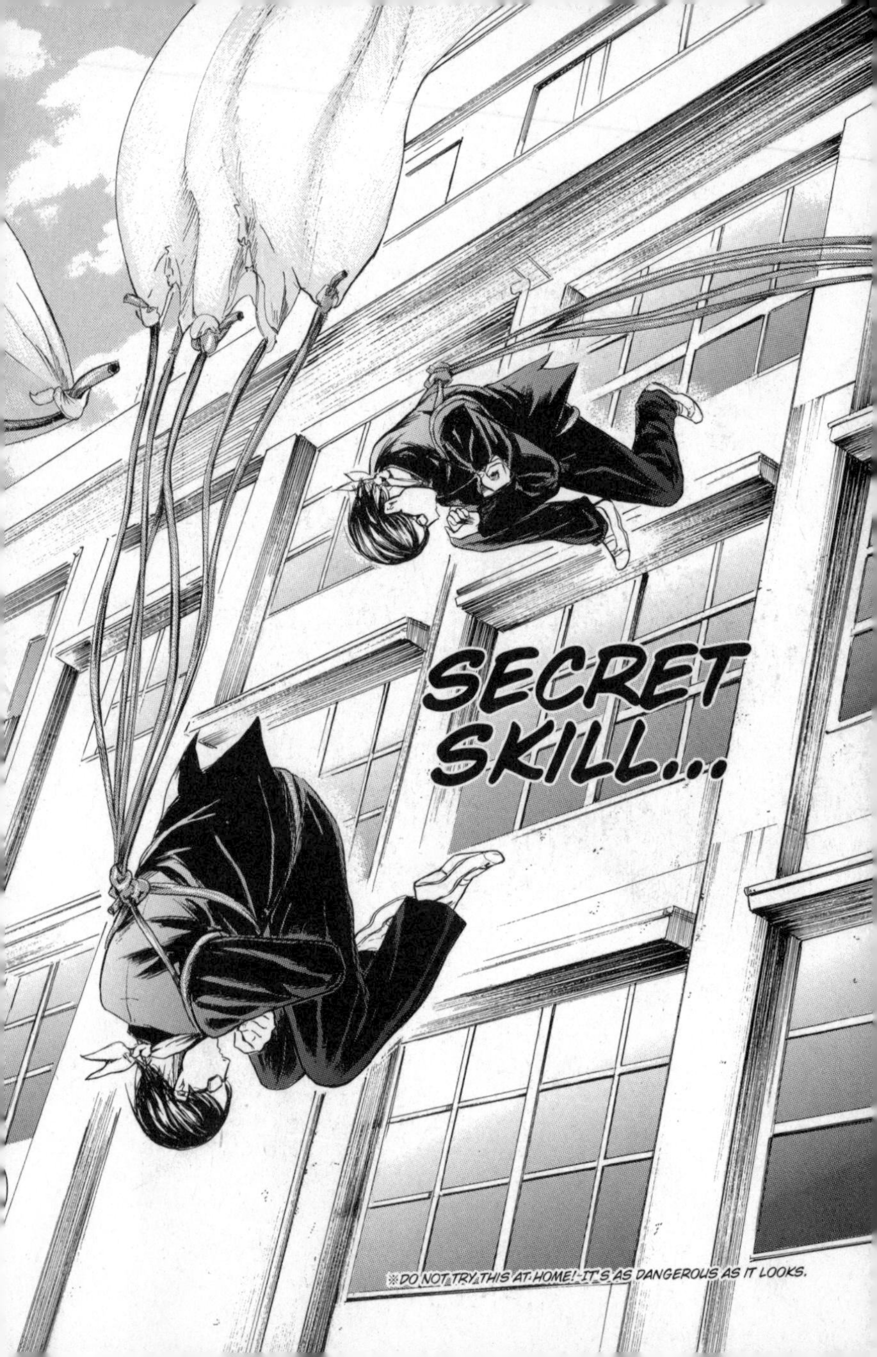
SECRET SKILL...
※DO NOT TRY THIS AT HOME!-IT'S AS DANGEROUS AS IT LOOKS.

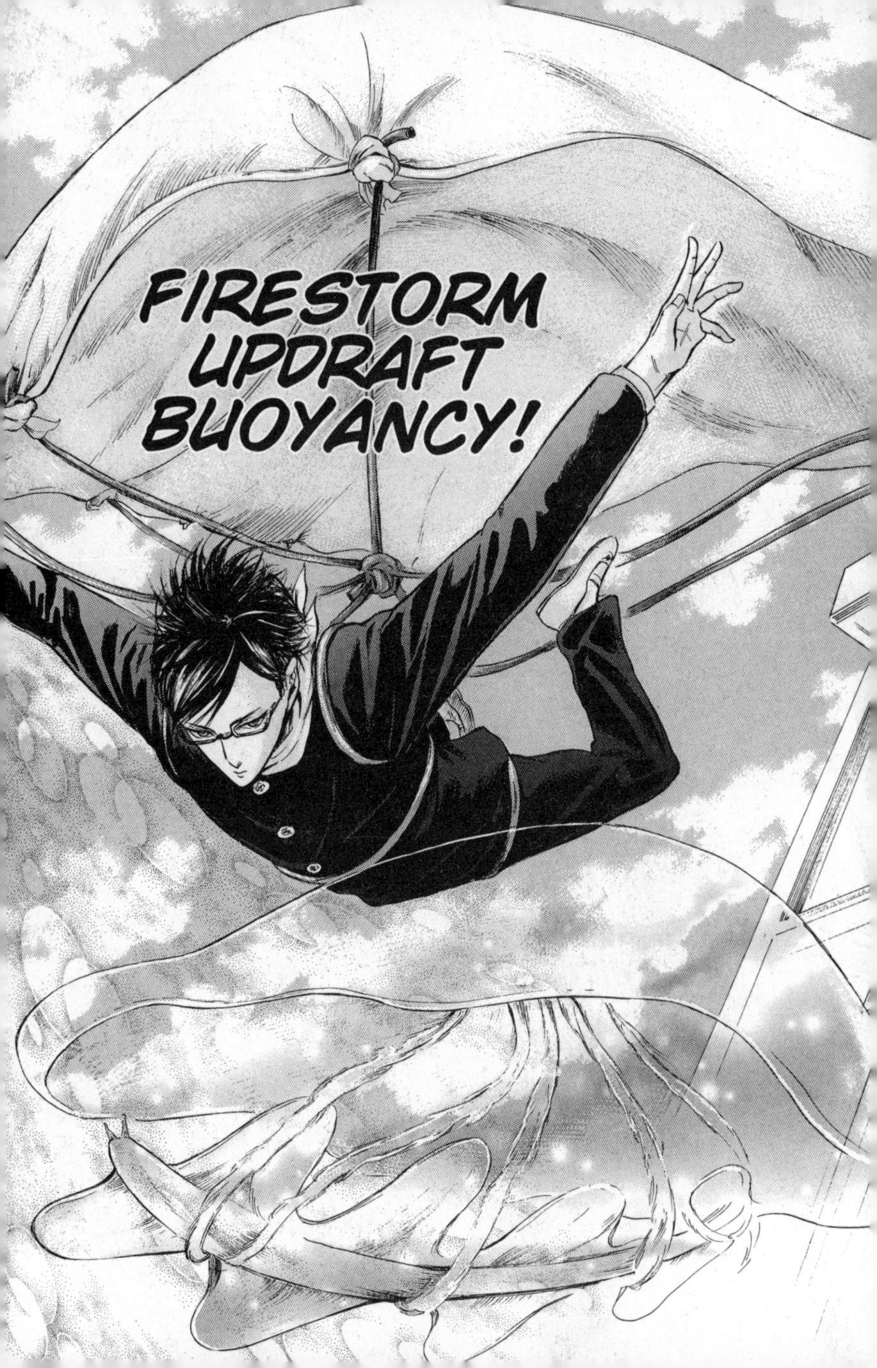
FIRESTORM UPDRAFT BUOYANCY!

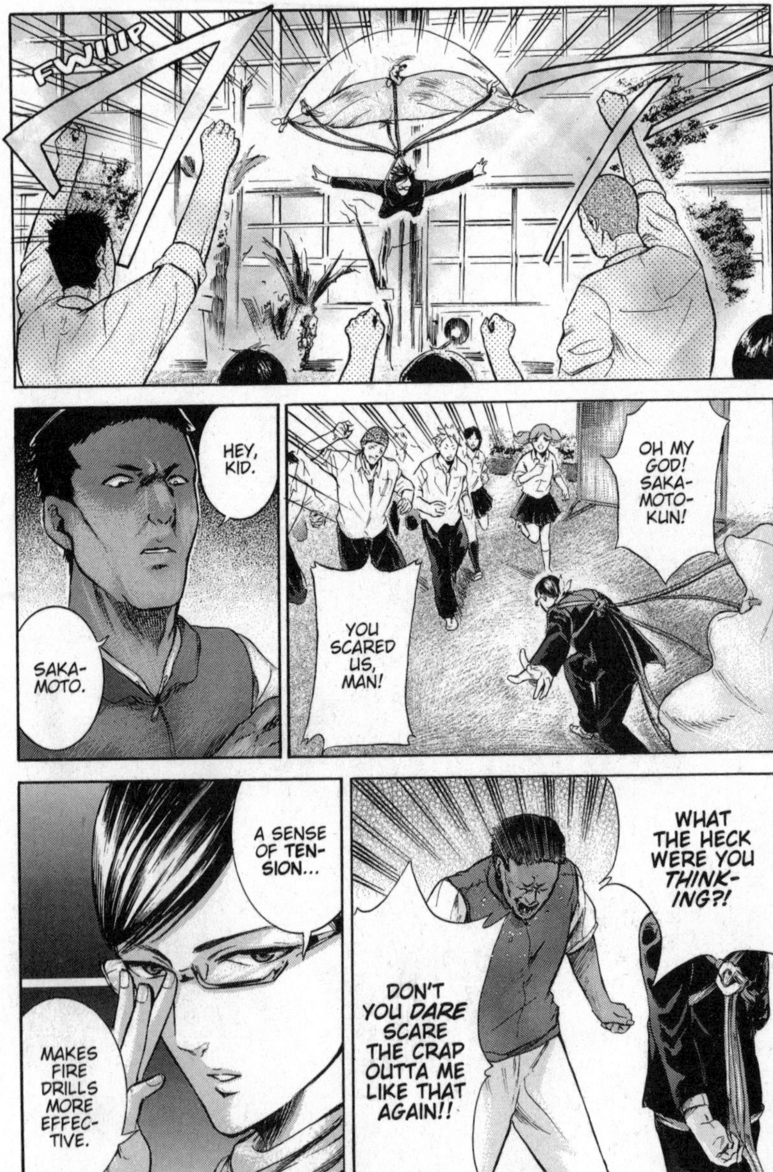
FWIIIP
OH MY GOD! SAKA-MOTO-KUN!
YOU SCARED US, MAN!
HEY, KID.
SAKA-MOTO.
WHAT THE HECK WERE YOU *THINK-ING?!*
DON'T YOU *DARE* SCARE THE CRAP OUTTA ME LIKE THAT AGAIN!!
A SENSE OF TEN-SION...
MAKES FIRE DRILLS MORE EFFEC-TIVE.

End of Chapter 8

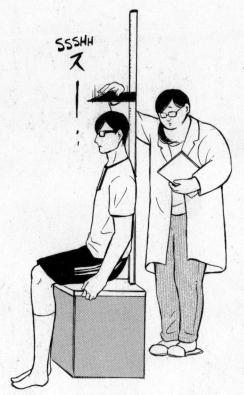

SSSHH
ス

Physical Exam #3:
Sitting Height

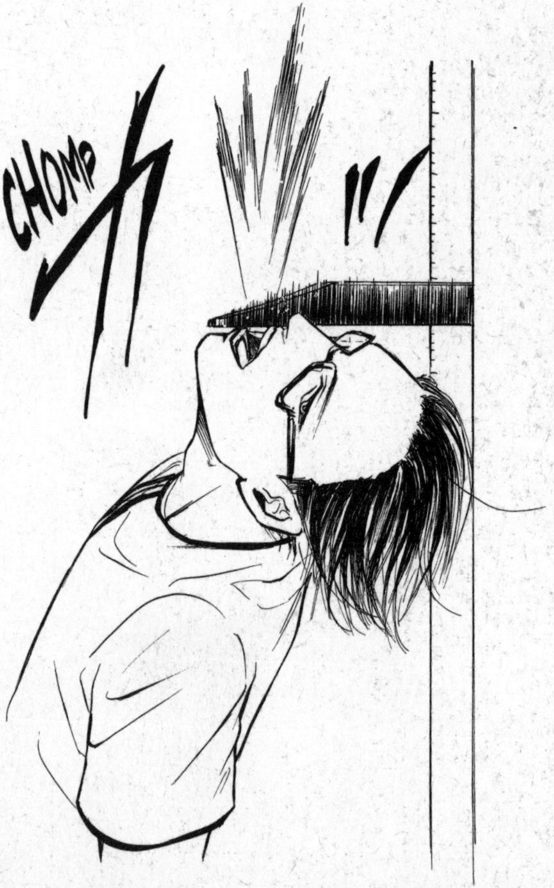
CHOMP

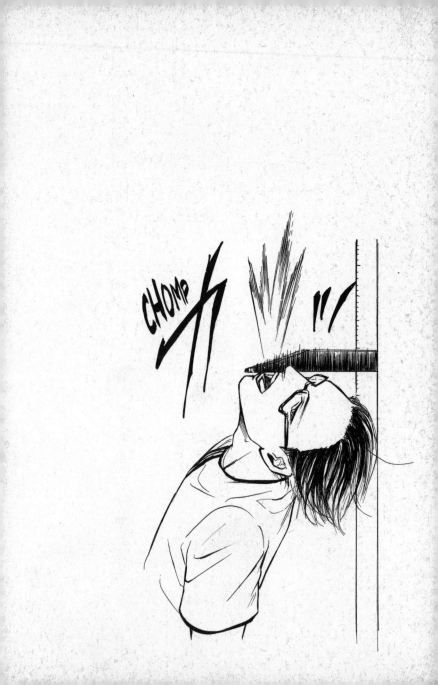

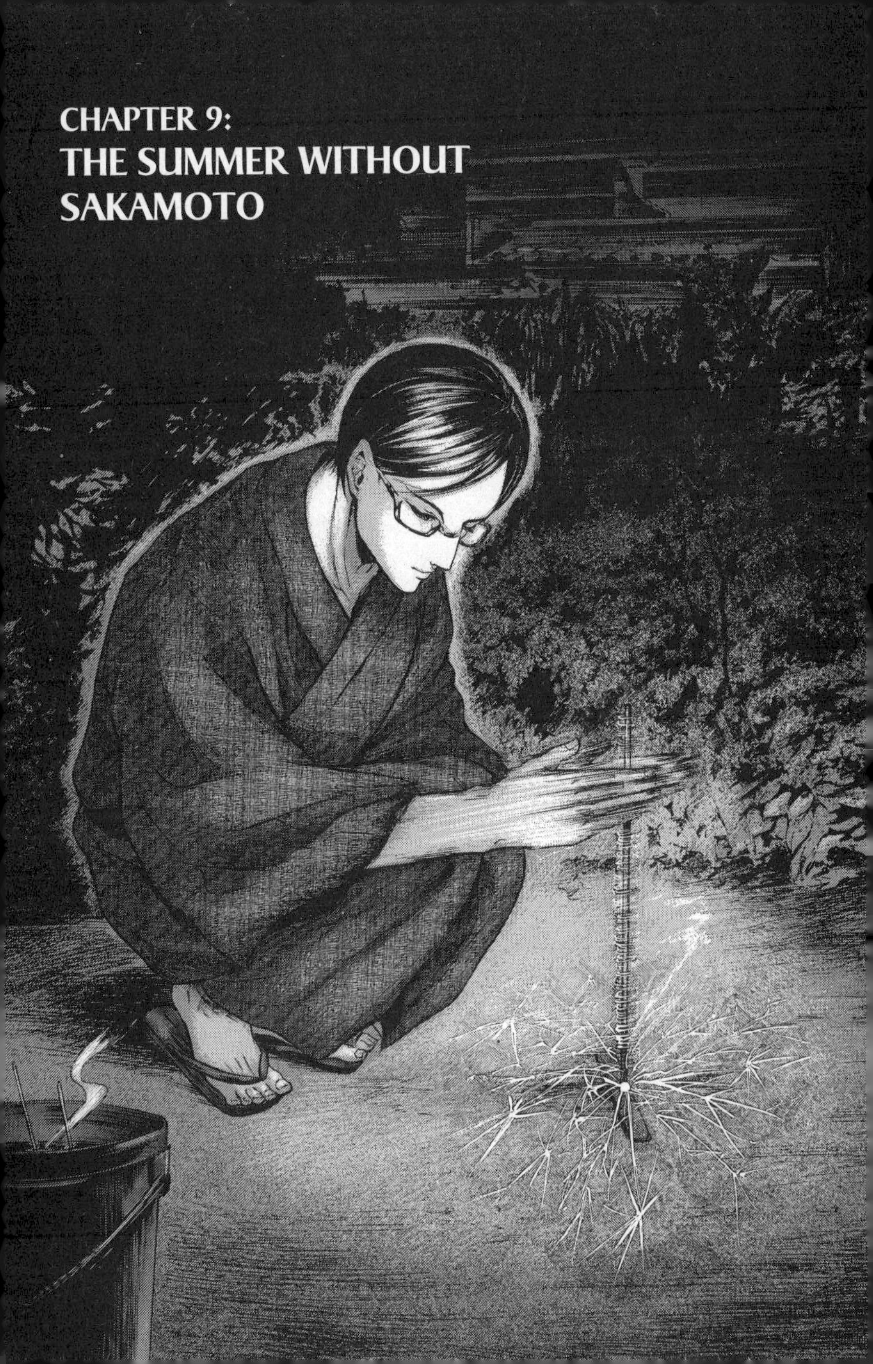
CHAPTER 9:
THE SUMMER WITHOUT SAKAMOTO

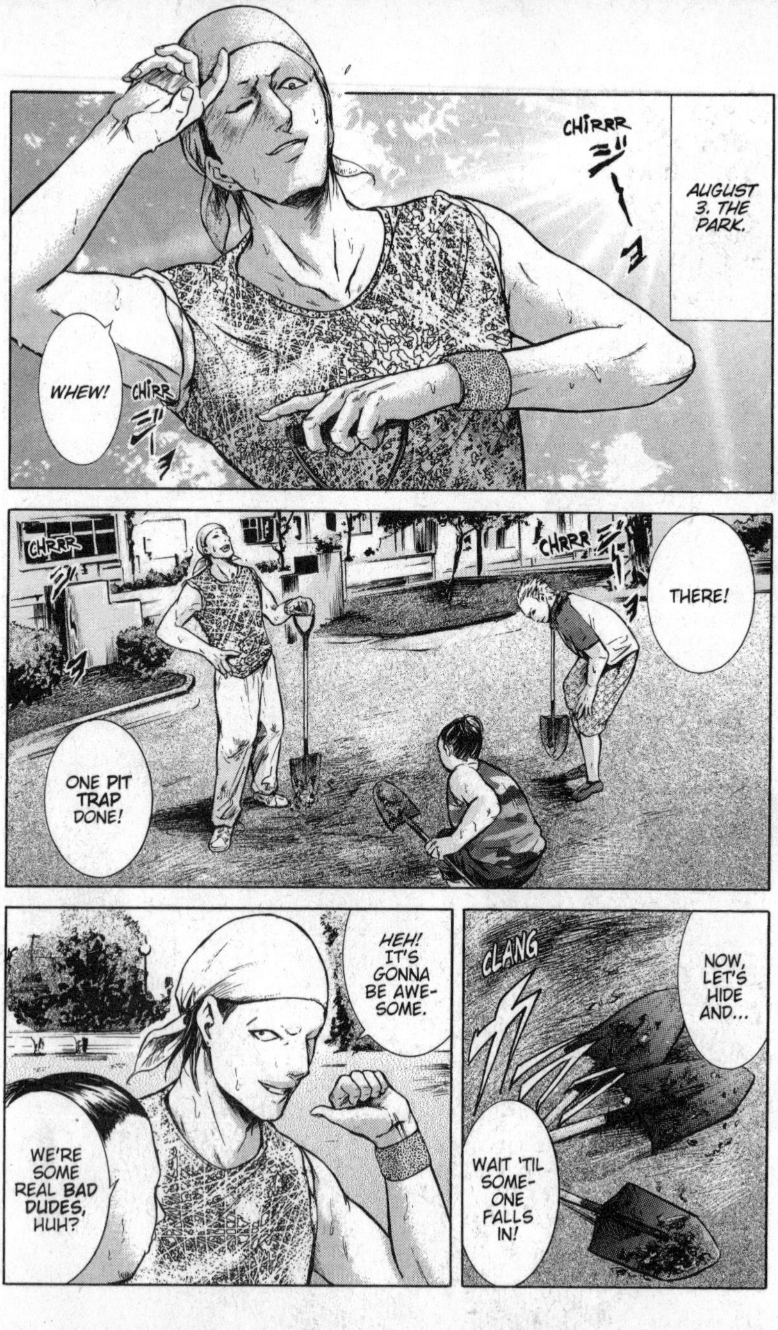
CHIRRR
AUGUST 3. THE PARK.
WHEW!
CHIRR
THERE!
CHRRR
CHRRR
ONE PIT TRAP DONE!
NOW, LET'S HIDE AND...
CLANG
WAIT 'TIL SOME-ONE FALLS IN!
HEH! IT'S GONNA BE AWE-SOME.
WE'RE SOME REAL BAD DUDES, HUH?

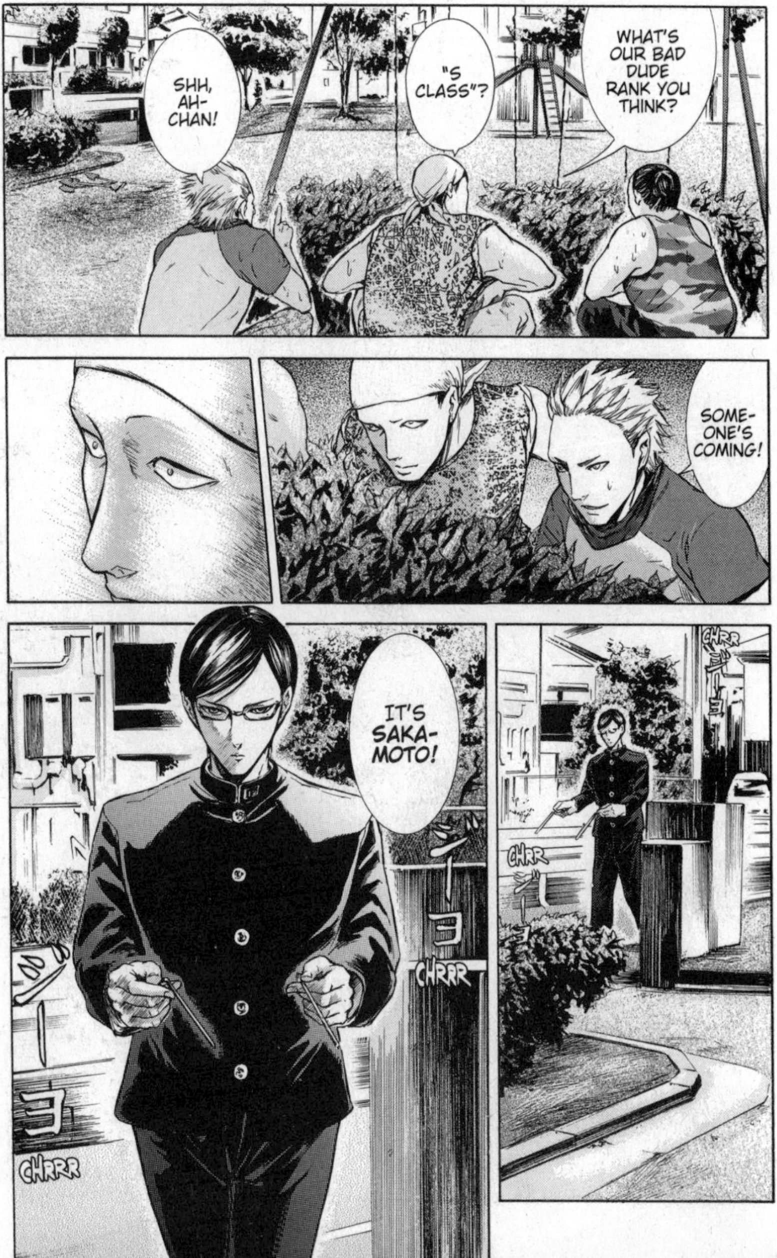
WHAT'S OUR BAD DUDE RANK YOU THINK?
"S CLASS"?
SHH, AH-CHAN!
SOME-ONE'S COMING!
CHRR
CHRR
IT'S SAKA-MOTO!
CHRRR
CHRRR

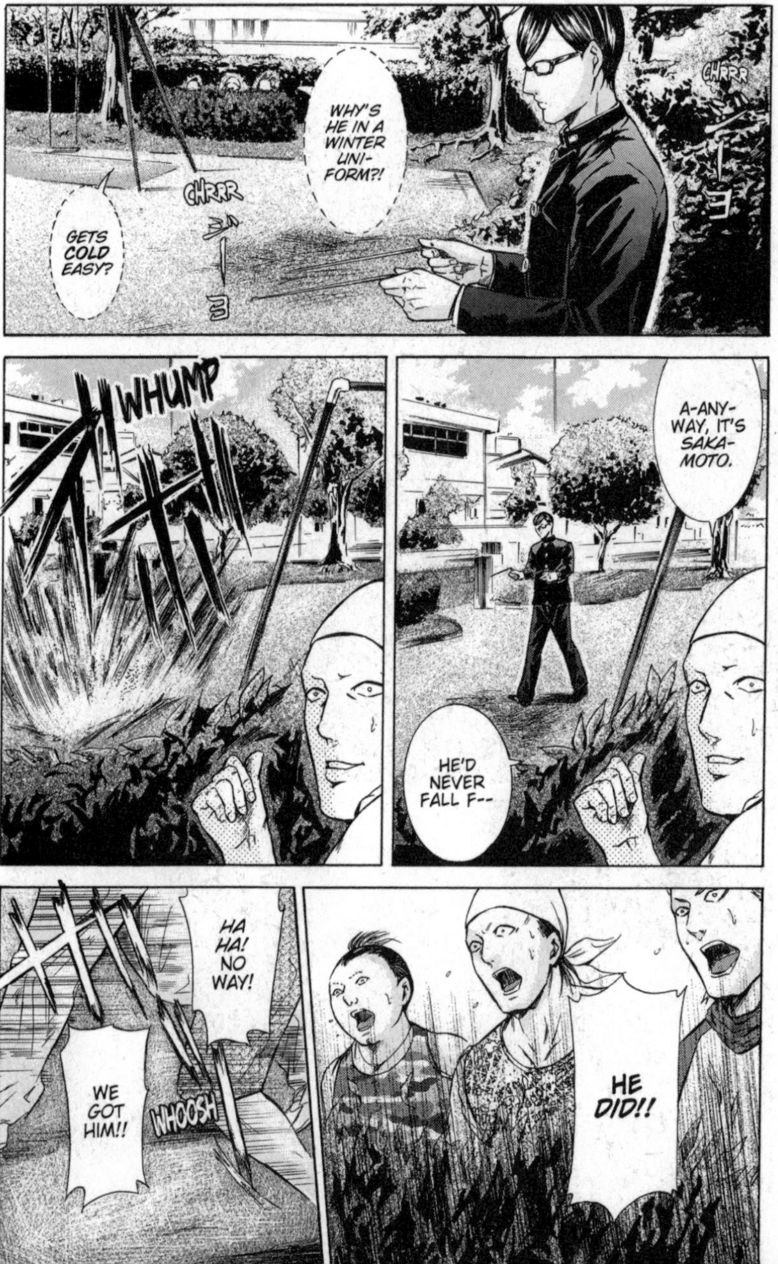
CHRRR
WHY'S HE IN A WINTER UNI-FORM?!
CHRRR
GETS COLD EASY?
A-ANYWAY, IT'S SAKAMOTO.
HE'D NEVER FALL F--
WHUMP
HE DID!!
HA HA! NO WAY!
WE GOT HIM!!
WHOOSH

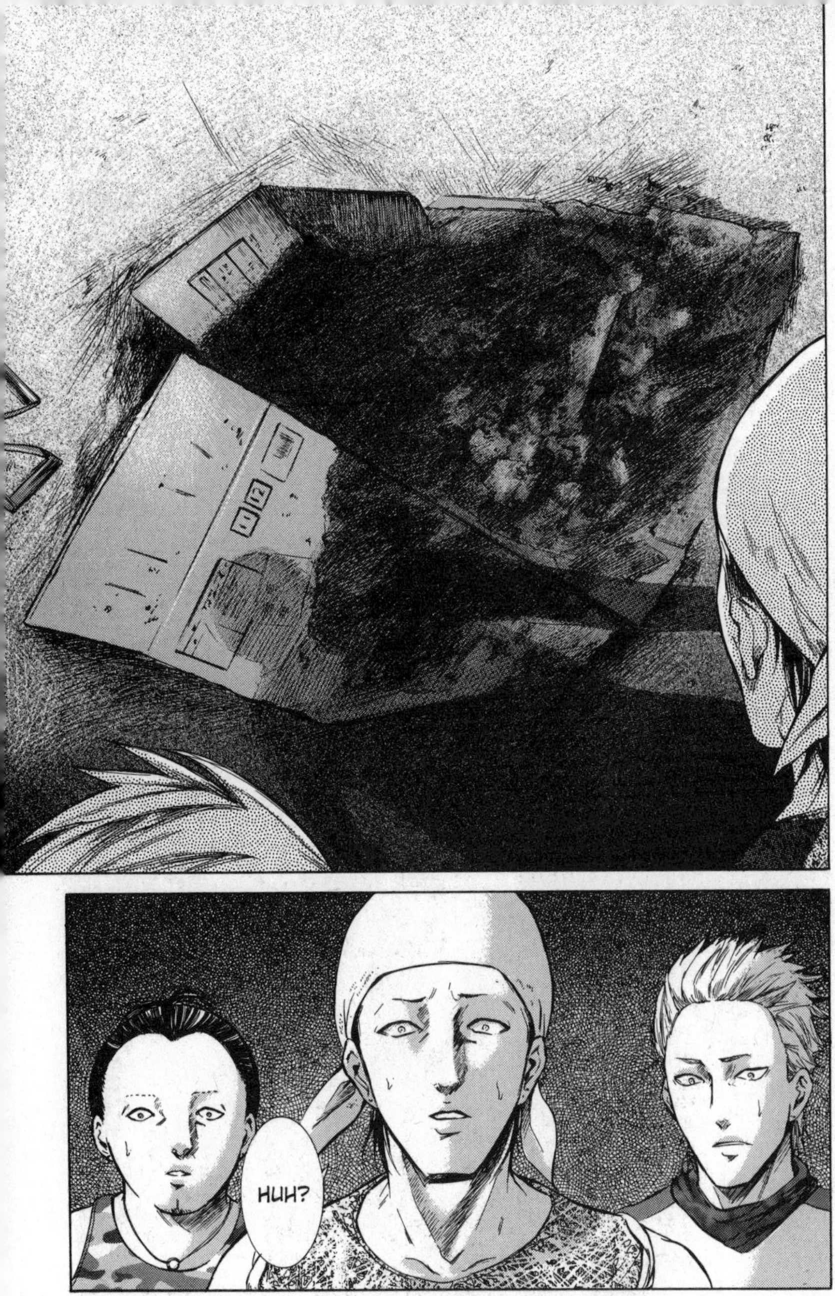
HUH?

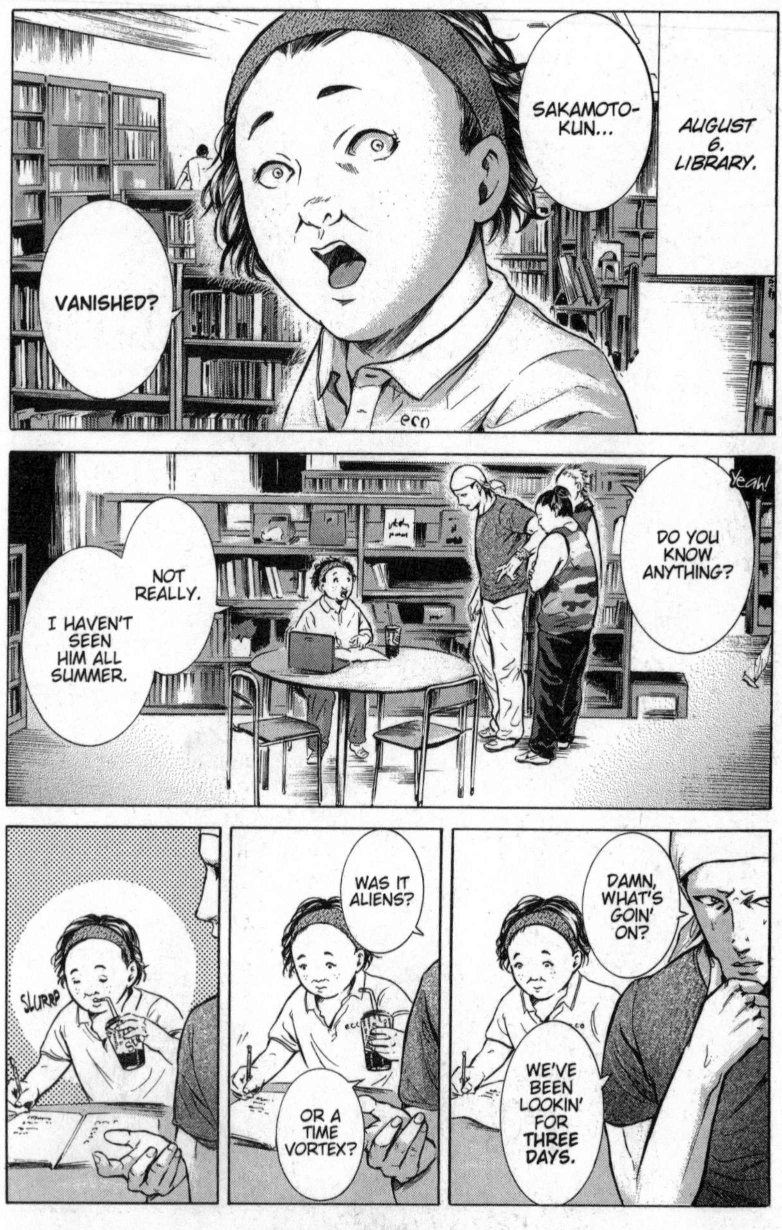
AUGUST 6. LIBRARY.
SAKAMOTO-KUN...
VANISHED?
Yeah!
DO YOU KNOW ANYTHING?
NOT REALLY.
I HAVEN'T SEEN HIM ALL SUMMER.
DAMN, WHAT'S GOIN' ON?
WE'VE BEEN LOOKIN' FOR THREE DAYS.
WAS IT ALIENS?
OR A TIME VORTEX?
SLURRP

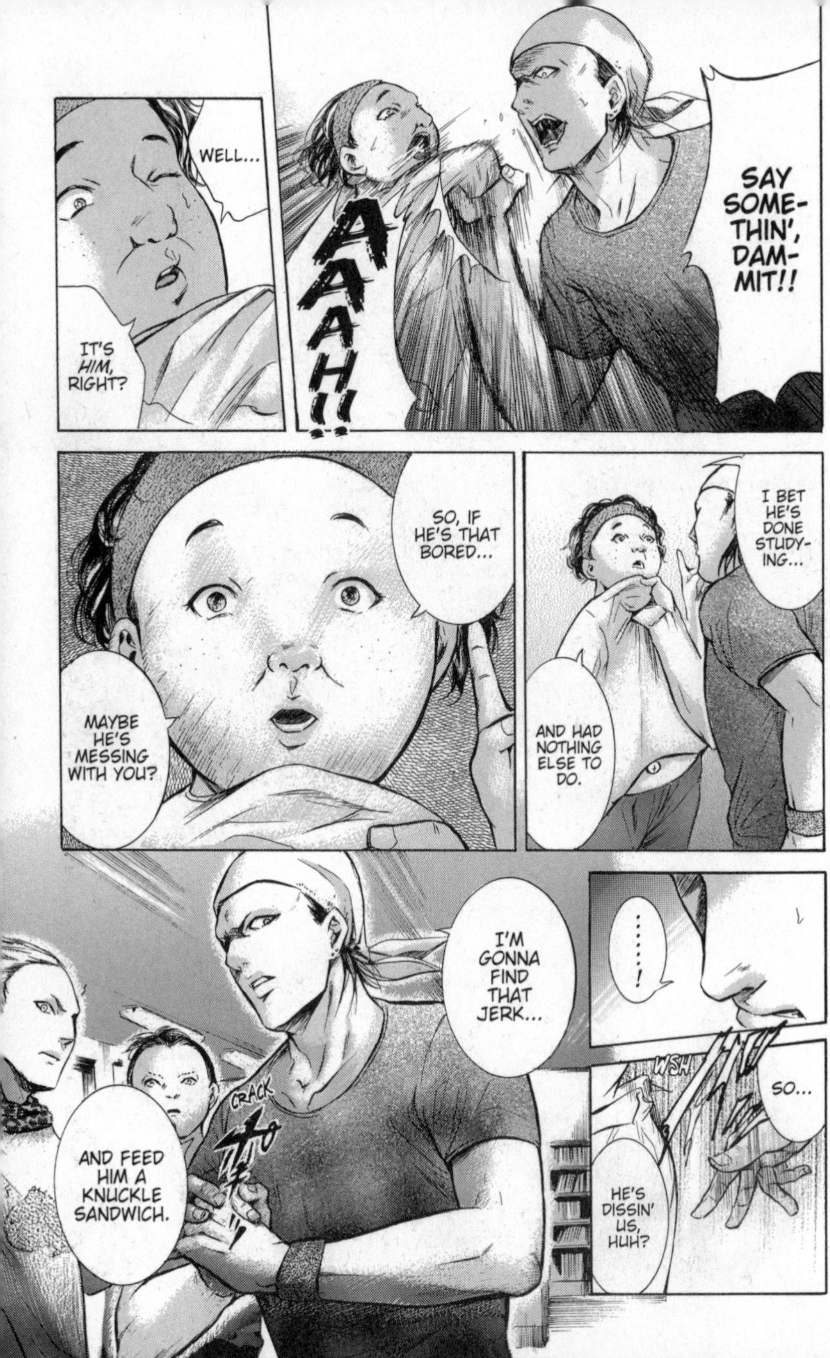
SAY SOMETHIN', DAMMIT!!
AAAH!!
WELL...
IT'S *HIM*, RIGHT?
I BET HE'S DONE STUDYING...
AND HAD NOTHING ELSE TO DO.
SO, IF HE'S THAT BORED...
MAYBE HE'S MESSING WITH YOU?
......!
WSH
SO...
HE'S DISSIN' US, HUH?
I'M GONNA FIND THAT JERK...
CRACK
AND FEED HIM A KNUCKLE SANDWICH.

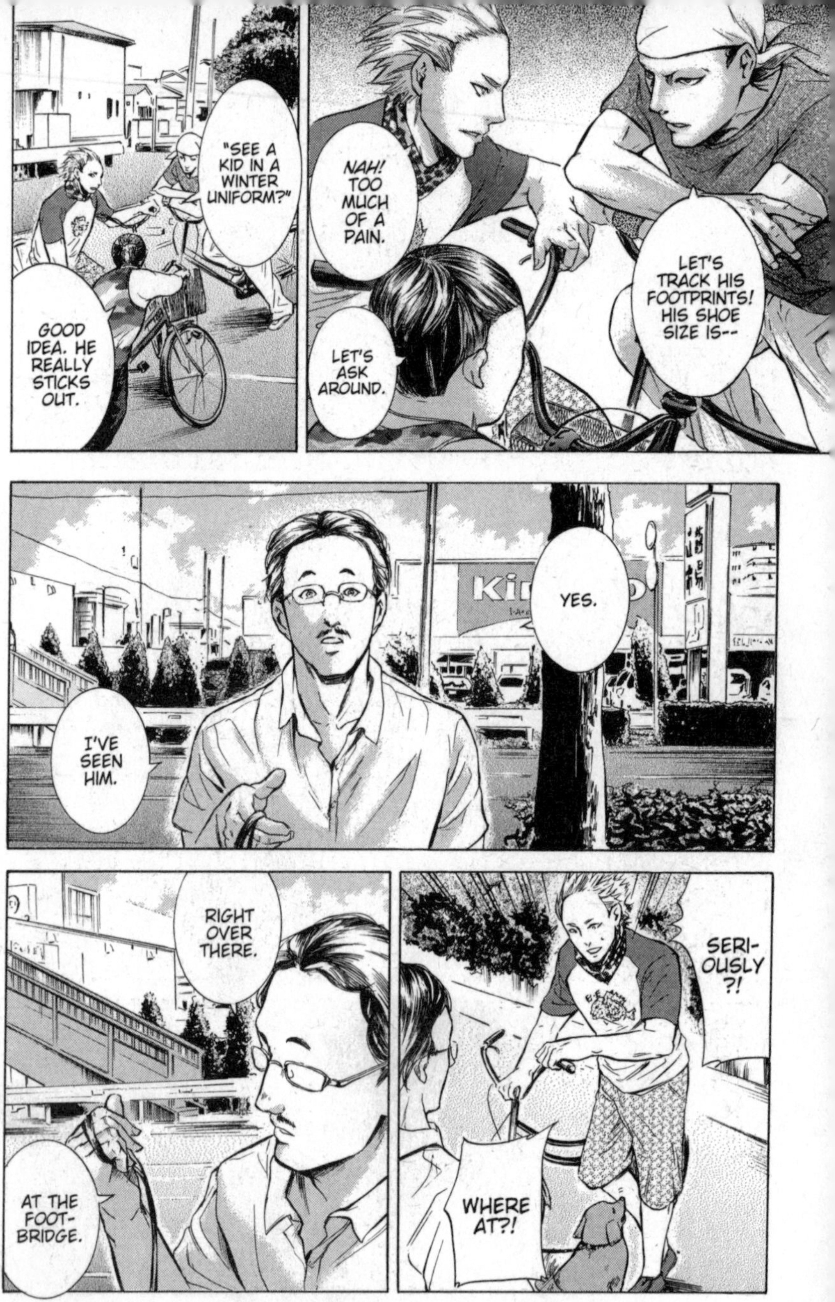
LET'S TRACK HIS FOOTPRINTS! HIS SHOE SIZE IS--
NAH! TOO MUCH OF A PAIN.
LET'S ASK AROUND.
"SEE A KID IN A WINTER UNIFORM?"
GOOD IDEA. HE REALLY STICKS OUT.
YES.
I'VE SEEN HIM.
SERI-OUSLY?!
WHERE AT?!
RIGHT OVER THERE.
AT THE FOOT-BRIDGE.

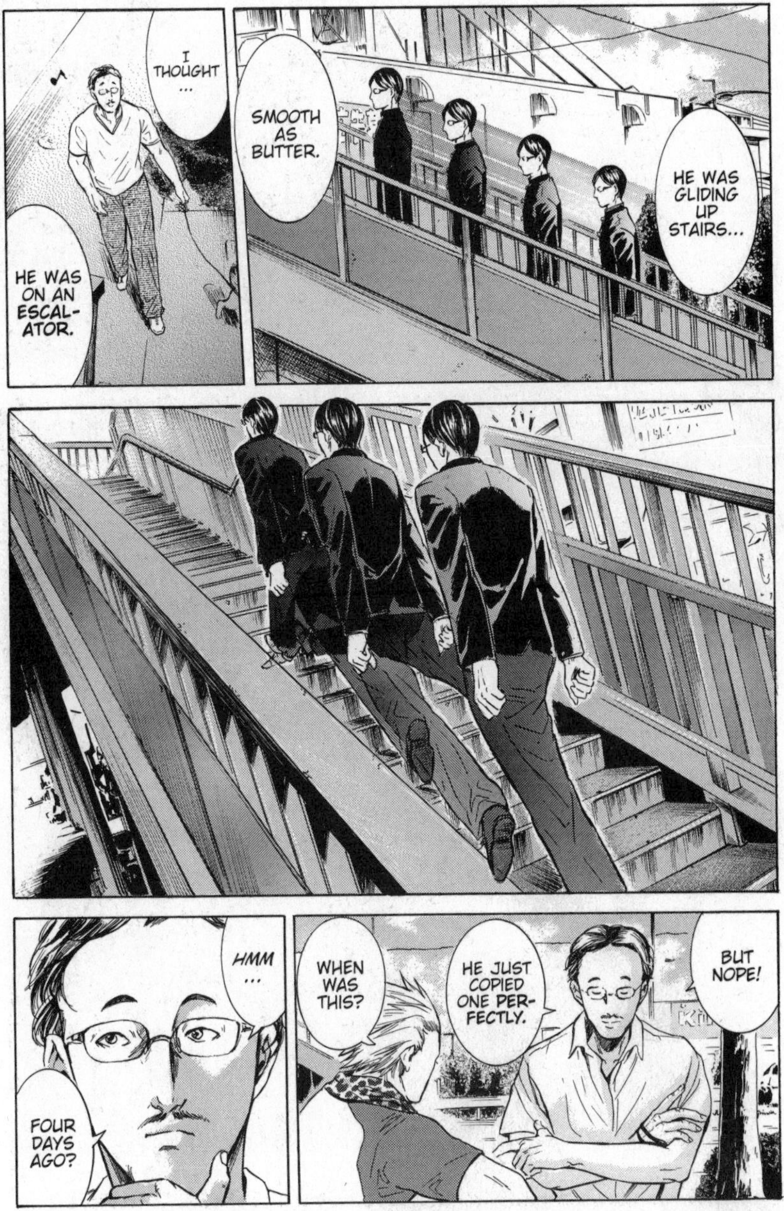
HE WAS GLIDING UP STAIRS...
SMOOTH AS BUTTER.
I THOUGHT...
HE WAS ON AN ESCALATOR.
BUT NOPE!
HE JUST COPIED ONE PERFECTLY.
WHEN WAS THIS?
HMM...
FOUR DAYS AGO?

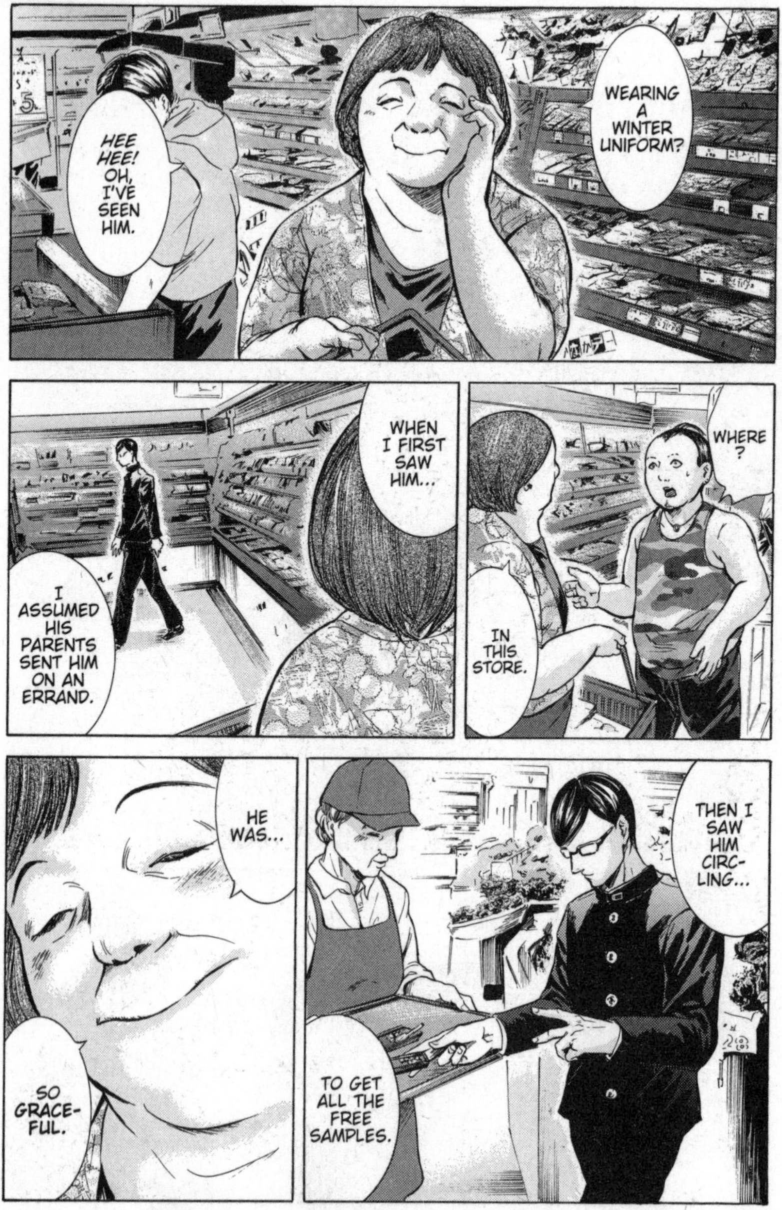
WEARING A WINTER UNIFORM?
HEE HEE! OH, I'VE SEEN HIM.
WHERE?
IN THIS STORE.
WHEN I FIRST SAW HIM...
I ASSUMED HIS PARENTS SENT HIM ON AN ERRAND.
THEN I SAW HIM CIRCLING...
TO GET ALL THE FREE SAMPLES.
HE WAS...
SO GRACEFUL.

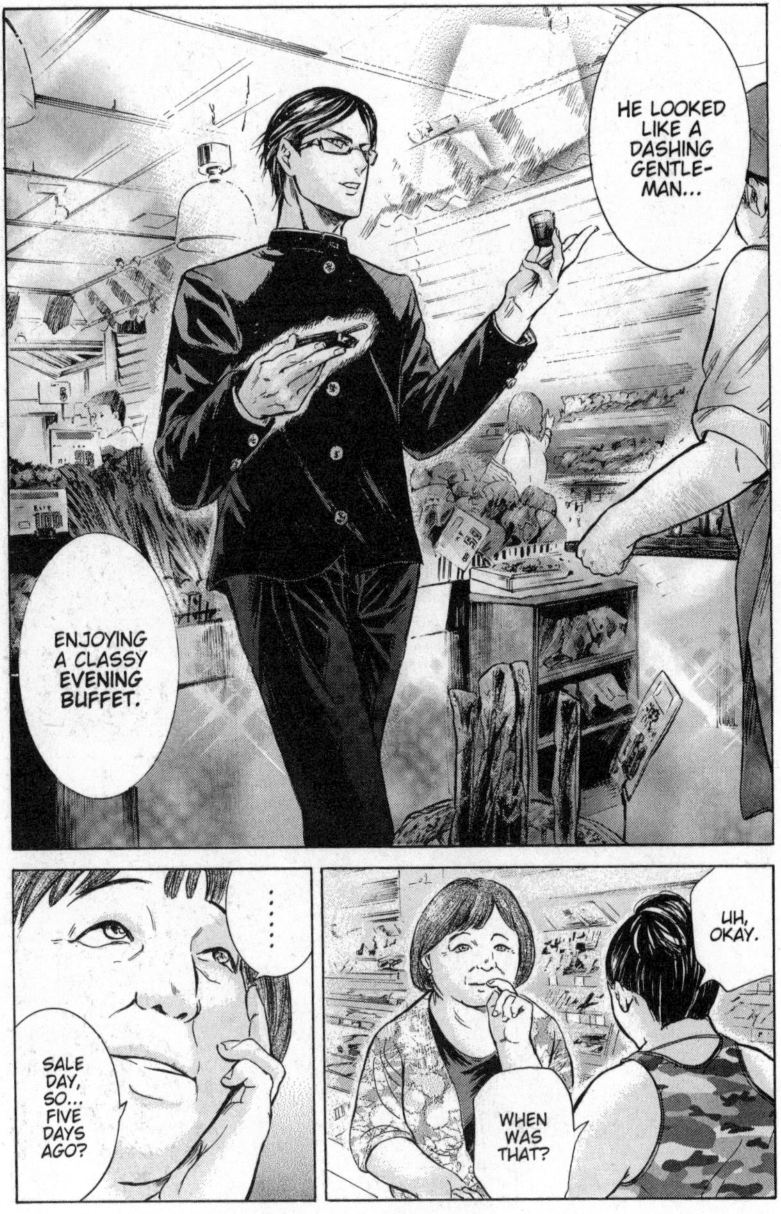
HE LOOKED LIKE A DASHING GENTLE-MAN...
ENJOYING A CLASSY EVENING BUFFET.
UH, OKAY.
WHEN WAS THAT?
......
SALE DAY, SO... FIVE DAYS AGO?

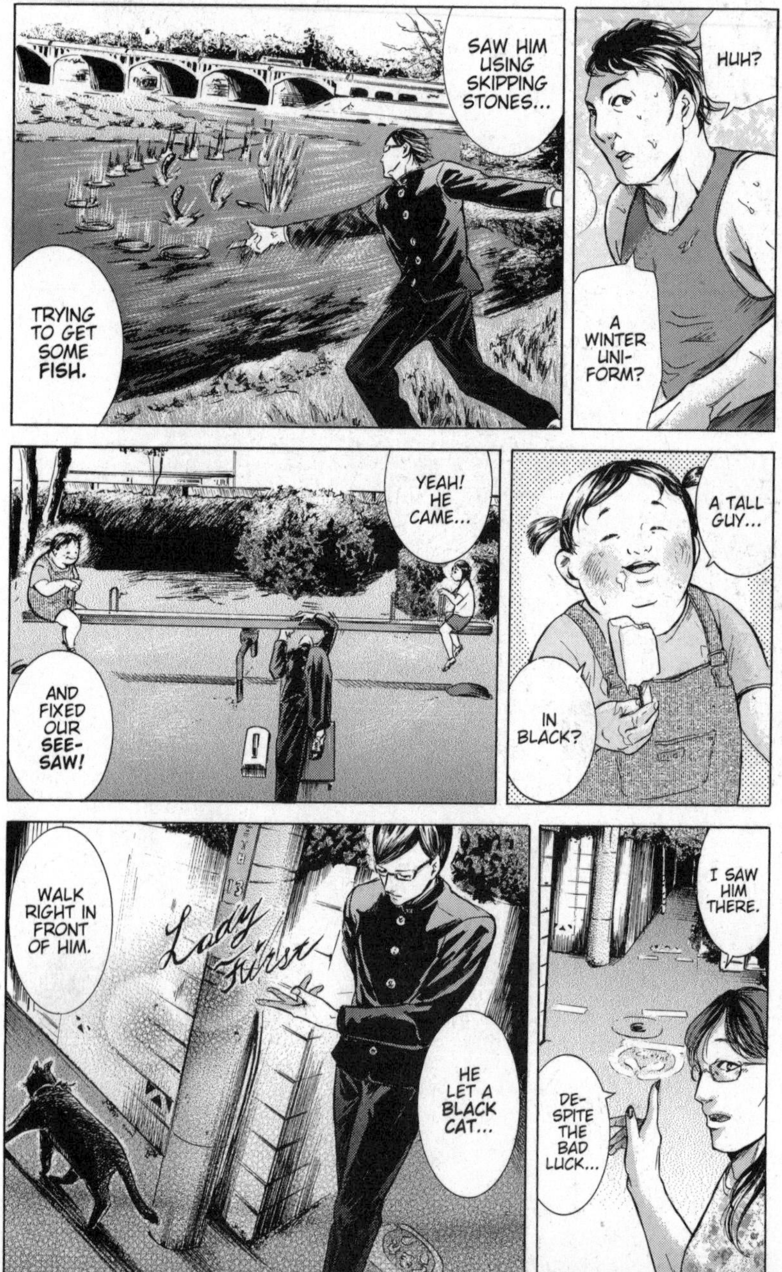
HUH?
A WINTER UNI-FORM?
SAW HIM USING SKIPPING STONES...
TRYING TO GET SOME FISH.
A TALL GUY...
IN BLACK?
YEAH! HE CAME...
AND FIXED OUR SEE-SAW!
I SAW HIM THERE.
DE-SPITE THE BAD LUCK...
Lady First
HE LET A BLACK CAT...
WALK RIGHT IN FRONT OF HIM.

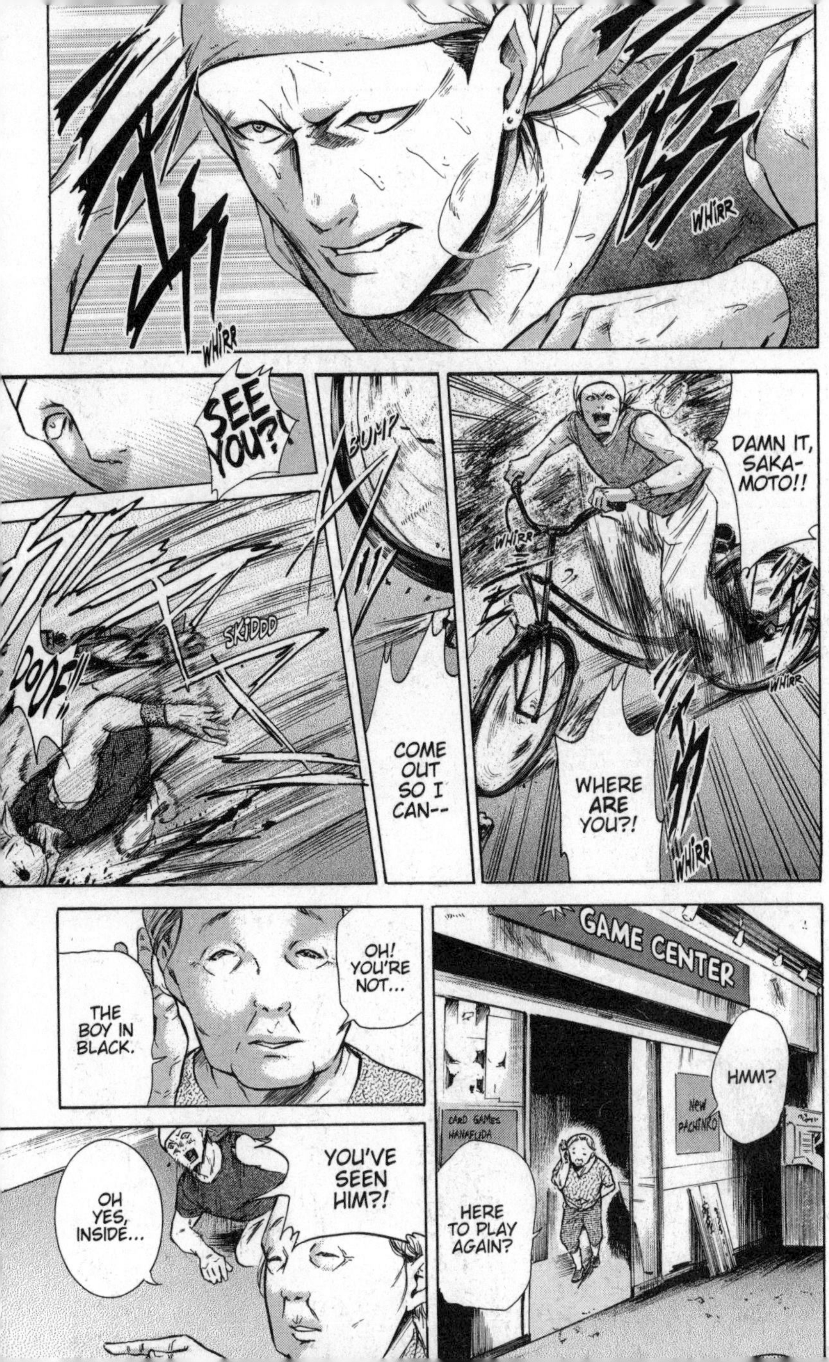
WHIRR
WHIRR
DAMN IT, SAKA-MOTO!!
WHIRR
WHIRR
WHERE ARE YOU?!
WHIRR
BUMP
COME OUT SO I CAN--
SEE YOU?!
SKIDDD
DOOF!!
GAME CENTER
HMM?
NEW PACHINKO
CARD GAMES HANAFUDA
HERE TO PLAY AGAIN?
OH! YOU'RE NOT...
THE BOY IN BLACK.
YOU'VE SEEN HIM?!
OH YES, INSIDE...

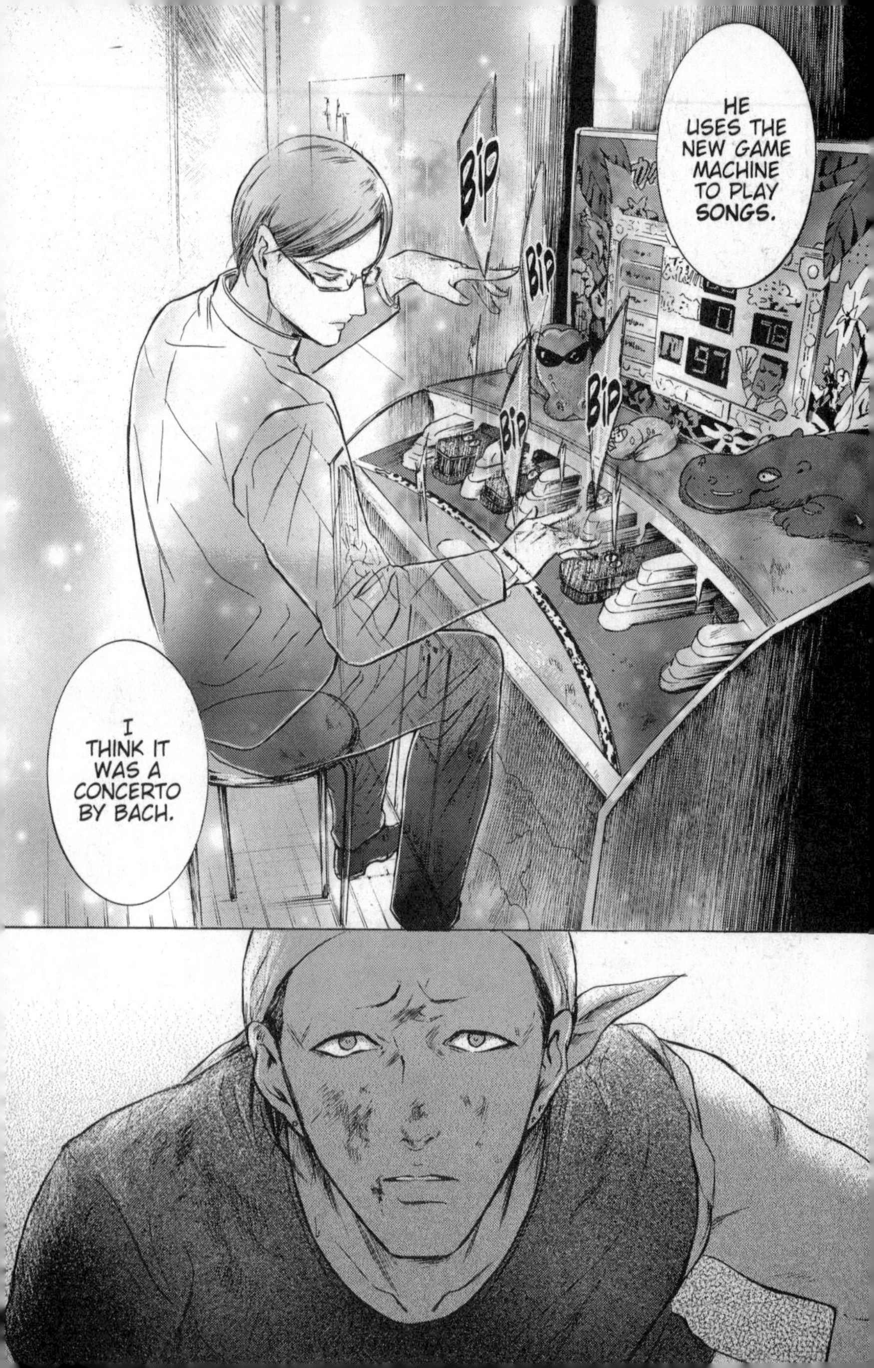
HE USES THE NEW GAME MACHINE TO PLAY SONGS.
BIP
BIP
BIP
BIP
I THINK IT WAS A CONCERTO BY BACH.

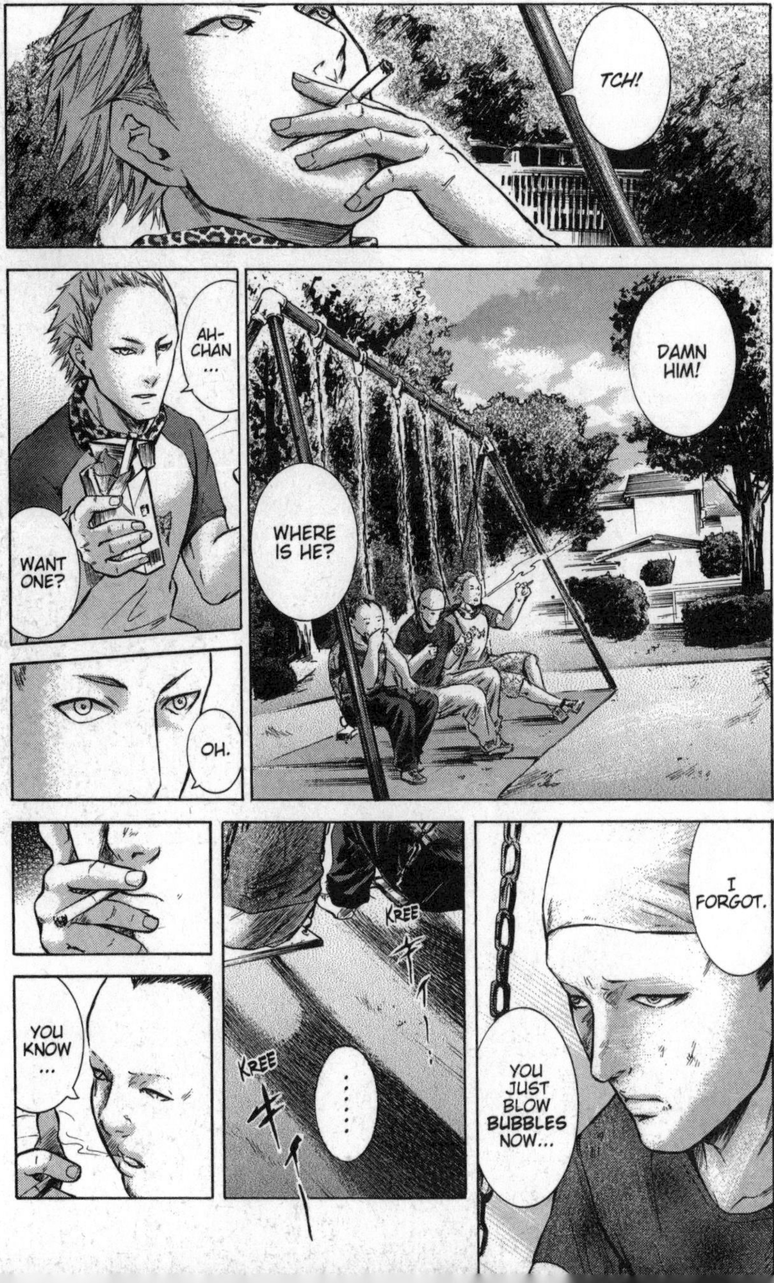
TCH!
DAMN HIM!
WHERE IS HE?
AH-CHAN ...
WANT ONE?
OH.
I FORGOT.
YOU JUST BLOW BUBBLES NOW...
KREE
......
KREE
YOU KNOW ...

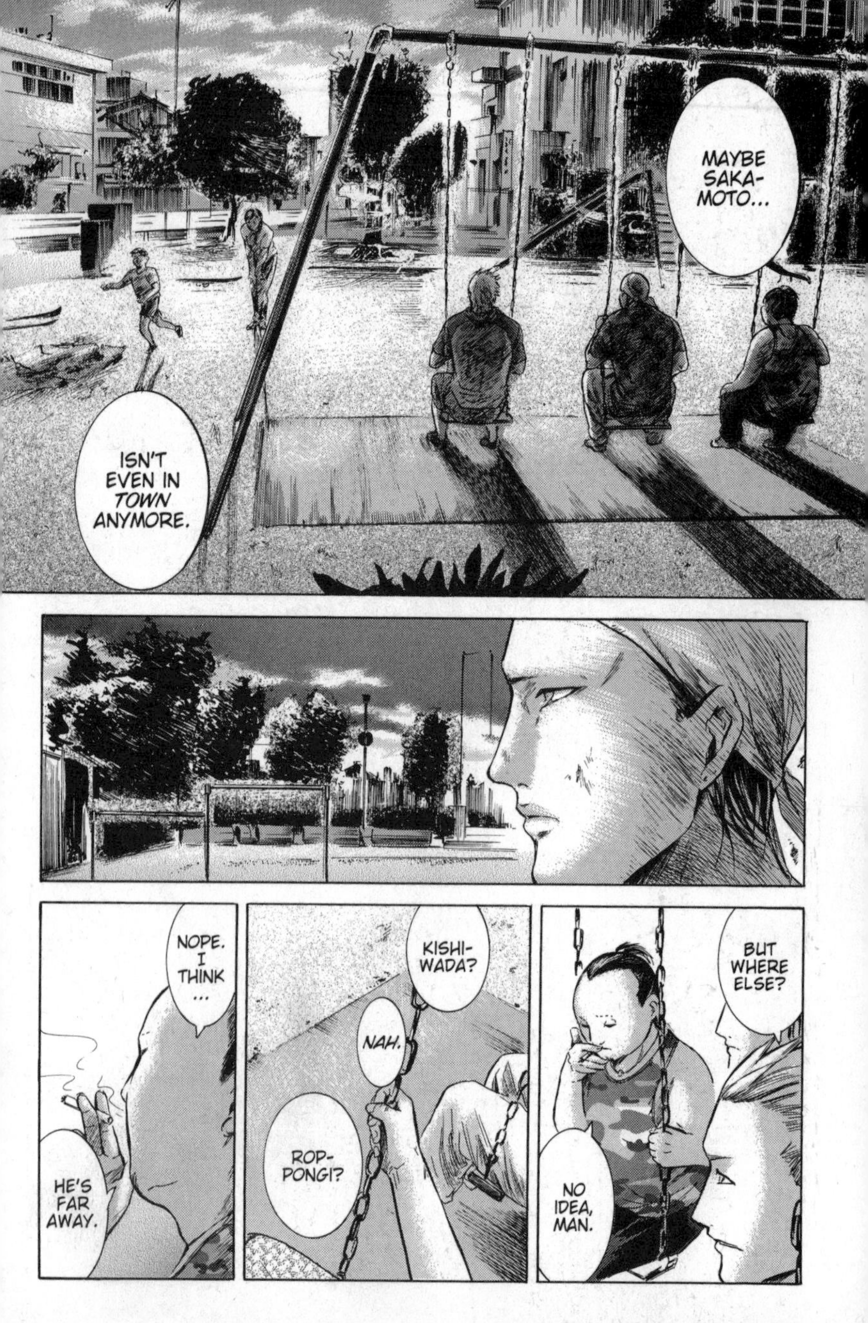
MAYBE SAKAMOTO...
ISN'T EVEN IN *TOWN* ANYMORE.
BUT WHERE ELSE?
NO IDEA, MAN.
KISHIWADA?
NAH.
ROPPONGI?
NOPE. I THINK...
HE'S FAR AWAY.

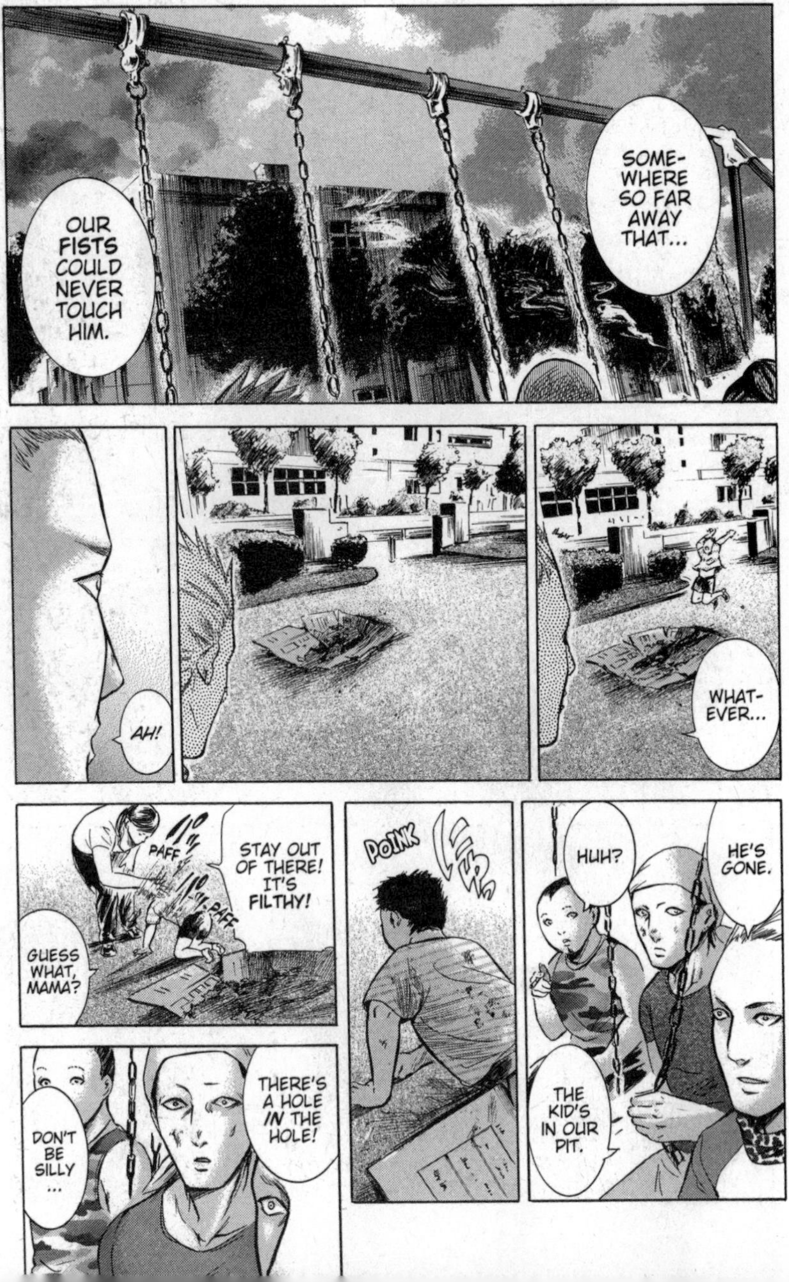
SOME-WHERE SO FAR AWAY THAT...
OUR FISTS COULD NEVER TOUCH HIM.
WHAT-EVER...
AH!
HE'S GONE.
HUH?
THE KID'S IN OUR PIT.
POINK
STAY OUT OF THERE! IT'S FILTHY!
PAFF
PAFF
GUESS WHAT, MAMA?
THERE'S A HOLE *IN* THE HOLE!
DON'T BE SILLY ...

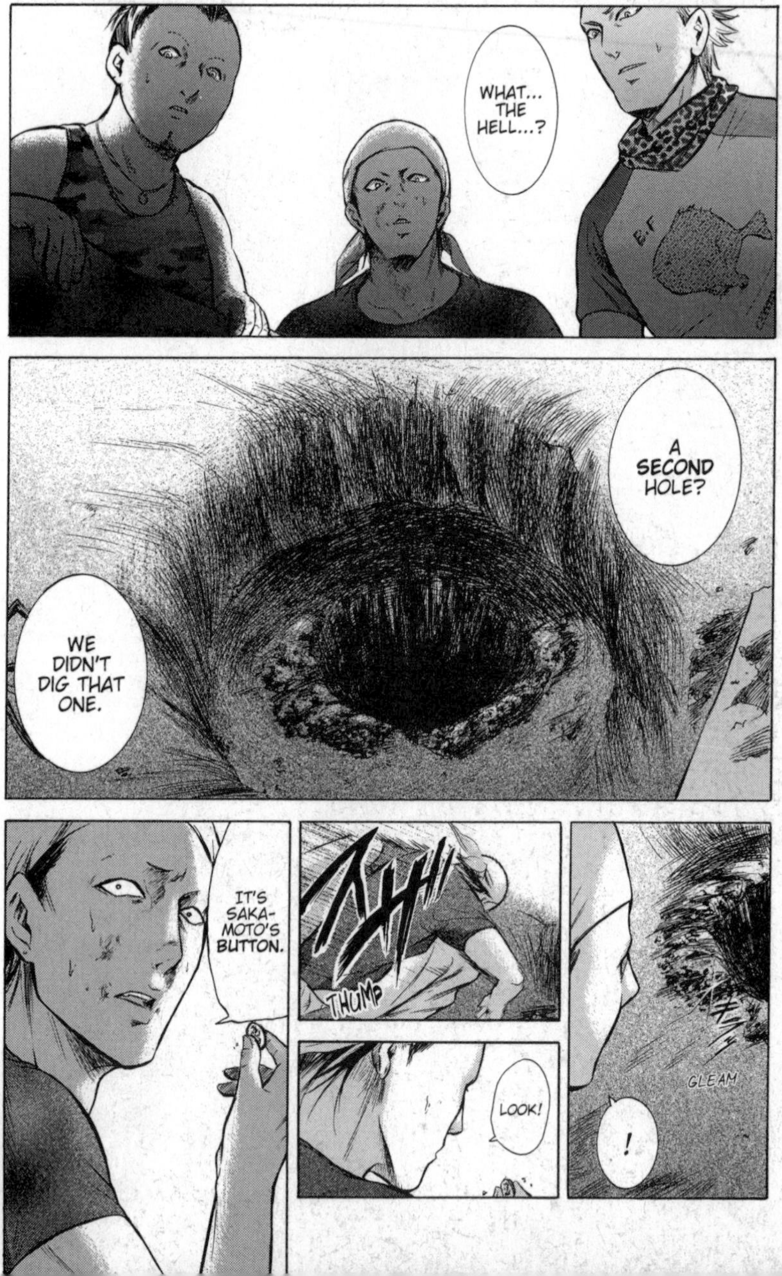
WHAT... THE HELL...?
A SECOND HOLE?
WE DIDN'T DIG THAT ONE.
GLEAM
!
THUMP
LOOK!
IT'S SAKA-MOTO'S BUTTON.

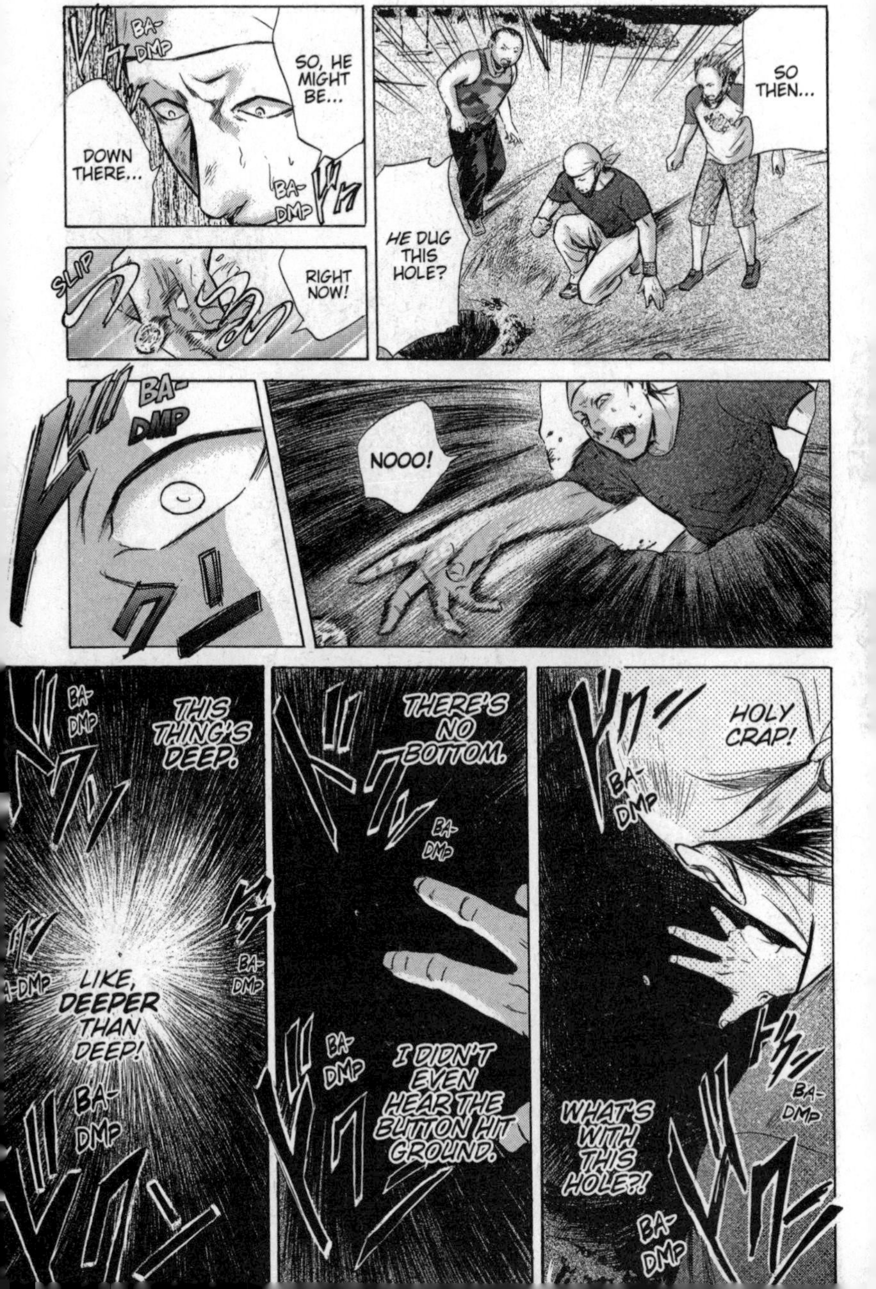
SO THEN...
HE DUG THIS HOLE?
BA-DMP
SO, HE MIGHT BE...
DOWN THERE...
BA-DMP
SLIP
RIGHT NOW!
NOOO!
BA-DMP
HOLY CRAP!
BA-DMP
WHAT'S WITH THIS HOLE?!
BA-DMP
BA-DMP
THERE'S NO BOTTOM.
BA-DMP
BA-DMP
I DIDN'T EVEN HEAR THE BUTTON HIT GROUND.
BA-DMP
THIS THING'S DEEP.
BA-DMP
LIKE, DEEPER THAN DEEP!
BA-DMP

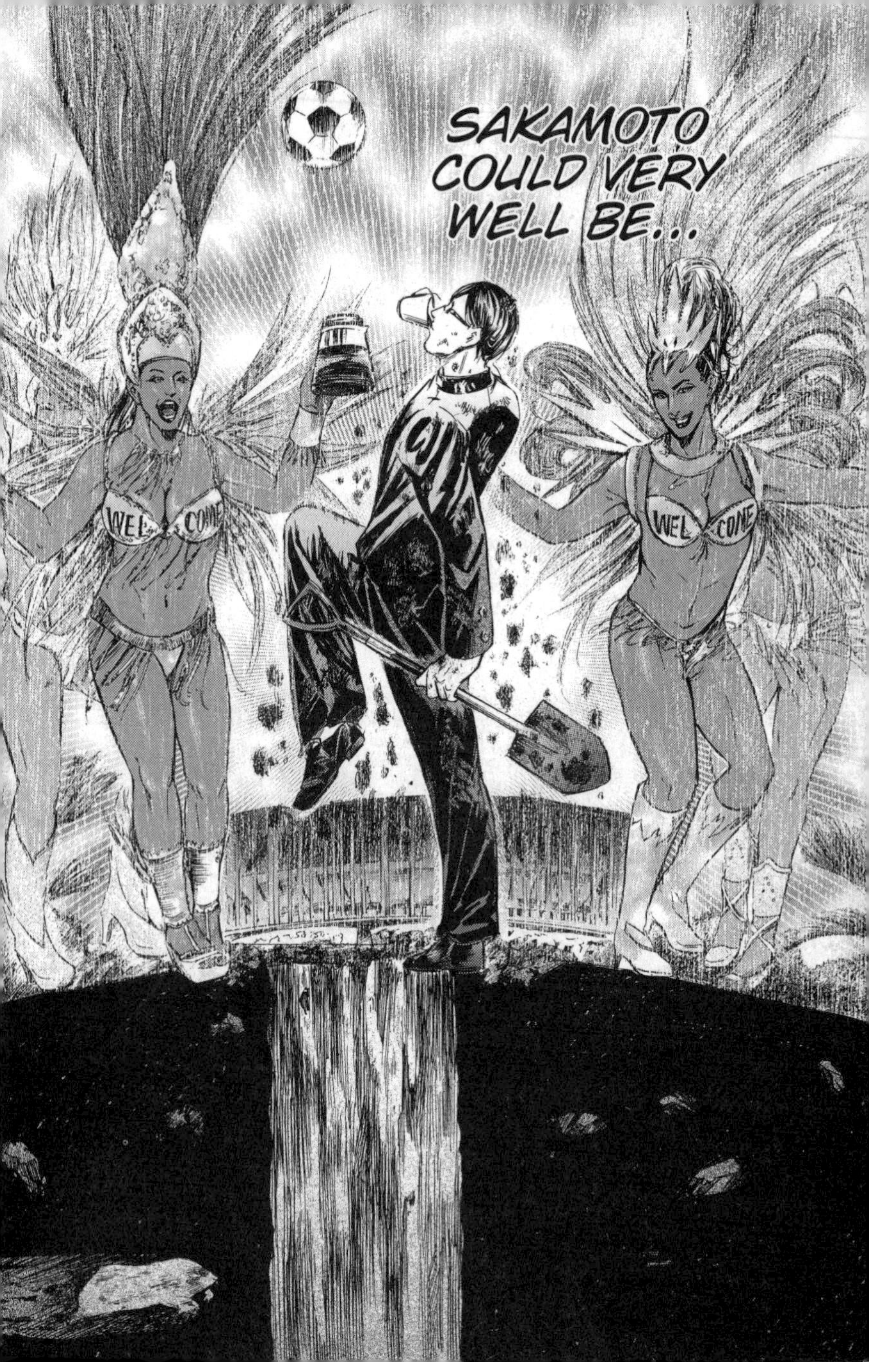
SAKAMOTO COULD VERY WELL BE...
WEL COME
WEL COME

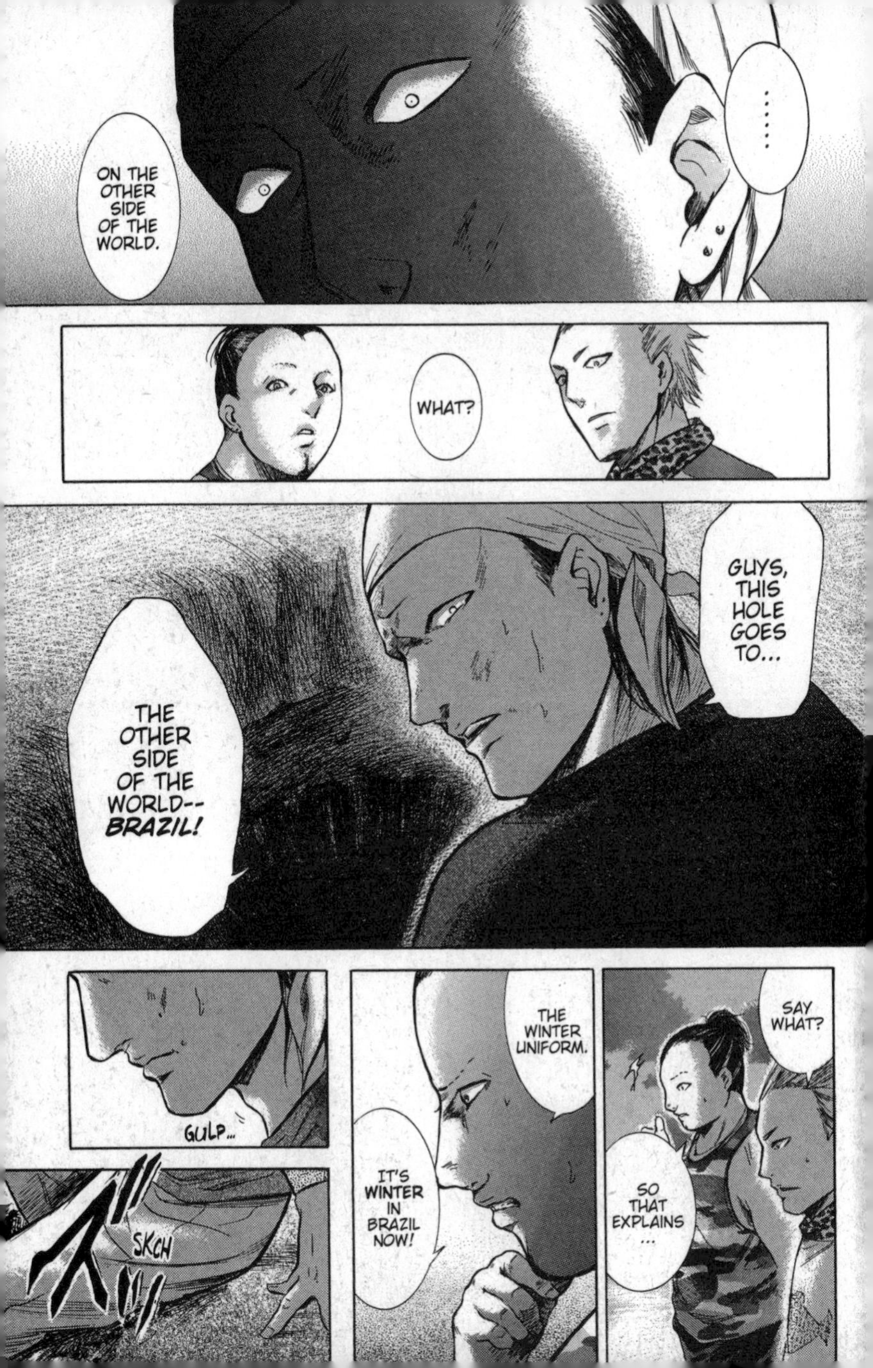
......
ON THE OTHER SIDE OF THE WORLD.
WHAT?
GUYS, THIS HOLE GOES TO...
THE OTHER SIDE OF THE WORLD-- *BRAZIL!*
SAY WHAT?
SO THAT EXPLAINS ...
THE WINTER UNIFORM.
IT'S WINTER IN BRAZIL NOW!
GULP...
SKCH

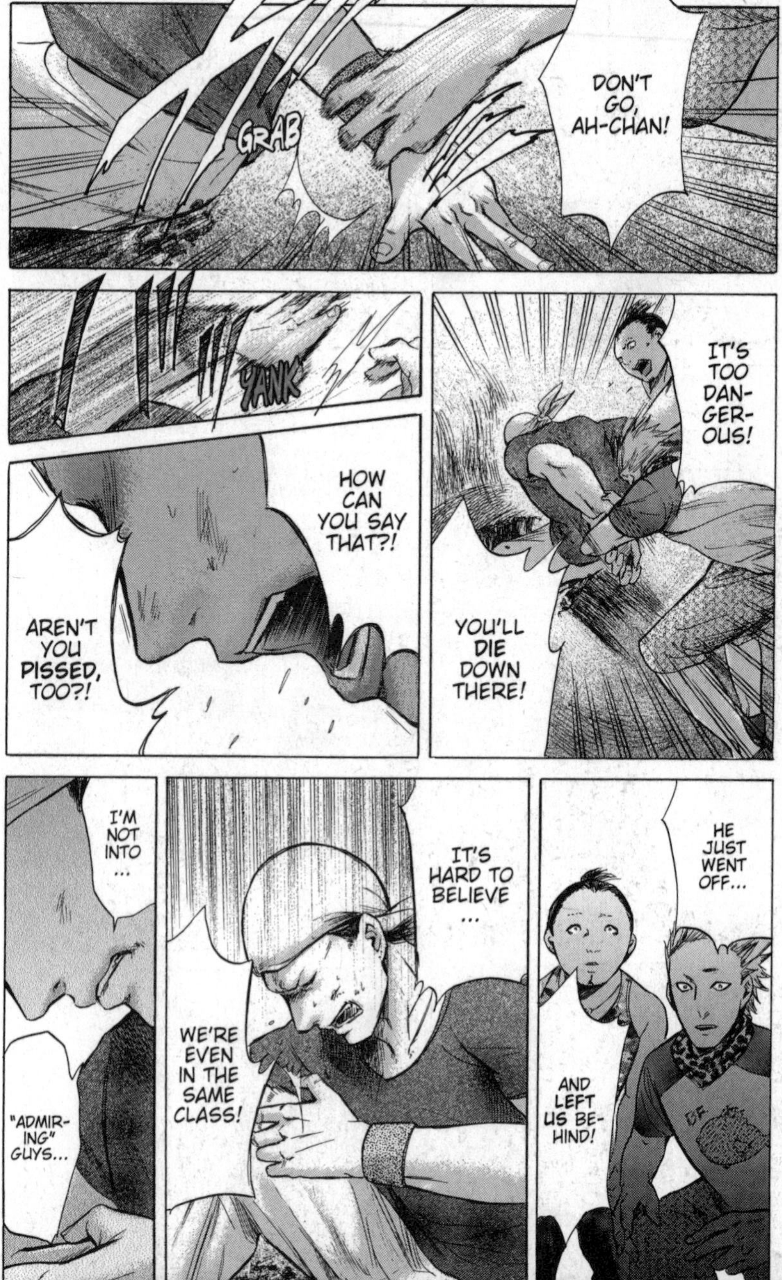
DON'T GO, AH-CHAN!
GRAB
IT'S TOO DAN-GER-OUS!
YOU'LL DIE DOWN THERE!
YANK
HOW CAN YOU SAY THAT?!
AREN'T YOU PISSED, TOO?!
HE JUST WENT OFF...
AND LEFT US BE-HIND!
IT'S HARD TO BELIEVE...
WE'RE EVEN IN THE SAME CLASS!
I'M NOT INTO...
"ADMIR-ING" GUYS...

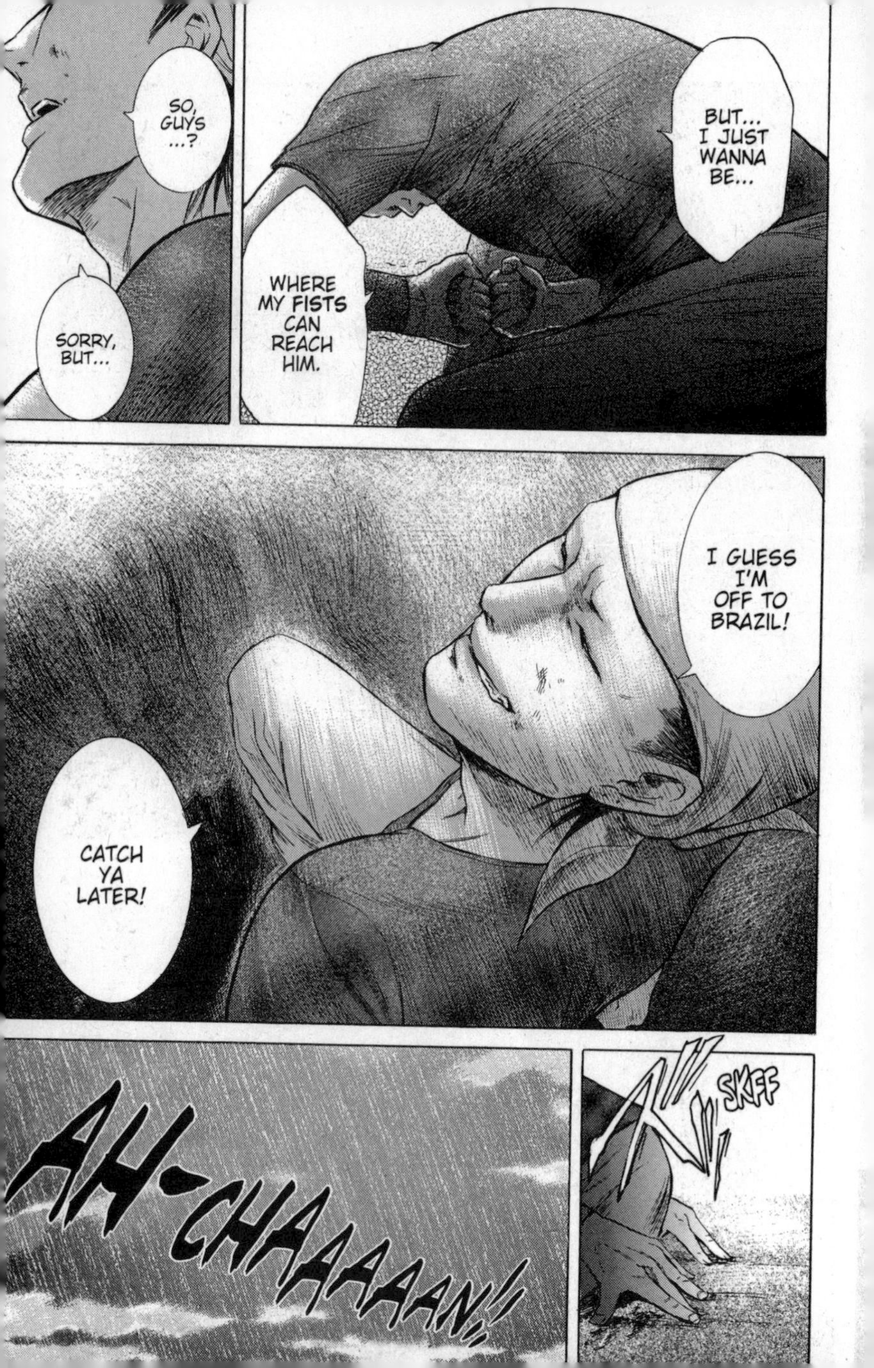
BUT... I JUST WANNA BE...
WHERE MY FISTS CAN REACH HIM.
SO, GUYS ...?
SORRY, BUT...
I GUESS I'M OFF TO BRAZIL!
CATCH YA LATER!
SKFF
AH-CHAAAAAN!!

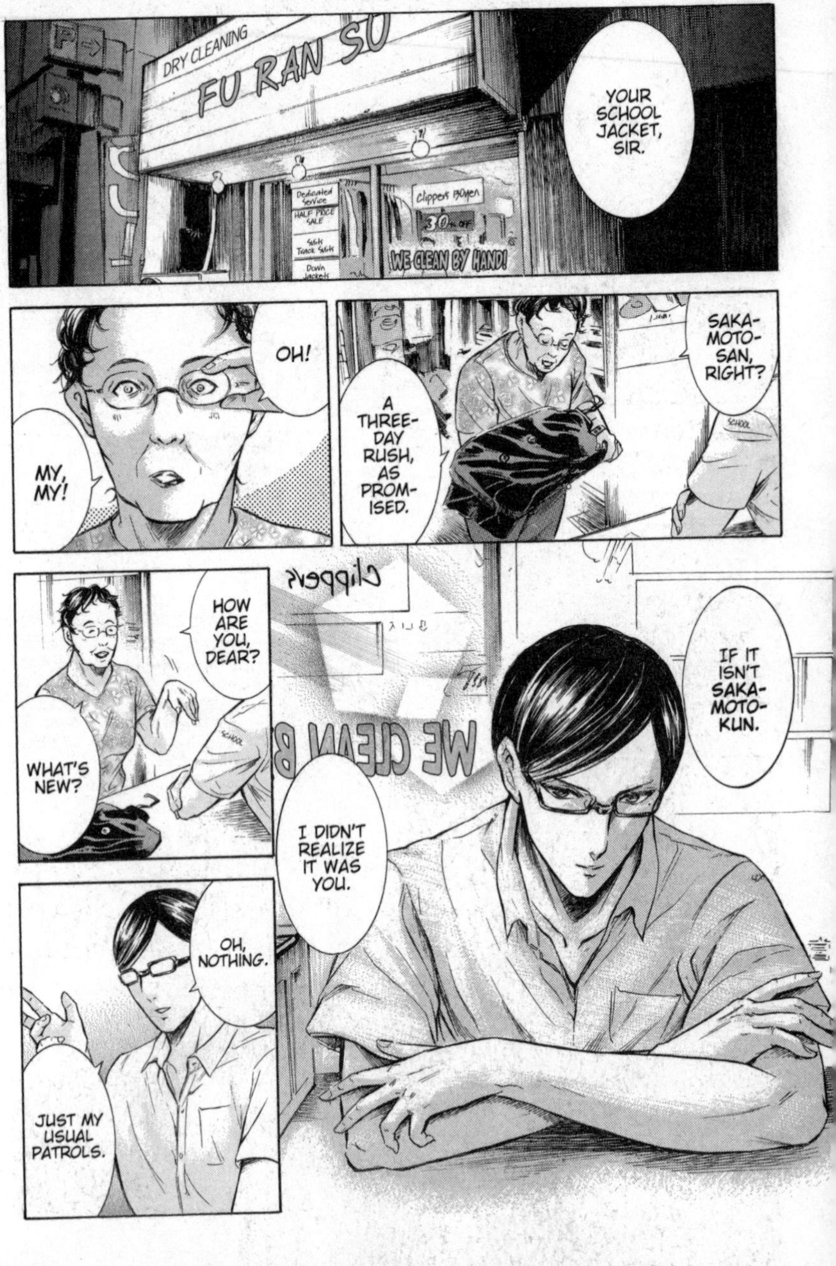
DRY CLEANING
FU RAN SU
Dedicated Service
HALF PRICE SALE
Suits Track Suits
Down Jackets
Clippers 130yen
30% OFF
WE CLEAN BY HAND!
YOUR SCHOOL JACKET, SIR.
SAKA-MOTO-SAN, RIGHT?
A THREE-DAY RUSH, AS PROMISED.
OH!
MY, MY!
IF IT ISN'T SAKA-MOTO-KUN.
I DIDN'T REALIZE IT WAS YOU.
HOW ARE YOU, DEAR?
WHAT'S NEW?
OH, NOTHING.
JUST MY USUAL PATROLS.

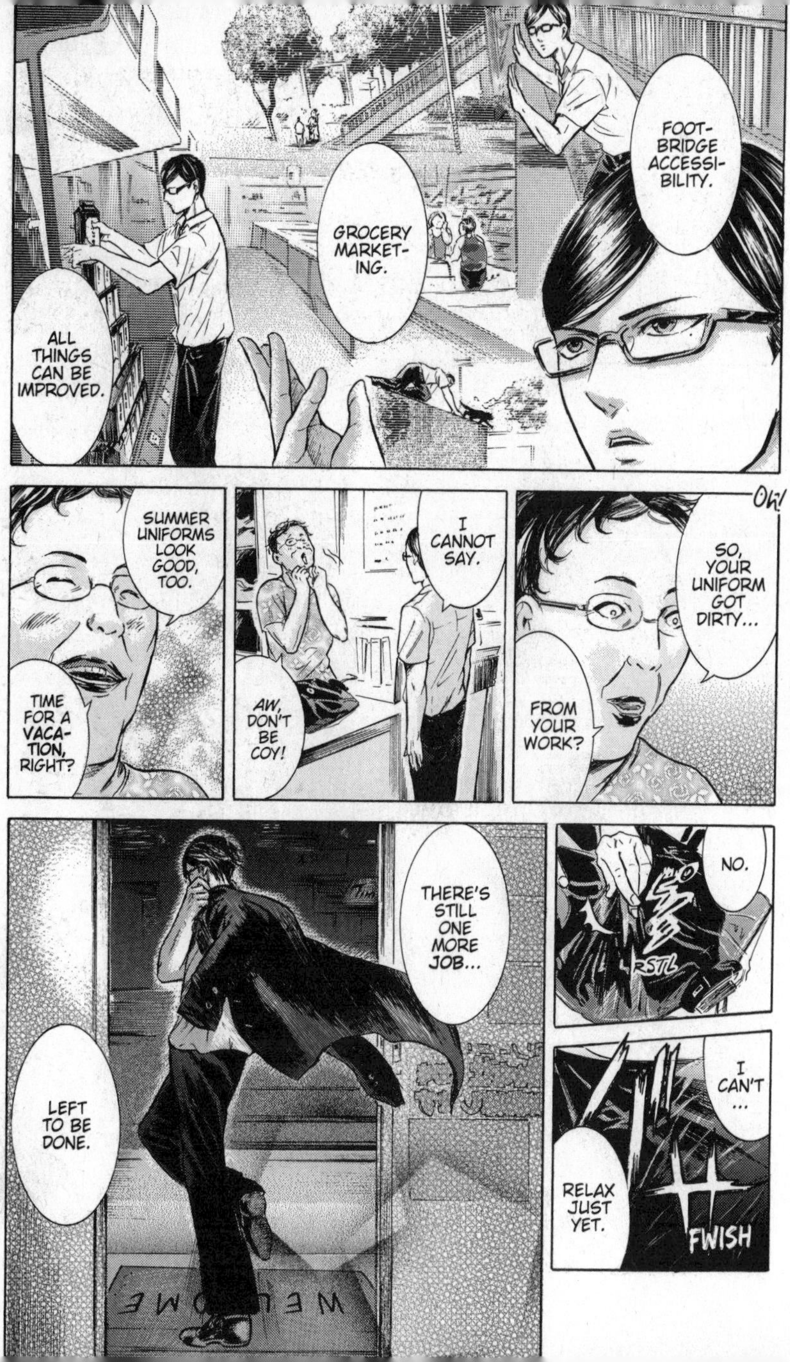
FOOT-BRIDGE ACCESSI-BILITY.
GROCERY MARKET-ING.
ALL THINGS CAN BE IMPROVED.
Oh!
SO, YOUR UNIFORM GOT DIRTY...
FROM YOUR WORK?
I CANNOT SAY.
AW, DON'T BE COY!
SUMMER UNIFORMS LOOK GOOD, TOO.
TIME FOR A VACA-TION, RIGHT?
NO.
RSTL
I CAN'T...
RELAX JUST YET.
FWISH
THERE'S STILL ONE MORE JOB...
LEFT TO BE DONE.

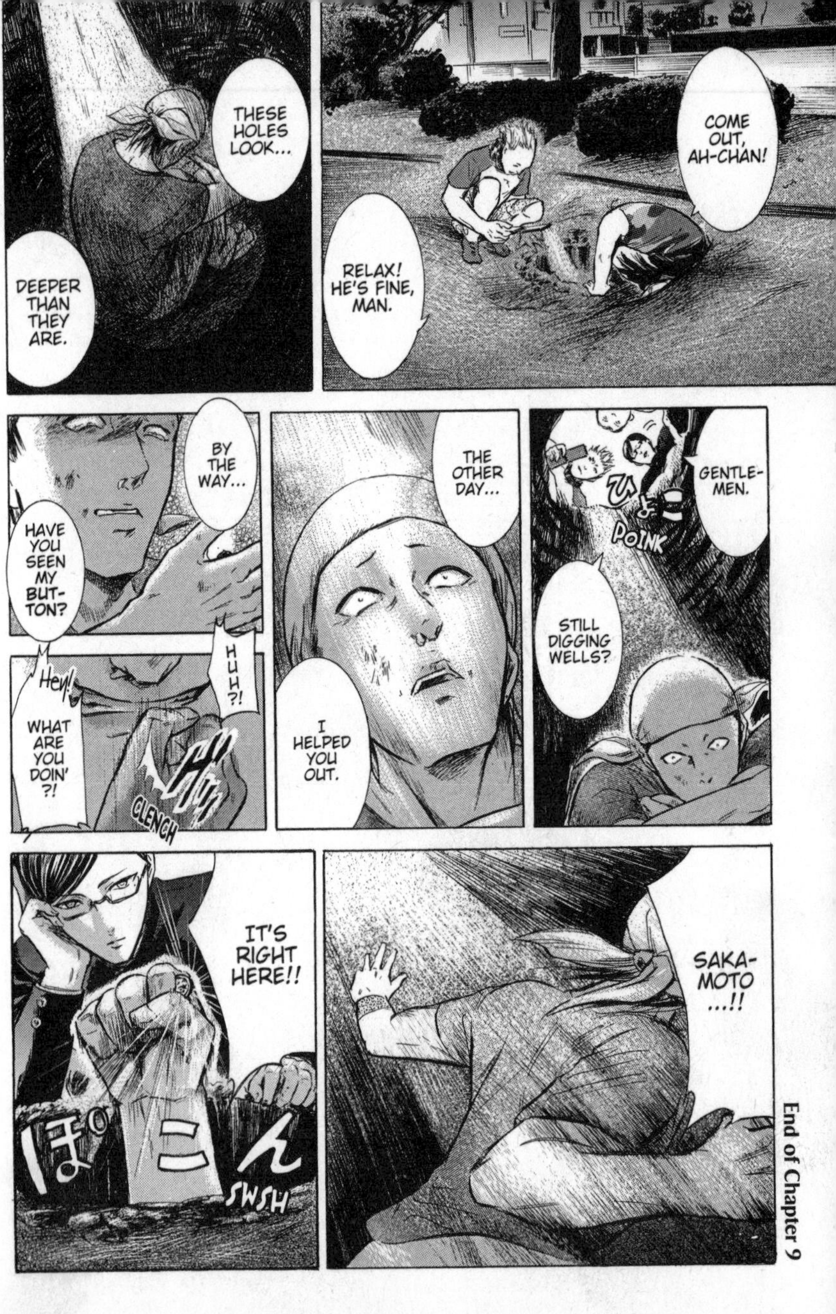
COME OUT, AH-CHAN!
RELAX! HE'S FINE, MAN.
THESE HOLES LOOK...
DEEPER THAN THEY ARE.
GENTLE-MEN.
POINK
STILL DIGGING WELLS?
THE OTHER DAY...
I HELPED YOU OUT.
BY THE WAY...
HAVE YOU SEEN MY BUT-TON?
HUH?!
Hey!
WHAT ARE YOU DOIN'?!
CLENCH
SAKA-MOTO ...!!
IT'S RIGHT HERE!!
SWSH

End of Chapter 9

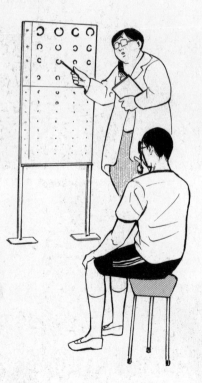

Physical Exam #4:
Vision

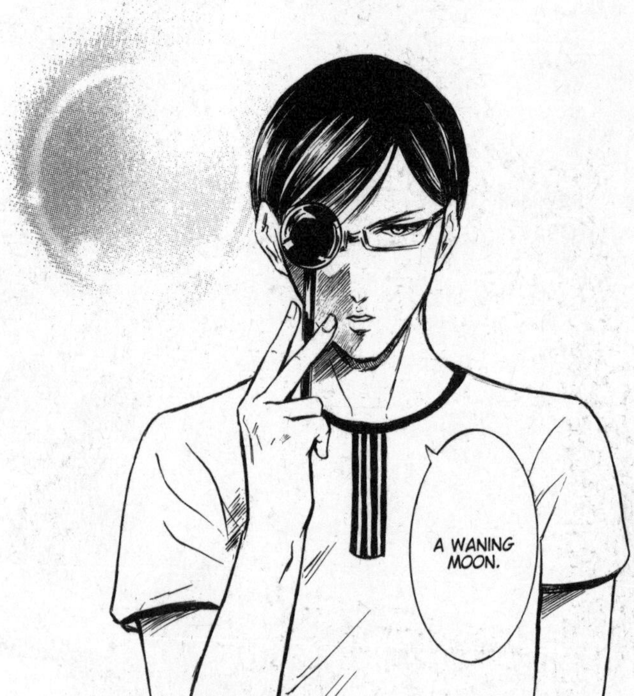
A WANING MOON.

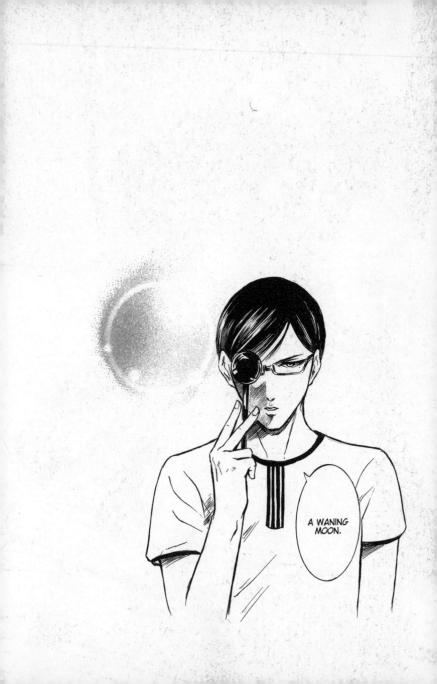

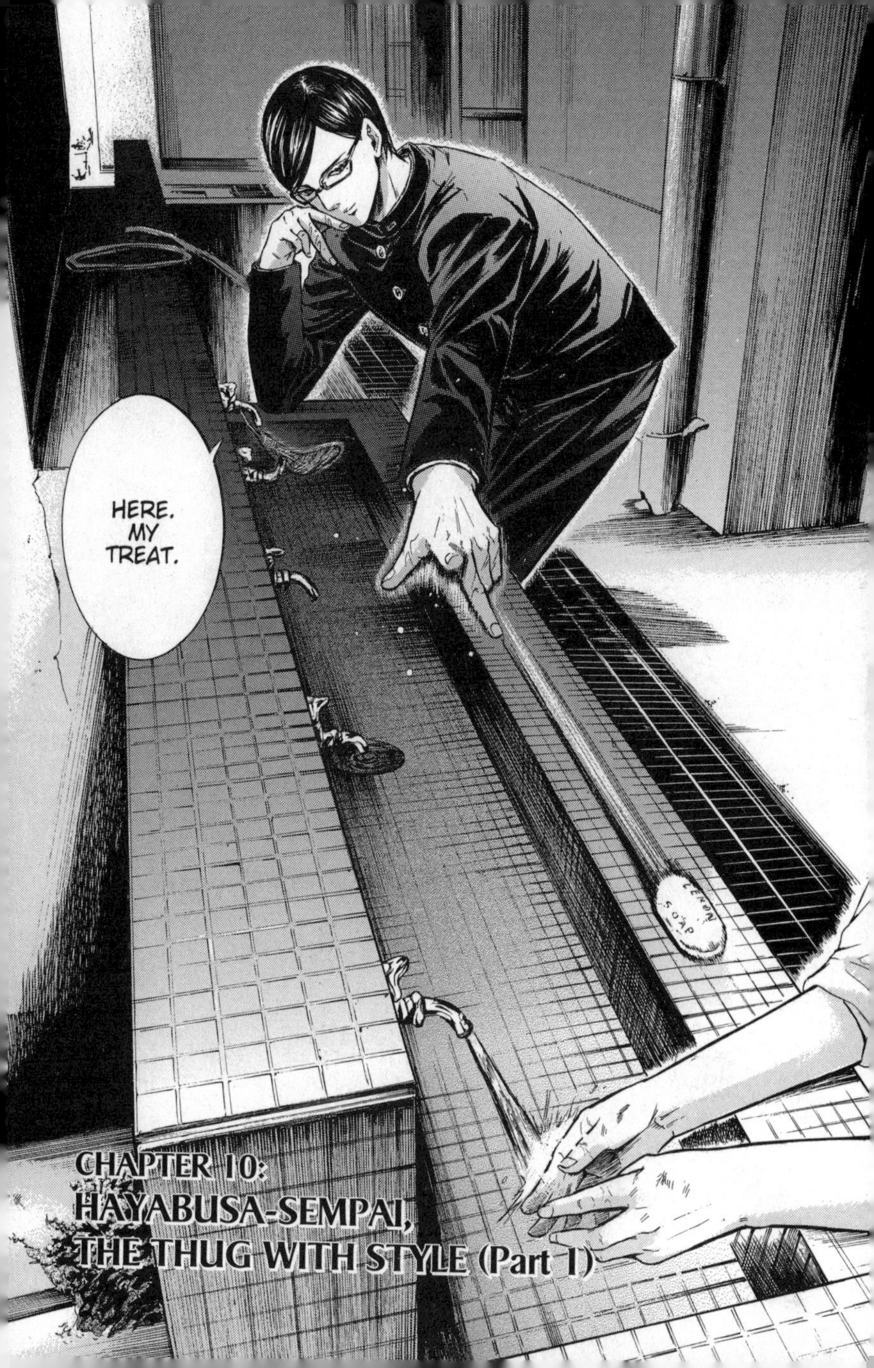
HERE. MY TREAT.
LEMON SOAP
CHAPTER 10: HAYABUSA-SEMPAI, THE THUG WITH STYLE (Part 1)

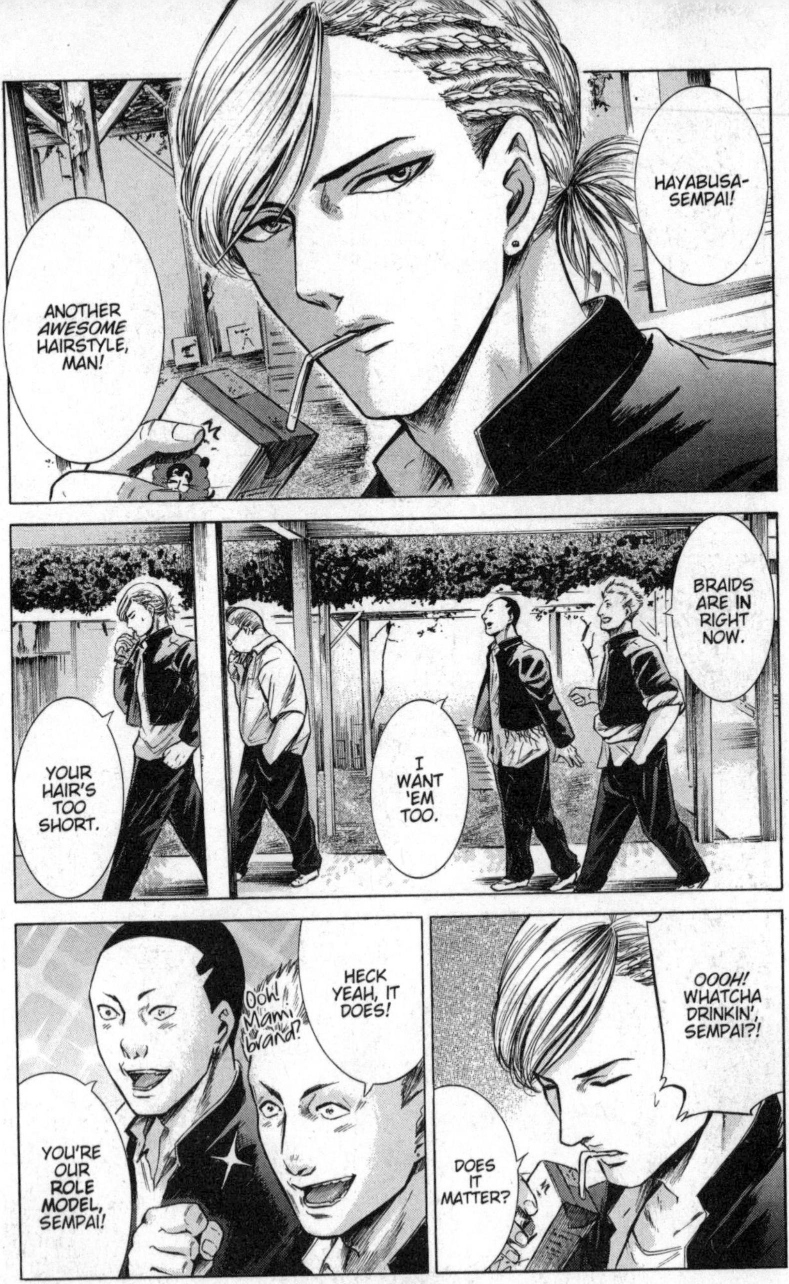
HAYABUSA-SEMPAI!
ANOTHER *AWESOME* HAIRSTYLE, MAN!
BRAIDS ARE IN RIGHT NOW.
I WANT 'EM TOO.
YOUR HAIR'S TOO SHORT.
OOOH! WHATCHA DRINKIN', SEMPAI?!
DOES IT MATTER?
HECK YEAH, IT DOES!
Ooh! Mami brand?
YOU'RE OUR ROLE MODEL, SEMPAI!

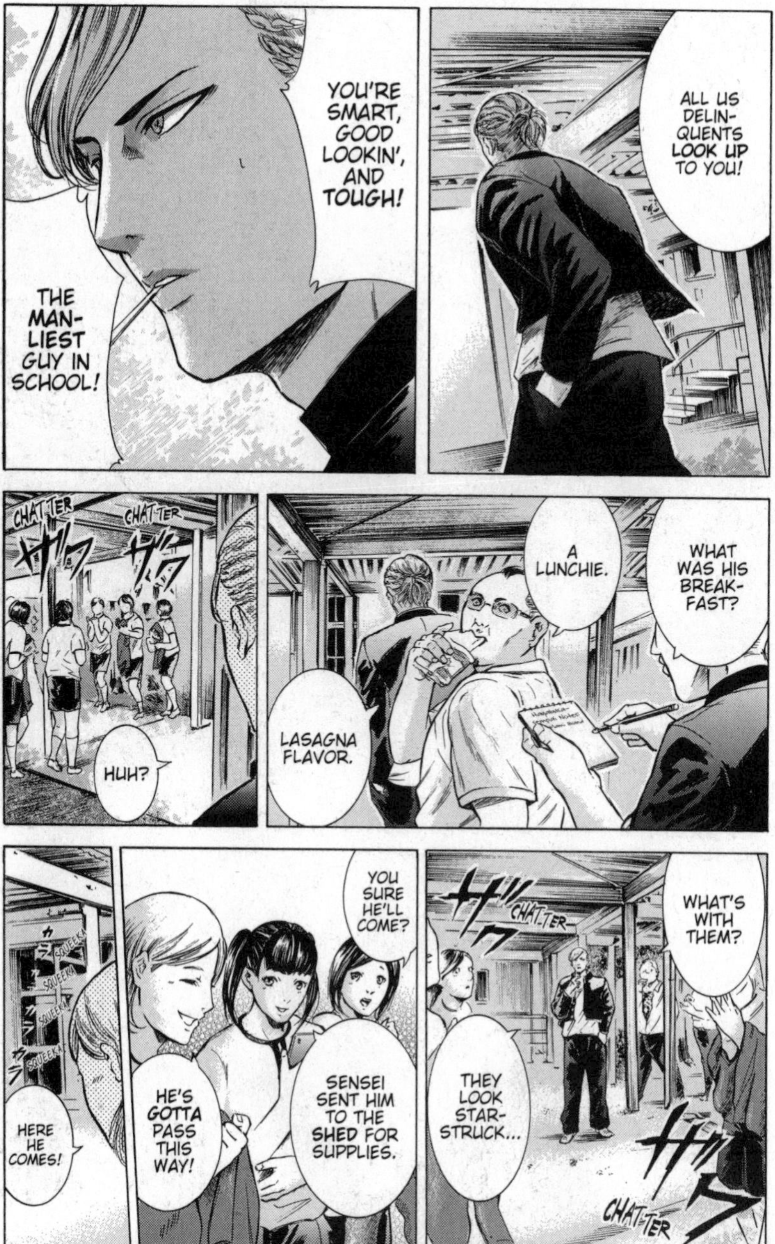
ALL US DELIN-QUENTS LOOK UP TO YOU!
YOU'RE SMART, GOOD LOOKIN', AND TOUGH!
THE MAN-LIEST GUY IN SCHOOL!
WHAT WAS HIS BREAK-FAST?
A LUNCHIE.
LASAGNA FLAVOR.
CHAT-TER
CHAT-TER
HUH?
WHAT'S WITH THEM?
CHAT-TER
THEY LOOK STAR-STRUCK...
CHAT-TER
YOU SURE HE'LL COME?
SENSEI SENT HIM TO THE SHED FOR SUPPLIES.
HE'S GOTTA PASS THIS WAY!
SQUEEK
SQUEEK
SQUEEK
SQUEEK
HERE HE COMES!

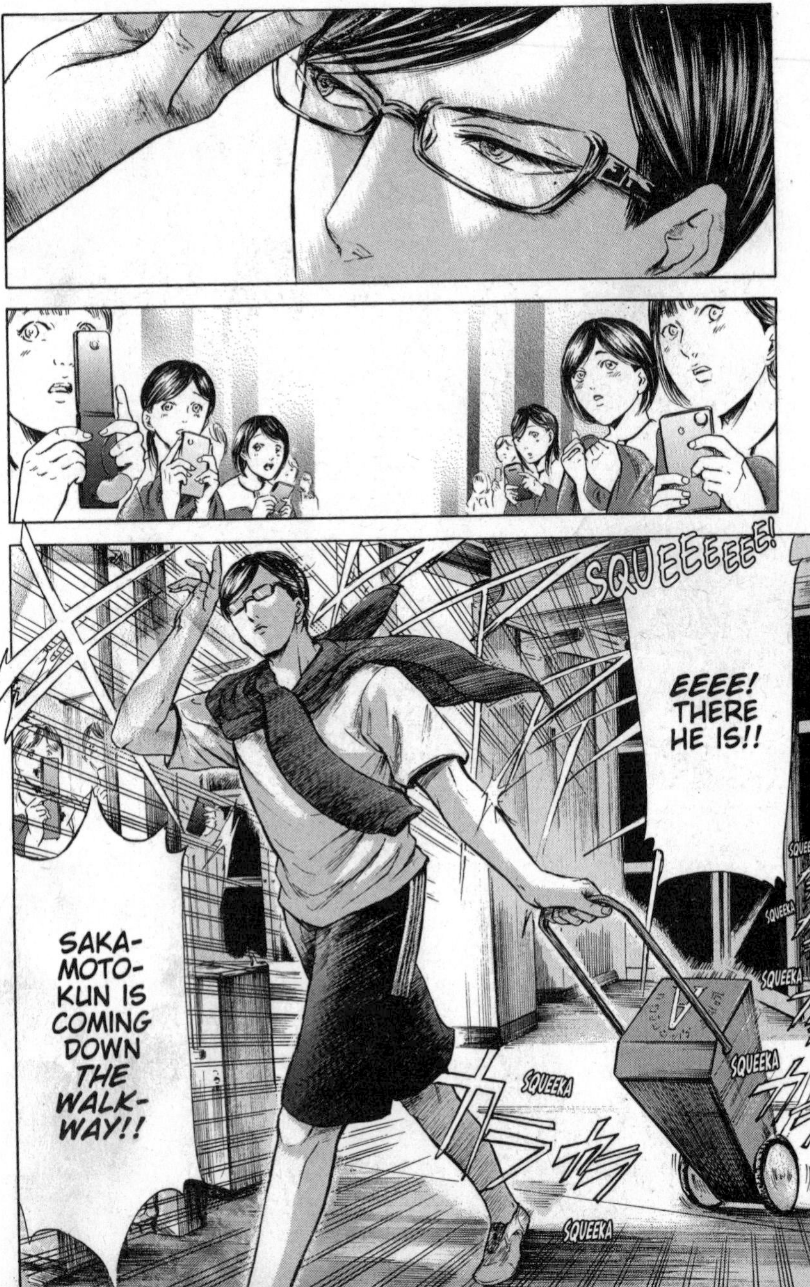
SQUEEEEEEE!
EEEE! THERE HE IS!!
SQUEEKA
SQUEEKA
SQUEEKA
SQUEEKA
SAKA-MOTO-KUN IS COMING DOWN THE WALK-WAY!!
SQUEEKA
SQUEEKA

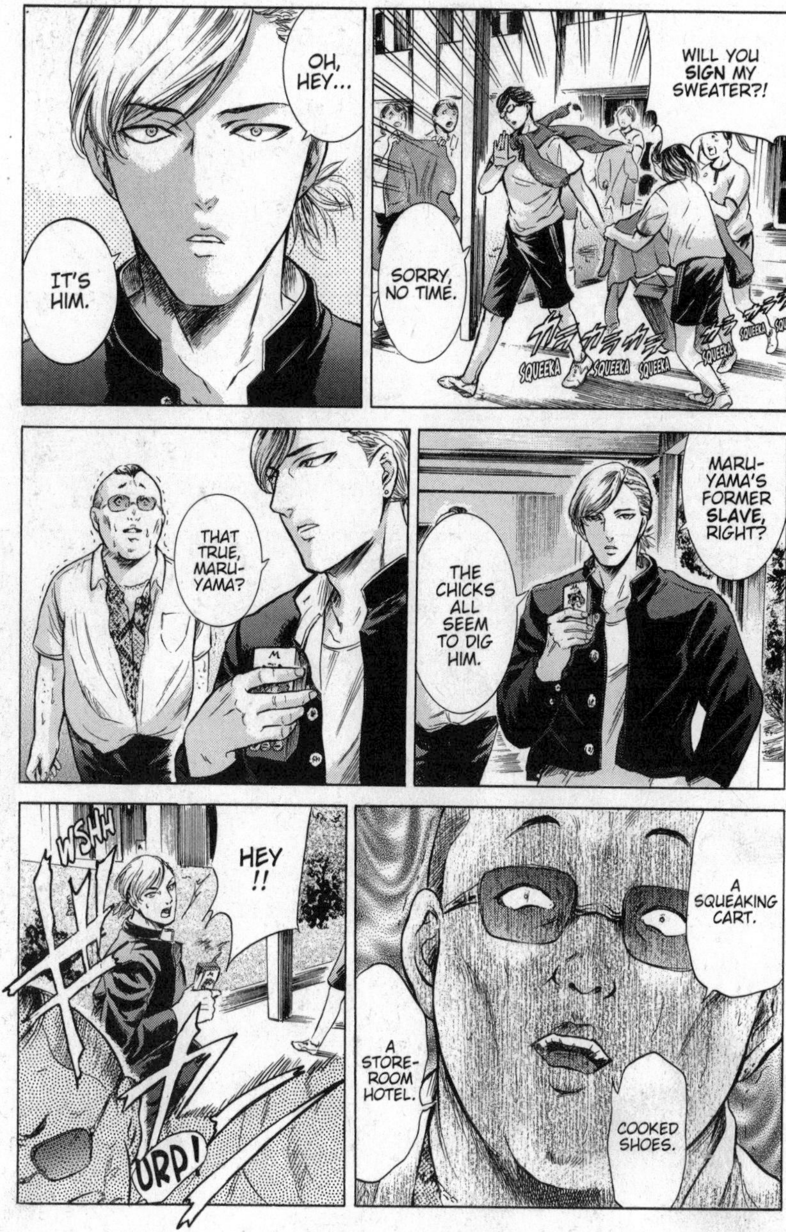
WILL YOU SIGN MY SWEATER?!
SORRY, NO TIME.
SQUEEKA
SQUEEKA
SQUEEKA
SQUEEKA
SQUEEKA
OH, HEY...
IT'S HIM.
MARU-YAMA'S FORMER SLAVE, RIGHT?
THE CHICKS ALL SEEM TO DIG HIM.
THAT TRUE, MARU-YAMA?
A SQUEAKING CART.
A STORE-ROOM HOTEL.
COOKED SHOES.
WSHH
HEY !!
URP!

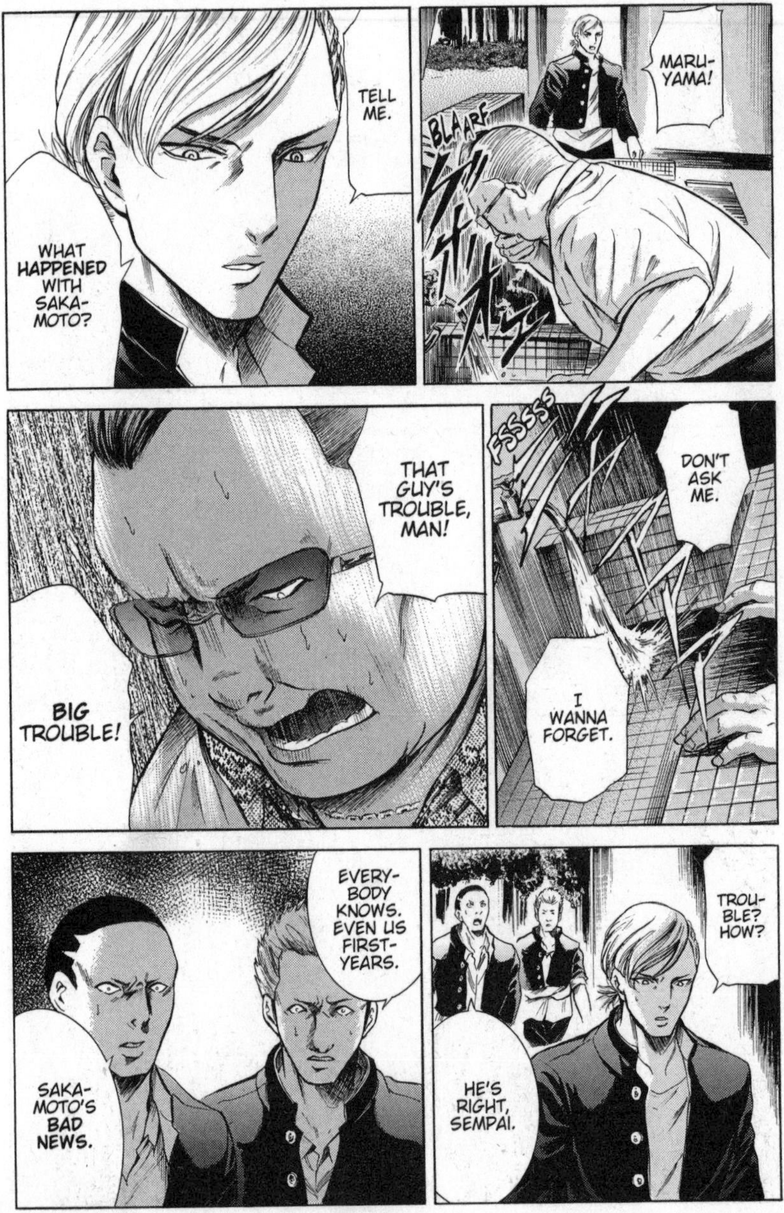
MARU-YAMA!
BLAARF
TELL ME.
WHAT HAPPENED WITH SAKA-MOTO?
FSSSSS
DON'T ASK ME.
I WANNA FORGET.
THAT GUY'S TROUBLE, MAN!
BIG TROUBLE!
TROUBLE? HOW?
HE'S RIGHT, SEMPAI.
EVERY-BODY KNOWS. EVEN US FIRST-YEARS.
SAKA-MOTO'S BAD NEWS.

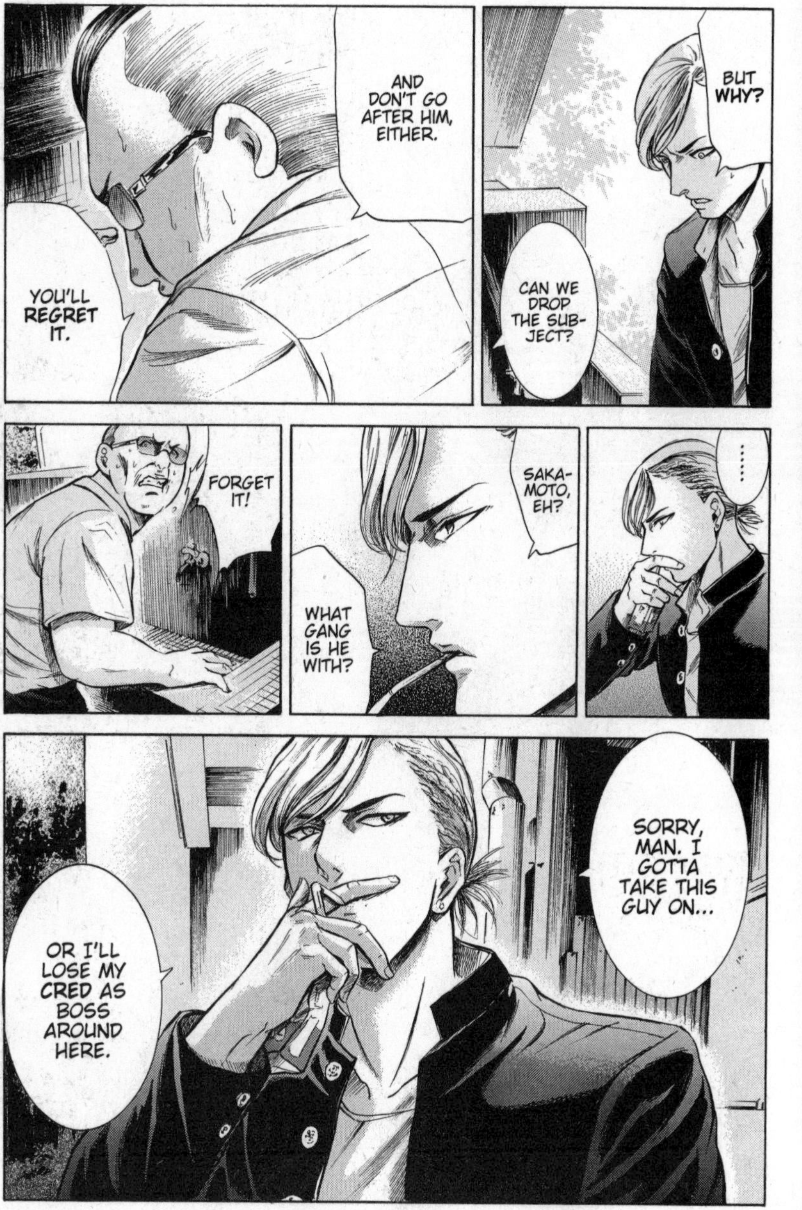
BUT WHY?
CAN WE DROP THE SUBJECT?
AND DON'T GO AFTER HIM, EITHER.
YOU'LL REGRET IT.
……
SAKAMOTO, EH?
WHAT GANG IS HE WITH?
FORGET IT!
SORRY, MAN. I GOTTA TAKE THIS GUY ON...
OR I'LL LOSE MY CRED AS BOSS AROUND HERE.

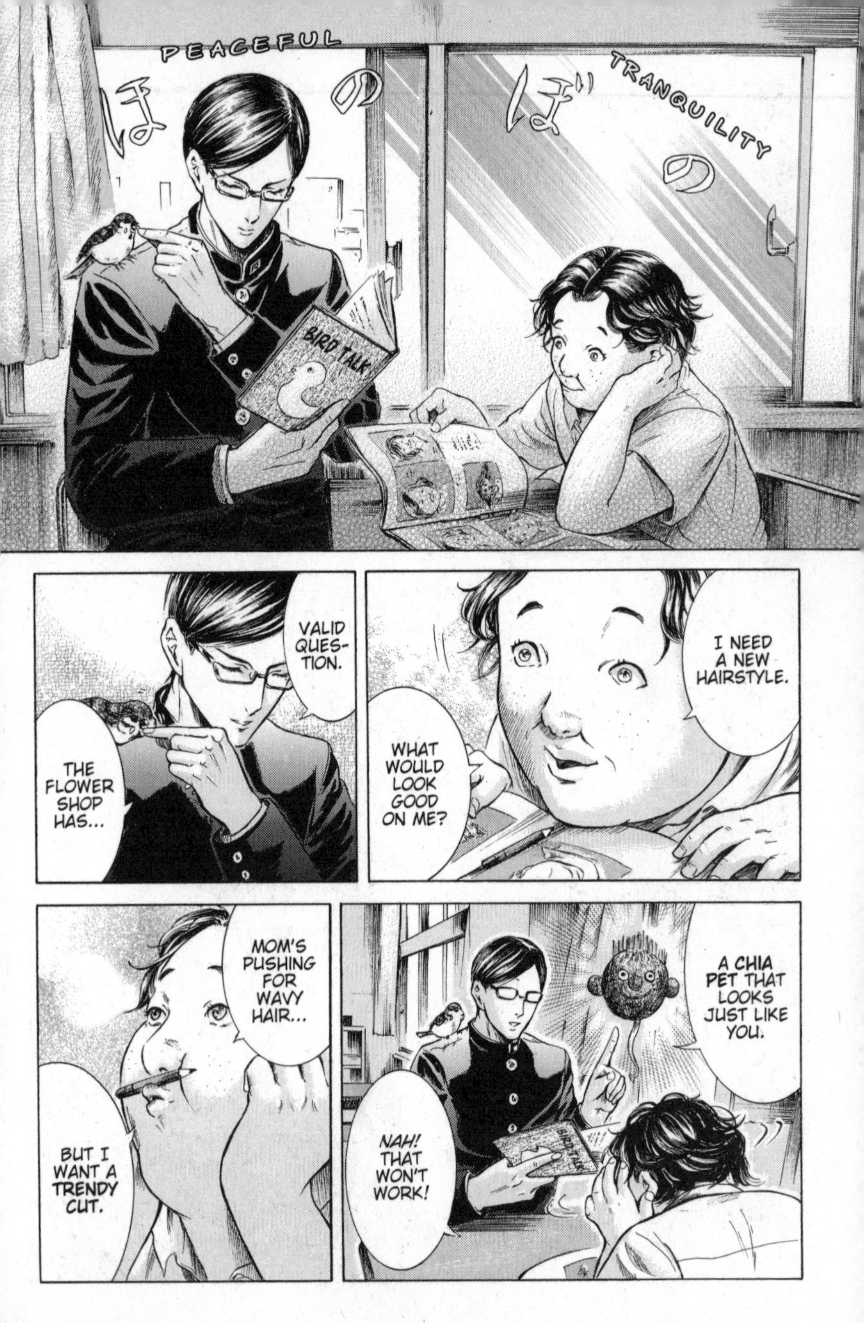
PEACEFUL
TRANQUILITY
ほのぼの
BIRD TALK
I NEED A NEW HAIRSTYLE.
WHAT WOULD LOOK GOOD ON ME?
VALID QUESTION.
THE FLOWER SHOP HAS...
A CHIA PET THAT LOOKS JUST LIKE YOU.
NAH! THAT WON'T WORK!
MOM'S PUSHING FOR WAVY HAIR...
BUT I WANT A TRENDY CUT.

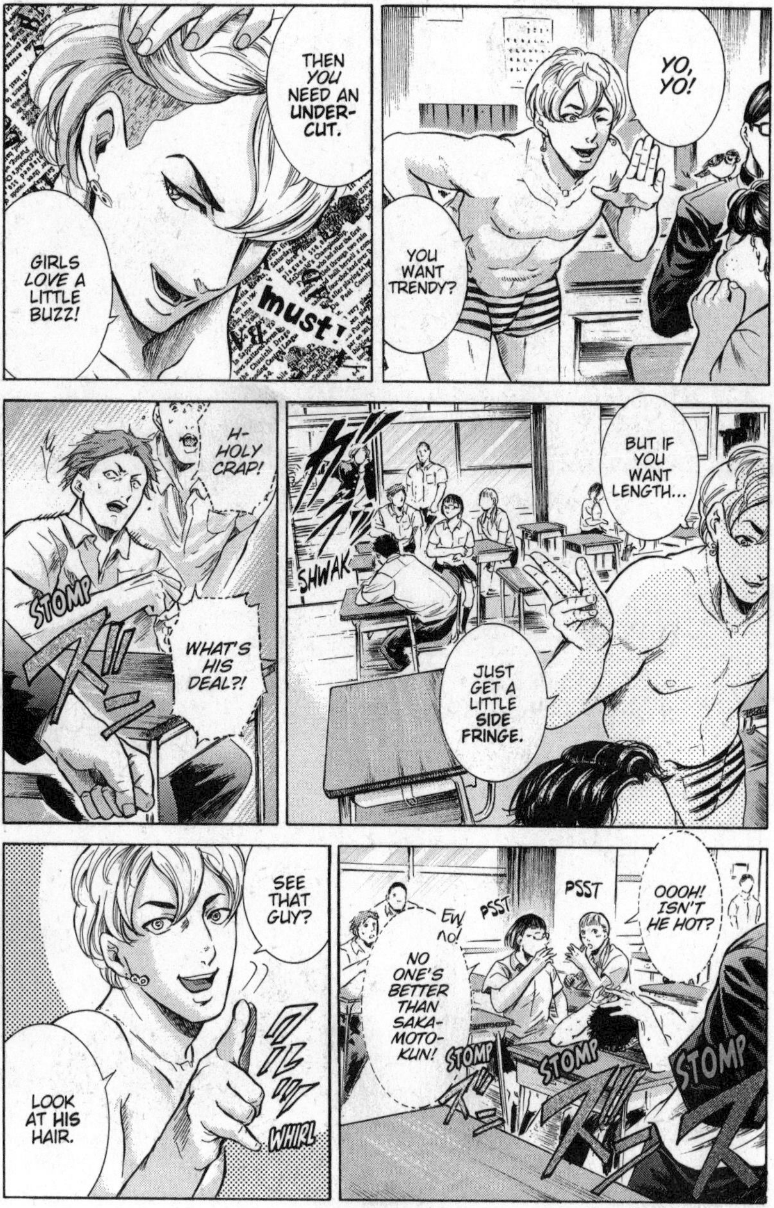
YO, YO!
YOU WANT TRENDY?
THEN YOU NEED AN UNDER-CUT.
must!
GIRLS LOVE A LITTLE BUZZ!
SHWAK
BUT IF YOU WANT LENGTH...
JUST GET A LITTLE SIDE FRINGE.
H-HOLY CRAP!
STOMP
WHAT'S HIS DEAL?!
OOOH! ISN'T HE HOT?
PSST
STOMP
EW no!
PSST
NO ONE'S BETTER THAN SAKA-MOTO-KUN!
STOMP
STOMP
SEE THAT GUY?
WHIRL
LOOK AT HIS HAIR.

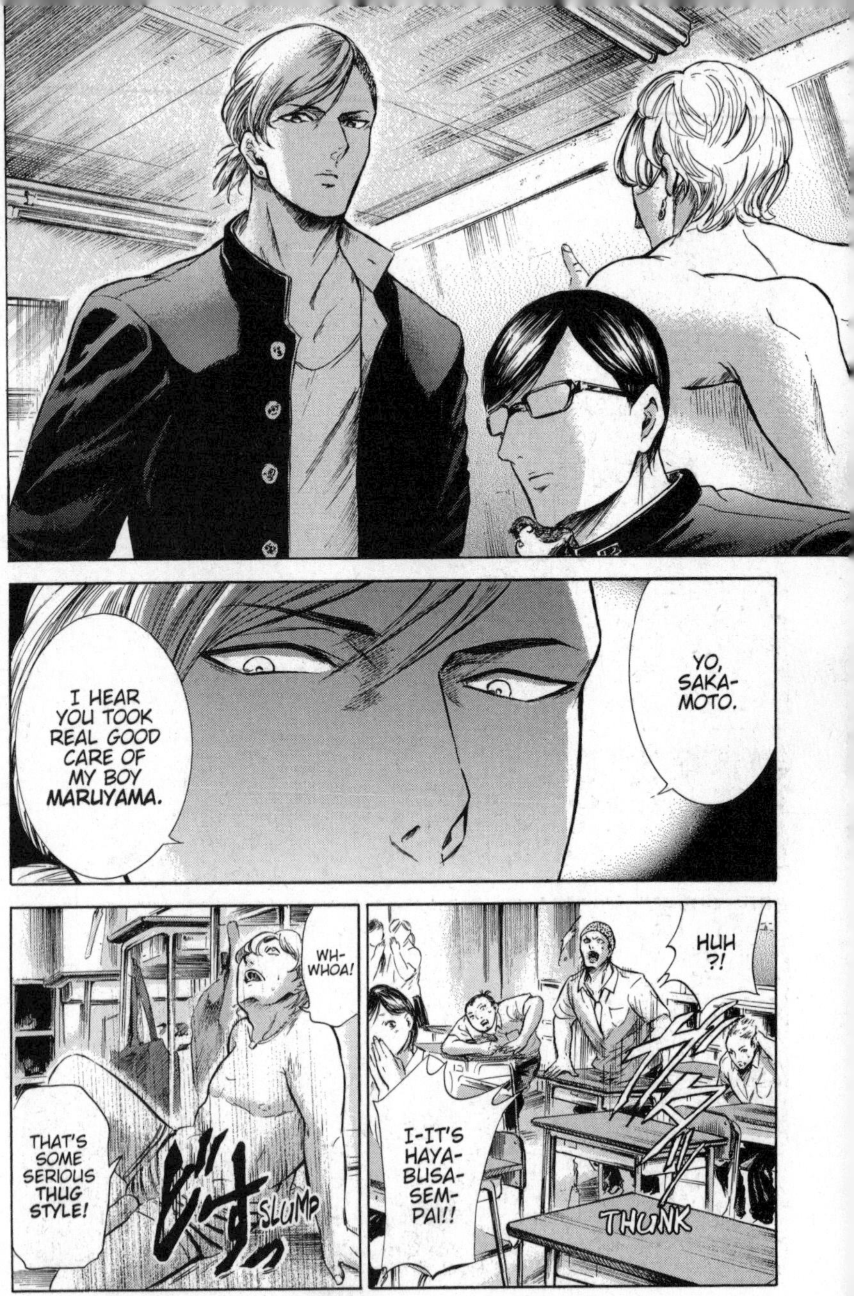
YO, SAKA-MOTO.
I HEAR YOU TOOK REAL GOOD CARE OF MY BOY MARUYAMA.
HUH?!
I-IT'S HAYA-BUSA-SEM-PAI!!
THUNK
WH-WHOA!
THAT'S SOME SERIOUS THUG STYLE!
SLUMP

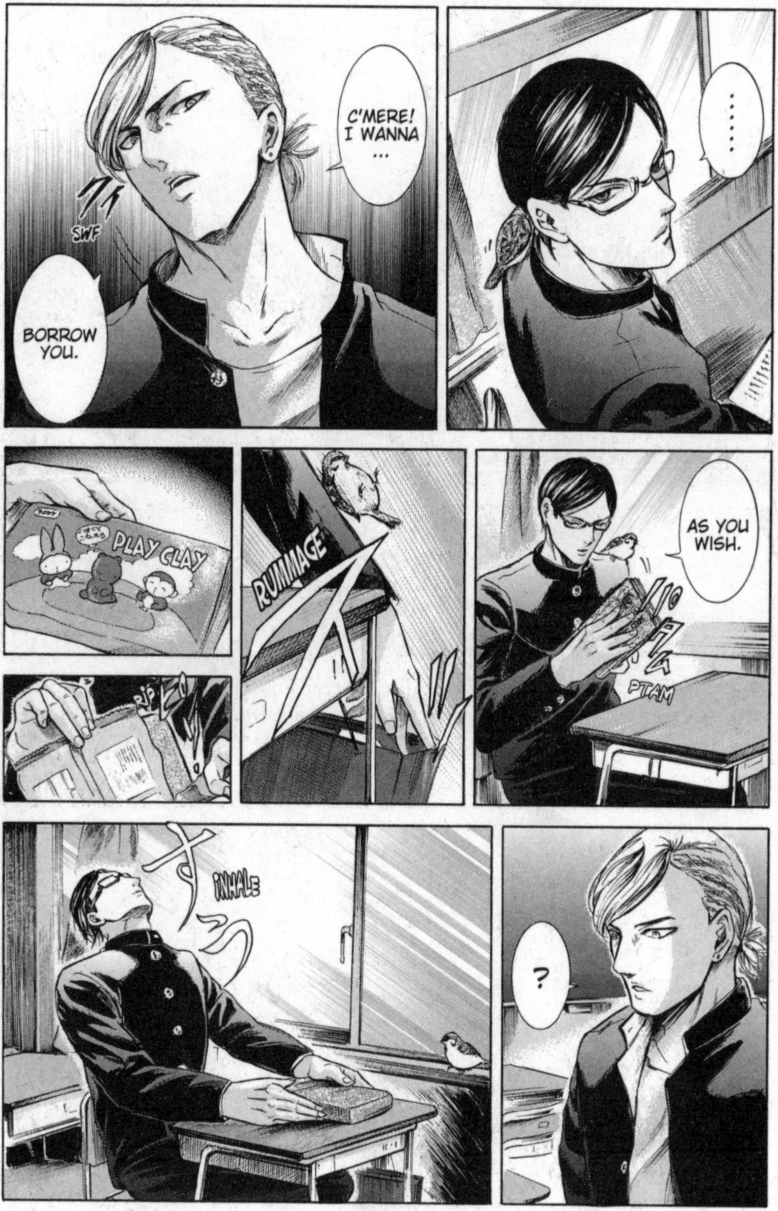
......
C'MERE! I WANNA ...
SWF
BORROW YOU.
AS YOU WISH.
PTAM
RUMMAGE
PLAY CLAY
RIP
?
INHALE

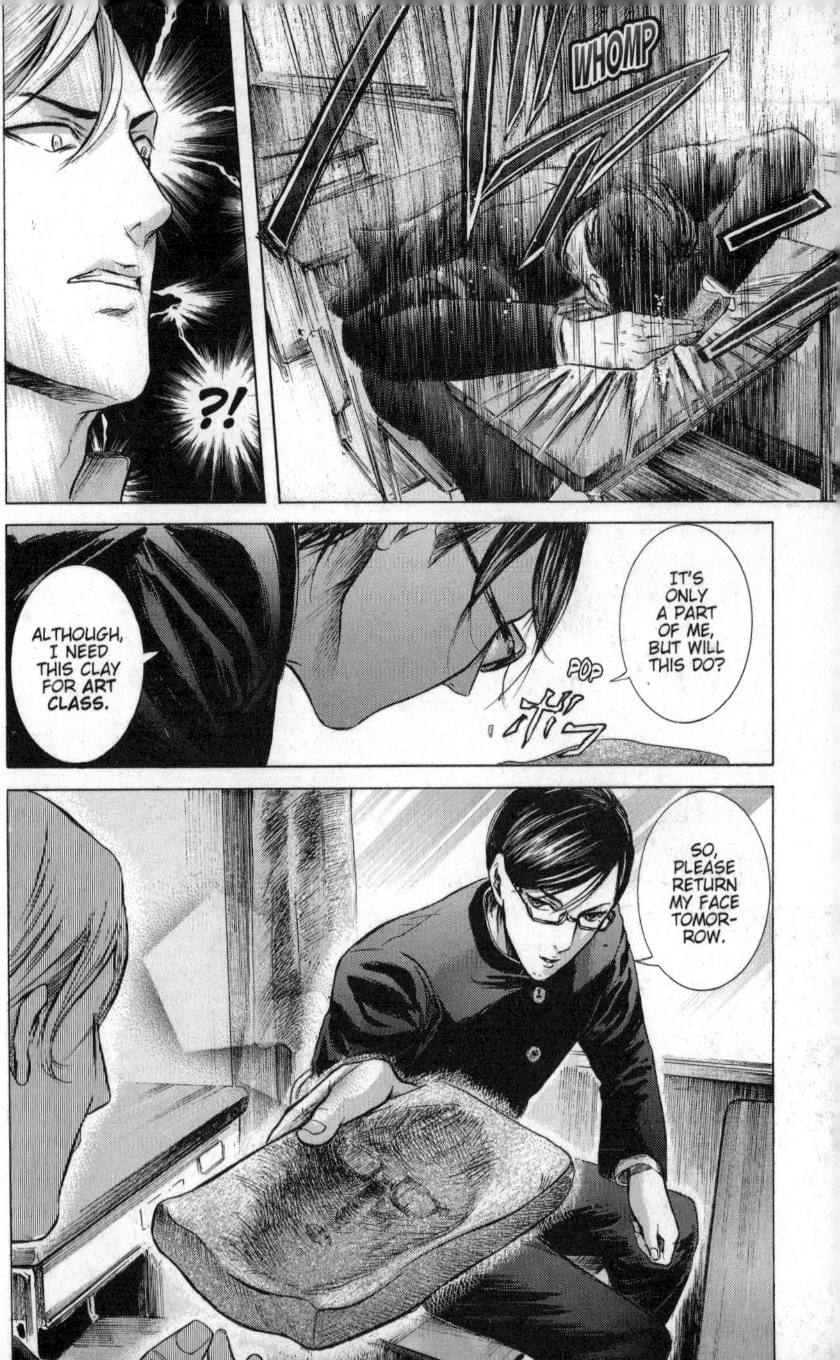
WHOMP
?!
IT'S ONLY A PART OF ME, BUT WILL THIS DO?
POP
ALTHOUGH, I NEED THIS CLAY FOR ART CLASS.
SO, PLEASE RETURN MY FACE TOMORROW.

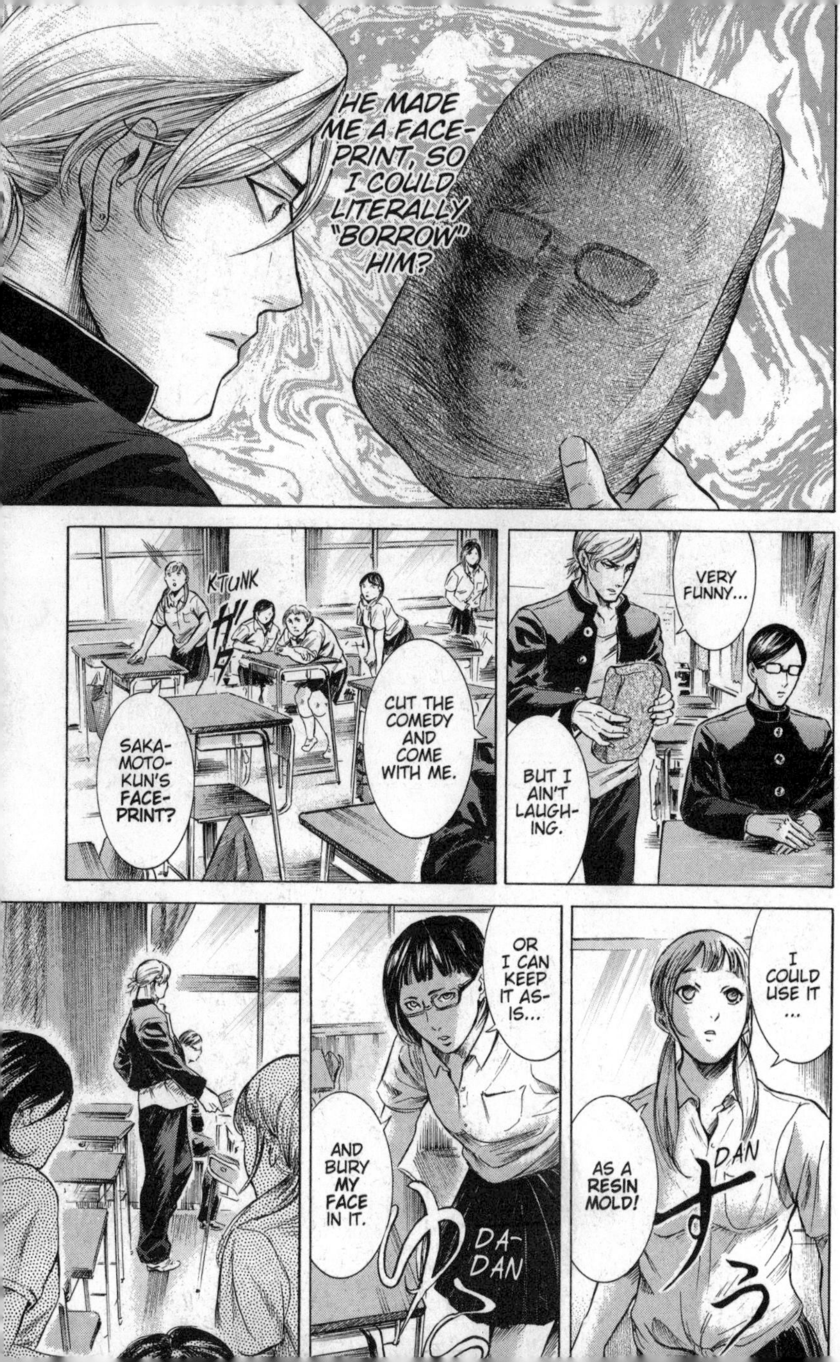
HE MADE ME A FACE-PRINT, SO I COULD LITERALLY "BORROW" HIM?
VERY FUNNY...
BUT I AIN'T LAUGHING.
CUT THE COMEDY AND COME WITH ME.
KTUNK
SAKAMOTO-KUN'S FACE-PRINT?
I COULD USE IT ...
DAN
AS A RESIN MOLD!
OR I CAN KEEP IT AS-IS...
AND BURY MY FACE IN IT.
DA-DAN

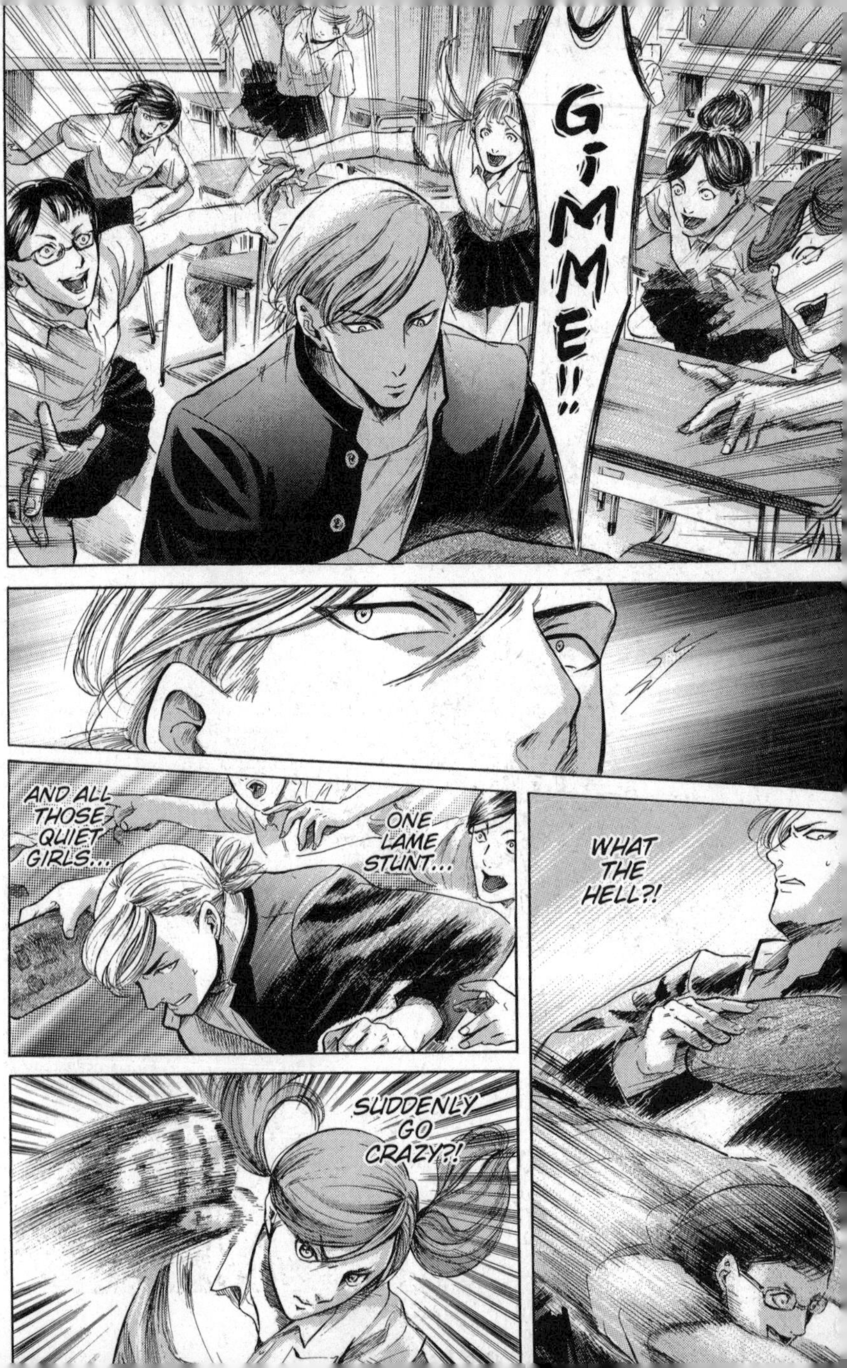
GIMME!!
WHAT THE HELL?!
ONE LAME STUNT...
AND ALL THOSE QUIET GIRLS...
SUDDENLY GO CRAZY?!

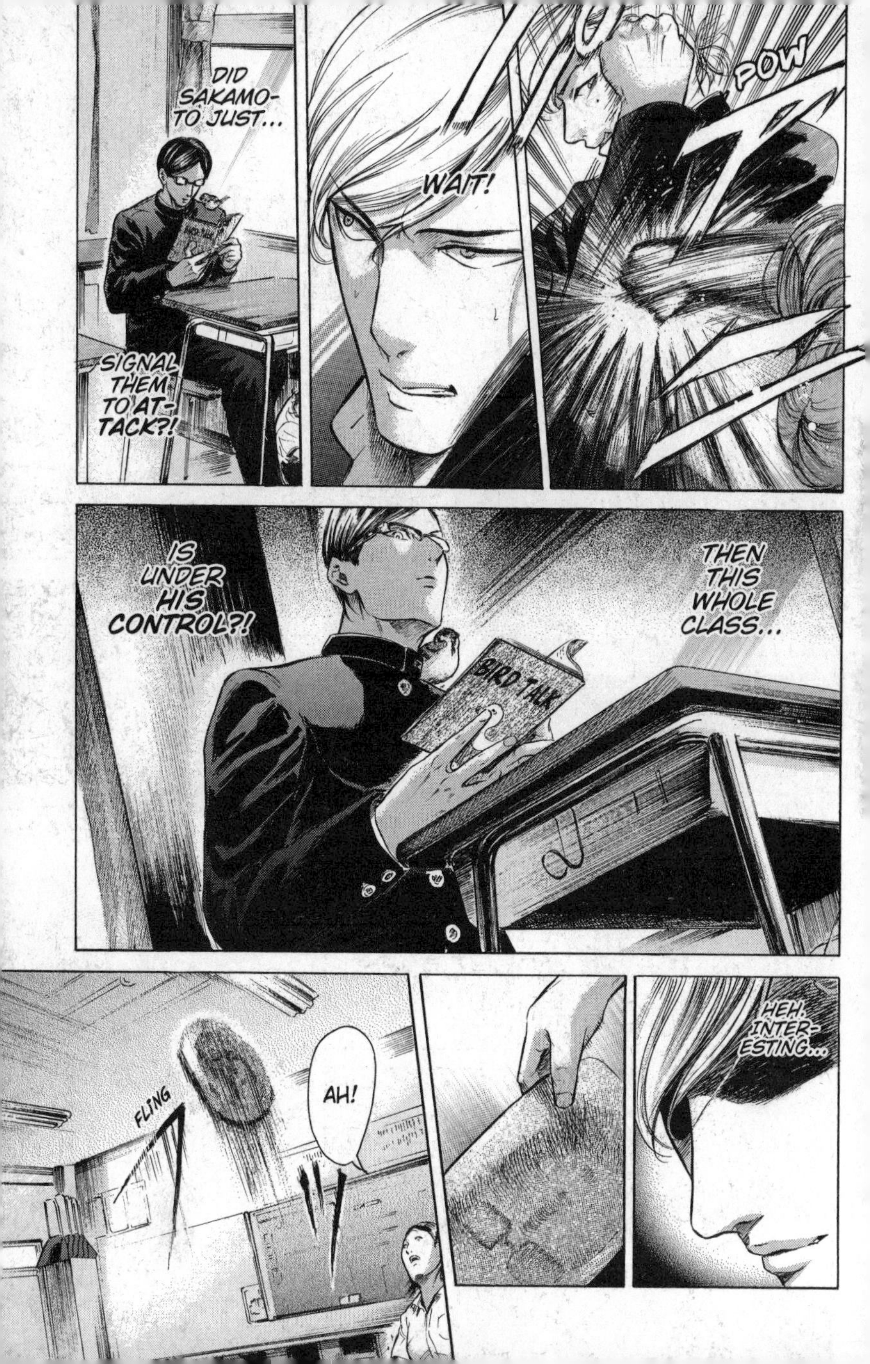
POW
WAIT!
DID SAKAMO-TO JUST...
SIGNAL THEM TO AT-TACK?!
THEN THIS WHOLE CLASS...
IS UNDER HIS CONTROL?!
BIRD TALK
HEH. INTER-ESTING...
AH!
FLING

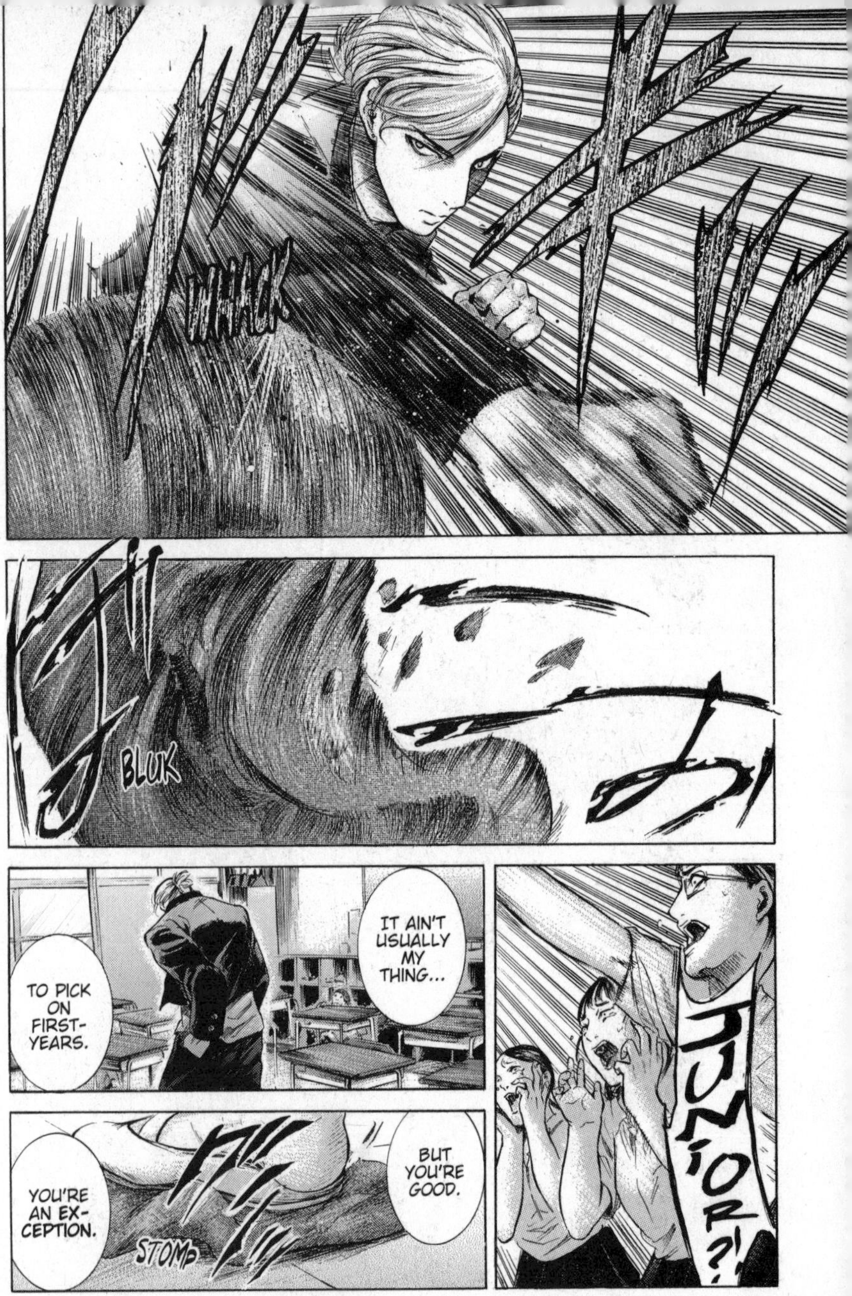
WHACK
BLUK
JUNIOR?!
IT AIN'T USUALLY MY THING...
TO PICK ON FIRST-YEARS.
BUT YOU'RE GOOD.
YOU'RE AN EXCEPTION.
STOMP

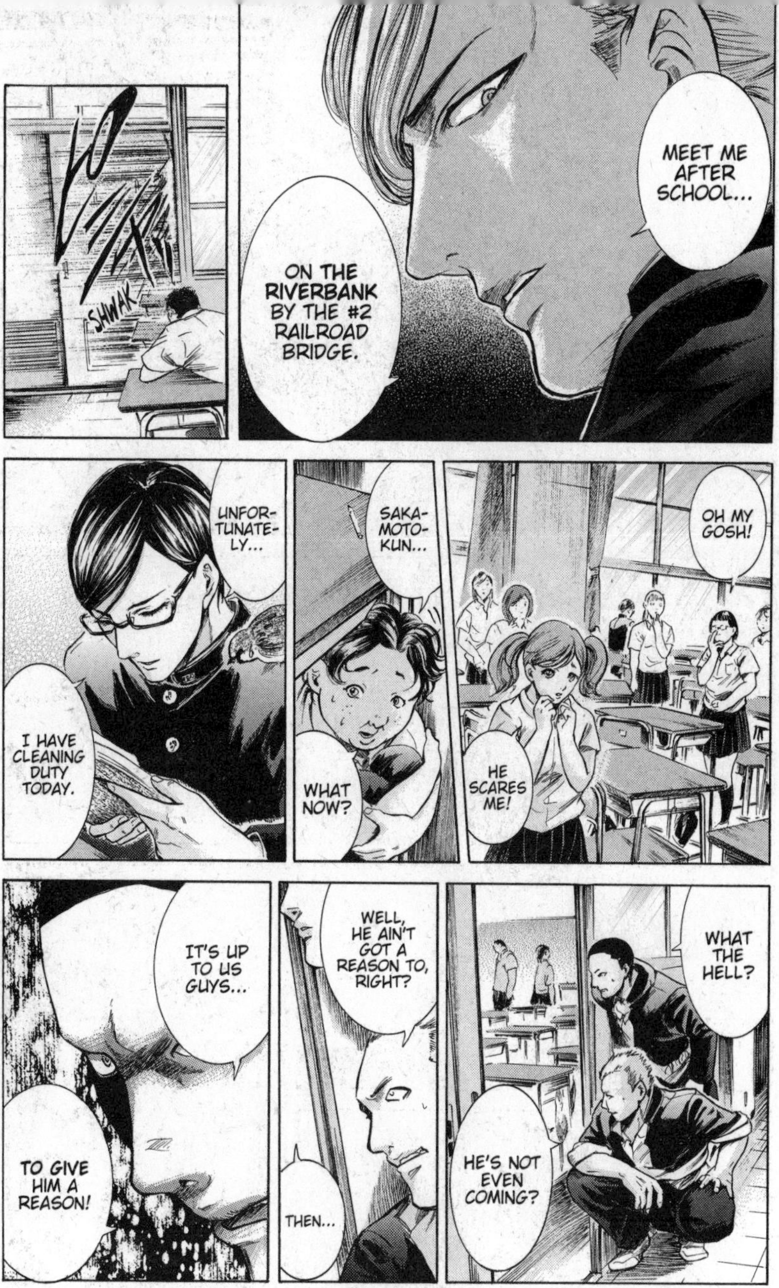
MEET ME AFTER SCHOOL...
ON THE RIVERBANK BY THE #2 RAILROAD BRIDGE.
SHWAK
OH MY GOSH!
HE SCARES ME!
SAKA-MOTO-KUN...
WHAT NOW?
UNFOR-TUNATE-LY...
I HAVE CLEANING DUTY TODAY.
WHAT THE HELL?
HE'S NOT EVEN COMING?
WELL, HE AIN'T GOT A REASON TO, RIGHT?
THEN...
IT'S UP TO US GUYS...
TO GIVE HIM A REASON!

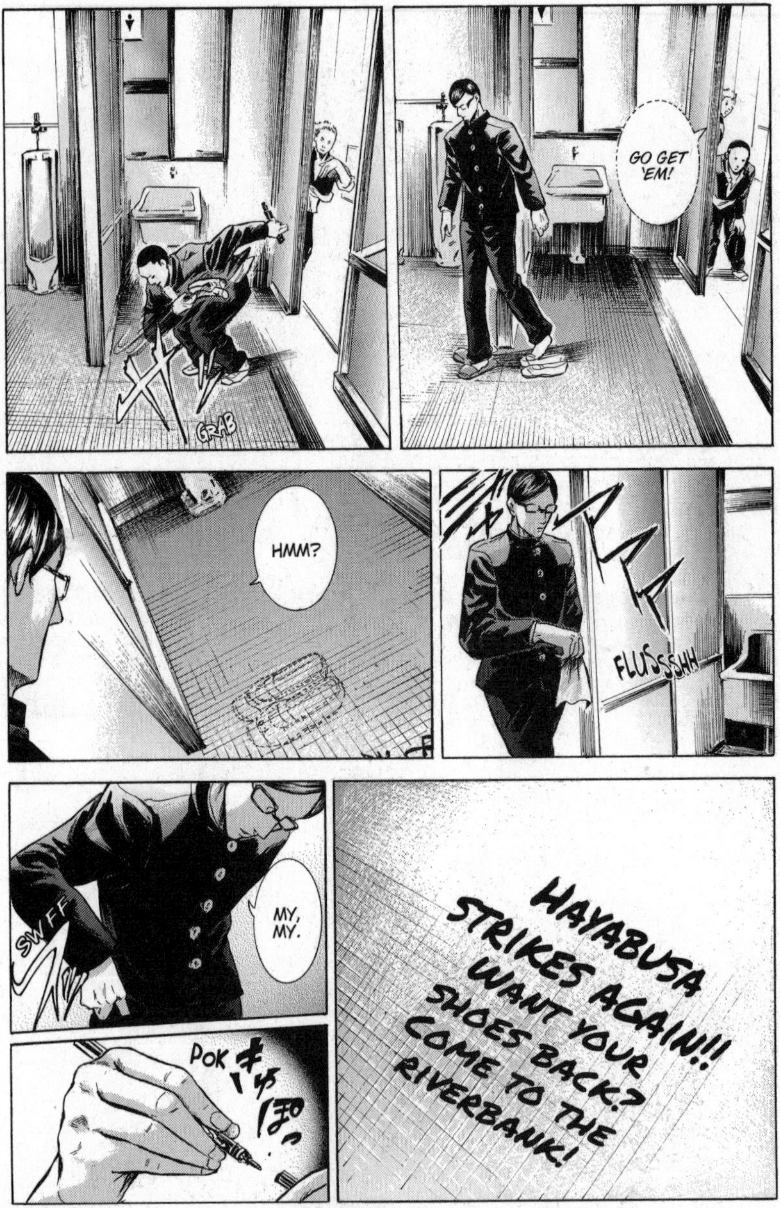
GO GET 'EM!
GRAB
FLUSSSHH
HMM?
HAYABUSA STRIKES AGAIN!! WANT YOUR SHOES BACK? COME TO THE RIVERBANK!
SWFF
MY, MY.
POK

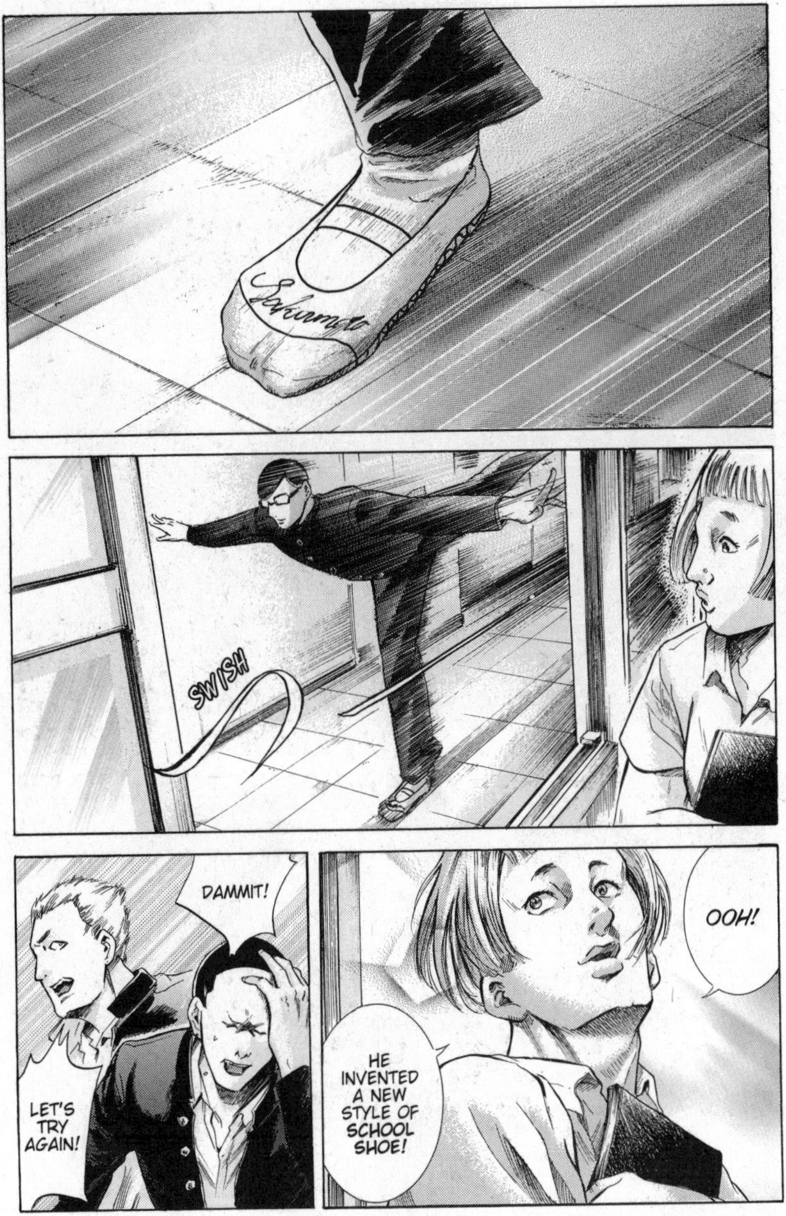
Sakamoto
SWISH
OOH!
HE INVENTED A NEW STYLE OF SCHOOL SHOE!
DAMMIT!
LET'S TRY AGAIN!

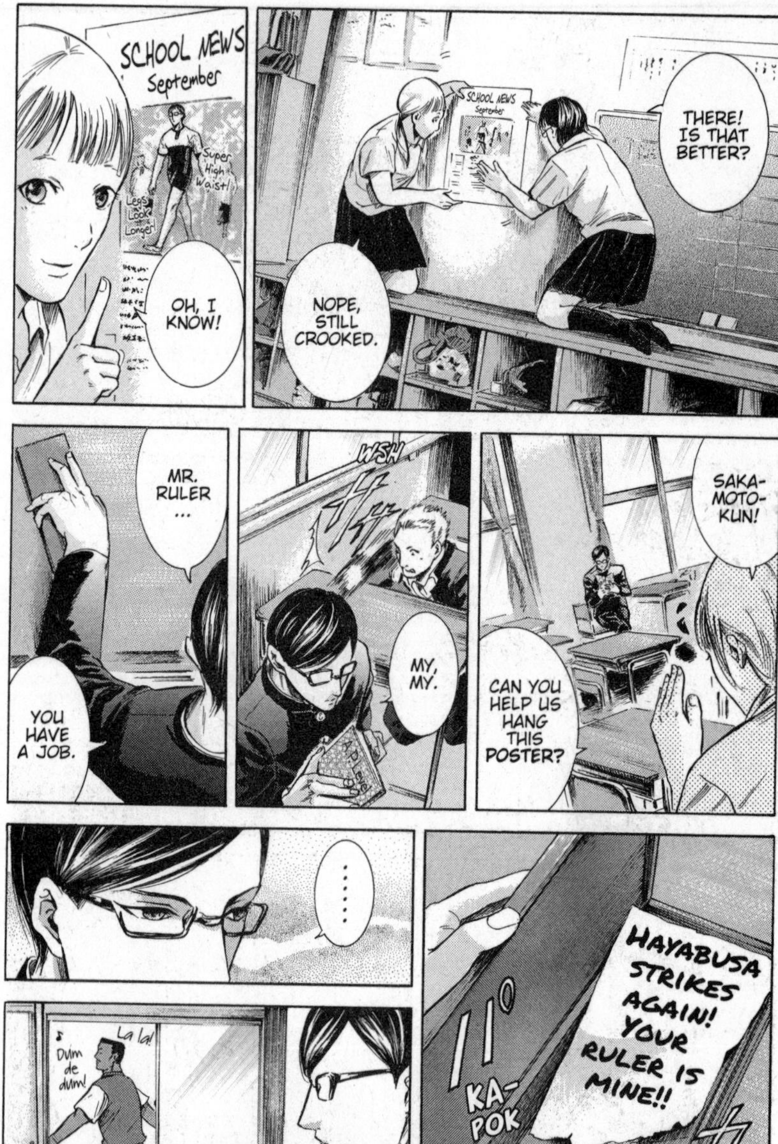
SCHOOL NEWS September
THERE! IS THAT BETTER?
NOPE, STILL CROOKED.
SCHOOL NEWS September
Super High Waist!
Legs Look Longer!
OH, I KNOW!
SAKA-MOTO-KUN!
CAN YOU HELP US HANG THIS POSTER?
WSH
MY, MY.
MR. RULER ...
YOU HAVE A JOB.
HAYABUSA STRIKES AGAIN! YOUR RULER IS MINE!!
KA-POK
......
La la!
Dum de dum!

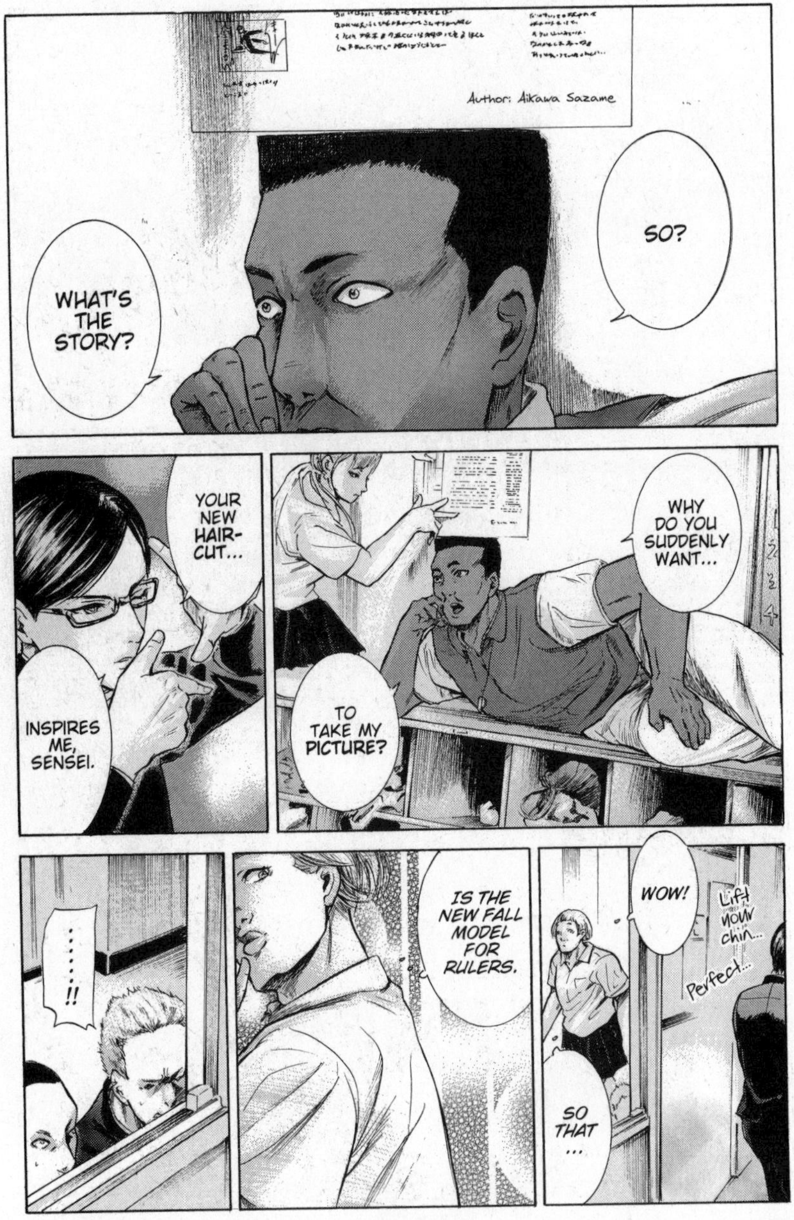

Author: Aikawa Sazame
SO?
WHAT'S THE STORY?
WHY DO YOU SUDDENLY WANT...
TO TAKE MY PICTURE?
YOUR NEW HAIR-CUT...
INSPIRES ME, SENSEI.
WOW!
Lift your chin...
Perfect...
SO THAT ...
IS THE NEW FALL MODEL FOR RULERS.
......!!

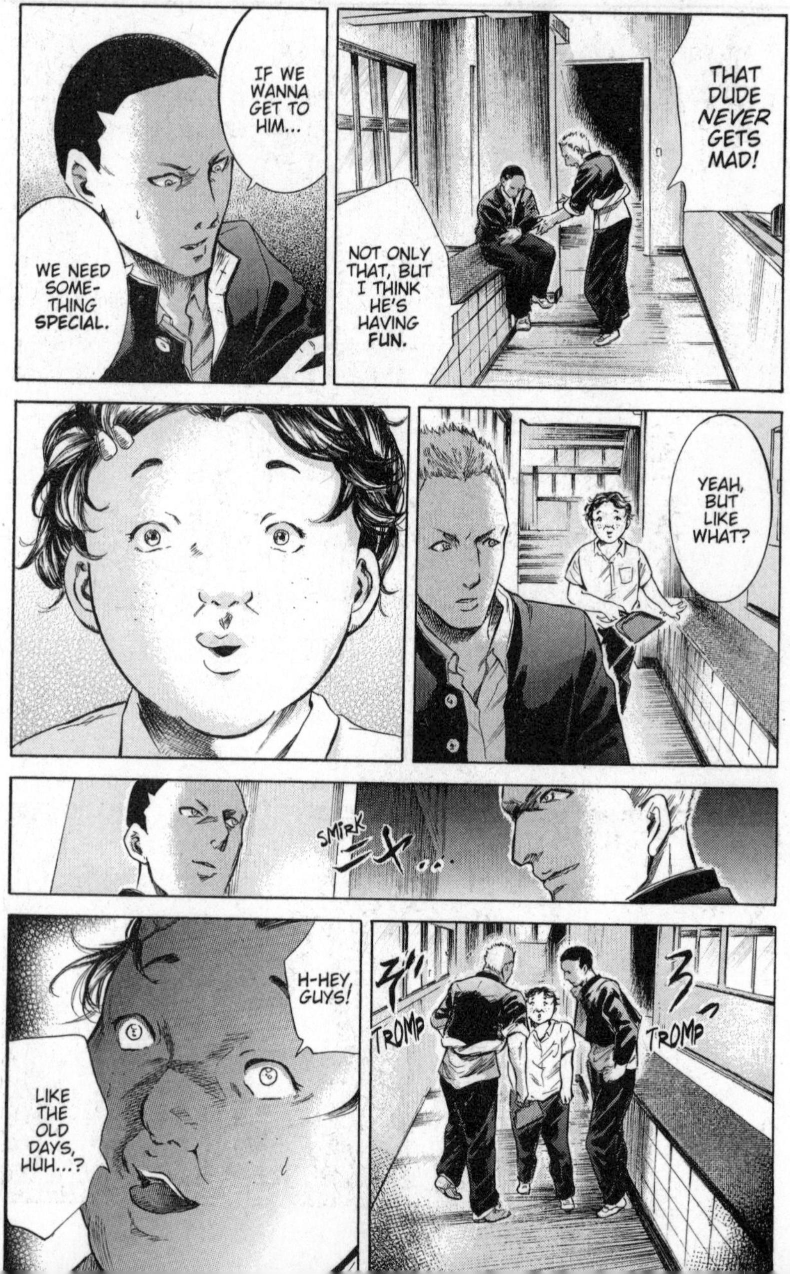
THAT DUDE NEVER GETS MAD!
NOT ONLY THAT, BUT I THINK HE'S HAVING FUN.
IF WE WANNA GET TO HIM...
WE NEED SOME-THING SPECIAL.
YEAH, BUT LIKE WHAT?
SMIRK
TROMP
TROMP
H-HEY, GUYS!
LIKE THE OLD DAYS, HUH...?

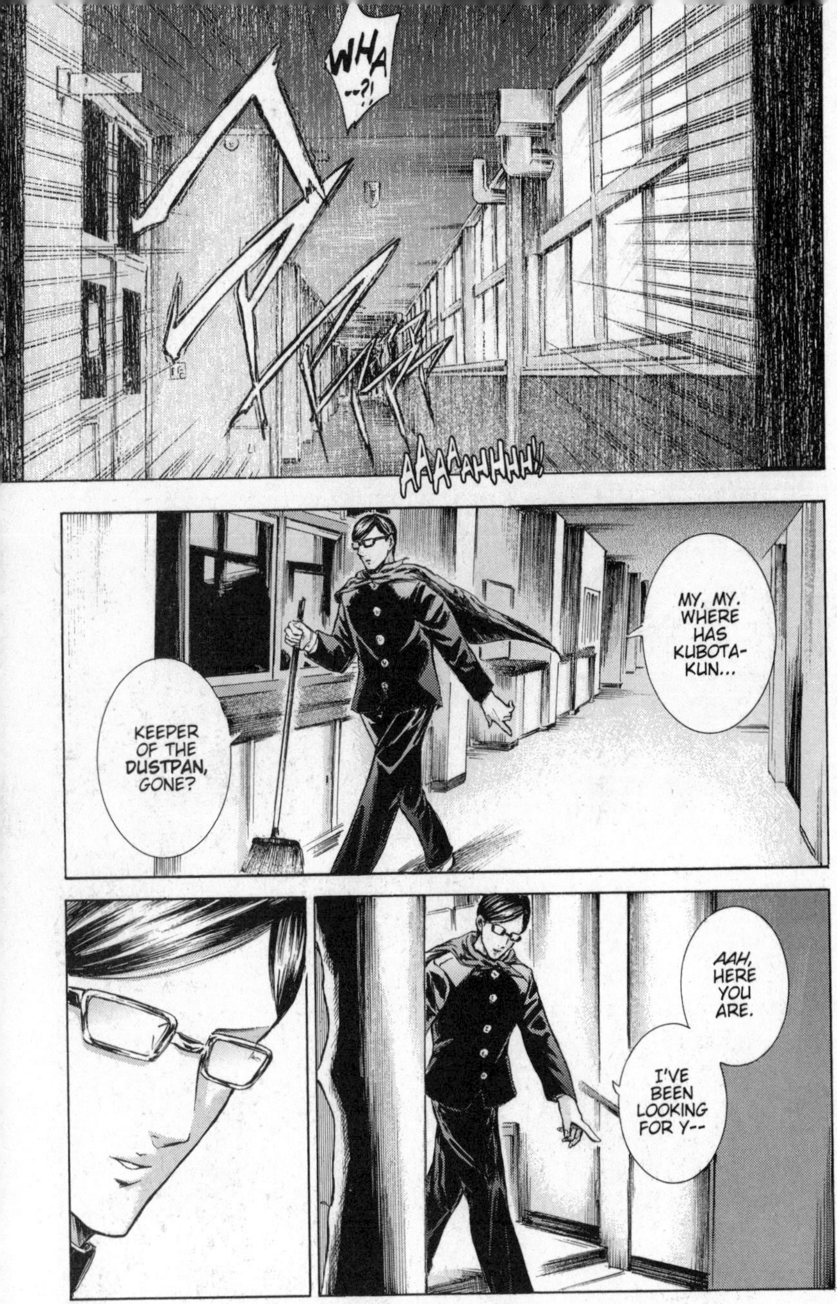
WHA--?!
AAAAHHHHH!!
MY, MY. WHERE HAS KUBOTA-KUN...
KEEPER OF THE DUSTPAN, GONE?
AAH, HERE YOU ARE.
I'VE BEEN LOOKING FOR Y--

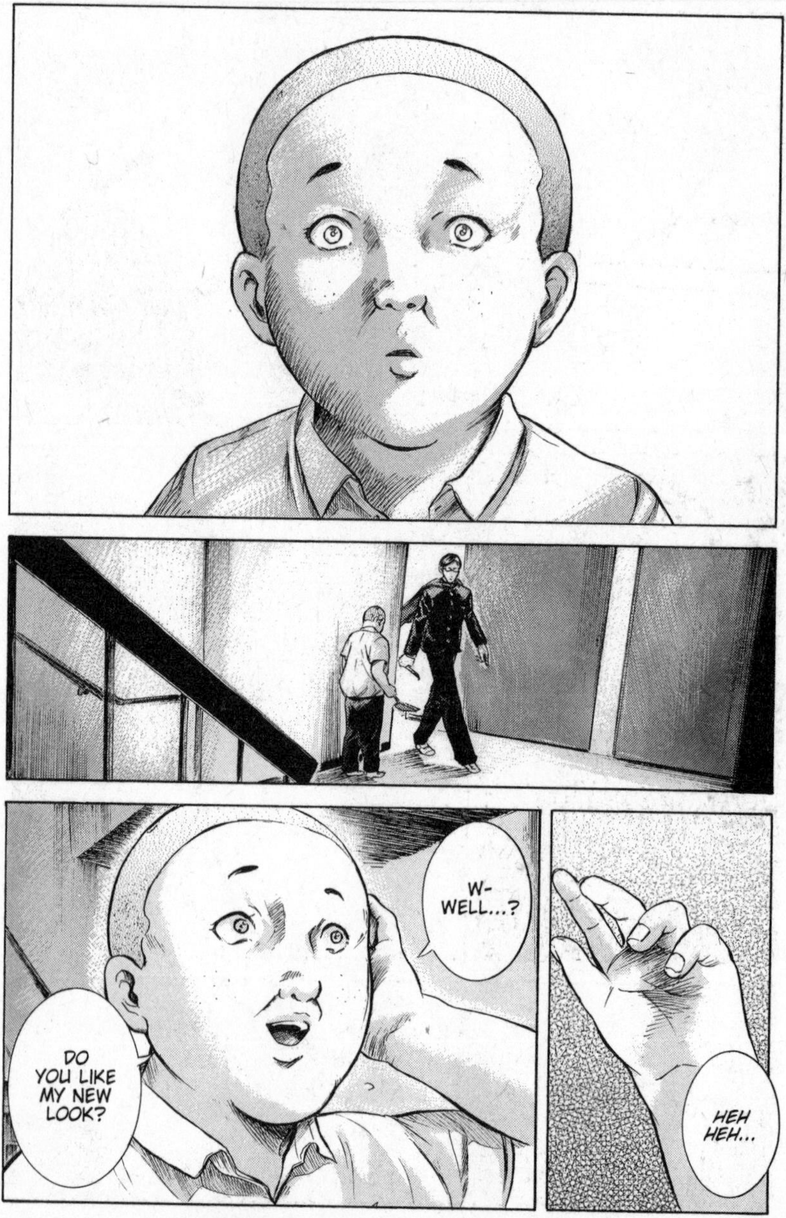
HEH HEH...
W-WELL...?
DO YOU LIKE MY NEW LOOK?

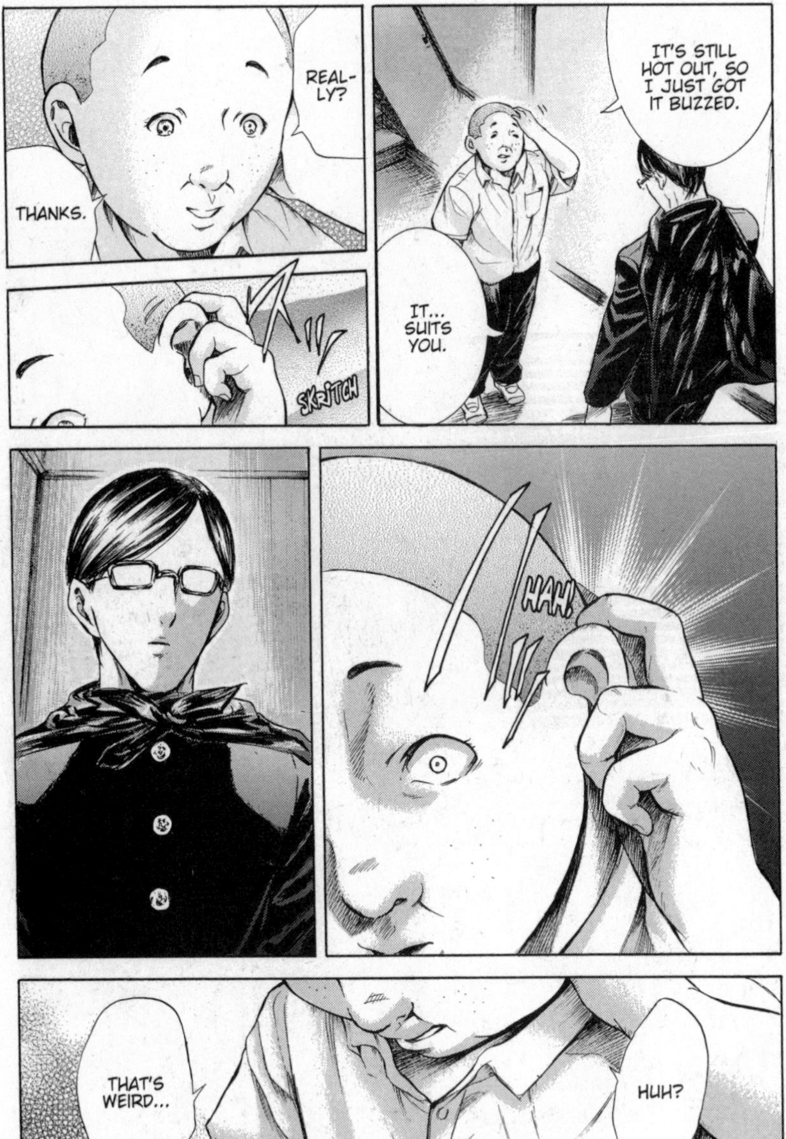
IT'S STILL HOT OUT, SO I JUST GOT IT BUZZED.
IT... SUITS YOU.
REAL-LY?
THANKS.
SKRITCH
HAH!
HUH?
THAT'S WEIRD...

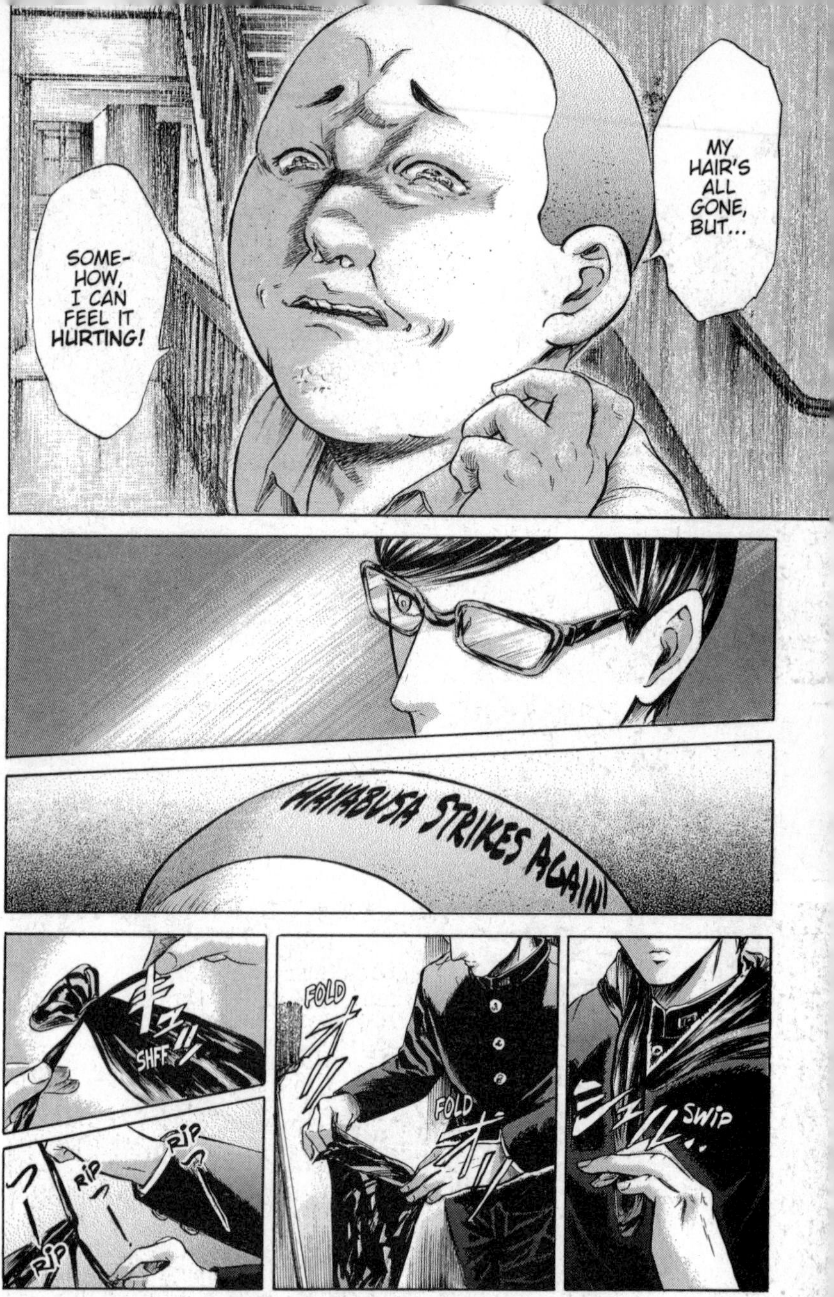
MY HAIR'S ALL GONE, BUT...
SOME-HOW, I CAN FEEL IT HURTING!
HAYABUSA STRIKES AGAIN!
SWIP
FOLD
FOLD
SHFF
RIP
RIP
RIP

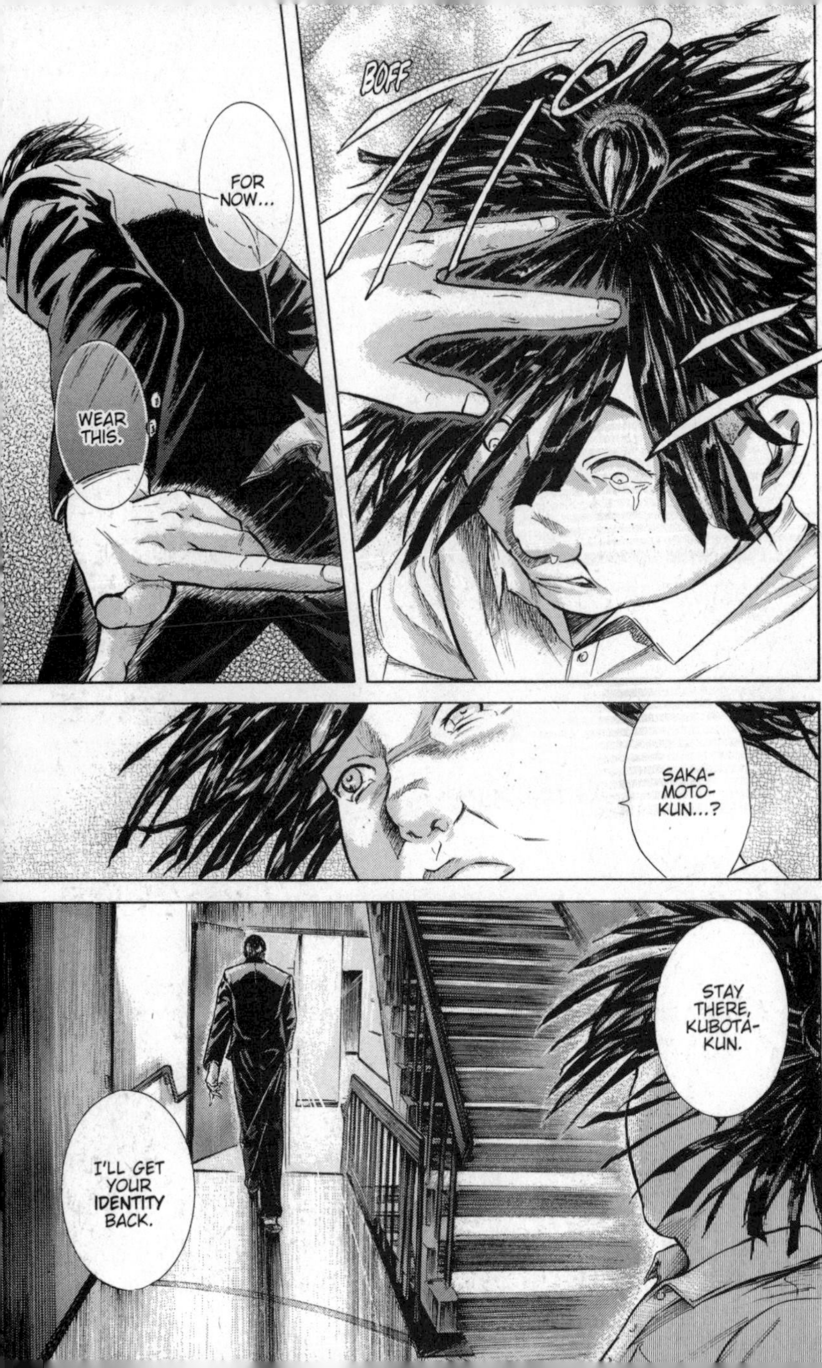
BOFF
FOR NOW...
WEAR THIS.
SAKAMOTO-KUN...?
STAY THERE, KUBOTA-KUN.
I'LL GET YOUR IDENTITY BACK.

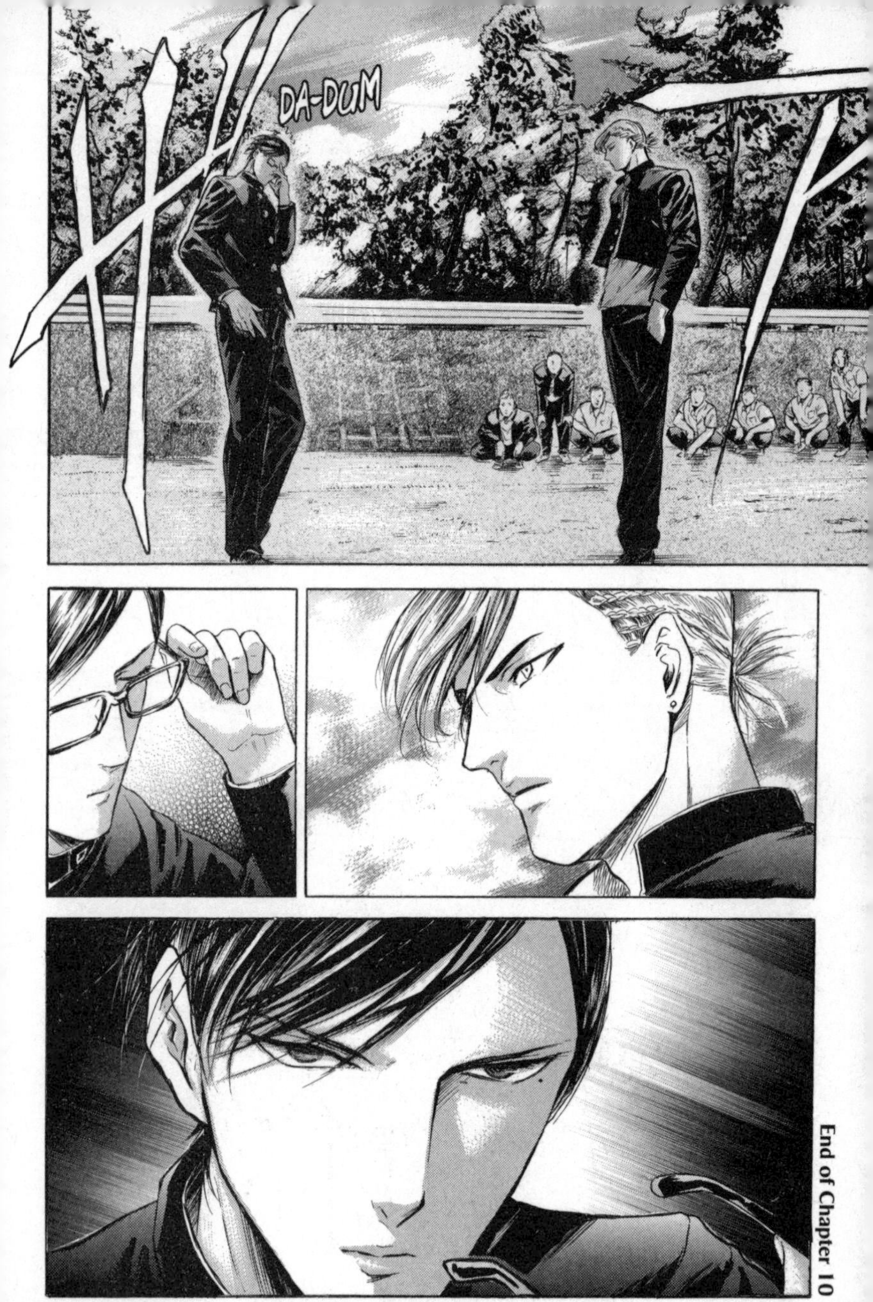
DA-DUM

End of Chapter 10

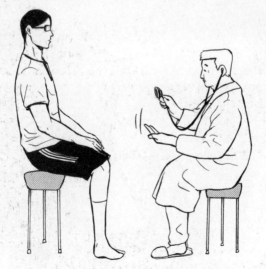

Physical Exam #5:
Heart &
Respiration

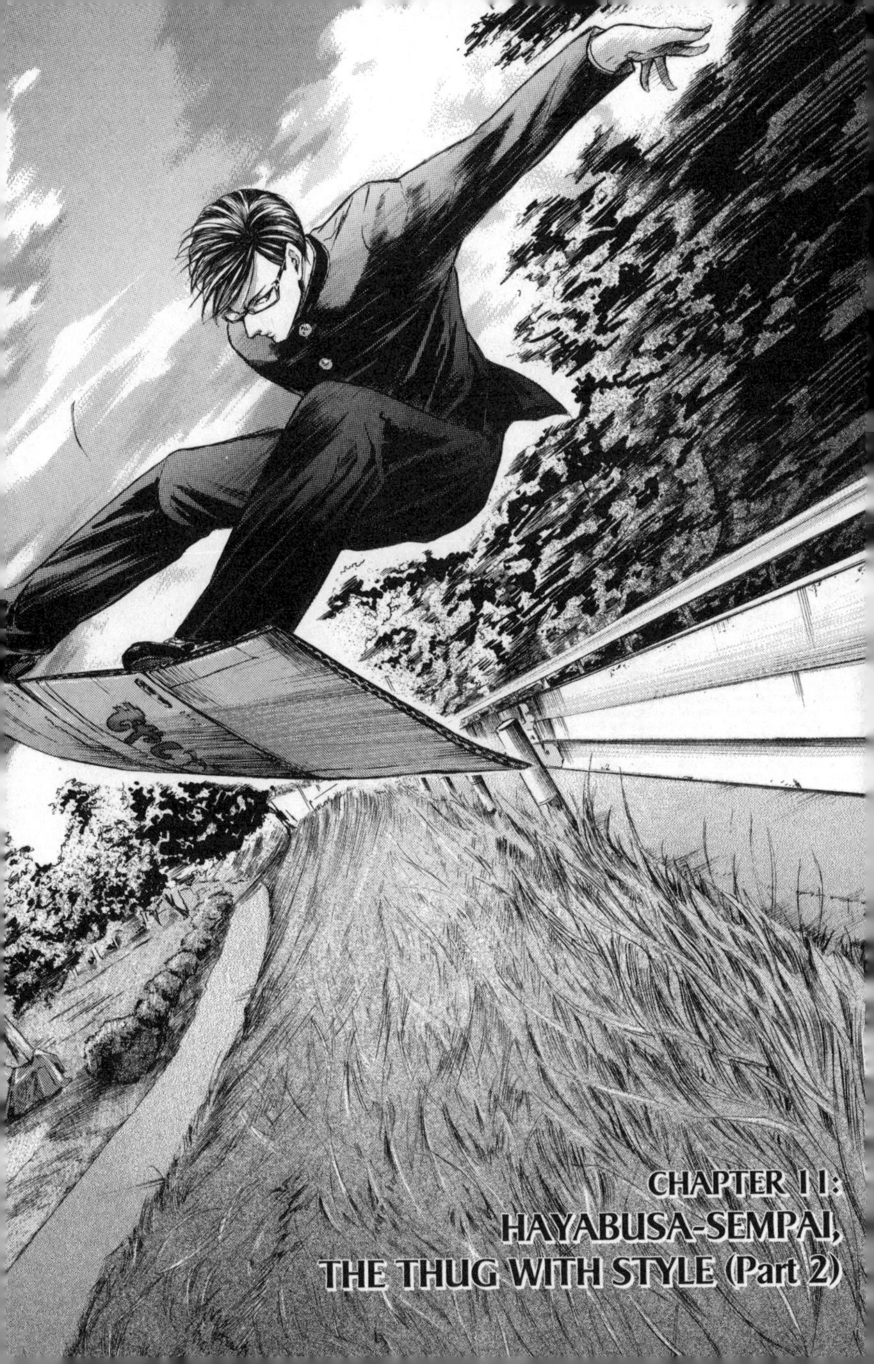

CHAPTER 11:
HAYABUSA-SEMPAI, THE THUG WITH STYLE (Part 2)

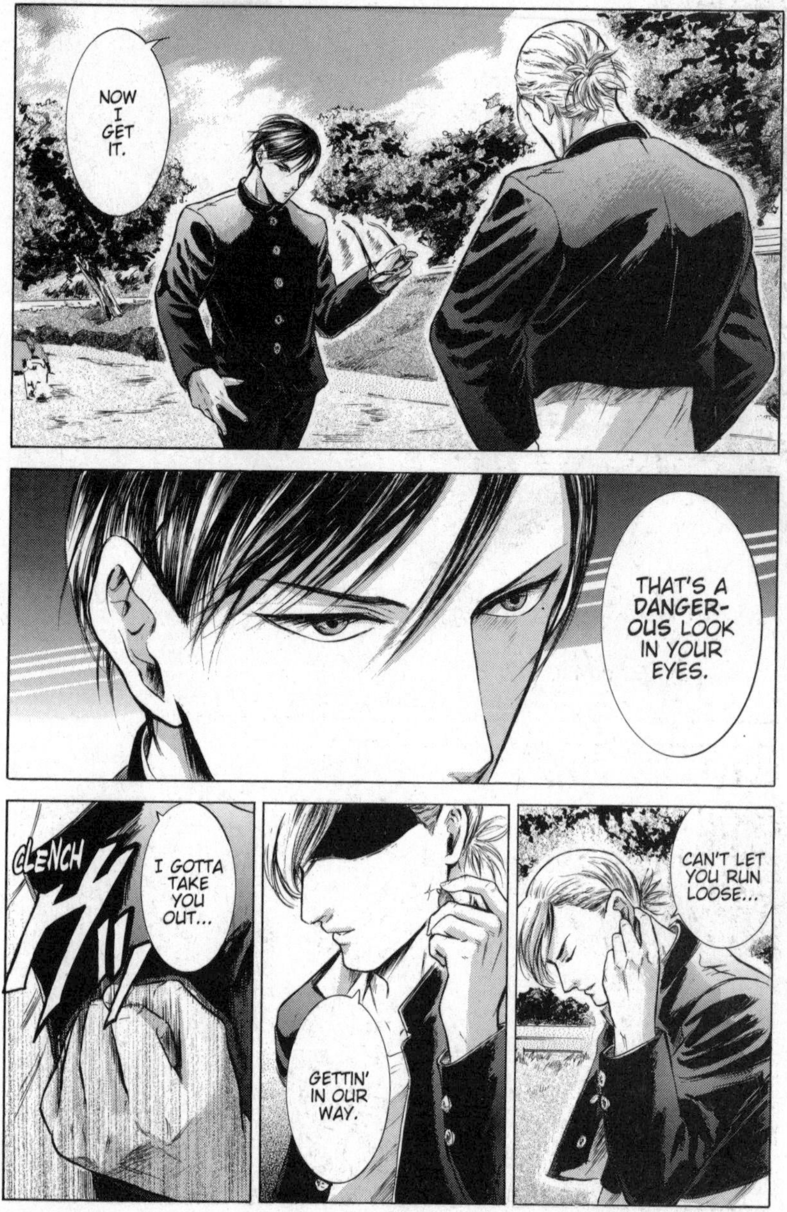
NOW I GET IT.
THAT'S A DANGER-OUS LOOK IN YOUR EYES.
CAN'T LET YOU RUN LOOSE...
GETTIN' IN OUR WAY.
I GOTTA TAKE YOU OUT...
CLENCH

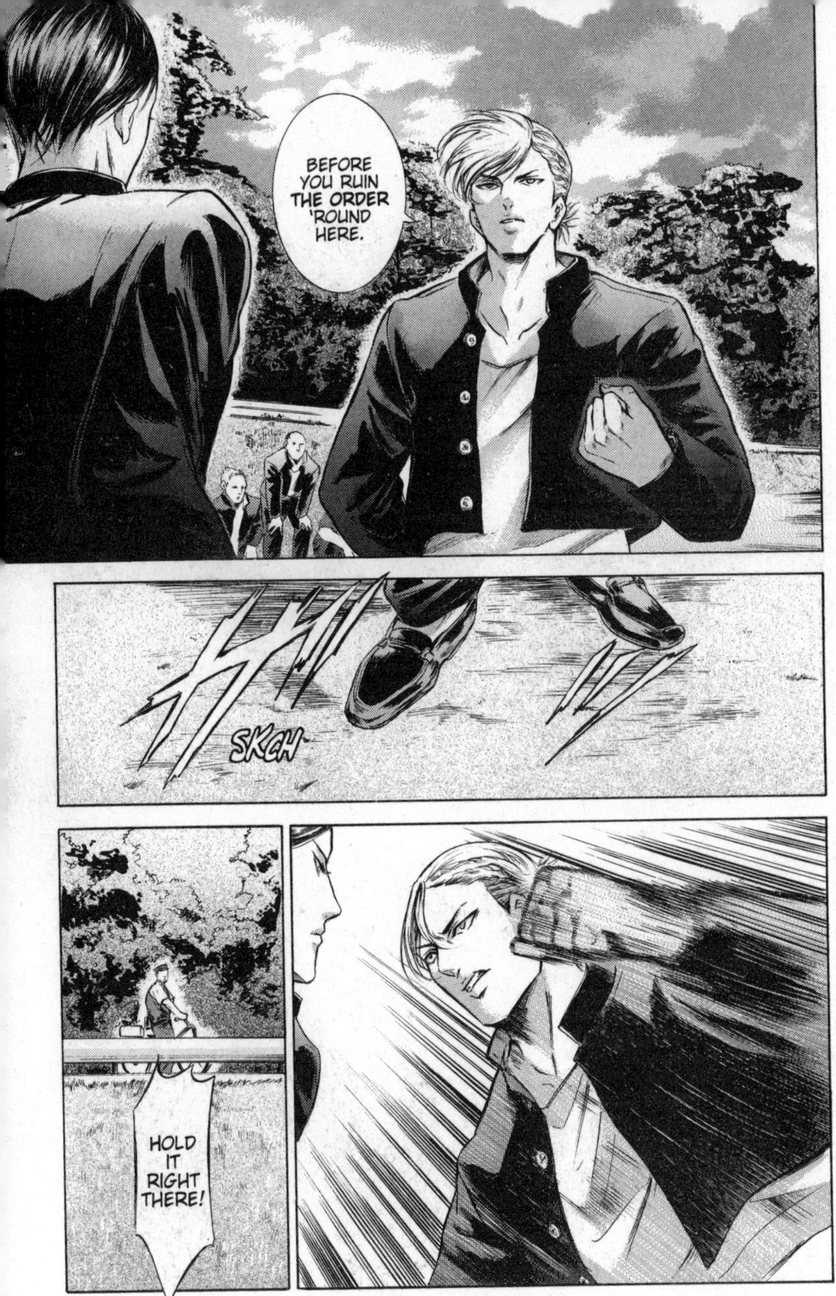
BEFORE YOU RUIN THE ORDER 'ROUND HERE.
SKCH
HOLD IT RIGHT THERE!

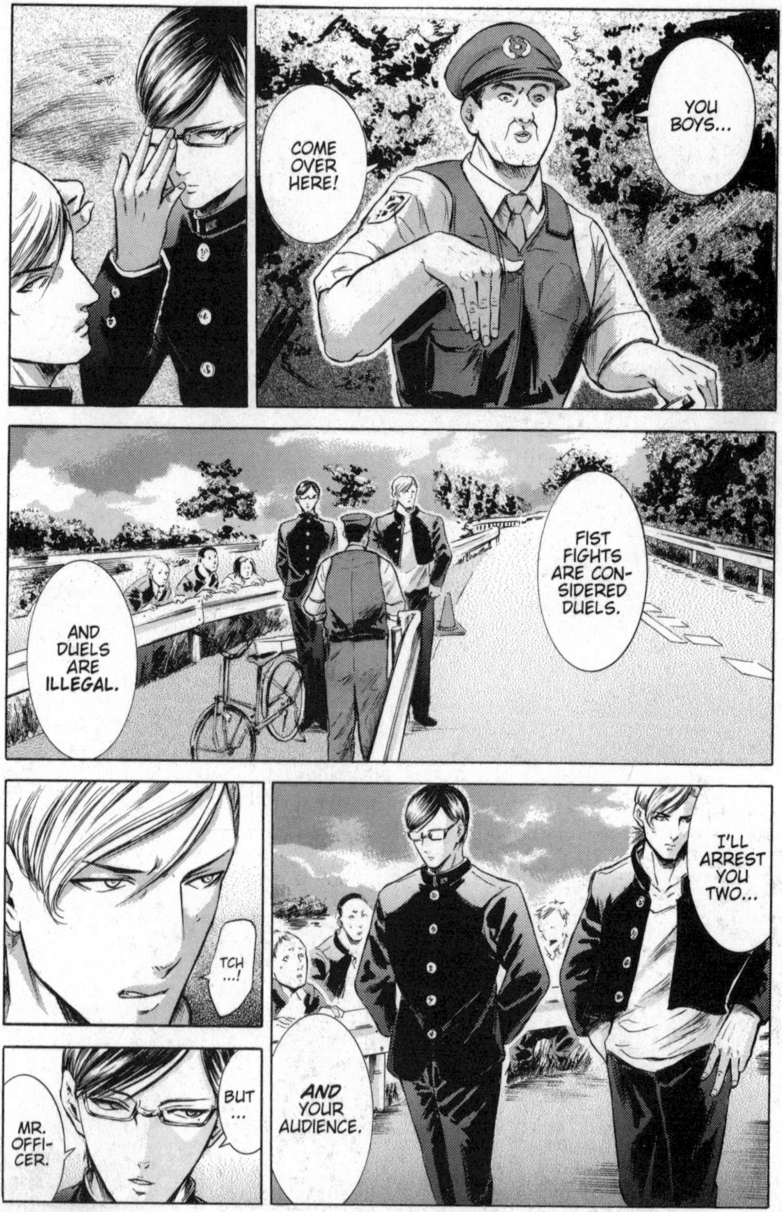
YOU BOYS...
COME OVER HERE!
FIST FIGHTS ARE CON-SIDERED DUELS.
AND DUELS ARE ILLEGAL.
I'LL ARREST YOU TWO...
AND YOUR AUDIENCE.
TCH ...!
BUT ...
MR. OFFI-CER.

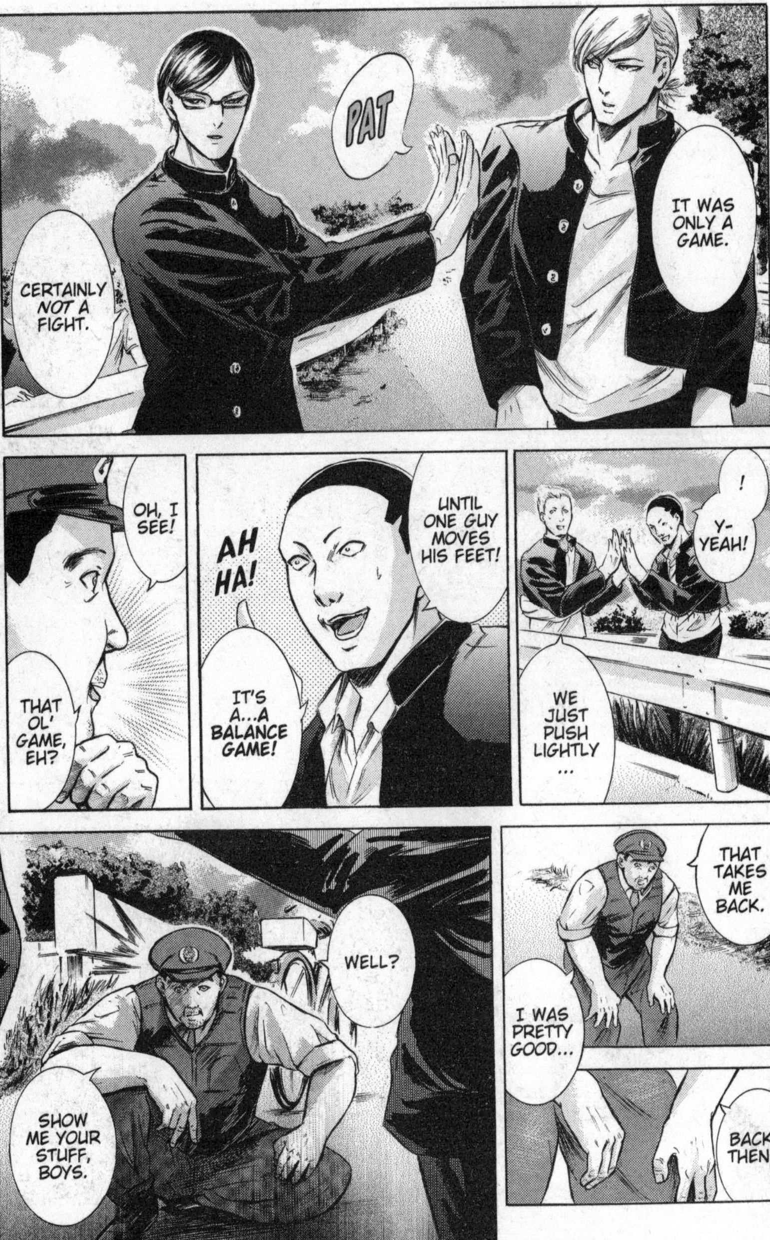
IT WAS ONLY A GAME.
PAT
CERTAINLY *NOT* A FIGHT.
!
Y-YEAH!
WE JUST PUSH LIGHTLY ...
UNTIL ONE GUY MOVES HIS FEET!
AH HA!
IT'S A...A BALANCE GAME!
OH, I SEE!
THAT OL' GAME, EH?
THAT TAKES ME BACK.
I WAS PRETTY GOOD...
BACK THEN.
WELL?
SHOW ME YOUR STUFF, BOYS.

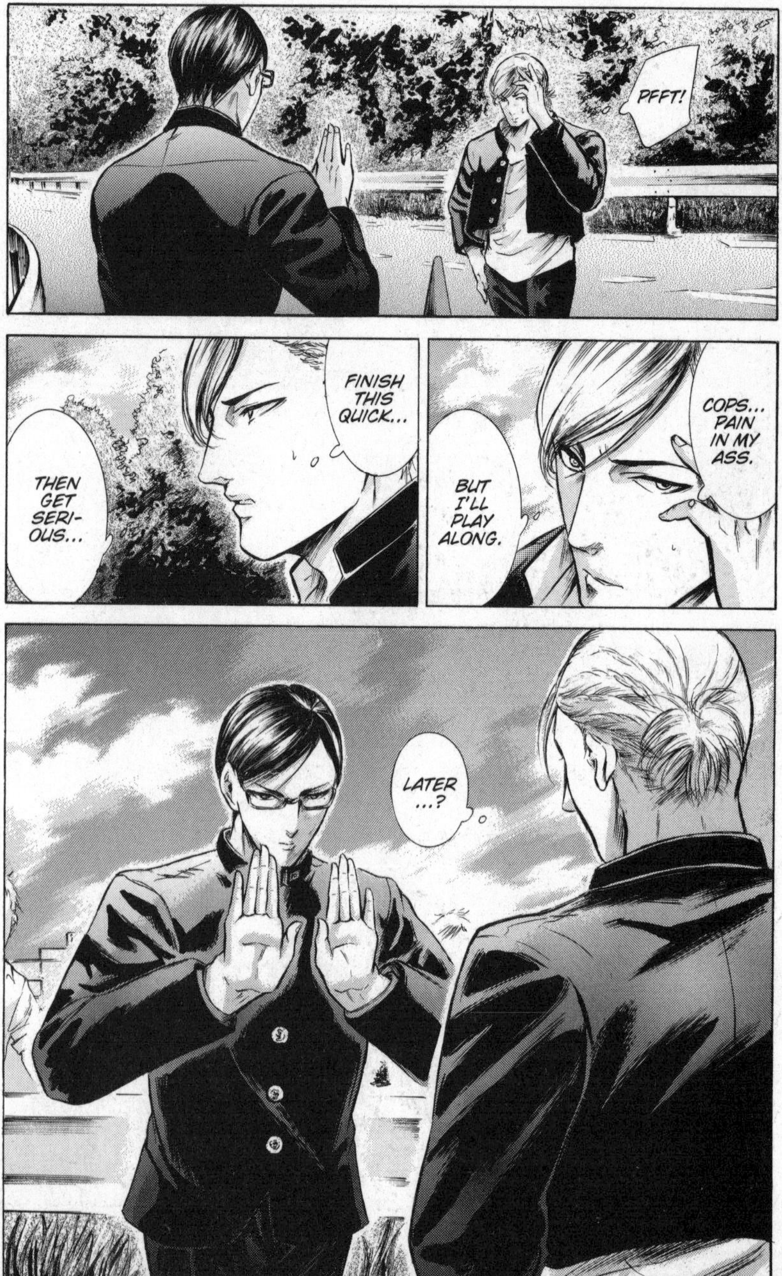
PFFT!
COPS... PAIN IN MY ASS.
BUT I'LL PLAY ALONG.
FINISH THIS QUICK...
THEN GET SERI-OUS...
LATER ...?

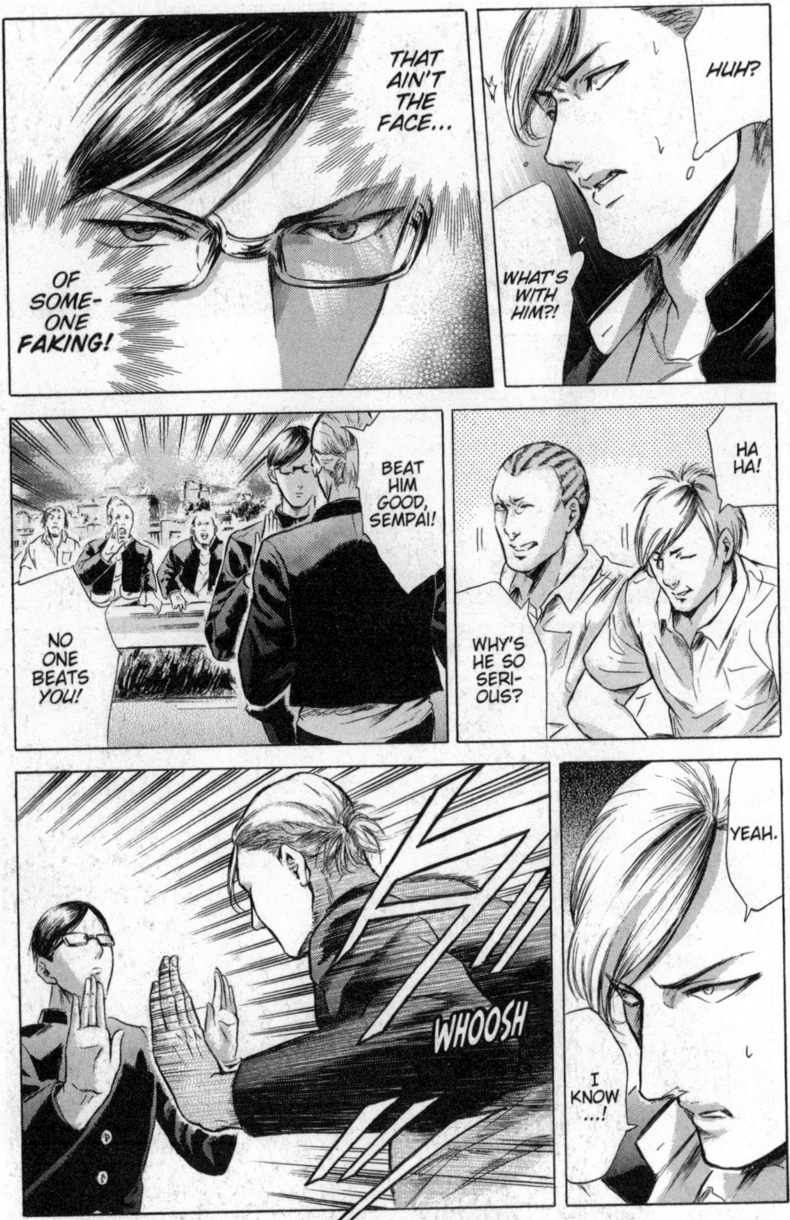
HUH?
WHAT'S WITH HIM?!
THAT AIN'T THE FACE...
OF SOME-ONE FAKING!
HA HA!
WHY'S HE SO SERI-OUS?
BEAT HIM GOOD, SEMPAI!
NO ONE BEATS YOU!
YEAH.
I KNOW ...!
WHOOSH

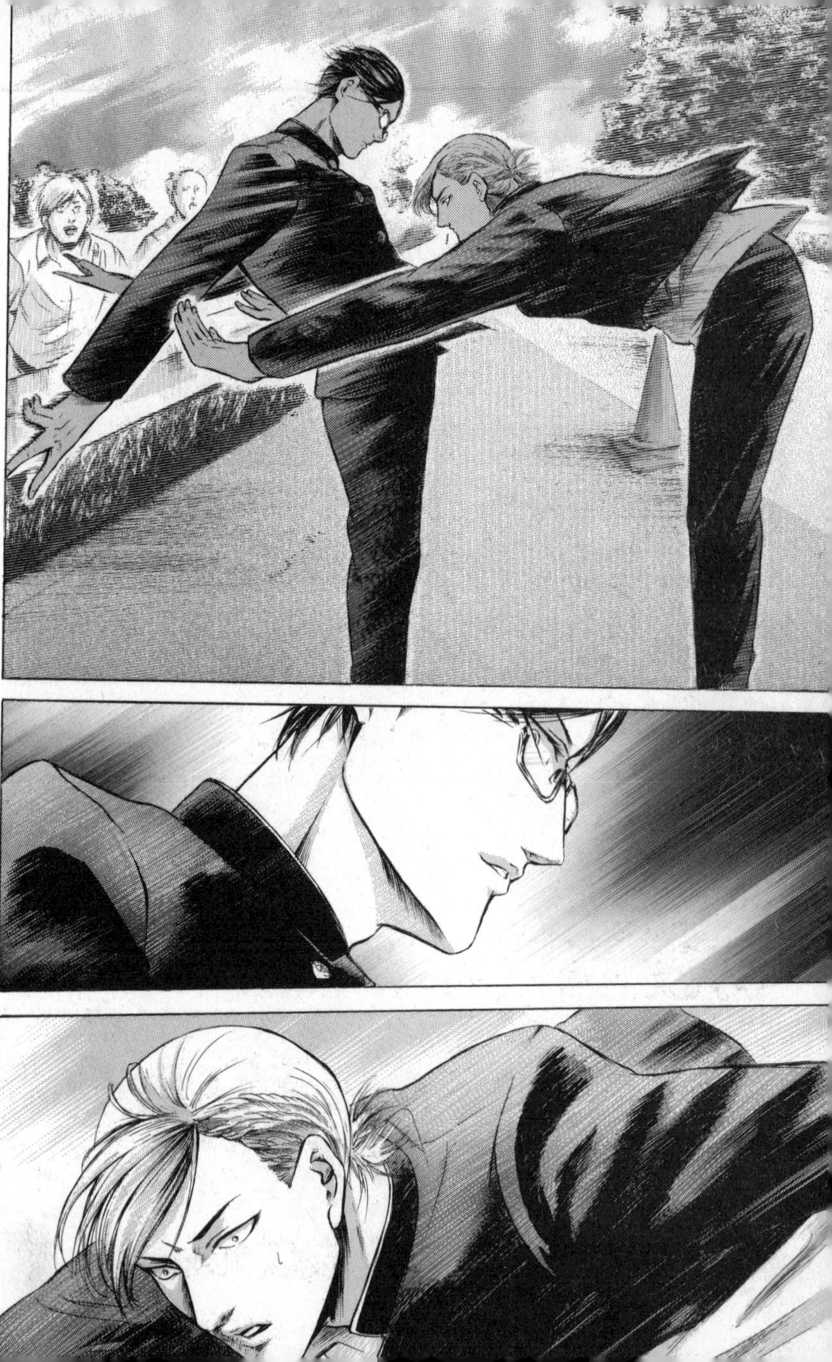

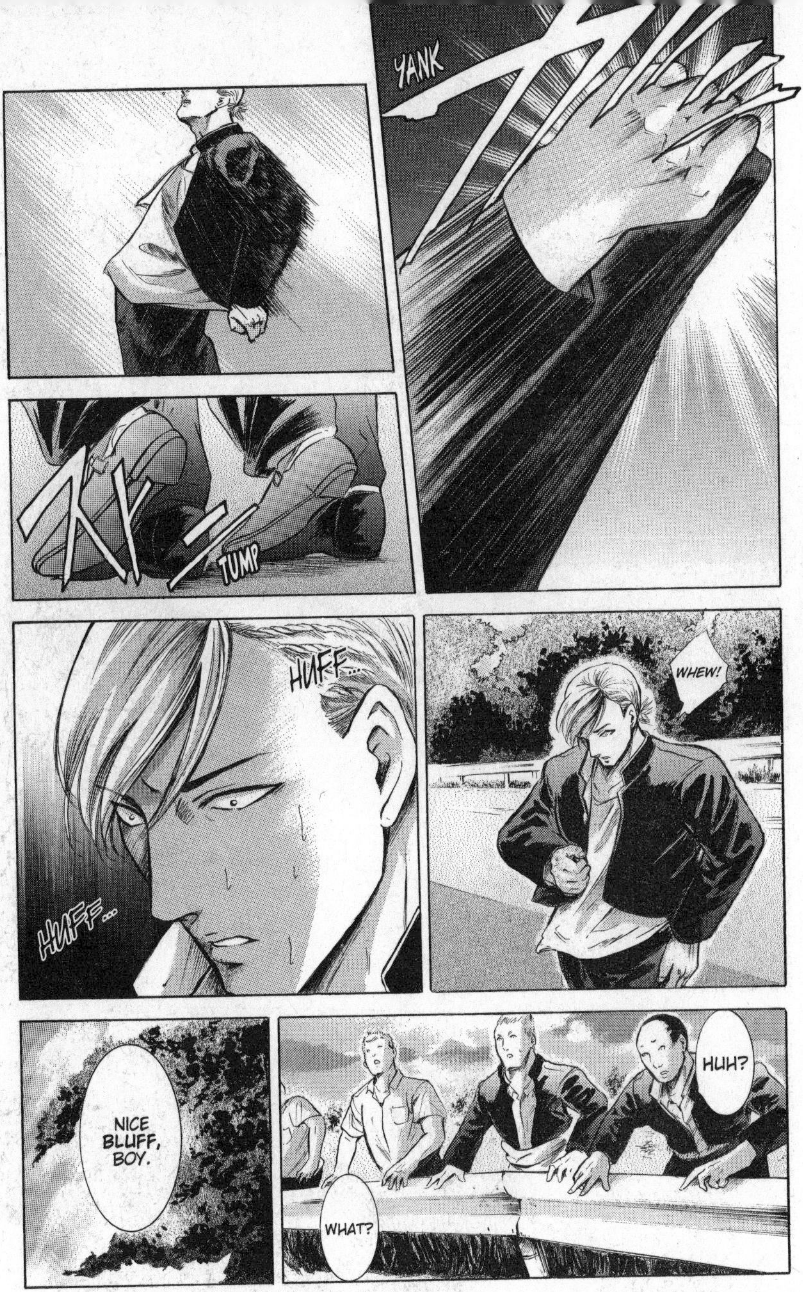
YANK
TUMP
WHEW!
HUFF...
HUFF...
HUH?
WHAT?
NICE BLUFF, BOY.

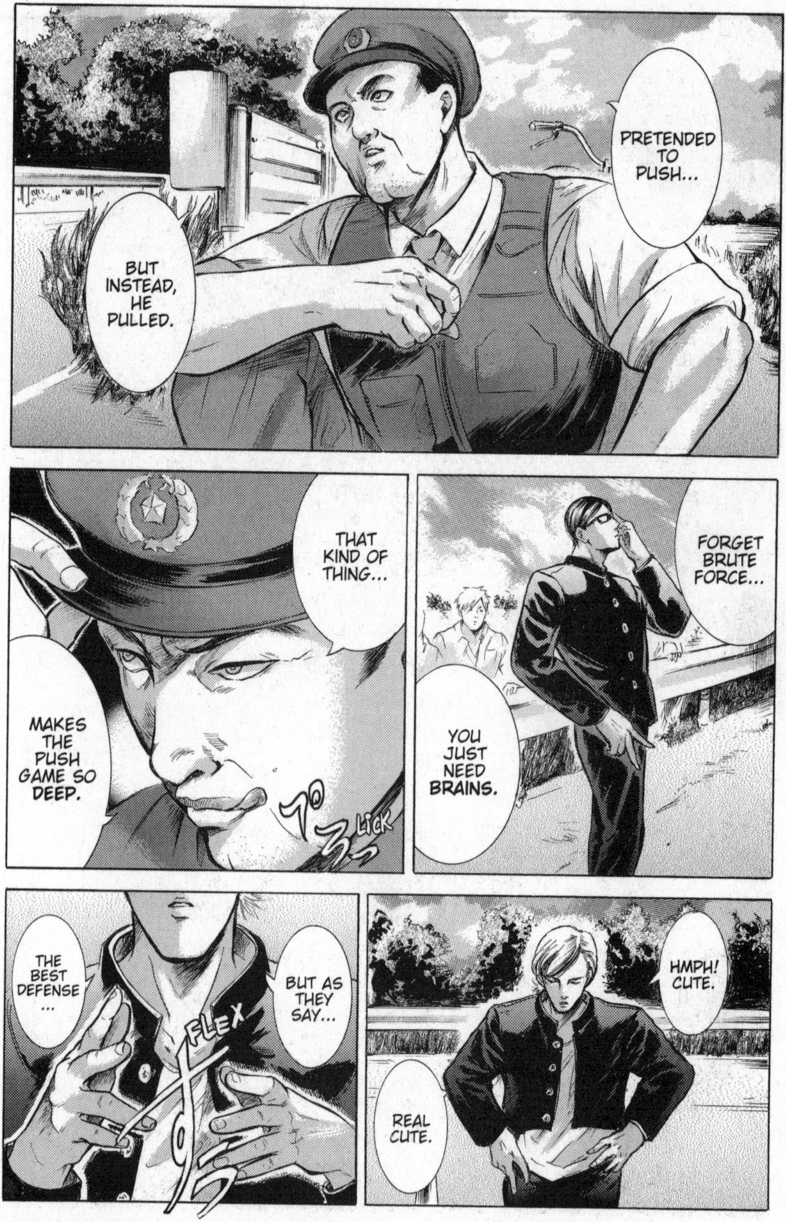
PRETENDED TO PUSH...
BUT INSTEAD, HE PULLED.
FORGET BRUTE FORCE...
YOU JUST NEED BRAINS.
THAT KIND OF THING...
MAKES THE PUSH GAME SO DEEP.
LICK
HMPH! CUTE.
REAL CUTE.
BUT AS THEY SAY...
THE BEST DEFENSE ...
FLEX

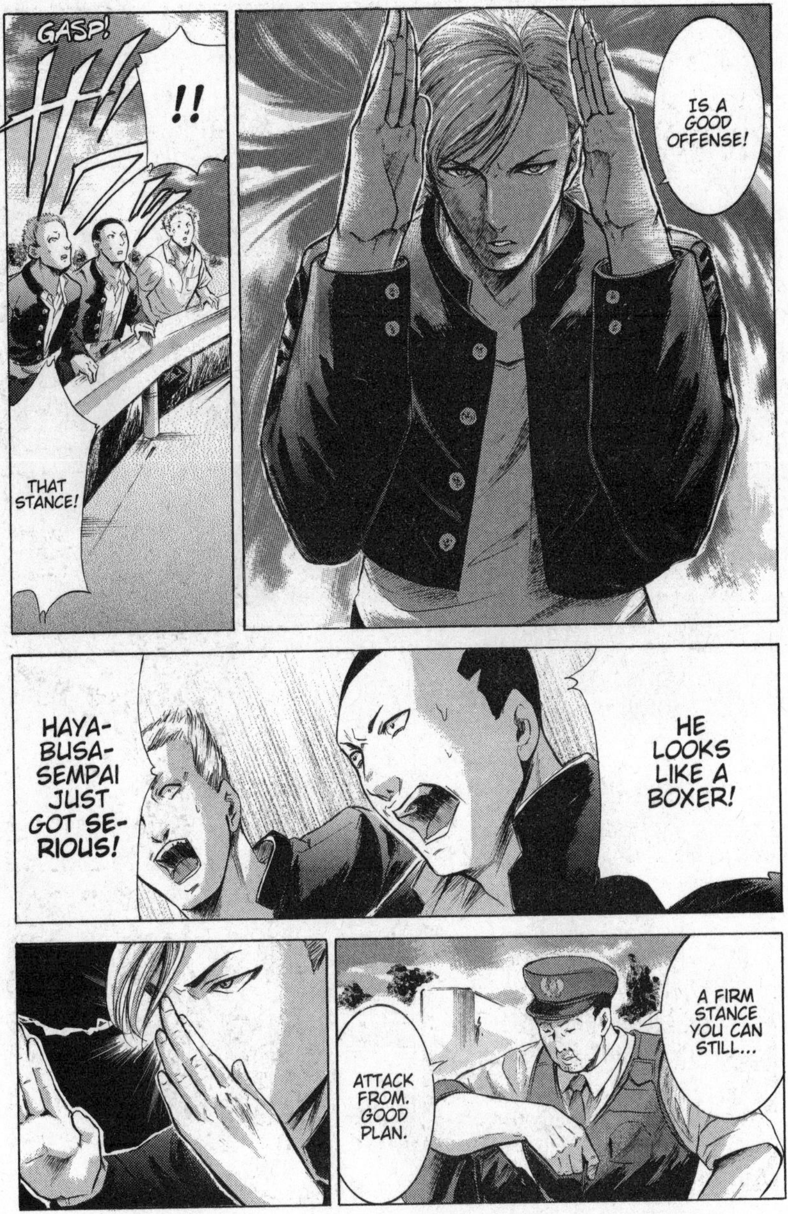
IS A GOOD OFFENSE!
GASP!
!!
THAT STANCE!
HE LOOKS LIKE A BOXER!
HAYA-BUSA-SEMPAI JUST GOT SE-RIOUS!
A FIRM STANCE YOU CAN STILL...
ATTACK FROM. GOOD PLAN.

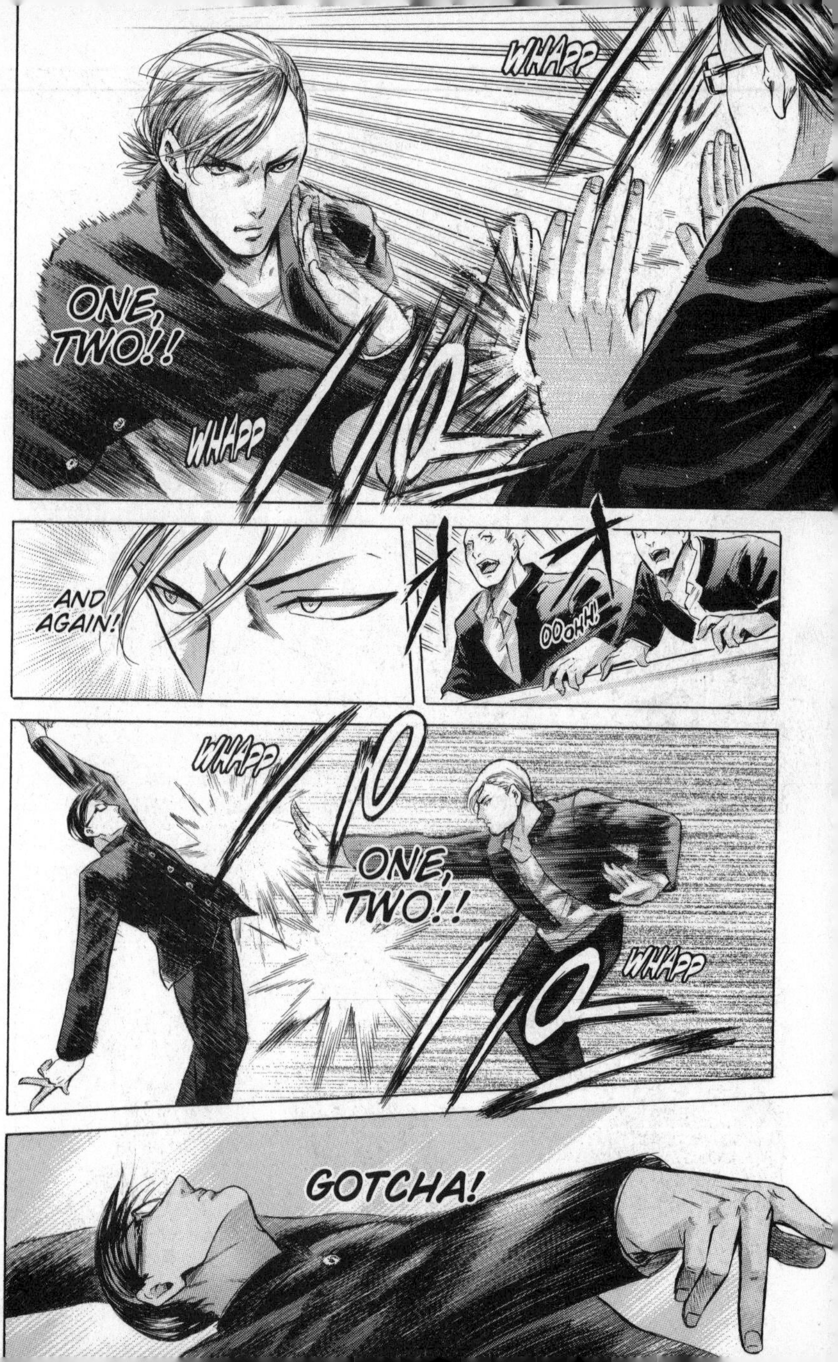
WHAPP
ONE, TWO!!
WHAPP
OOOHH!
AND AGAIN!
WHAPP
ONE, TWO!!
WHAPP
GOTCHA!

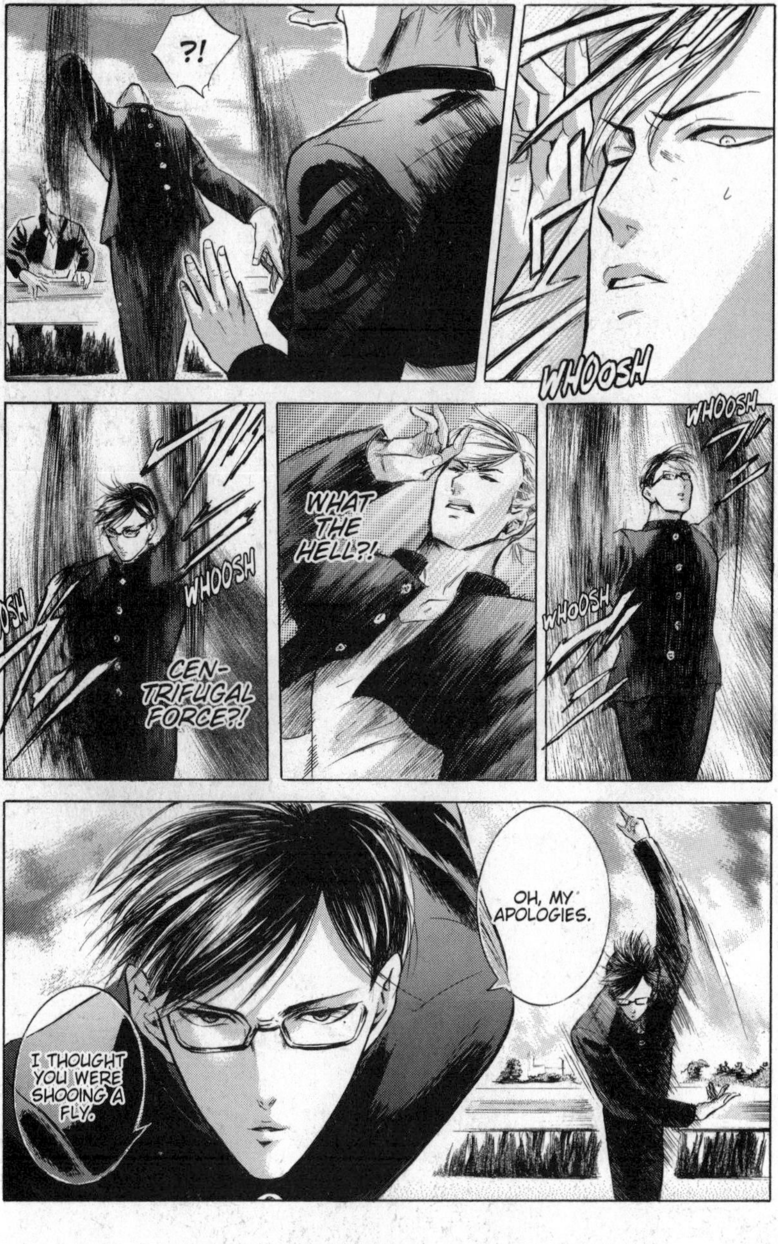
WHOOSH
?!
WHOOSH
WHOOSH
WHAT THE HELL?!
WHOOSH
WHOOSH
CEN-TRIFUGAL FORCE?!
OH, MY APOLOGIES.
I THOUGHT YOU WERE SHOOING A FLY.

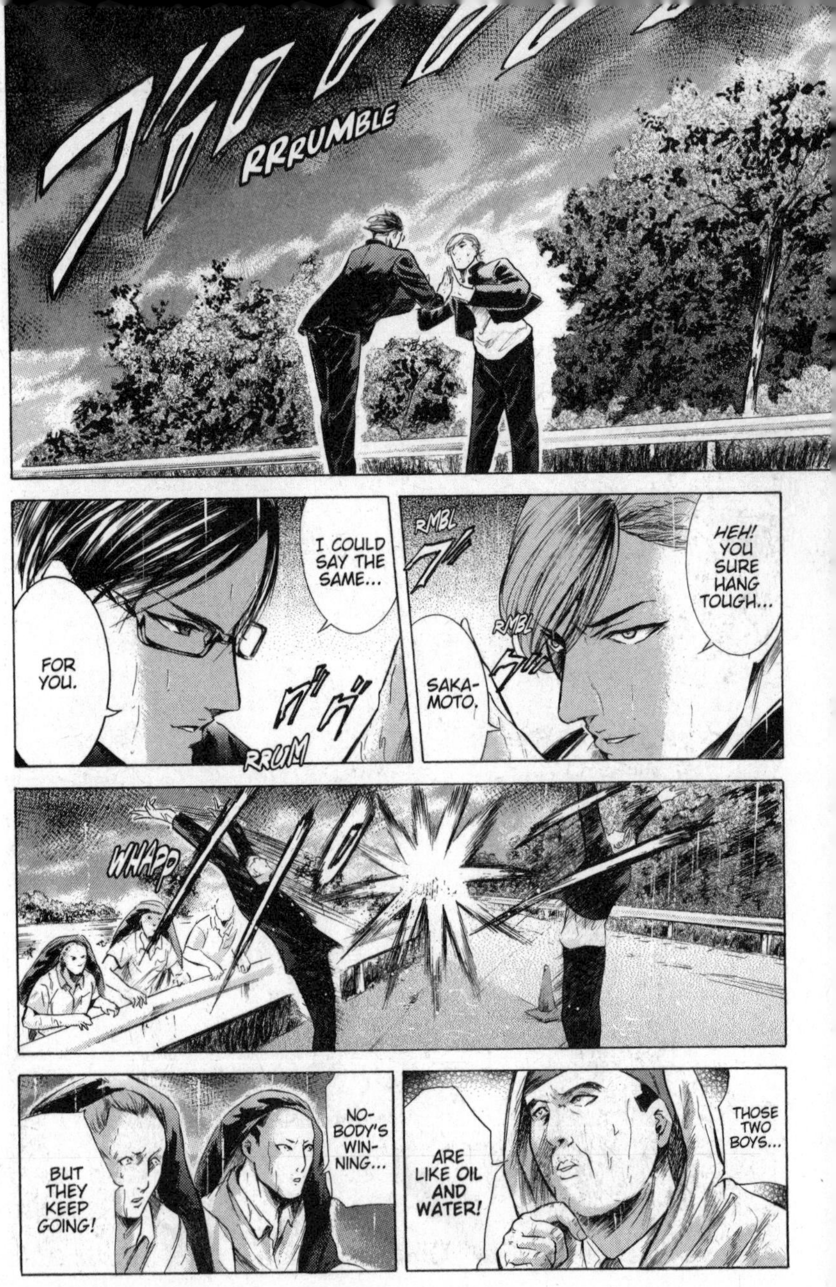
RRRUMBLE
RMBL
HEH! YOU SURE HANG TOUGH...
RMBL
SAKAMOTO.
I COULD SAY THE SAME...
FOR YOU.
RRUM
WHAPP
THOSE TWO BOYS...
ARE LIKE OIL AND WATER!
NO-BODY'S WIN-NING...
BUT THEY KEEP GOING!

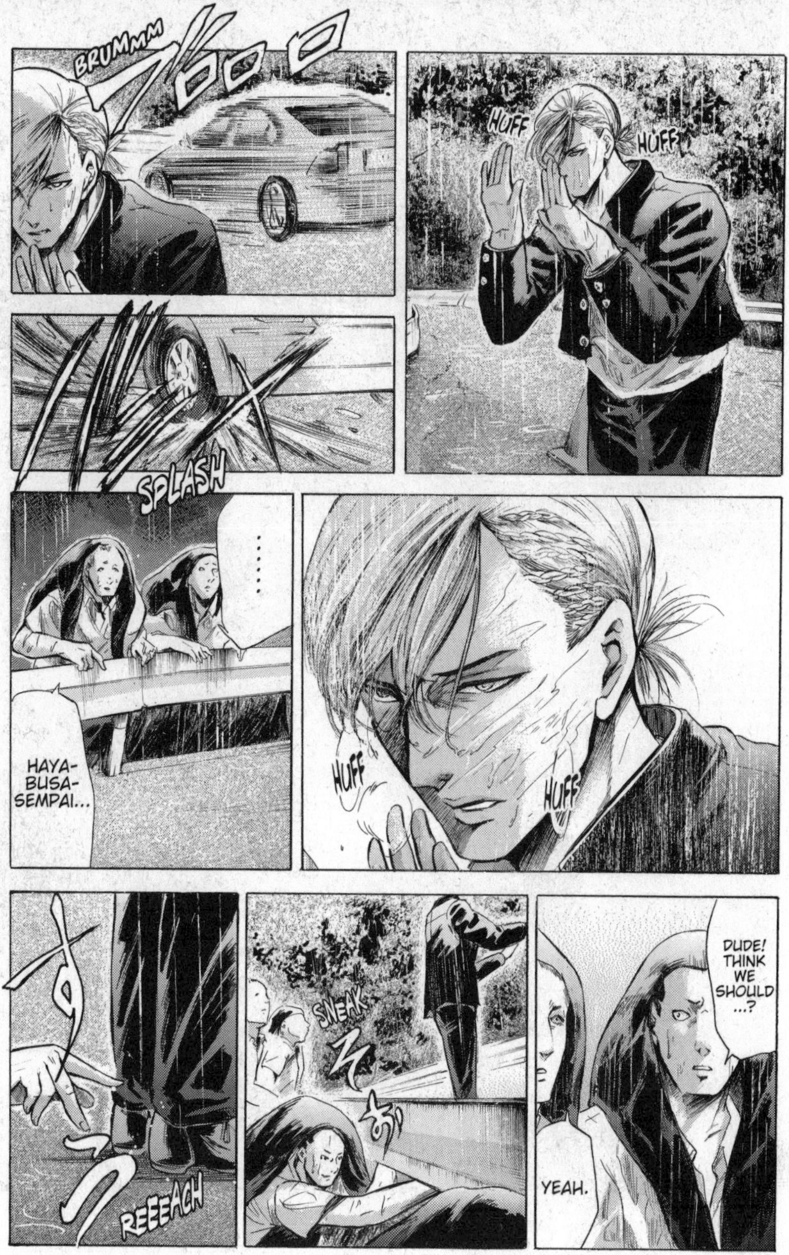
HUFF
HUFF
BRUMMM
SPLASH
HUFF
HUFF
.....
HAYA-BUSA-SEMPAI...
DUDE! THINK WE SHOULD ...?
YEAH.
SNEAK
REEEACH

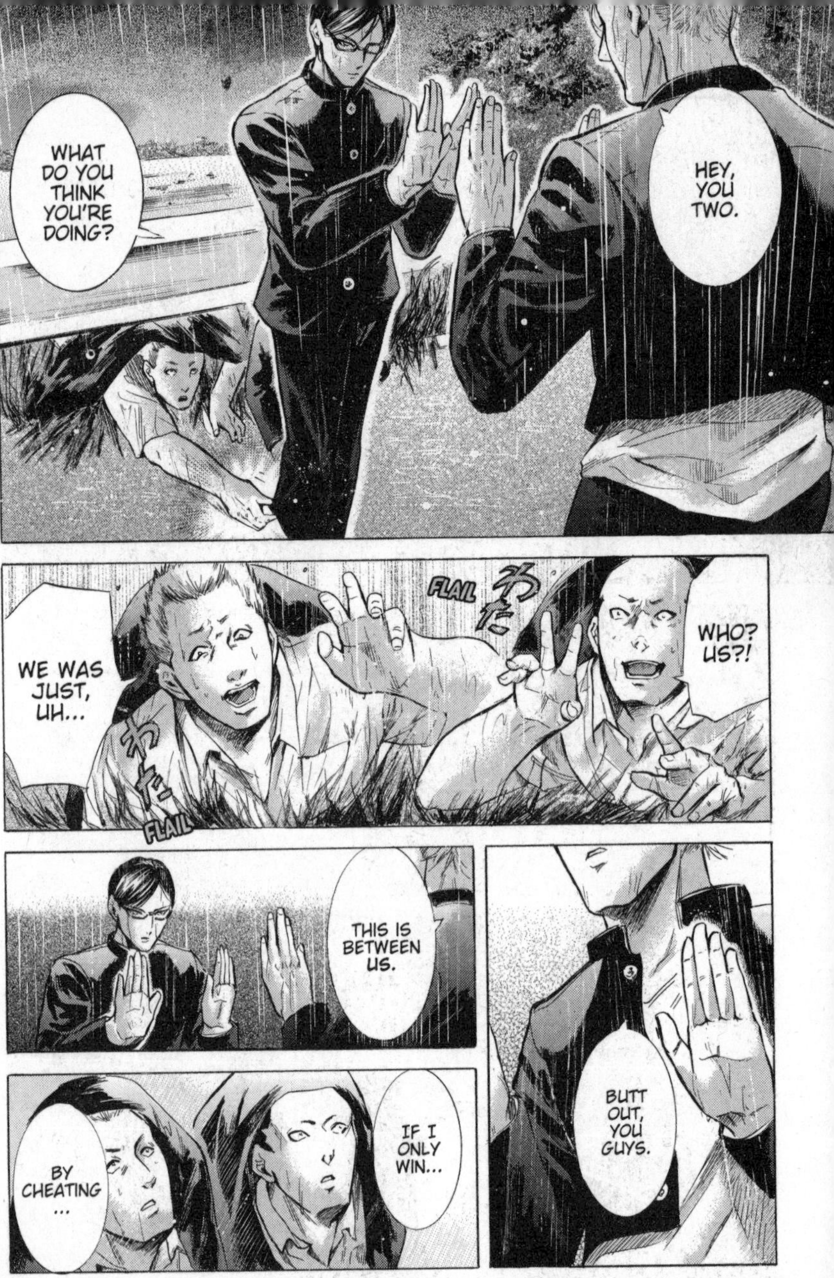

HEY, YOU TWO.
WHAT DO YOU THINK YOU'RE DOING?
WHO? US?!
わた
FLAIL
WE WAS JUST, UH...
わた
FLAIL
BUTT OUT, YOU GUYS.
THIS IS BETWEEN US.
IF I ONLY WIN...
BY CHEATING...

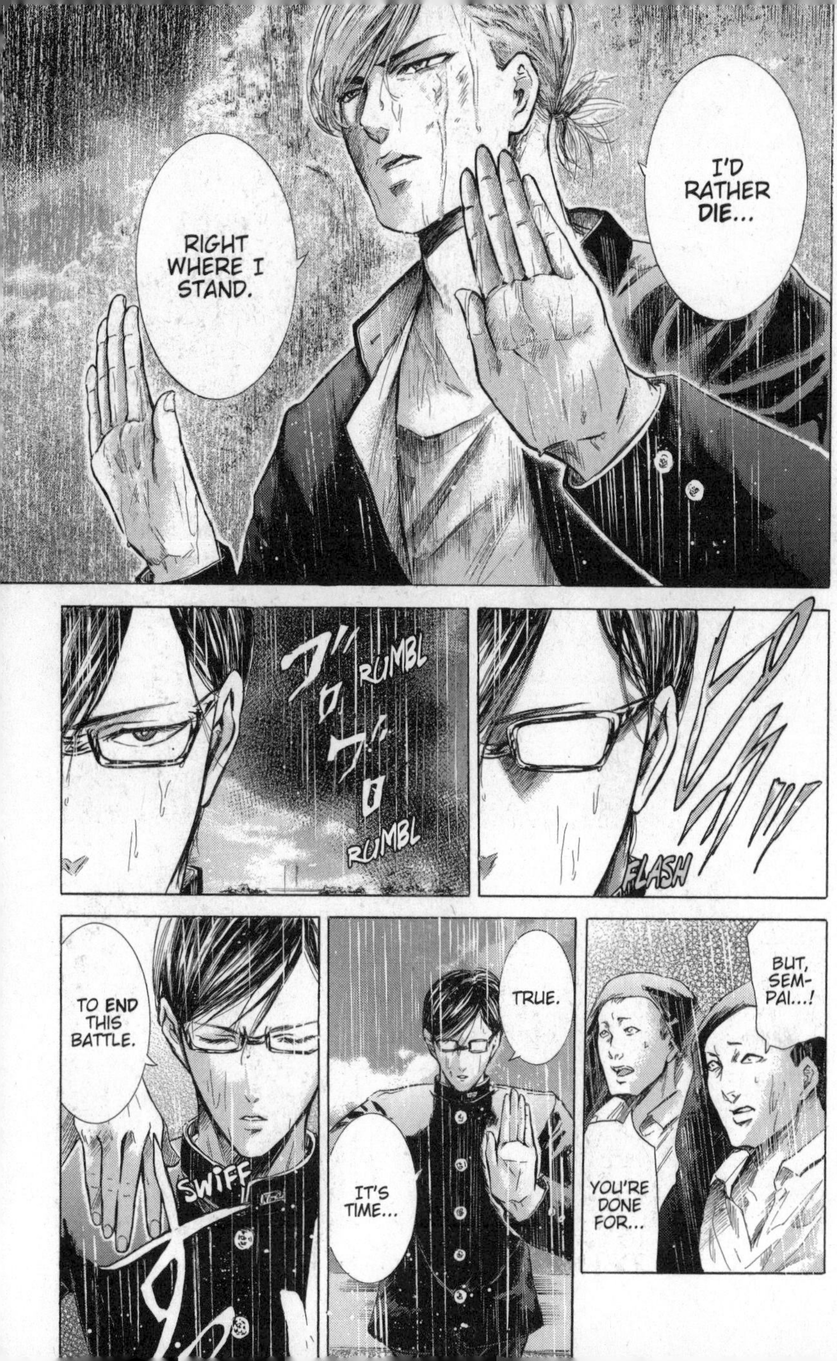
I'D RATHER DIE...
RIGHT WHERE I STAND.
FLASH
RUMBL
RUMBL
BUT, SEMPAI...!
YOU'RE DONE FOR...
TRUE.
IT'S TIME...
TO END THIS BATTLE.
SWIFF

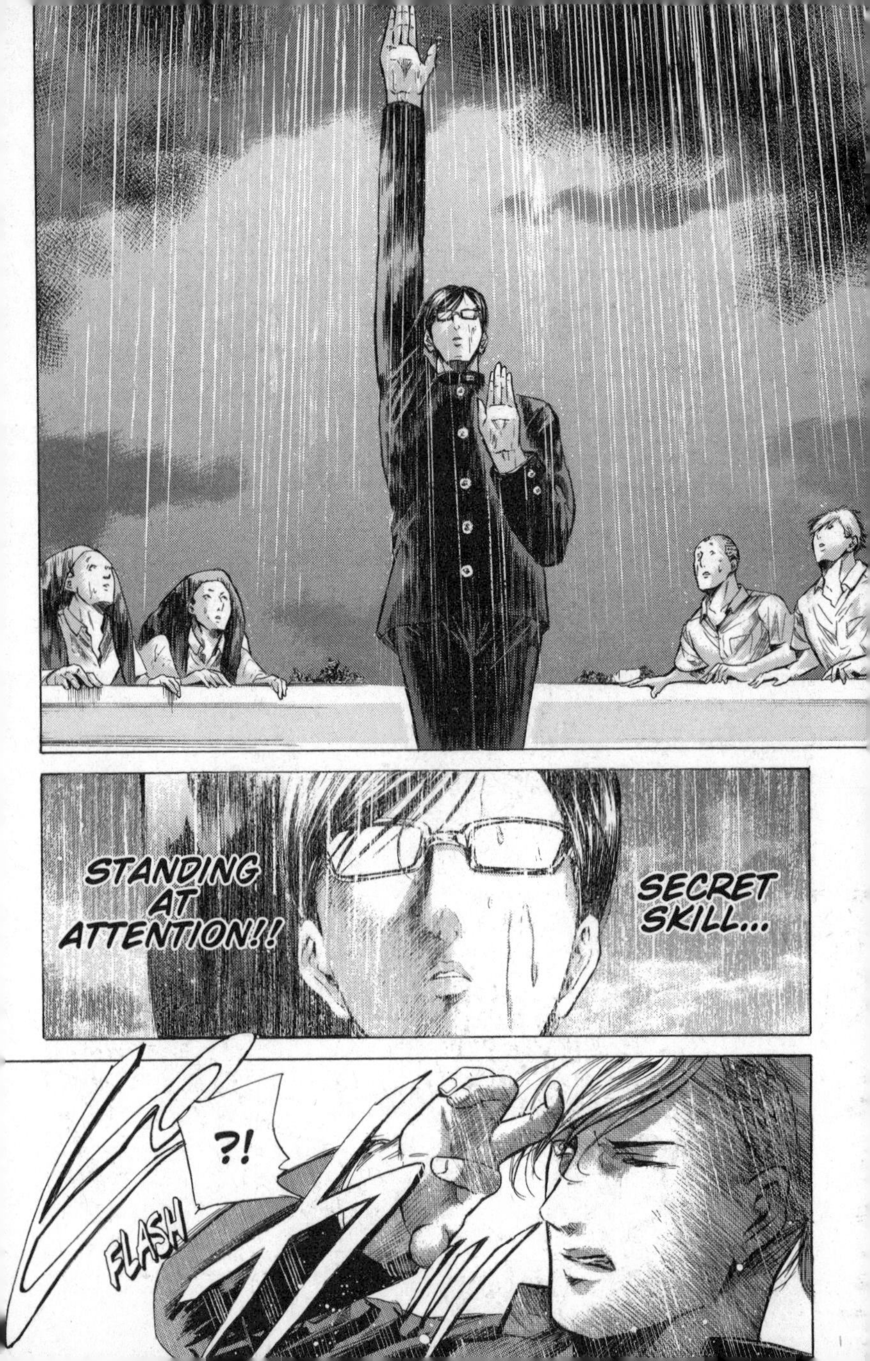
SECRET SKILL...
STANDING AT ATTENTION!!
?!
FLASH

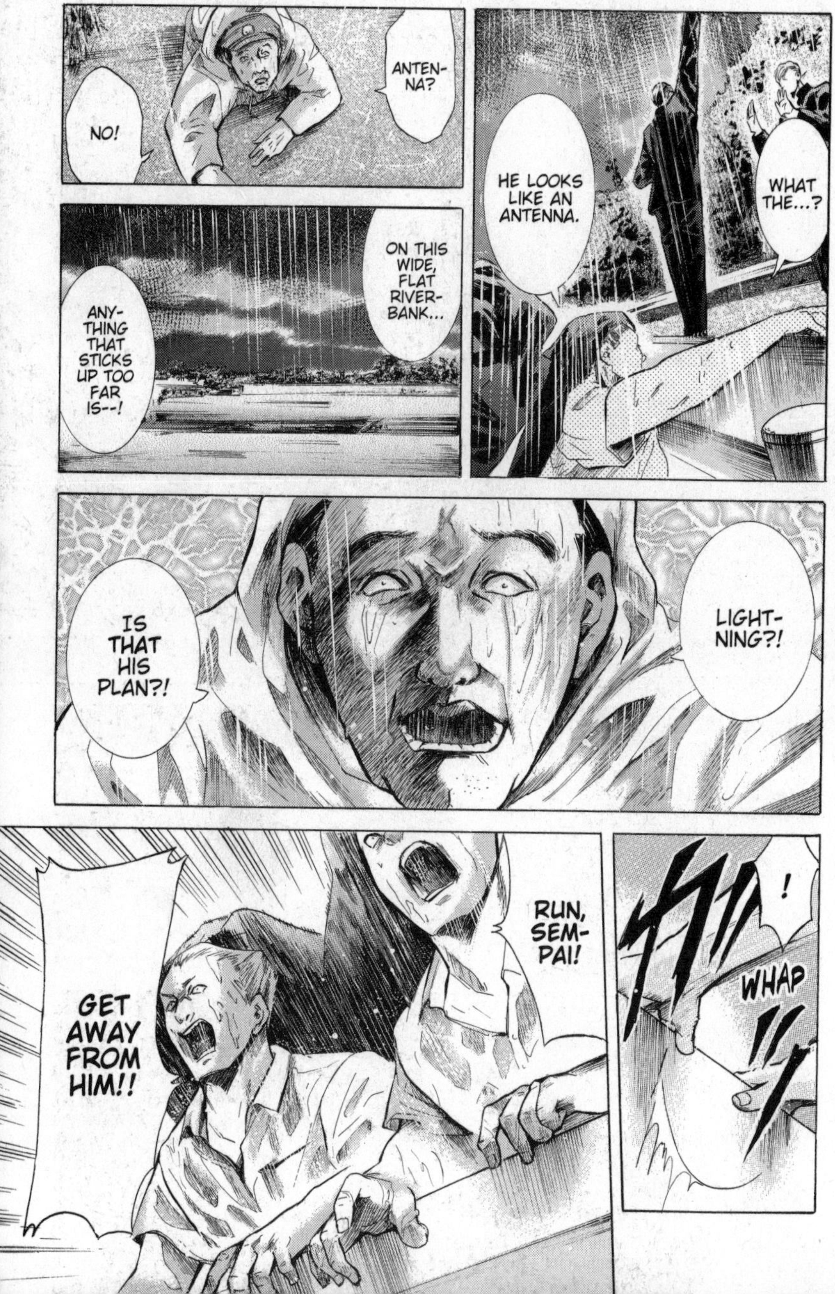
WHAT THE...?
HE LOOKS LIKE AN ANTENNA.
ANTEN-NA?
NO!
ON THIS WIDE, FLAT RIVER-BANK...
ANY-THING THAT STICKS UP TOO FAR IS--!
LIGHT-NING?!
IS THAT HIS PLAN?!
!
WHAP
RUN, SEM-PAI!
GET AWAY FROM HIM!!

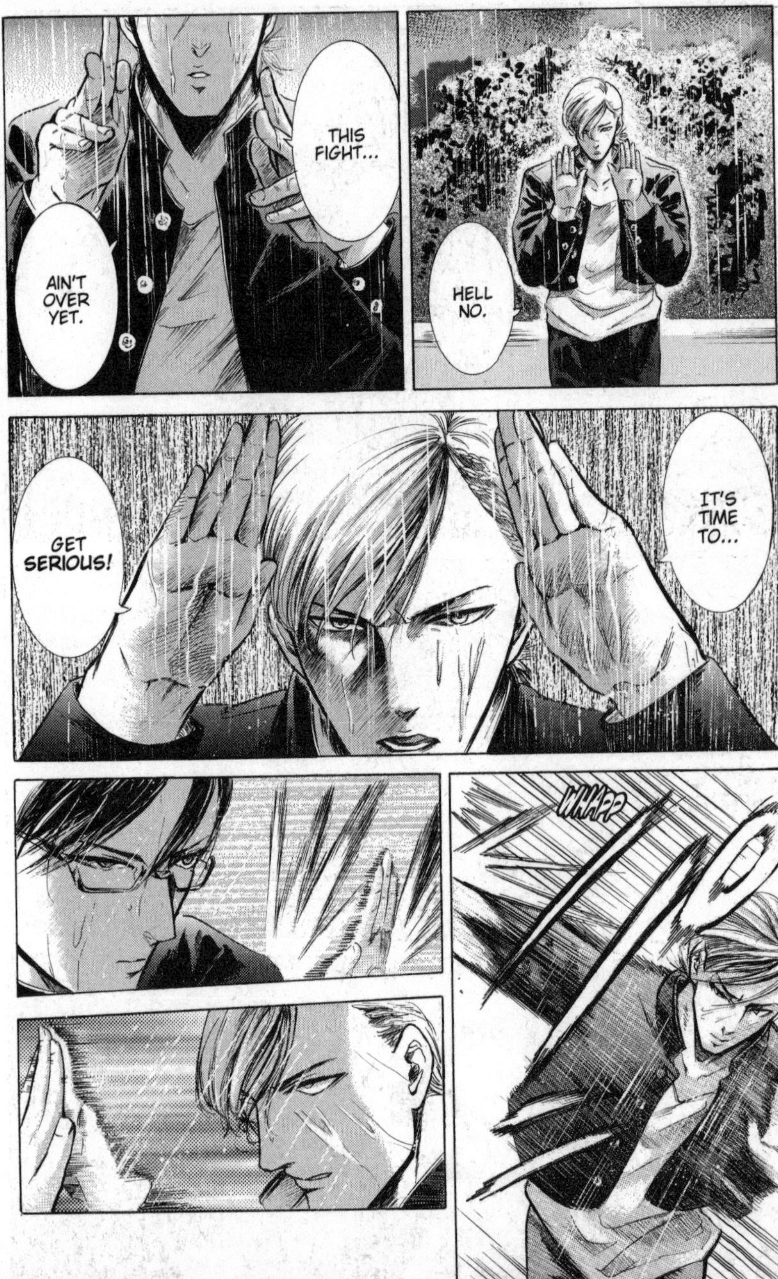
HELL NO.
THIS FIGHT...
AIN'T OVER YET.
IT'S TIME TO...
GET SERIOUS!
WHAPP

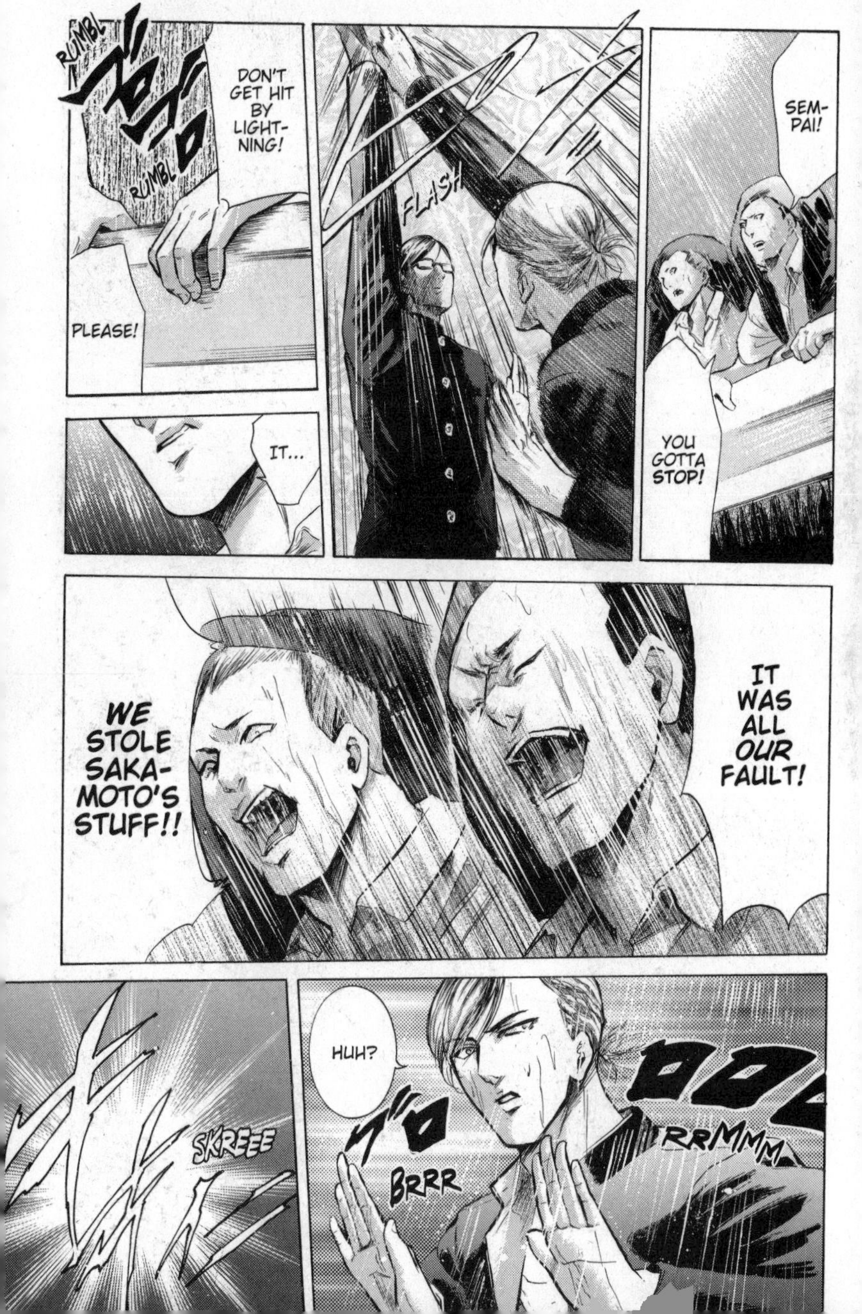
SEM-PAI!
YOU GOTTA STOP!
FLASH
RUMBL
DON'T GET HIT BY LIGHT-NING!
RUMBL
PLEASE!
IT...
IT WAS ALL OUR FAULT!
WE STOLE SAKA-MOTO'S STUFF!!
HUH?
BRRR
RRMMM
SKREEE

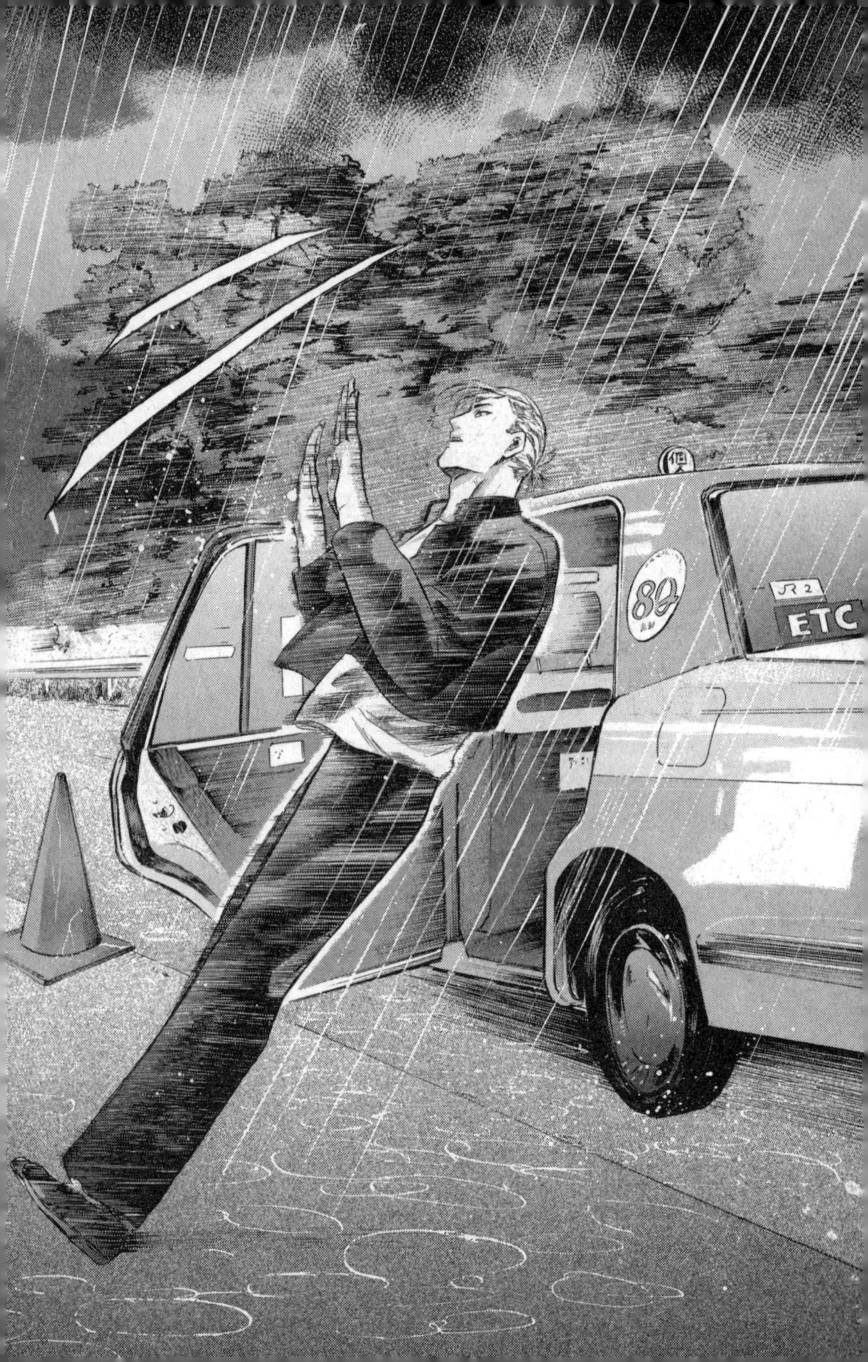
JR 2
ETC

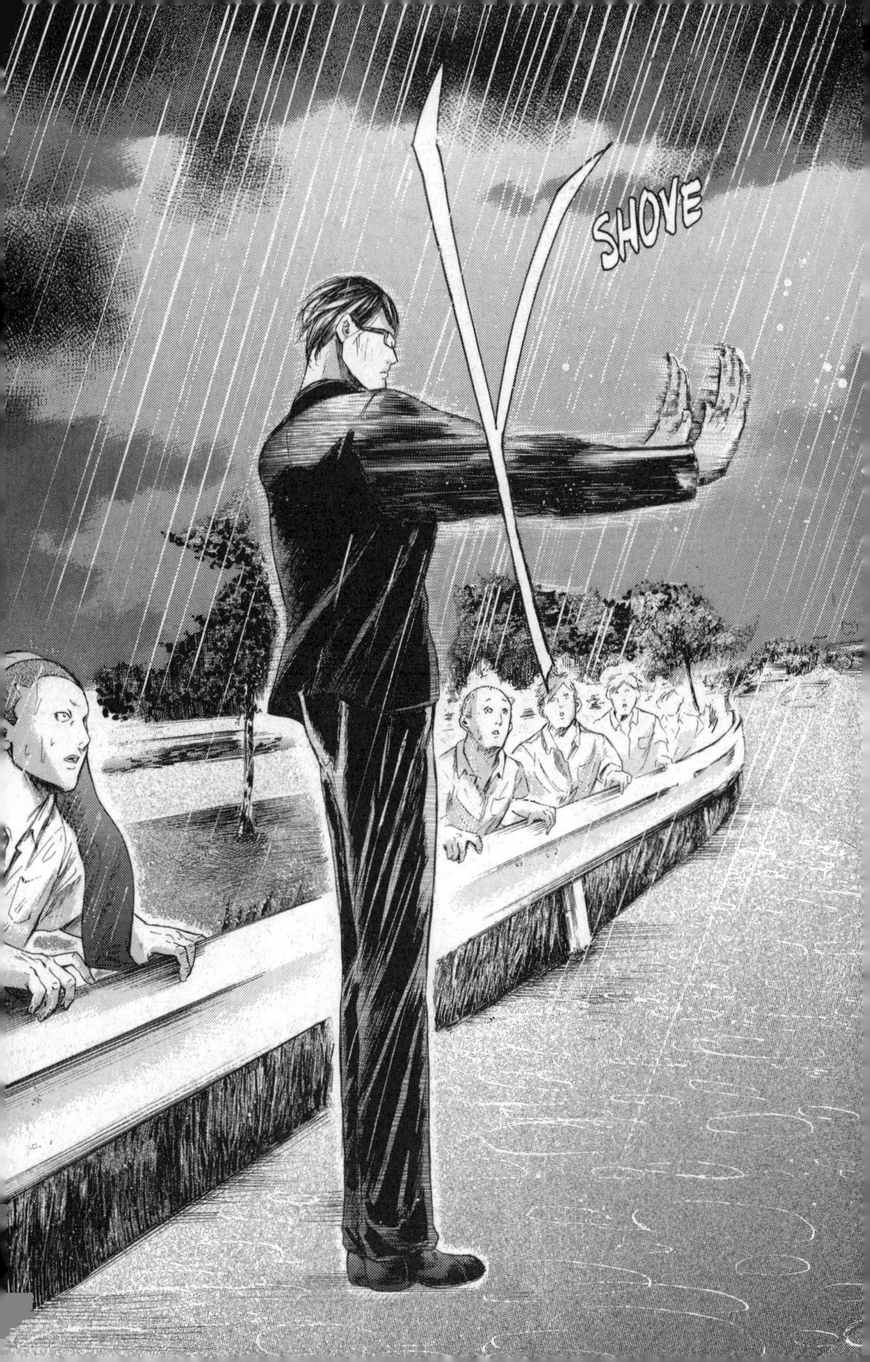
SHOVE

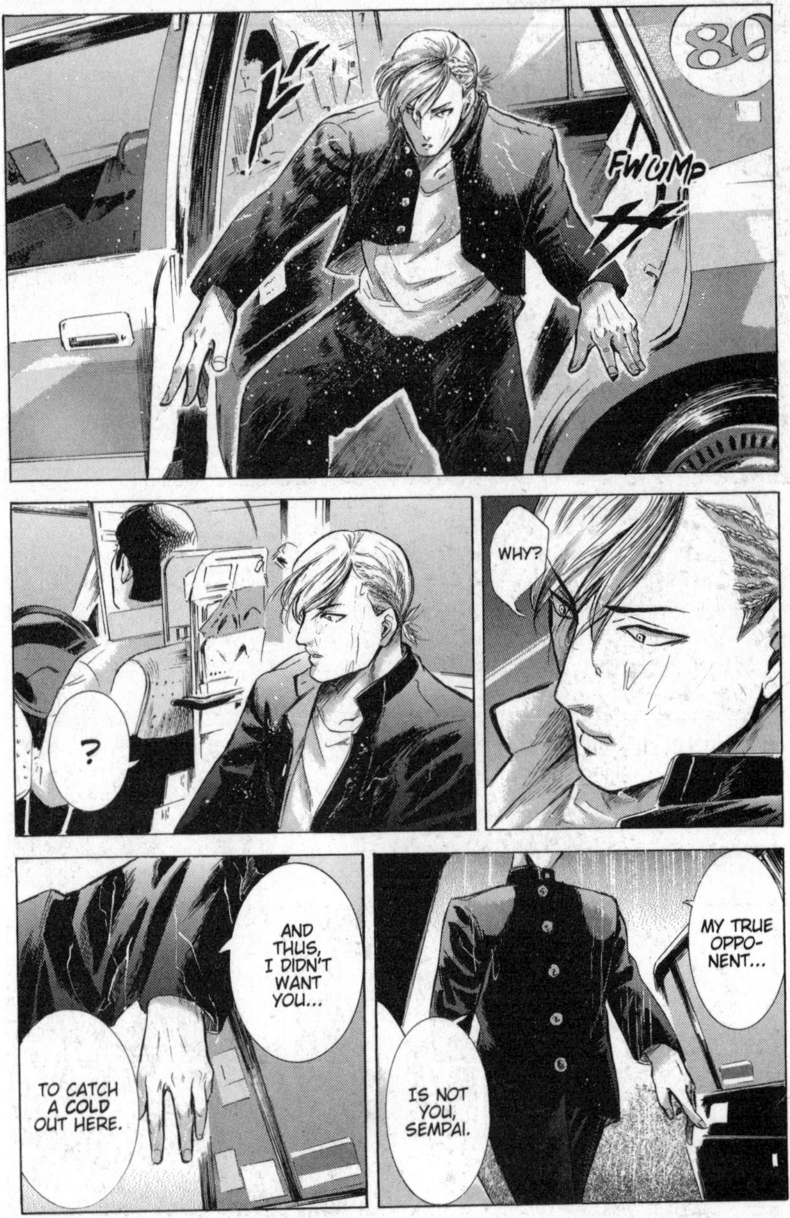
80
FWUMP
WHY?
?
MY TRUE OPPO-NENT...
IS NOT YOU, SEMPAI.
AND THUS, I DIDN'T WANT YOU...
TO CATCH A COLD OUT HERE.

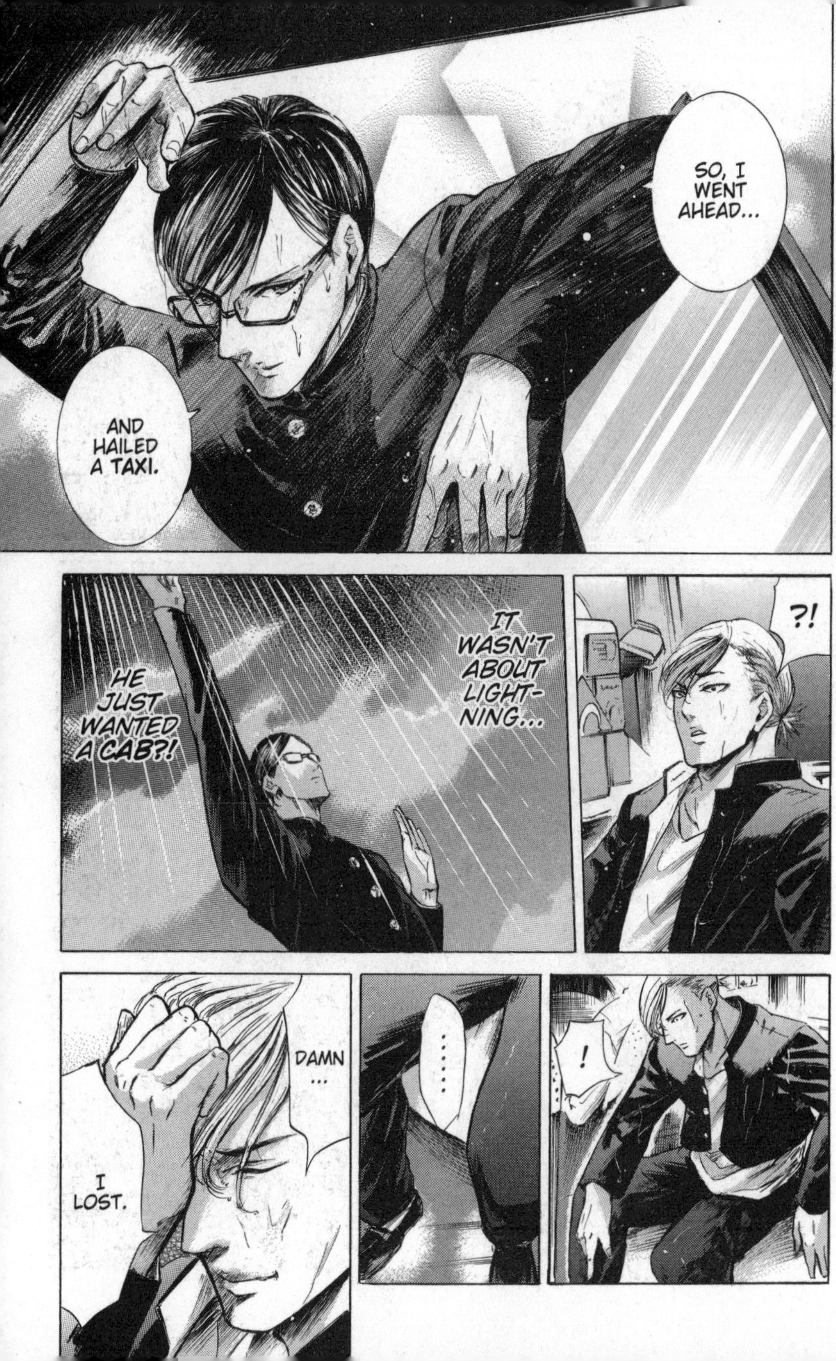
SO, I WENT AHEAD...
AND HAILED A TAXI.
?!
IT WASN'T ABOUT LIGHT-NING...
HE JUST WANTED A CAB?!
!
......
DAMN ...
I LOST.

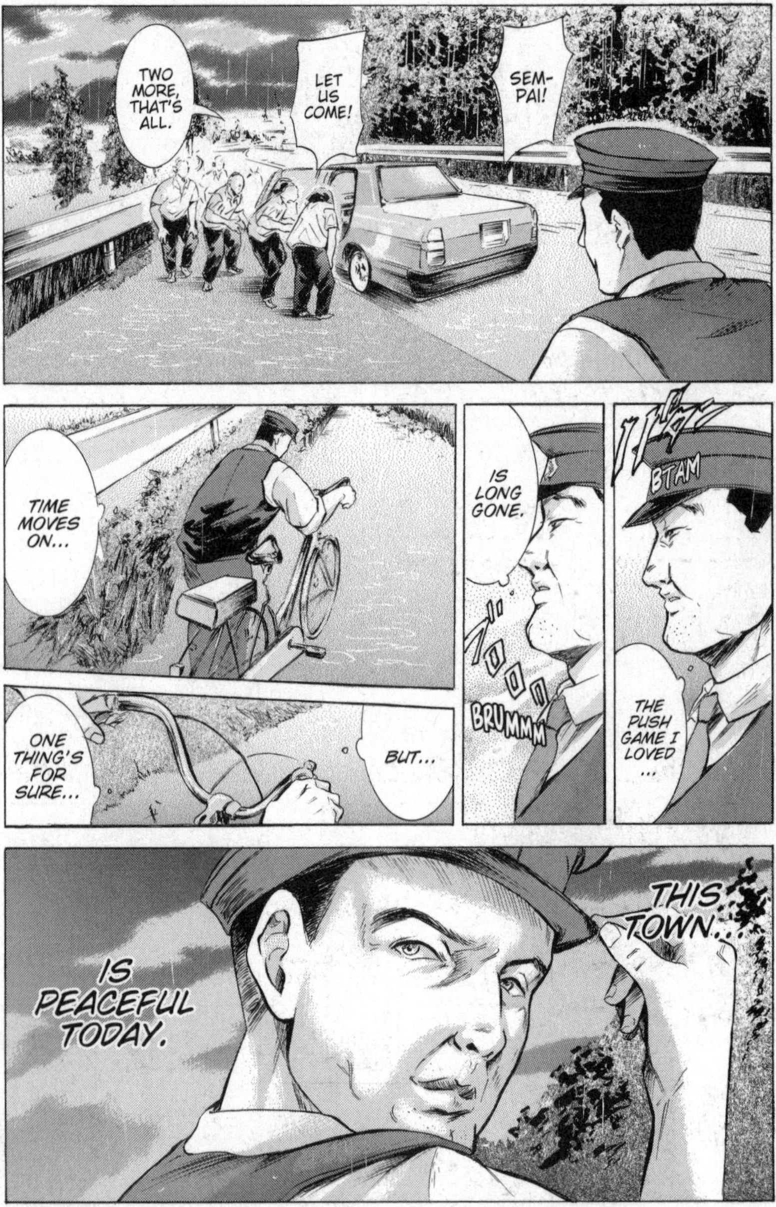
SEM-PAI!
LET US COME!
TWO MORE, THAT'S ALL.
BTAM
THE PUSH GAME I LOVED ...
IS LONG GONE.
BRUMMM
TIME MOVES ON...
BUT...
ONE THING'S FOR SURE...
THIS TOWN...
IS PEACEFUL TODAY.

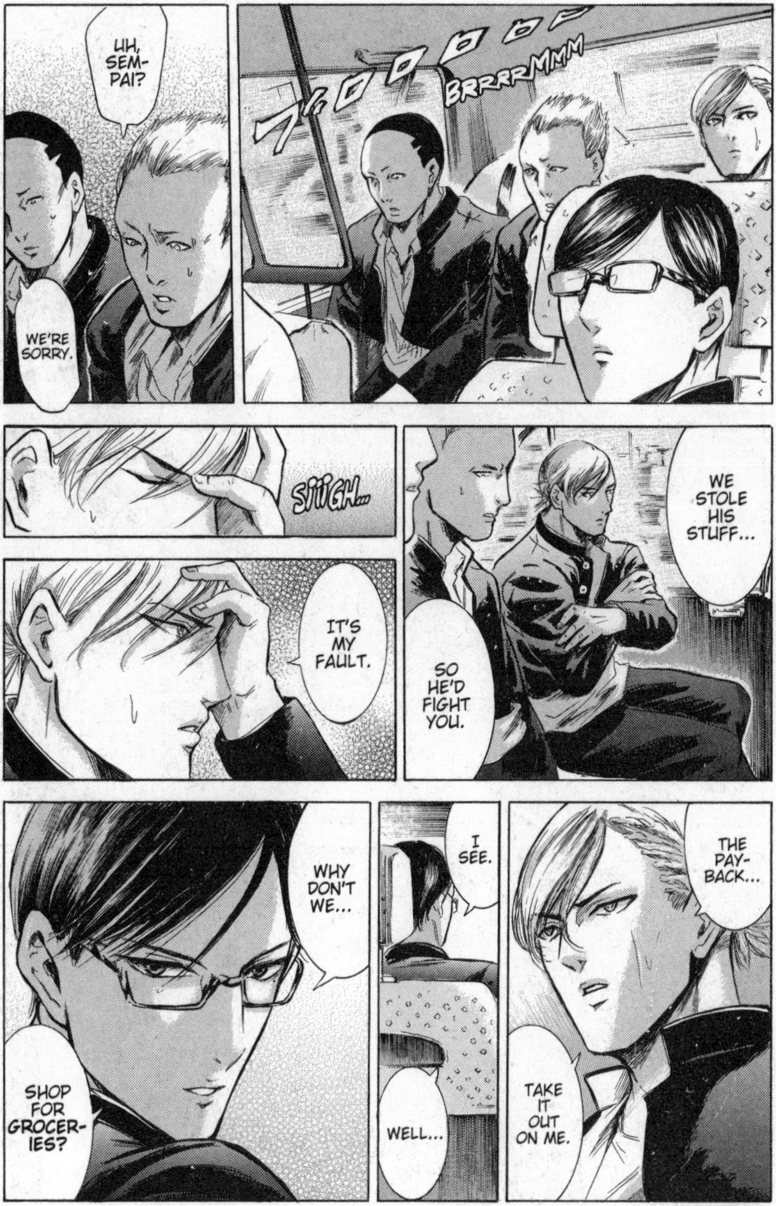
BRRRRMMMM
UH, SEMPAI?
WE'RE SORRY.
WE STOLE HIS STUFF...
SO HE'D FIGHT YOU.
SIIIGH...
IT'S MY FAULT.
THE PAY-BACK...
TAKE IT OUT ON ME.
I SEE.
WELL...
WHY DON'T WE...
SHOP FOR GROCER-IES?

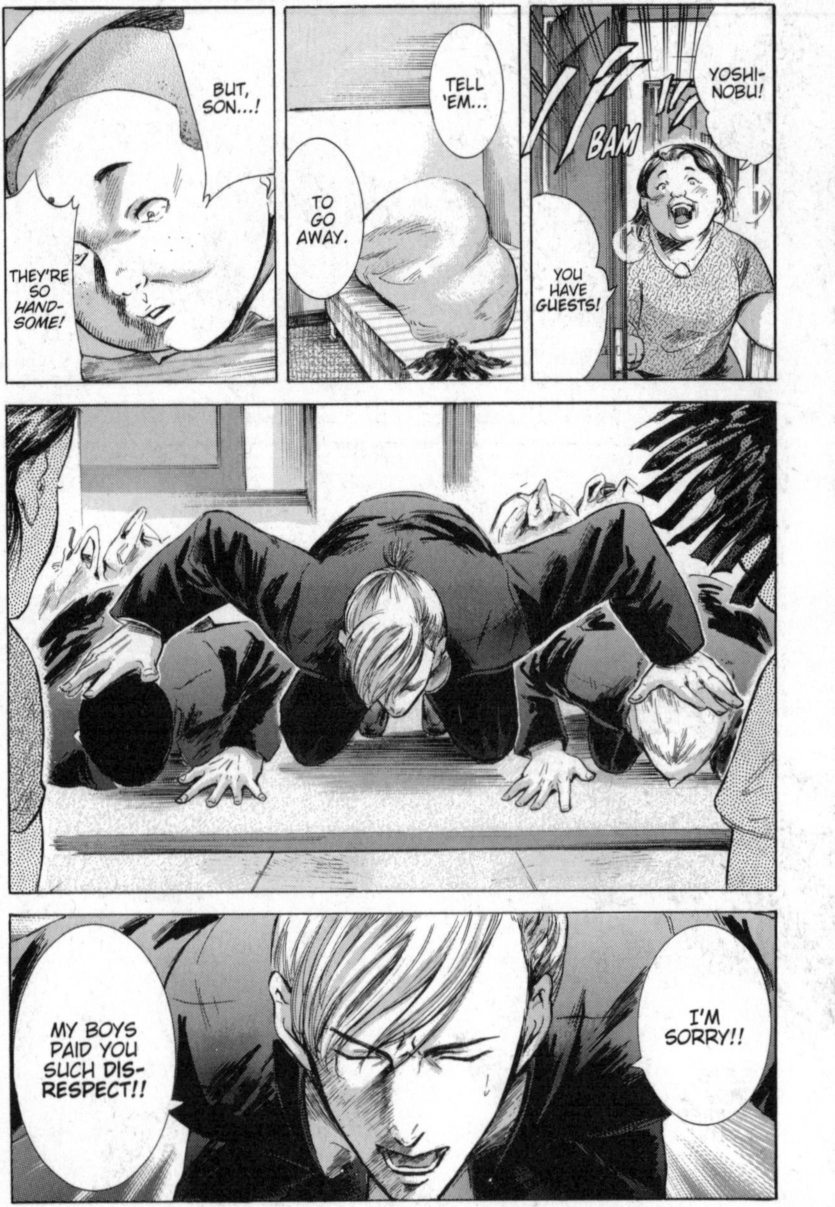
YOSHI-NOBU!
BAM
YOU HAVE GUESTS!
TELL 'EM...
TO GO AWAY.
BUT, SON...!
THEY'RE SO HAND-SOME!
I'M SORRY!!
MY BOYS PAID YOU SUCH DIS-RESPECT!!

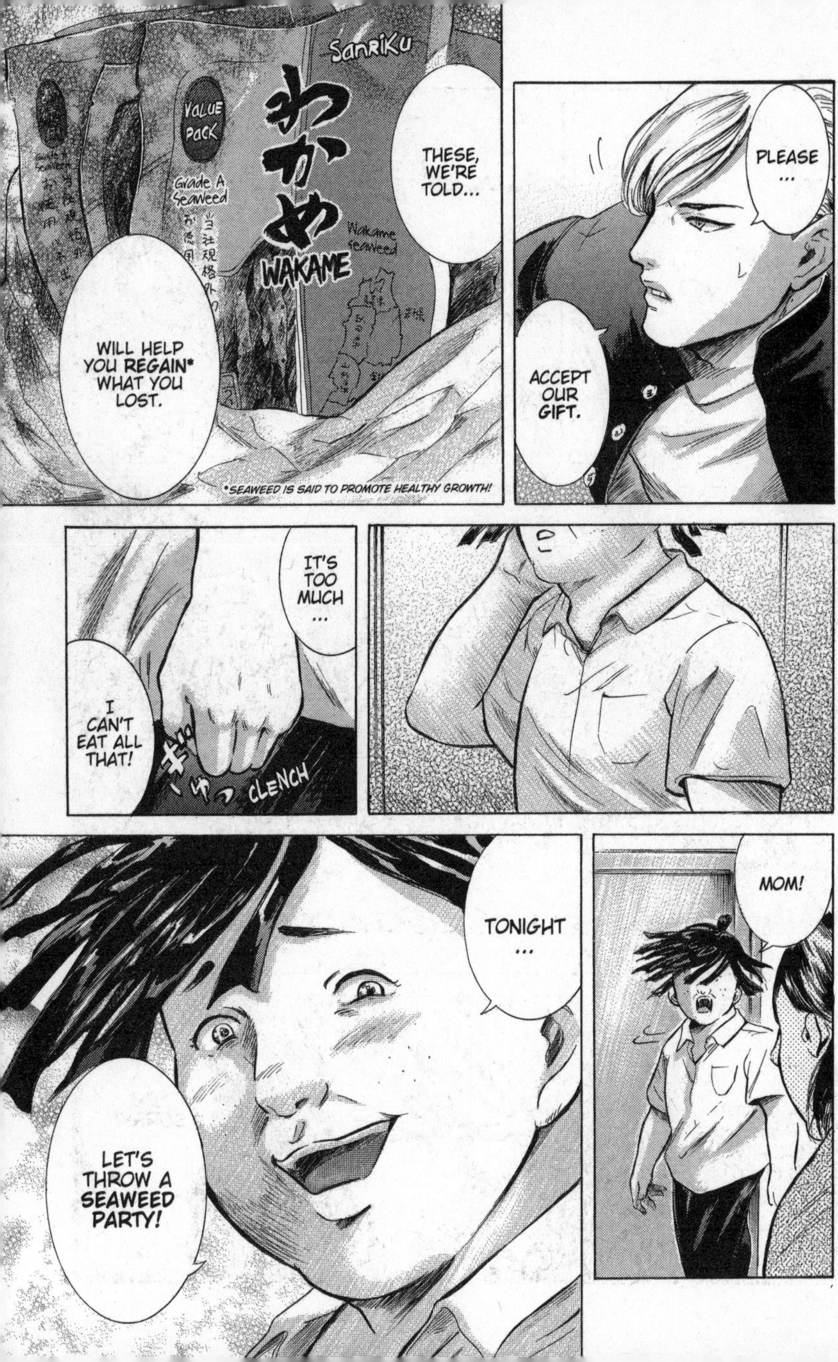
PLEASE ...
ACCEPT OUR GIFT.
Sanriku
わかめ
WAKAME
VALUE PACK
Grade A Seaweed
Wakame seaweed
THESE, WE'RE TOLD...
WILL HELP YOU REGAIN* WHAT YOU LOST.
*SEAWEED IS SAID TO PROMOTE HEALTHY GROWTH!
IT'S TOO MUCH ...
I CAN'T EAT ALL THAT!
CLENCH
MOM!
TONIGHT ...
LET'S THROW A SEAWEED PARTY!

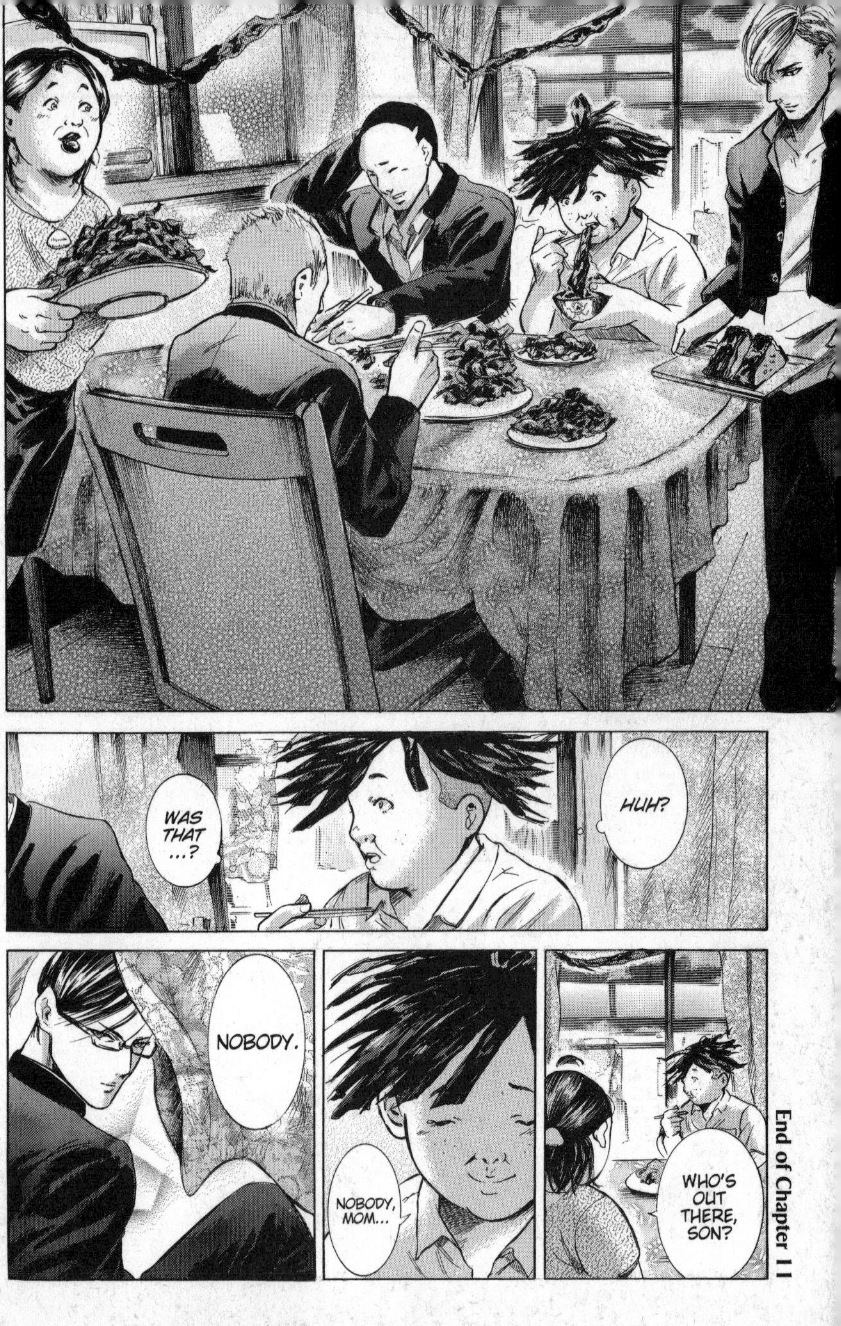
HUH?
WAS THAT ...?
WHO'S OUT THERE, SON?
NOBODY, MOM...
NOBODY.

End of Chapter 11

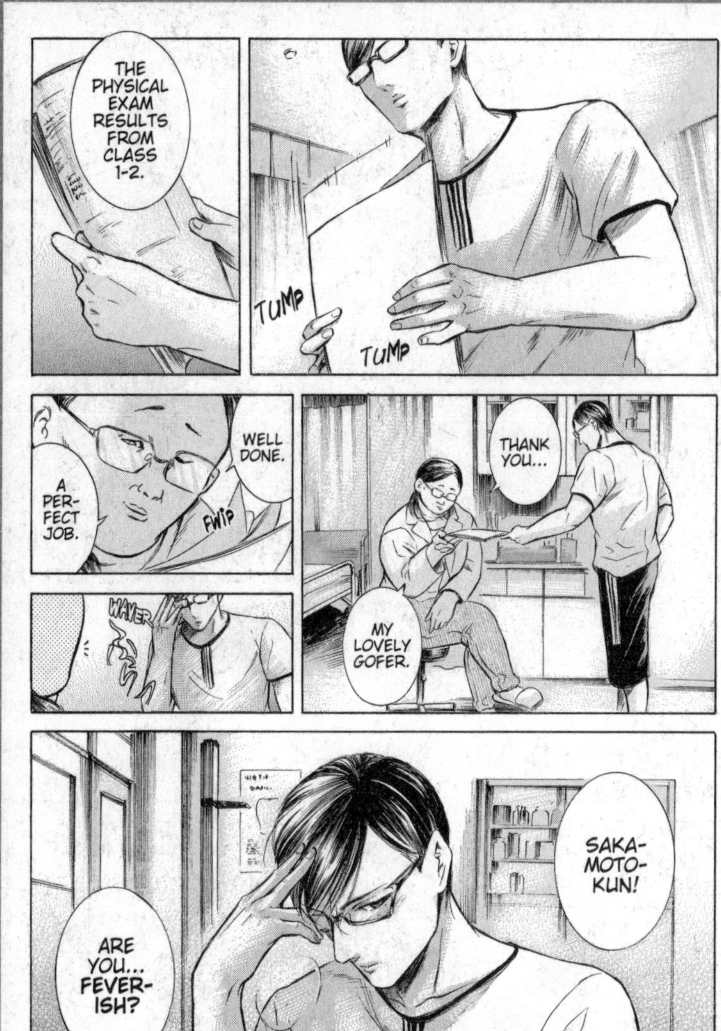
TUMP
TUMP
THE PHYSICAL EXAM RESULTS FROM CLASS 1-2.
THANK YOU...
MY LOVELY GOFER.
WELL DONE.
A PERFECT JOB.
FWIP
WAVER
SAKA-MOTO-KUN!
ARE YOU... FEVER-ISH?

Bonus Manga: Health Conscious

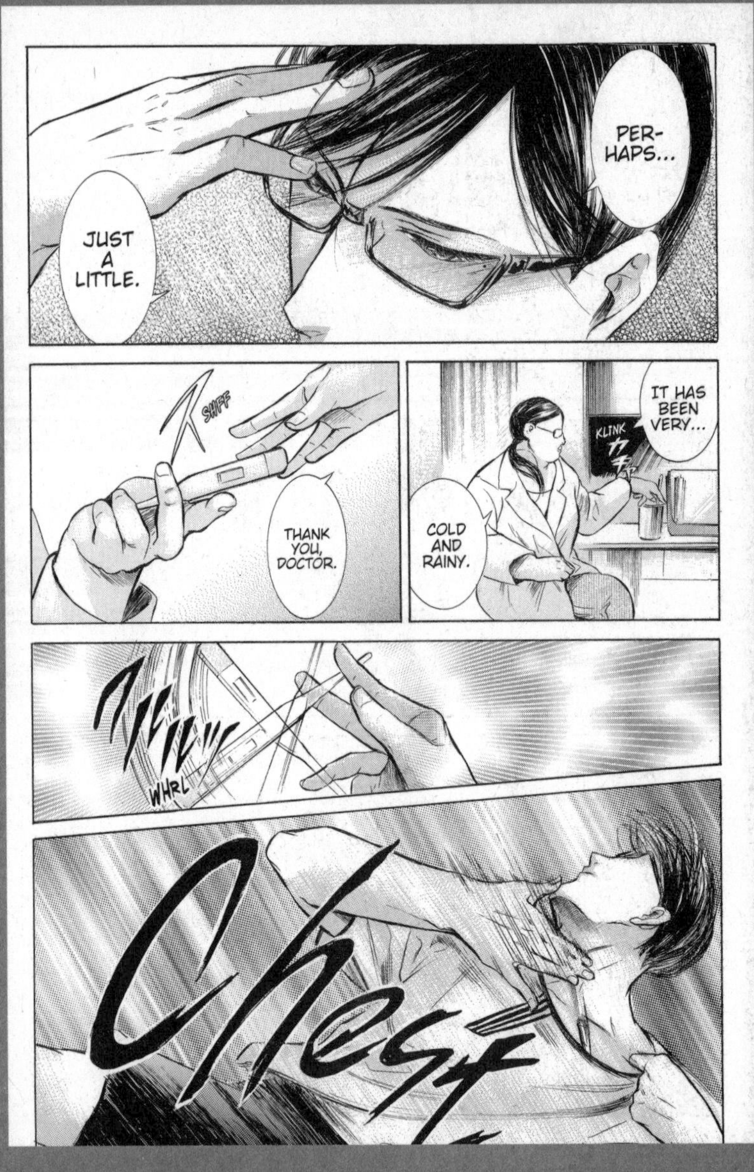
PER-HAPS...
JUST A LITTLE.
IT HAS BEEN VERY...
KLINK
COLD AND RAINY.
SHFF
THANK YOU, DOCTOR.
WHRL

BE-
BE-
BEEP
※101°F
I WAS RIGHT!
Gasp!
SUCH A HIGH FEVER!
YOU NEED REST...
GLANCE
AND A COLD...
COM-PRESS.
SWIFF
WAIT!
TOTTER
TOTTER
YOU NEED TO LIE DOWN!!
HOME EC
WAP
TOTTER
TOTTER
KA-POK

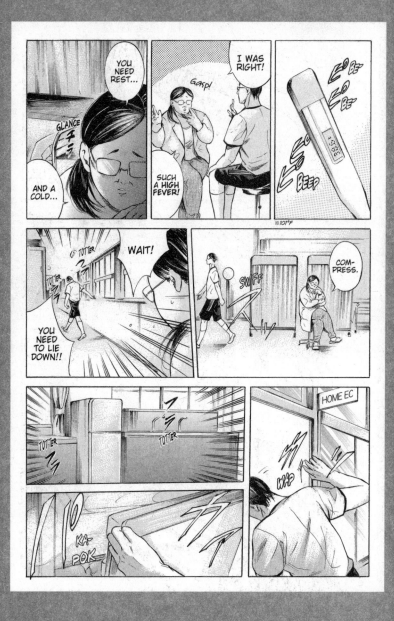

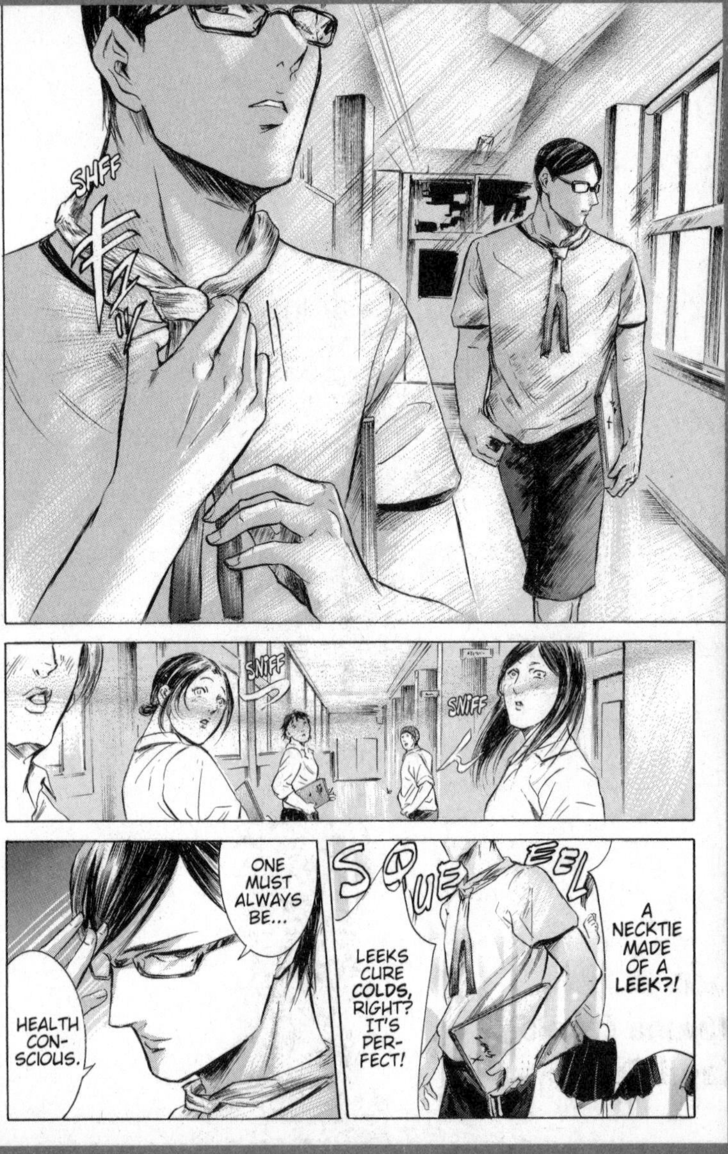
SHFF
SNIFF
SNIFF
SQUEEEL
A NECKTIE MADE OF A LEEK?!
LEEKS CURE COLDS, RIGHT? IT'S PERFECT!
ONE MUST ALWAYS BE...
HEALTH CONSCIOUS.

End of Bonus Manga

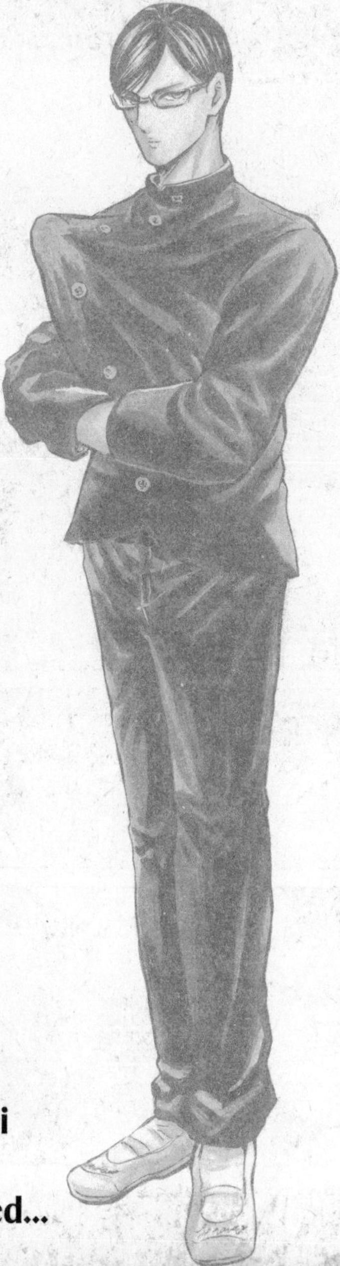

‹Staff›
Haruna Onoki
Kaori Sakagami

To be continued...

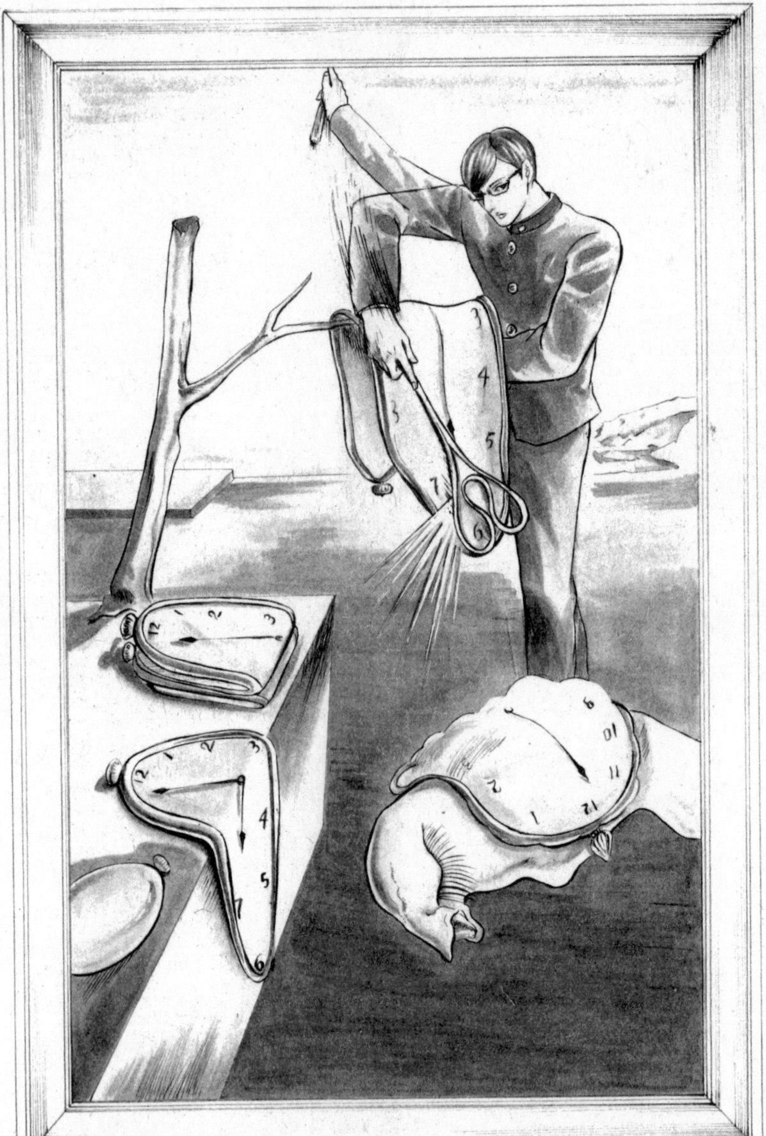